AF526662

# UNDERDOGS END EMPIRES

*A Memoir*

# UNDERDOGS END EMPIRES

*A Memoir*

I.P. KHOSLA

KONARK PUBLISHERS PVT LTD

KONARK PUBLISHERS PVT LTD
A-149, Main Vikas Marg, Delhi-110092 (India)
e-mail: konarkpublishers@hotmail.com



ISBN 81-220-0780-5



Typeset by The Laser Printers, New Delhi, and
Printed at ASK Advertising Aids Pvt Ltd, New Delhi.

# Preface

This book is a memoir extracted from my years in the Indian Foreign Service (IFS), which started in 1960. But it is not about diplomatic finesse or negotiating skills, important and interesting people encountered, difficult or trivial decisions taken or sojourns in the busy or boring capitals of the world.

Amongst those of us who joined the IFS in the early 1960s there were several who used to get together and talk at lunch time or otherwise; most often this happened at headquarters in the Ministry of External Affairs, New Delhi, sometimes in missions abroad also. This was not a fixed group; it varied all the time, with the place, over the years. Usually, as was to be expected, the talk turned to one or other aspect of international relations (IR) and India's foreign policy.

And our thinking changed from time to time; in fact, there was a particular way to think about these subjects that evolved during those years, call it the way of the underdog or, as Ranajit Guha would put it in the early 1980s, the subaltern way. In this book it is also called the traditional story. When Indira Gandhi became the Prime Minister belief in the truth of this way was particularly strong but, also to be expected, several of those who joined the talk disagreed, often strongly, as indeed, I should mention, did many commentators and foreign policy analysts from outside the IFS.

Over the years I found that diplomats from many countries shared this way of thinking about IR. There was a *joie de vivre* about getting freedom which pervaded most African and Asian societies in the 1960s and 1970s and was very perceptible among their diplomats: a conviction that they were not going to remain underdogs for long. One of my earliest assignments, to give one example, was to Algeria, within months of its achieving independence as the result of winning a long and bloody war; and it was one of the most stimulating. But, in fact, most of the diplomats from nonaligned and developing countries agreed with this way to think about IR.

So, within the IFS and with diplomats from other countries in Asia and Africa, we talked of many things, all those in this book and many others: experiences of colonialism and freedom struggles; incidents in the Cold War, where tensions seemed to rise and fall and of how it was used to pressurise smaller countries; of the way India should respond to all this. And we read about them. The diplomats from countries which had been through a violent freedom struggle had an especial experience of what I have written here. Freedom for them was not a boon, benevolently bestowed by the colonial power, as it is now generally portrayed to be; it was a rightful appropriation, wrested violently from a colonial power determined to use all its military might to deny it. Most of them also agreed on the thinking here outlined about what is called the years of the Cold War: that IR in the world after 1945 was not about a tense but entirely peaceful competition between two great powers and their allies but a number of struggles, often violent, between one or the other of them or those who they hired, against the weaker countries of Asia and Africa, with the other supporting, not the latter but the former. These struggles determined the course of events after 1945, so in fact there was no Cold War.

This way to think was neither a carefully argued theory nor an elaborate structure. There was some, but quite little, literature based on it. It was dwarfed by the standard theories that came out of the West, based on what is here called the modernity story, and which argued the exact opposite, which produced reams of rigorously argued texts, liberally strewn with examples, seamless theoretical foundations holding up elaborate structures. But it was fairly consistent; above all it explained a great deal more of what was actually happening on the ground than the standard theories. Some day, I thought, along with many other diplomats from Africa and Asia, this way, this traditional story, would dominate the field.

Anyway, it did appear to be the right way to think about IR. The assignments that I did in Algeria, Afghanistan, Myanmar, Bangladesh, the things that I heard and saw there, confirmed that it was the right way. The first two are the subject of separate chapters in this book; two more chapters are devoted to specific countries: Indonesia, since I learnt much about it during an assignment in the Netherlands; and Vietnam, where I paid an extended visit. In any case, a book like this cannot be properly written without a great deal about Afghanistan and Vietnam, each of which put more body into the traditional story than any combination of a dozen other countries.

But our way didn't get to dominate the field. On the contrary it became moribund; once the Cold War ended it was going to die, or at best, stay moribund. That's a pity; it didn't deserve that fate.

So this book is a memoir which recalls that particular way to think about IR, that story, and to which I have added notes and references over the years and wherever appropriate. Some sections are longer than might appear appropriate; others are too short or even missing. There is probably a lot more within quotation marks than would be usual; this seems to give authenticity to a forgotten story that now seems not really believable; and a lot more about national histories, but the strength of nationalism is at the heart of the traditional story. Anyway, the contents are based on personal experience, discussions and reading, not on systematic research. By way of contrast, and mainly to show how the two are polar opposites, I have included some chapters and a few sections in some other chapters on the modernity story, the way IR is usually presented to us; but these are few and short since the material in them is familiar from our daily reading.

Towards the end, I was tempted to project that underdog way into the post-Cold War World and did that; but it's not an appealing picture that emerged. So perhaps I'm wrong. Maybe it did deserve that fate.

Here I would like to thank my colleagues in the IFS, senior and junior, for all the friendship, of course, but also quite specially for keeping alive and prosperous, whenever they get together, the great Indian argumentative tradition and the heterodoxy it generates. Thanks go also to the many diplomats from Africa and Asia who have clarified during discussions many of the ideas in this book;

and to Konark Publishers, who have been publishing books on IR of a consistently high quality for many years and have done a superb job on this one.

Any errors and inaccuracies which remain are entirely the responsibility of the author.

*New Delhi*
*January 2010*

**I.P. Khosla**

# Contents


| | | |
|---|---|---|
| | *Preface* | v |
| | *Introduction* | xi |
| 1 | War and Power: The Pre-Colonial Era | 1 |
| 2. | Peace Plans | 19 |
| 3. | War, Power and Making Empires | 30 |
| 4. | Modernity in the Colonial Era | 65 |
| 5. | Indonesia | 91 |
| 6. | Algeria | 116 |
| 7. | The 'Cold War' that wasn't—I | 149 |
| 8. | The 'Cold War' that wasn't—II | 172 |
| 9. | The Other Story: the Cold War | 215 |
| 10. | Vietnam | 236 |
| 11. | Afghanistan | 275 |
| 12. | The US Goes into Afghanistan | 315 |
| 13. | Iraq: the 2003 Invasion and After | 336 |
| 14. | Modernity: the Post-Cold War Era | 372 |
| | *INDEX* | 393 |

# Introduction

In the chapters that follow, two ways of looking at international relations (IR) are described, two world-views or stories that are told about this subject, and that are polar opposites: they are here called the traditional story and that of modernity respectively. Over the years the opposition between them appears in the discrepancy between the way power actually operates at ground level and the conceptions or misconceptions that are prevalent about the way it operates. This discrepancy makes states and governments do things they should not. It makes them continue the slaughter of war long after the war itself has been lost, or won; it makes them hang on as colonial rulers after they know they have no option but to quit; it makes them, among the many other things that could be included in this list, invade smaller countries, thinking it will be a walkover. The traditional story is about the way power actually operates; the modernity story is the one that leads to all the misconceptions about the way it operates.

This introduction starts by giving examples of world-views.

There are then notes on the traditional way of looking at the world and at IR, which is the one used to describe the content of all except four of the subsequent chapters.

A description of the modernity world-view or story comes next; this way of looking at the world is now most commonly used. In fact the modernity world-view dominates all contemporary intellectual activity and, of course, almost all IR today is based on the story of modernity. It is as well, therefore, to understand its geographically confined origins and shaky foundations. References are also made to the remaining four chapters of the book which are based on modernity.

## The Need to Select

Since there can be no full description of any datum or event, far less of a collection of data or series of events, we are compelled to select and arrange. This is so even in the world of numbers, as mathematicians aver.

The question is how to eliminate, select and arrange. There could be many different theories or models, sets of rules or procedures for deciding this; each of these yields a world-view. So there are also a very large number of world-views. Over the centuries, ways of classifying them have been suggested. But the main point is that different world-views lead to differing narratives about the same thing.

Here is an example of the way narratives can differ.

Kautilya's *Arthashastra*[1] is a detailed text that documents every aspect of life in Mauryan India: the state and the people, the ruler and the officials under him, political economy, foreign policy as also personal life. It is both descriptive and prescriptive.

Kautilya is rigorously analytical in his description of the facts as well as his advocacy of what needs to be done, so rigorous in fact as to be quite contemporary in his world-view. In what concerns IR closest, for instance, he gives the elements of sovereignty in great detail: the king, the minister, the country and so on, eight elements in all. Then he gives a list of what are the best qualities in each of these elements: the king should be born of a high family; possessed of valour; virtuous; truthful; of resolute mind and not addicted to procrastination; and so on. Then he describes the best qualities of a minister of the country as well as of others. Then comes the analysis of the situation or the circle of states in which the sovereign finds himself: the neighbour, who is the enemy; the enemy's friend; the enemy's friend's friend; the neighbour's neighbour, who is the friend; the rearward enemy; the rearward friend; and in each case it has to be determined whether the friend or enemy is assailable, destructible, a natural friend or an acquired friend and so on. In the detailed analysis of this situation as a whole Kautilya finds there are four primary circles of states, twelve kinds of kings, sixty elements of sovereignty, and seventy-two elements of states.

This leads to the analysis of what one can do with the situation in which one finds oneself, what is the list of possibilities of action, and there are six: make peace; make war; observe neutrality; marching meaning making preparations for war; alliance, meaning seeking the protection of another; and making peace with one while waging war with another. Then each of these is discussed in some detail. Finally comes the analysis of what you should do, which of the six options are to be selected in a given situation. Here Kautilya is quite categorical. If you are superior you shall wage war, but if you are inferior you shall make peace, meanwhile building up your strength so that you become superior. The whole of Book VII, comprising eighteen chapters, is devoted to the question of how to analyse your situation accurately and then how to decide the most appropriate policy to choose: what kind of alliances to enter into; when precisely to make war and peace; what sort of agreements to make and under which conditions and so on.

We can contrast this precise and analytical account with that given by Megasthenes. He was the ambassador sent by Seleucus Nicator, successor to Alexander's empire, to the court of Chandragupta Maurya, or Sandracotta, as the Greeks called him. Kautilya and Megasthenes are writing about the same place, the same court and empire, and at the same time: the first wrote the *Arthashastra* around 300 BC or perhaps some years earlier, the second wrote his account, the *Indika*, around the same time or a little later. It is quite impossible, just by reading the two, to discover that they are writing about the same place and time.[2]

Although not one line of Megasthenes work survives, paraphrases by different authors agree sufficiently for us to be sure we do have a good idea of the reports he sent. He does give general particulars about the society and politics of the time, but then he goes on to specifics. The result is, as Strabo[3] tells us, stories of wild men, "their heels are in front, and instep and toes are turned backward"; or the Okupedes, "people who in running could leave the horse behind"; and then the Enotokoitai who had ears reaching down to their feet so that they could sleep in them, not to mention the Monommatoi, "who have the ears of a dog, their one eye set in the middle of their forehead" and that "on many of the mountains there lives a race of men having heads like those of dogs"; and the Astomi, "who have no mouth." And that list of marvels is a sampling of just the human race. There are also serpents that fly about by night dropping their urine or sweat onto unsuspecting people down below, which blister their skin; giant winged scorpions; trees that grow in the sea. And, of course, the well-known and oft-repeated story of the gold digging ants, which being "larger than foxes make their burrows proportionately larger. But the ground is impregnated with gold and Indians thence obtain their gold."[4]

The ancient Greeks, including many of his contemporaries, understandably called Megasthenes a liar. Strabo calls him the second biggest liar writing about India, and writes that "generally speaking, the men who have hitherto written on the affairs of India were a set of liars – Deimachos[5] holds the first place in the list, Megasthenes comes next." More contemporary historians are skeptical but gentler, judging that "much of this account could have been gathered from conversations and travellers' tales, rather than from personal knowledge."[6]

When Megasthenes writes that in the Southern parts of India shadows fall in opposite directions, north and south, at different times of the year, we can believe that he did pick up the story in India, since this is what would happen south of the Tropic of Cancer, somewhere along the latitude of present-day Bhopal; but when he goes on to report that in the southern part of India the constellation of the bear (*Ursa Major*) disappeared from view, then you have to wonder who he has been talking to, for that constellation, with a declination averaging 50 degrees plus, is visible round the year, no matter how far south you go in India. Actually it is visible, though close to the horizon, even as far south as the Cape of Good Hope.

So, on the one hand, it is true that in the world we are today familiar with any ambassador who sent the kind of report Megasthenes did would probably not get another assignment; but it is equally true and more relevant that within the Greek world-view, which he is so well qualified to serve, Megasthenes makes sense and even Aristotle, whose logic (and philosophy) reigned in the Western world for two millennia, told us many of the same tales, though he lived too early to have read Megasthenes. For within that pre-modern story monsters, flying serpents and those who sleep on their own ears are possible components of a world of miracle and wonder. It is this wondrous world that is depicted again and again in the magnificent art of renaissance Europe.

## The Origins of the Traditional Story

Getting closer to the contrast between the traditional world-view and that of modernity as far as IR is concerned, we may take the example of Michel Foucault who has proposed one of the best-known classifications of world-views. This is called episteme or an epistemological field.[7] I have borrowed a great deal from it in what follows.

The episteme is concerned entirely with practical application, with how, at a particular period of time and within a particular cultural and civilisational context, we put data and events together in such a way that the resulting picture helps us cope with the world outside through a scientific approach, or, as Foucault says, with "those configurations within the space of knowledge which have given rise to the diverse forms of empirical science."[8] The episteme is always also concerned with the way ethics and morality on the one hand, and hierarchy and power, on the other, fit into the picture. We look at this now.

Up to the end of the sixteenth century, according to Foucault, resemblance or similitude was the determining factor through which the world was seen. This may also be called the renaissance episteme. Things and events, the raw data around us, were put together according to adjacency of place or juxtaposition giving rise to similitude from close quarters, emulation at a distance, analogy and sympathy. Emulation at a distance, to cite one example, makes the human face resemble the sky, its eyes reflect the sun and the moon; it "enables things to imitate one another from one end of the universe to the other without connection or proximity."[9] And sympathy, to cite another, is what draws things to one another so that the course of a man's life may be compared to, or be determined by, the movements of the planets and stars or the darkness of battle to the frequency of eclipses. The episteme was always open to change as new similitudes, analogies and sympathies between different kinds of things were discovered or suggested; the focus had to be on the concrete more than the abstract, the local more than the universal, the timely more than the timeless.

This episteme actually predates the renaissance. In the fifth century BC, Thucydides noted how unprecedented was the Peloponnesian War, its sheer length, the numbers of cities captured and devastated, the number of exiles, and then adds that wide areas were at the time affected by earthquakes; and there were more frequent eclipses of the sun than had ever been recorded.[10] His writing is a clear instance of what Foucault noted: "Sympathy creates communication between our bodies and the heavens, and transmits the movement of the planets to the affairs of men."[11] Magic and divination were integral parts of the renaissance episteme. These were not a different kind of knowledge or one without proper foundations in observation and analysis; they were part of the main body of knowledge itself.

Machiavelli, centuries later, is, of course, part of the renaissance and very much part of this episteme. He asserts that "the affairs of the world are controlled by fortune and by God in such a way that the prudence of men cannot match them, and indeed cannot improve them at all." And, to the extent a Prince has discretion, he should fit his mode of proceeding to be in tune with the times in order to be successful.[12] The fluctuations in the power and standing of a principality are to be taken as the interplay of chance and ability; adversity is the prelude to success, as was happening to Italy at the time. Sympathy with fortune and being in tune with the times is what Machiavelli recommends, not getting a higher GNP or defence expenditure or any of the other indices that have become so much a part of the episteme of modernity.

Within the renaissance episteme the norms of ethics and morality, and the effects of power, work in a very specific way. On the first a healthy skepticism about the universality of ethical standards was the norm. So you may adopt a particular viewpoint about right and wrong, "but you cannot deny others the right to adopt different working positions for themselves."[13] This leads to a more liberal and tolerant attitude, for instance, to different ethnic groups in contrast with the Social Darwinist attitude, which is so typical of the modernity episteme. On the second, power leads to war, as it should.

By the way, if we compare the renaissance story or episteme with that which framed the writing of Kautilya's *Arthashastra,* we note that there is no question in the rigorously analytical narrative of the latter of communicating with the heavens or of being in tune with the times; and the reliance on fortune would be the worst mark, that of an enemy easily uprooted.

## The Traditional Story in IR

Now we can outline the contrast between the traditional story and that of modernity.

The central idea of the traditional story is that for most of human history the possession of power and the making of war were inseparable in three ways: empirically, the possession of power was defined by the ability to make war successful which in turn brought more power; secondly, and normatively, the most desirable course of action was that the possession of power would (and should) translate periodically into war-making; thirdly, the power equals war equals power equation was self-contained, for international morality, institutions and regimes, economics, society or culture flow from the equation, they are not cause but consequence. This central idea is brought out in chapter 1.

In implication the idea brings us close to the renaissance narrative: there are no immutable laws governing the relations between societies and nations since the interplay of chance and ability will always determine the outcome of wars; there are no fixed hierarchies either, for hierarchies are the product of power and power is dependent on the outcome of war; so these relations are anything but stable; another effect of the play of chance and the unforeseen is that there is no irreversible movement forward according to some predetermined destiny.

A closely related idea, applied to colonial times, is discussed in chapter 3. The equation of war with power, adapted to the discussion on empire, could be rewritten as power equals empire equals war. By the middle of the nineteenth century the power and prestige of European great powers had come to depend on the acquisition of an empire and the size of that empire. Opposing those powers was the nationalism of those who were to be ruled, which generated the unyielding tenacity to be free of foreign rule. Examples of the encounter of these two opposing forces have been given.

Chapters 5 and 6 are specific illustrations of the ideas above, in the cases of Indonesia and Algeria. In each case there was the colonial power with war and military operations as its main instrument for making an empire and thence becoming powerful. On the other side, there were the colonised peoples who resisted. Nationalism was the main driving force in this resistance, and here we encounter the importance of leaders like Prince Depo Negoro in Indonesia and Amir Abdel Kader in Algeria, who gave inspiration to all those who finally succeeded in ousting the colonial powers in the twentieth century. Chapters 5 and 6 also illustrate the way the colonial powers continued the slaughter of the war to hang on long after that war had been lost.

Chapter 7 is about what happened after 1945, as far as the traditional story is concerned, and this is continued in chapter 8. These chapters illustrate the way the smaller countries use their resources, including those of nationalism, to resist the new empire builders. There were four great powers, the victors of World War II: France, Britain, the USA and the Soviet Union. They lost a great deal of their status as a result of wars against smaller powers; how the so-called rivalry between them, often called the Cold War, didn't really exist, is also described.

The French lost their great power status once they had lost the war for Algeria; the British lost it after they lost the war for South Yemen, which is discussed in chapter 7. That left the USA and the Soviet Union, with the former acknowledged to be in the lead, much more powerful than any other power, with the latter a distant second. Chapter 8 illustrates the way these two worked in cooperation to try pushing the smaller ones around.[14] Their efforts were not very successful for the smaller powers could with ever greater ease resist what the great powers tried to do to them; there are several examples of how this happened, more about the USA than about the Soviet Union, since the former tried harder.

Chapters 10 and 11 are again case studies from the years after 1945. The first is on Vietnam. When the US lost that war its politico-military structure began to crack. Indeed that war is a good illustration of the way in which the discrepancy between the way power operates on the ground and ideas about how it should operate prolongs slaughter. For five years, from 1968 to 1973, having already lost that war, the US continued to fight, years which were accompanied by massive destruction of the Vietnamese people and economy and what appeared to be the irreversible loss of US political, military and economic primacy. So the US lost its uncontested position at the top of the world's politico-military pecking order.

Later, of course, the US did recover to the extent of asserting its position as the sole superpower. But in the late 1970s it was the Soviet Union that was well on the way to becoming the most powerful country on the planet.

Then came the Soviet invasion of Afghanistan, covered in chapter 11. Losing that war meant the end of Soviet power, yet another example of the discrepancy; actually it meant the end of the status of the Soviet Union as a Union; it broke up. Soviet power dropped with cascading effect. Their geo-strategic position had ranged from Africa to Latin America, even the Gulf; their blue water navies operated across the world's oceans; all of which disappeared. In

Cuba and Vietnam, in South Yemen, Ethiopia and Angola there was no respect left for the power and ability of the Soviet Union. Then Hungary broke away from the Soviet orbit; then Poland, Bulgaria, Czechoslovakia, and all the others; that left the Soviet Union itself, and that too dissolved.

The next two chapters, 12 and 13, are about the American invasions of Iraq and Afghanistan, and are based on the presumption that the same trends which have been evident since 1945 will again assert themselves. If this happens the two smaller countries, driven by nationalism, will defeat the US, which will quickly, and as a direct result, lose its world status. But nationalism, as will be apparent from the previous chapters, comes in many varieties; so it will be in Afghanistan that the US will face defeat in a starker form than in Iraq.

## The Origins of the Modernity Story

The modernity world-view is covered in only four chapters, 2, 5, 9 and 14, each of them quite short.

This originated in an early 17th century European general crisis. England was heading for the civil war which Oliver Cromwell won, followed by an autocratic dictatorship. France was divided by religious conflict and a peasant rebellion. In Germany the several states were attempting to devour one another. There was a Europe wide economic slump and unemployment which led not only to distress among the people, but to the large scale recruitment of cheaply available mercenaries for the Thirty Years' War (1618-48), thus making that war far more bloody than had generally been the case during the renaissance. The countryside throughout Europe was devastated. Farming stopped as the farmers were force-drafted into one or other military order. To get supplies commanders raided towns and villages for whatever they could find; starvation was consequently widespread. Thousands of hungry women and children followed the armies hoping for scraps. That's the first ingredient of modernity.

The most eminent statesmen, philosophers, political thinkers, writers on ethics of the period lived through this violence, instability and uncertainty and responded with a generalised quest for certainty. So modernity eventually replaced the renaissance episteme. In such times of chaos it was no longer possible, as Machiavelli had suggested should be done, to fit the mode of proceeding to the times. It was necessary to discover abstract, timeless and universal principles based on pure theories. They would open the door to a wholly determinist world governed by laws based on pure reason and logic, which would reign supreme no matter how confused and chaotic the world around.

These should be applicable to science, philosophy, politics and ethics and, of course, to IR. They should provide for a fully found world of hierarchic ordering, irreversible movement in a predictable 'forward' direction, and stability as a constant feature. This again led to an emphasis on peace, to the making of plans for perpetual peace; war and its uncertainties had to be laid to rest for good. Modernity prepared the ground for making peace not just desirable, but an immutable and universal law for peoples and nations. Chapter 2 recounts some peace plans: those which were formulated before the coming of modernity, which were really war plans; and those formulated after, the real peace plans, the hopes for perpetual peace.

Anyway "by 1650, the humanist tolerance of uncertainty, ambiguity and diversity of opinion gave way to Puritan intolerance, rationalist insistence on universal and exact theory, and an emphasis on certainty in all things."[15] That was the second ingredient of modernity.

There was a group of men who framed and elaborated the new world-view or episteme that resulted from the European crisis. The sheer intellectual avoirdupois of these men was enough to ensure that the episteme endured. Over and above this they were known to each other by name or in person, interacted and influenced each other. The discoveries of Galileo Galilei, for instance, had a strong influence on Rene Descartes, as he himself tells us; Thomas Hobbes, too, was deeply influenced by Galileo; the ethical philosopher Spinoza based his theories on Cartesian materialism and determinism. So that avoirdupois was multiplied, not added. Some examples follow.

After Galileo our view of space became transformed; now it was peopled by a large number of objects which were not circling the earth, which thereby became small and somewhat insignificant; so did the human race. Human destiny was disconnected from the planets and stars. In effect the laws that governed space became bigger than the earth or its inhabitants; these laws were timeless, impersonal, universal, stable, immutable, and not subject to chance or the contingent. We shall see the way immutable and impersonal laws, laws impervious to the preferences of men, as pointed out in chapter 9, were sought for after 1945 in the world of IR. This included the measurement of power, which was now done solely by statistical analysis. You didn't have to do anything to show how powerful you were; it was all there in the books. After 1945 great tables of economic and other statistics, published by the UN, the World Bank and so on established the power hierarchy of nations.

Descartes did this for philosophy, building a whole structure which is irrefutable because it is derived from incontestable premises by pure reasoning; thereafter it was taken for granted that this structure built from necessary truths would be an isomorph of that built to describe the natural world; practical physics would become geometry in motion, following which colonialism became Social Darwinism in motion, the practical implementation of a natural, immutable or God-given hierarchy; while IR during the Cold War became the super power balance in motion. Western philosophy, incidentally, has still not recovered from Descartes obsession with how we can be certain that we know what we know.

Spinoza did it for ethics. Pure logic rules in his *Ethics*; there are definitions, axioms, theorems; all the theorems are proved by deductive argument; ethics is to be discovered by reasoning alone. Timeless and universal principles govern the decisions about what is good and what is just. But there could be hiccups; some nations may take a route which modernity does not prescribe, in which case intervention may be necessary to re-establish the transcendental, the ordered progress of the world. Chapter 9 gives more details about how this happened after 1945.

As for the political Thomas Hobbes is the best representative of this new episteme. Until the middle of the 17th century politics had been only about city states, kingdoms, principalities and so on, their historical experience and what one could learn from it. Thereafter (*Leviathan* was published in 1651) humans in nature are the starting point for politics; they are like objects in space, without morality or justice. Each man uses his own power to do whatever he likes to preserve his life. Result: a perpetual war of every man against his neighbour. To overcome this men arrive at a contract to give sovereign power to one man or an assembly and that power has to be unlimited in order successfully to overcome the state of war in which nature has left man. As the Canadian political economist C.B.

Macpherson wrote in the introduction to one edition of Hobbes Leviathan, "he had truly caught the spirit of the new science that was transforming men's understanding of the natural world ... bold hypothesis and closely reasoned deduction from it..."[16]

The sheer eminence of those who created it was the third ingredient of modernity further explaining its strength and resilience.

## Modernity and IR

All the three ingredients described above went into the shaping of IR today. As one of the classics of the field has it, which claims to have discovered the final theory on the subject, there are laws by which society lives and these are objective laws. "Realism, believing as it does in the objectivity of the laws of politics, must also believe in the possibility of developing a rational theory that reflects ... these laws."[17]

For IR purposes as for world-views in general the divide between the renaissance story and that of modernity is conceptually clear: the Peace Treaty of Westphalia that brought an end to the Thirty Years' War.

Before Westphalia a multiplicity of authorities had or claimed jurisdiction over a given people and territory: the Pope; lay rulers or Kings; the monastic orders, not always under the control of the Pope, such as the Teutonic Knights; city states like Florence; city leagues like the Hanseatic League that signed treaties with monarchs, raised and used armed forces; and, among others, there were the feudal barons who disputed the authority of the Kings. This kaleidoscope of authorities constantly tried to encroach on each other's territories and populations, for recruitment into their militias and armies, for taxes, for religious loyalty.

Westphalia changed all that. One ruler came to hold all power over one territory and people. Absolute kings replaced even the representative institutions that had characterised several principalities and the kings were able to set about unifying the people, giving them one set of mutually consistent laws and obligations, and above all creating nations. Given the depredations of war, especially by the thousands of hired mercenaries, the practice quickly spread of recruiting only fully professional soldiers, thus for the first time separating the civilian from the soldier. Now a body of troops, recruited on a long-term basis and whose only task was to fight wars could be trained and disciplined to fight for the state.

This was the fourth ingredient of modernity and the one specific to IR. So was made possible the emergence of IR as we know it, not as an academic discipline, for that came in the twentieth century, but as practice.

Social Darwinism and the entire body of thought that accompanied and justified colonialism also had its beginning here; so did the entire business of dividing time into eras, like the pre-colonial, the colonial, the Cold War, the post-Cold War, each later era being an advance on the previous one. Today it is difficult to think of history without dividing it up into eras, one world-wide consequence of that mid-seventeenth century European crisis. Chapter 4 points out the consequences of all this for the colonial years: the empire-makers' belief that the wars to establish colonies were really quite insignificant, since it was primitive peoples against whom they were fought; indeed the natives of the colonies didn't matter, for it was the empire-makers that decided everything of any significance. In any case the empires were acquired more or less by accident. And they were lost for reasons that had nothing to do with the colonised people. In fact nationalism in the colonies was largely the creation of the empire-makers. In every aspect, thus, this story is the polar opposite of the traditional story. Chapter 4 also points out that Marxism, then as now, is in tandem with the modernity of other western thinking, not in opposition.

Chapter 9 is about the Cold War. During this period war was separated completely from power. At the time empires were being acquired wars between the great powers could and did happen. Once the Cold War began, even these wars were no more possible, meaning there was a final severing of the equation of war with power. The end of the Cold War happened, according to the modernity story, because the US won it, but this argument is so well known that it is not dwelt on.

Chapter 14 takes these trends beyond the Cold War. War had already been diffracted and scattered as a concept, while academic efforts were made to bring its study on to a mathematical basis. Now, after the Cold War, it became even more diffuse. As for power it was proclaimed that there was now a new structure of international relations: unipolar, with the United States alone at the head. The chapter ends with a projection of the way things will turn out in Afghanistan and Iraq according to the modernity story.

## Endnotes

This is not an academic or research work. It's a memoir. The endnotes are thus not a bibliography but a selection of comments which do not really belong to the text and a list of readings done mostly during but also after my diplomatic career. These have been placed at the end of each chapter, rather than all together at the end of the book; I have always found this to be more convenient while reading any book. For further convenience the endnotes contain all the references in that chapter even if some of these are duplications from other chapters; this means each chapter is self-contained and the reader will not have to refer from one chapter to another. This also means there is some overlap, but since the material used for any one chapter is pretty much widely different from any other, not much.

Some grouping of references has been done, where one or a few successive paragraphs have references to different pages of the same work. This makes for a shorter list. Right through the book there are references to people and places; where appropriate these are explained in the text, but brief particulars are there in the index

And some of the references have been used in support of one story, then in support of its opposite; see chapter 3 for the why and how of this happening.

### ENDNOTES

[1] Kautilya's *Arthashastra,* translated by R. Shamasastry, Mysore Printing and Publishing House, Mysore, 1967.

[2] Though there is no dearth of scholars who have compared the two. Of course, almost all take Megasthenes as the more authoritative, which is also in accordance with the traditional story!

[3] The Greek historian and geographer, circa 63 BC to 23 AD.

[4] *Ancient India as described by Megasthenes and Arrian,* Transl. J.W.McCrindle, Chuckervertty, Chatterjee & Co. Ltd, Calcutta, 1960, pp. 54, 61, 75-80.

[5] The Greek Ambassador to the court of Bindusara, successor to Chandragupta Maurya.

[6] Romila Thapar, *Early India, From the Origins to AD 1300*, Allen Lane, London, 2002, p. 177.

[7] This is distinct from epistemology, which is the philosophical theory of knowledge and looks at the varieties of knowledge, the separation of deductive from inductive knowledge or how certain we can be that we know something. Epistemology is solely theoretical and unconcerned with

practical application. The episteme is a specific epistemological field; it is concerned primarily with practical knowledge, the way it is applied to a particular society. This is a little bit like the difference between the study of cricket as a sport and the watching of a particular match.

[8] Michel Foucault, *The Order of Things, An Archaeology of the Human Sciences*, Vintage Books, New York, 1994, p. xxii.

[9] Michel Foucault, op. cit., p. 19.

[10] Thucydides, *History of the Peloponnesian War*, Penguin Books, London, 1972, p. 48.

[11] Michel Foucault, op. cit., pp. 27-28.

[12] Niccolo Machiavelli, *The Prince*, Wilco Publishing House, Mumbai, 2004, p. 116-119. He does add that fortune is the arbiter of only half our actions; we control the other half.

[13] Stephen Toulmin, *Cosmopolis, The Hidden Agenda of Modernity*, University of Chicago Press, 1990, p. 29, discussing 16th century or renaissance humanism.

[14] Sometimes this argument is attributed to Chinese thinking after the 1963 break with the Soviet Union, or with the Cultural Revolution of the late 1960s; also to those who led the revolutions of 1968 in Europe. It is more correct to say that the Chinese and revolutionaries learnt all this from the independence struggles of the former colonies and then used it for their own ends.

[15] Stephen Toulmin, op. cit., p. 160.

[16] Thomas Hobbes, *Leviathan*, edited with an introduction by C.B.Macpherson, Penguin Books, London, 1985, p. 10.

[17] Hans Morgenthau, *Politics Among Nations, The Struggle for Power and Peace*, Scientific Book Agency, Calcutta, 1966, p. 4. His theory, realism, is certainly the most widely accepted one, as explained in chapter 9.

# 1

# War and Power: The Pre-Colonial Era

Power is the central organising concept in the world of IR. It occupies the place that money occupies in the world of economics, or dates and the passage of time in the world of history.

The traditional story, as outlined in this chapter, tells us that if at all it was necessary and useful to rank states/rulers/Kings in an order which shows their position in the hierarchy of power, this was done by the results of war, which was, of course, an uncertain and unpredictable way. But for most of human history the possession of power and the making of war were inseparable. Within the epistemological space of relations between Kings or rulers or states the link between war and power has through the ages occupied a central position.

After 1945, as a result of the increasing destructiveness of war, the resort to ever larger deployments of men to the battlefield and of the propaganda necessary to induce them to fight there were changes in public postures, but the link remained.

## The Three-Way Link between War and Power

There has always been a three-way link between war and power. This is also true today.

In the first place, in what concerns the empirical, war has throughout history been taken to be a normal part of the life of kings and rulers; for them the possession of power meant the ability to make successful war; the judgment of how much power you had depended on the extent to which you made war successful or not; one ruler or king was more powerful than another if, and only if, the former was victorious in war against the latter. There is not a separation of the latency of power from the exercise of it; power is to be seen and measured only in action; and it is the moment when you inflict defeat on your enemy, and by virtue of that defeat, that your greater power is to be seen.

Secondly, as concerns the normative, that is to say, the most desirable course of action, before 1945 the classical thinkers were clear that the possession of power would (and should) translate periodically into war-making which, in turn, would translate into greater power; the converse was equally true, for the less powerful ruler or king would, and should, be attacked by the more powerful. Only submission could avoid this. The idea that peace could be desirable in itself, or that some version of a Kantian perpetual peace is something that statesmen should work for would have been strange to Kautilya or Machiavelli or Clausewitz. Indeed in "most of the societies known to history, war has been an established and usually rather enjoyable social rite. In Western Europe until the first part of the seventeenth century, warfare was a way of life for considerable sections of society, its termination was for them a catastrophe, and its prolongation, official or unofficial, was the legitimate objective of every man of spirit."[1] This implied also that war is a normal part of the human condition, something that was, even if not at all times desirable, to be accepted.

Thirdly, the power equals war equals power equation was self-contained. Neither international morality, institutions and regimes, nor economics, society nor culture had any influence on it. Indeed they all flow from the equation, they are not cause but consequence; war leads to power and it is that power which determines the kind of morality, institutions, society or culture we should have. As one recent commentator puts it, "the harsh fact is that the state structure of the international system as it exists today is not the result of peaceful, teleological growth, the evolution of nations whose seeds have germinated in the womb of time and have come to a natural fruition. It is the result of conflicts that might, in very many cases, have been resolved differently ..."[2]

Those ancients who thought about war accepted it as part, or even the most important part of the life of man once he is organised into communities. We can start with the Greeks, since they have a lot to say on the subject.

Heraclitus of ancient Greece thought that war "is the father of all and the king of all"; adding "we must know that war is common to all and strife is justice".[3]

In Sparta, during the fifth and sixth centuries BC, to give the most obvious example, the entire machinery of government was devoted to the sole aim of greater efficiency in war; the citizens were trained only for war, all the business of land cultivation and so on being done by slaves; only healthy children were allowed to live; while women were schooled to harden their bodies so that their children would be strong. Whereas the Greek states in general took war as a normal part of the daily business of state and citizen, in Sparta the entire devotion of the state was to war for the sake of war and power and preserving freedom and conquest; in other words, Sparta took this to the extreme and, of course, was admired by all the other Greek states. Plato thought it was the nearest approach to the ideal.

Plato didn't actually go all the way with Heraclitus; he was more matter of fact, accepting that as mankind gathers into cities and makes governments, he also has to learn the art of war; while Aristotle, Plato's pupil, disapproved of war, suggesting that it is mainly tyrants who make war, to keep their subjects from opposing their tyranny. But Aristotle was for three years tutor to Alexander, one of the greatest warriors the world has seen, and he could not entirely disapprove. So he suggested two things: that rulers may make war if it was necessary to live in peace; and that war may be made on those people who are naturally suited to be slaves but are unwilling to accept that status. This becomes a justification for any war, turning Aristotle's disapproval on its head; but it is still a justification, meaning war is not a part of normal life but requires special justification.

But Aristotle was an exception. Take one of the most famous passages in Greek history, Pericles funeral oration. Here Thucydides the Athenian, writing nearly two and a half millennia ago, around 400 BC, quotes him as starting with a reference to "the warlike deeds by which we acquired our power" and it is that which enables them to enjoy a constitutional democracy, a free and open political life and the benefits of beauty and good taste; so all these benefits of life flowed from the power that successful war-making entailed. The heart of Pericles oration is to praise the Athenian ability to make offensive and defensive war. Continuing with this normative approach, Thucydides takes up the question of morality when the Athenians face the Melians and tell them that the "standard of justice depends on the equality of power to compel and that in fact the strong do what they have the power to do and the weak accept what they have to accept." When the Melians appeal to morality, to the possibility of a "principle that is to the general good of all men" the Athenians reply that there is no difference between right and wrong and only those can prevail who are strong.[4] In other words, morality is consequence, not cause, where war is concerned.

In India, too, war has always been accepted as part of life, even as the most important part. One of the leading authorities on the sources of Indian traditions writes that "with very few exceptions, Indian thinkers looked on warfare as legitimate." One school, of the *Mahabharata*[5] and the *Law book* of Manu "looked on war as good in its own right, as a very exciting, if very grim, sort, and sometimes even as a religious duty". The other school, of Kautilya, looked on war as "a legitimate last resort in achieving the aims of statecraft".[6] Somadeva, a political commentator of the Gupta period (early fourth to mid-sixth century AD), looked on war "as a normal activity of the King". Even in Jainism, founded in the fifth century BC, which has traditionally had the most extreme commitment to non-violence, it has been remarked that no Jain King gave up war, unlike Asoka, and that Jain literature nowhere advocates peace between Kingdoms as a desirable goal.[7]

The law-giver, Manu,[8] was quite clear about the equation of war and power, that "when challenged by rivals – whether they are stronger, weaker, or of equal strength – as he protects his subjects, a King must never back away from battle, recalling the Law of Ksatriyas ...", and there was a bonus, for "when Kings fight each other in battles with all their strength, seeking to kill each other and refusing to turn back, they go to heaven". Furthermore, insofar as it concerns the normative, "the King should seek to acquire what he has not acquired, and what he has not acquired he should seek to acquire by military force ... he should keep his military force in constant readiness, constantly display his might, constantly guard his secrets, and constantly probe his enemy's weakness ... it is with military force, therefore, that he should subdue all creatures". He should never use guile; however, a little further on Manu does add that war should be avoided since victory and defeat are uncertain, so the King should use conciliation, gifts, and fomenting dissensions among his enemies.[9]

Kautilya, who came somewhat later, affirmed the first and second points above, in essence, when he asserted that there are only two forms of policy, peace and war, and adds that "whoever is inferior to another shall make peace with him; whoever is superior in power shall wage war". It is only if you cannot destroy the other in war and he cannot destroy you that you should make peace, bide your time, meanwhile build up your strength, ensure that it gets to be greater than that of your opponent, if need be by seeking allies, and then make war. "Whoever is rising in power may break the agreement of peace"; in other words, peace is a temporary, atypical state of affairs during which preparations are being made for war. And war is the resource of first resort, once you are reasonably sure you can win it. As for the third point, morality and virtue, he clearly linked this with making war, but again as consequence, not cause. Morality follows results on the battlefield. Good character means conquering. The king who is possessed of good character "is termed the conqueror".[10]

## The Conduct of War

So much for the ancients.

War has been equally, or perhaps even more central to the Islamic faith. Here the world is divided into Dar al-Islam, the House of Faith, comprising the community of believers; and Dar al-Harb, the House of War, which consisted of everyone else. Jihad is the obligation of every Muslim ruler to strive to convert or subjugate all those in the Dar al-Harb. The leading Islamic scholar Bernard Lewis clarifies that between the two houses "there is a morally necessary, legally and religiously obligatory state of war, until the final and inevitable triumph of Islam over unbelief"; such a war is the first duty of those who hold power, and is morally justified under all conditions. Even within the Islamic fold might becomes right: if one person assumes the Imamat by force and military supremacy, "and thereafter there arises another who overcomes the first by his might and his armies, then the first is deposed and the second becomes Imam ..."[11]

Furthermore, even when the realities of relative military power showed little hope of success "the jurists were careful to insist that the obligation of Jihad survived every change of government or regime";[12] and it survived peace, which is to be regarded, the way Kautilya and Machiavelli would have, as a temporary truce or ceasefire before the resumption, inevitably, of hostilities. But this obligation goes much further than either Kautilya or Machiavelli would have taken it since it is there regardless of the likely result, which, of course, led to the sanctity of the suicide mission. In the history of Islam the fidayeen, those who are not only willing to lay down their lives for the cause, but volunteer for missions from which they are unlikely to return alive, occupy a special place of honour for their heroism.

Coming to a later period, Renaissance Europe, it continues to be a fundamental truth that war should be the aim of every ruler; that war is equal to power; that the universe of morality, religion, institutions and so on flows from war and not vice versa.

Machiavelli, whose *The Prince* was published in 1513, makes the point forcefully: that, where the empirical is concerned (and given that you are in tune with the times), only the possession of one's own arms gives security. Only the prince who has "sufficient power and resources", meaning "a sufficient supply of men or of money to put an adequate army in the field" can be an independent prince; and, as regards the normative, he must have no other objective than war: "no other objective, no other thought, nor take up any other profession but that of war". And "he must never turn his attention away from military matters. Indeed, he should devote himself to them in time of peace even more than in time of war", which, of course, echoes Kautilya.

As for morality and the universe of values, Machiavelli notes with approval how useful religion was in directing armies, in animating the people, and that "where there is religion, it is easy to introduce military discipline" and that, therefore, rulers should enhance religious belief "even if they themselves judge it to be false". War, therefore, takes precedence over all of virtue and morality, over truth and social values. Indeed the universe of all such things, matters of belief, is the product of war and of the use of force: "all armed prophets have succeeded and all unarmed ones have failed"; in the universe of belief it is necessary that when the people "no longer believe, they can be forced to believe".[13]

For Thomas Hobbes, of course, writing during the middle of the seventeenth century and soon after the end of the Thirty Years'

War, it is in the very nature of men, that "they are in that condition which is called Warre; and such warre, as is of every man, against every man"; in other words, *bellum omnium contra omnes*. If they are under a sovereign authority, then "in all times, Kings, and Persons of Soveraigne authority, because of their Independency, are in continual jealousies, and in the state and posture of Gladiators; having their weapons pointing, and their eyes fixed on one another ... which is a posture of war ... but because they uphold thereby the industry of their subjects; there does not follow from it, that misery which accompanies the Liberty of particular men."[14] In other words, it is better for people to be under a sovereign authority and in a state of potential or actual war at all times than to be without any authority to live under.

But change was in the air. The change had two related components which interfered with the idea that war is, and should be, part of our day-to-day existence: firstly with time an ever increasing number of soldiers got on to ever more bloody battlefields; and secondly an ever longer list of just causes or justifications for war had to be found to get them there.

As for the first, during and before the renaissance the conduct of war in Europe was the responsibility of princes and their hired, trained mercenaries. The latter often served one prince for one season, another for the next; they fought for money; war was a profession like other professions and a part of daily life, so casualties were avoided. Battles were often pretty much bloodless, a tradition that was well established in the time of Machiavelli. He refers to large-scale battles in which the total number killed was two or three; and others in which less than half a dozen persons died. Daniel Defoe wrote of armies of fifty thousand men each, which spent a whole campaign season just dodging one another and then, when winter came, marched off to their winter quarters.

One historian writes of the result of leaving the conduct of war to mercenaries, "that it came often to be waged as a mere tactical exercise or game of chess" the aim being to outmanoeuvre the enemy, not to engage him in battle. Even as late as the battle of Valmy between the French and the Prussians, fought in September, 1792, long after the Thirty Years' War, there was virtually no fighting, only manoeuvre of such consummate skill that the two adversaries were left at the end of it facing their respective bases, more or less with their backs to each other, with the result that the Prussians "skillfully withdrew from the last of the all but bloodless battlefields." The Prussian commander at that battle, Charles William Frederick Duke of Brunswick, had notably made his reputation "largely founded on his 1787 campaign in Holland, which was so completely bloodless that, in the eyes of his contemporaries, he was held to be the greatest soldier in Europe" Then there was another 'battle', the siege of Pizzeghetone in 1793, during which besieged and besieger got together, "all the officers entertained one another by turns ... there was nothing but balls, entertainment and concerts."[15]

This is reminiscent of the Chinese classic on the art of war in which Sun Tzu recommends there is no instance of a country having benefited from prolonged warfare, so to subdue the enemy without fighting is the acme of skill.

The Thirty Years' War initiated the change; it was, as pointed out in the introduction, both large-scale and particularly bloody; so it became a watershed in the transition to the story of modernity; now battles, with very few exceptions, could not be fought with few casualties. In general later wars were quite exceptionally bloody in comparison with what had been the norm during the renaissance. Such wars took the first step in preparing the ground for the eventual rejection, in the public statements of leaders and commentators, of the idea that war is normatively desirable or even acceptable as a part of the human condition; though that rejection didn't actually come until the twentieth century. Adam Smith, writing in the 1760s and 1770s, the father-figure of liberalism and proponent of the theory of 'the invisible hand' by which one man's self-interest serves society as a whole, who we could expect would be for peace, thought war is noble, "the art of war ... is certainly the noblest of all arts."[16]

Then comes Jean Jacques Rousseau in the latter part of the eighteenth century. Rousseau[17] continued the tradition that took success in war as a sign of merit. "Every force that is greater than the first succeeds to its right ... the strongest being always in the right, the only thing that matters is to act so as to become the strongest."[18] Here again, there is war for the sake of war and as a normal part of life. If you win the war right is on your side. So again, we have morality as consequence, not cause.

So it came slowly; but change was definitely in the air.

## The French Revolution: War Needs Justification

The French Revolution took it forward much more rapidly and brought both components of the change into the forefront.

Traditionally, when rulers couldn't, for whatever reason, get people to go to war they tried to find ways to encourage or force them to do so. The traditions of chivalry, of the glory and honour of war, of the brotherhood of comrades in arms, had always been there, as for example, in the story of King Arthur and his knights; or in the stirring lines of William Shakespeare in *Henry V*, as the king says "we few, we happy few, we band of brothers"; and in much romantic literature through the ages. The emotional call to arms was as old as history.

The just cause was another way of encouraging them to do so. In the fifth century AD St. Augustine, who famously said that we do not seek peace in order to be at war, but war that we may have peace, wrote of the just war, one conducted to right a wrong or avenge an injury. This was only a way of finding a road to bypass the biblical commandment not to kill; believers had to find an authority to sanction war and a justification for it.[19] But the sequence of events was that first the ruler or leader starts the war; then he gets the people emotionally involved by finding a justification for having done so. The historian of the Roman Empire reminds us that for the first crusade, launched at the end of the eleventh century by Christendom, Pope Urban the Second "proclaimed a *plenary indulgence* to those who should enlist under the banner of the cross; the absolution of *all* their sins", and so, "at the voice of their pastor, the robber, the incendiary, the homicide, arose by thousands to redeem their souls by repeating on the infidels the same deeds which they had exercised against their Christian brethren"[20]. So that was the sequence: first the war, then the just cause to get everybody on board.

One long sideways step will take this argument into peace plans, but here we are concerned with a different step: the number of people who fought and total casualties of the wars of the French Revolution put those wars into a different league. The actual conduct of war during and after the Revolution necessitated the raising of large-scale armies through conscription, for while revolutionary France was hemmed in by enemies on all sides, it was also too poor to pay volunteers. So in the France of the 1790s the entire nation became a potential armed force. On 23 August, 1793 a decree was issued in which article 1 provided that all Frenchmen are permanently requisitioned for service in the armies: the young to fight; the old to preach hatred against kings; the married men to forge weapons; the women to make tents; the children to make linen into lint. Thus far military recruits had been underpaid and reluctant to enlist; or you could get mercenary soldiers who had been costly; now the decree got large numbers of soldiers cheap, and they could be put into battles that were bloody. This made them even more reluctant to fight, with a greater need to rouse emotions. The recruits had to be convinced they were really fighting for *la patrie*, for liberty, equality and fraternity; you had to give them a justification for war.

It was also during the period of the French Revolution that the British constitutionalist and liberal utilitarian Edmund Burke (1729-97) advocated that war against revolutionary France was a religious duty, a Holy War, a war between the forces of Darkness and the forces of Light, a total war in which it was no longer necessary to observe any rules.

So on both sides, the Revolution and its opponents, war became not just an emotional call to arms, or a moral crusade; it became a cause for the entire nation, a prime-mover which could unify the people, cement the bond between state and people that would ensure the health of the state. In contrast to the Greek idea, now war had become a necessity for the protection (or the destruction) of the Revolution. So far war had been taken as a part of daily life; it needed a little call to heroism, perhaps some religious justification. But from now on war needed a much larger justification to ensure that the mass armies, forcibly drafted, paid little, would still fight with courage and commitment. And the next step was the generation of a cause, be it state necessity or Social Darwinism, as described below, or then at a later stage taking up the White Man's Burden or the safeguarding of the Aryan race, or, at an even later stage, the promotion of democracy: from an era in which war needed a cause, it came to be true in time that the cause needed the war.

Thus began the preparation of the ground for the rejection, at least in public, of the traditional normative link between war and power; and for the assertion, in another reversal of the historical links between war and power, of the need for morality, institutions, society, culture and the state to influence or even be determinative in the waging of war.

## War and the State

An important step was the linking of war and the state. War brought power to the state internally, greater control over people's lives; while victory brought international power. And so war became a necessity for the state, linked to its evolution; the history and function of the state became, in the hands of several philosophers and military thinkers, the history and function of war. We can trace this through three well-known writers of the nineteenth century, by way of example.

The philosophy is best characterised by Georg Wilhelm Friedrich Hegel, for whom the state is the highest achievement of man, the highest expression of rationality and the Divine idea as it exists on earth. Hence individual lives have no meaning, no spiritual reality, except as they are members of a state. States evolve through a dialectical process of history, a process in which war serves the essential function of revitalising the state. So war becomes both a necessary consequence of the emergence of the state and an estate, an integral contributor to the health of the body politic. For Hegel the emergence of the state justifies war.

Even the British utilitarians who were against war in general thought it could be justified. One of the most prominent among them and our second example, John Stuart Mill, scorned the decayed and degraded state of moral and patriotic feeling of those who think nothing is worth war; the person who has nothing for which he is willing to fight is a miserable creature with no chance of being free. And if they didn't justify it, they did accept that it was generally part of the functioning of the state. Jeremy Bentham, Mills' mentor, and the founder of the utilitarians, wrote in his proposal for a perpetual peace that "hitherto war has been the national rage: peace has always come too soon – war too late". To make the ministers accountable for war would be to deprive them of "numberless occasions of seizing those happy advantages that lead to war."[21]

Carl von Clausewitz, the third example, asserted that war was everything, and it was intimately connected to the state; and it should be bloody. Writing to his fiancée he said, "My country needs the war and – let us admit it openly – the war only can bring me to the happy goal".[22] Here again we have the argument that the emergence of the state (and his urge to get married!) justifies war. Now the renaissance idea of war as a genteel activity carried out with the minimum of casualties was no more acceptable. For Clausewitz demanded that "let us not hear of Generals who conquer without bloodshed. If a bloody slaughter is a horrible sight, then that is a ground for paying more respect to War, but not for making the sword we wear blunter and blunter by degrees from feelings of humanity ..."[23]

As put by Anatol Rapoport, himself a strategic thinker of note, and the editor of one of the recent editions of Clausewitz's *magnum opus*, his was a mind "which embraces war as an essential, productive, and inspiring component of human existence..." It was also, of course, not an independent thing in itself; it was "nothing but a continuation of political intercourse, a carrying out of the same with a mixture of other means", in the oft-quoted phrase.[24]

Later, in the lead up to the Franco-German war of 1870-71, political and military leaders from both sides welcomed and looked forward eagerly to the outbreak of hostilities, much as Clausewitz himself would have done. The French ideologue Ardant du Picq, to give just one example, wrote admiringly of the Prussian aristocracy that "it wants distinction through force; and to dominate, always to dominate more ... one dominates through war; it needs war ... it wants war".[25] And bloodshed, for others, after Clausewitz, were even more bloodthirsty than he was. The French Marshall Foch, for instance, wrote in 1911 that in battle there is no law but the offensive and the aim is to destroy the enemy, so "this result can only be obtained at the price of bloody sacrifice." And in 1914 a French officer is quoted as saying, "terrify, in order to terrify and destroy. The immediate object of fighting is to kill and to go on killing, until there is nothing left to kill".[26]

## War and Social Darwinism

A far stronger argument justifying war came with Charles Darwin. He is the fourth writer and the one who had an especially baneful influence on the colonial enterprise. War now became a necessity for the human race, linked not simply to the evolution of the state, but to evolution itself. It was a sort of final, irreducible cause justifying war. Social Darwinism provided a different and what appeared scientifically more rigorous justification for war based on universally valid reasoning: the survival of the fittest.

If, as Darwin so cogently elaborated, all species and their sub-species are locked forever in a war of nature, a struggle for existence in which natural selection ensures that only the fittest survive; and if, as he wrote so eloquently in the conclusion of his work, there is grandeur in this view of life for "from the war of nature, from famine and death, the most exalted object ... directly follows;"[27] then the glorification of war in inter-state relations could hardly have found a better advocate. The idea that while the affairs of men inside a state are governed by laws, regulations and rules framed by that state, the affairs of states within the international system are a war of all against all had already been popularized by Hobbes.

Military men, political leaders, philosophers found in Darwin the most powerful justification yet for war. The military men "found in Darwinism a boundless and apparently indisputable *raison d'etre* for their existence and interests – for a war of all nations against each and each against all"[28] Major Max Jahns, who was a leading teacher of military history in nineteenth century Germany, thought that war made for intellectual progress. And when General Friedrich von Bernhardi, who fought in the 1870-71 Franco-German war and was the first to ride through the Arch of Triumph in Paris when the Germans won, became chief of the Military History section of the General Staff, and then wrote a book *Germany and the Next War*, his reflections on war were only in biological terms. In his thinking war becomes a biological necessity of the first importance, a regulative element in the life of mankind which cannot be dispensed with, since without it an unhealthy development will follow, which excludes every advancement of the race, and, therefore, all real civilisation; it is the carrying out of "the natural law, upon which all the laws of nature rest, the law of the struggle for existence".[29] In war, that nation will conquer which can throw into the scale the greatest physical, mental, moral and political power; by giving that nation enlarged possibilities of expansion and widened influence, the progress of mankind will be promoted. And he quotes Goethe in support: to supplant or be supplanted is the essence of life.

It was not only the Germans who thought this way. The US War Department annual report of 1912 drew attention to the larger and larger proportions assumed by America's external problems. America was expanding, so were other nations; so "the contact between great nations and races tends to become constantly closer ... with this comes competition ... the evidence is clear that the nations and races capable of maintaining and protecting themselves are the only ones who can flourish in the world competition."[30]

Others agreed. Karl Pearson, who became the first Galton Professor of Eugenics at University College, London, in 1911, thought "life was struggle, and war was more than just a game – it was a form of natural selection"; and national progress, he thought, depended on racial fitness, of which the supreme test was war. When wars cease mankind will no longer progress for there will be nothing to check the fertility of inferior stock.[31]

In any case, regardless of this generally blood-thirsty attitude, the large-scale recruitment of soldiers, once Revolutionary France showed the way, was copied by every other western power right through the nineteenth century and into the twentieth. Along with the surge of causes for which war could be fought, the nation, the state, the survival of the fittest and so on, this meant bodies of men, larger than ever, all highly motivated, took to battlefields that were ever more bloody, as in 1914; and then again after 1939. The slaughter was immense. The trends set in motion by the Thirty Years' War were taken to the extreme during the two World Wars.

But, thereafter, such was the extreme to which they were taken, nobody could ever be seen to want that kind of slaughter any more, as shown in more detail in chapter 3.

## The Measure of Power

As for power, there was no need, in the view of those who wrote about these questions before 1945, for too much precision or exactness in measuring power. When you won the war you emerged more powerful. But there were some auguries of what was to come right into the centre of IR after 1945.

Quincy Wright, writing during the period between the two World Wars, is one authority who was clear about the relation between power and war, about "the positive correlation between the warlikeness of a state and its relative power" which happens also because of "the structure of the balance of power, which practically assures that all great powers will enter wars which threaten the balance in order to preserve it, a responsibility which smaller states do not have."[32]

But he did not define what he meant by smaller state. When he completed the research he had begun in 1926 on the causes of war and the nature of international relations he included some general indications about the elements that contributed to a nation's power, but saw no need for detailed and measurable indices. He had given a clue to what this could be, while analysing the chances of war. He suggested indices; more than military technology, power positions or ideologies, he prefers indices of attitude changes as measured by, for instance, newspaper opinions. But when analysts assert that power can be measured by indices, such as "available population, raw materials, industrial skill, and industrial plant capable of producing military power", he says "this is very difficult to realise in practice."[33]

But people like Bertrand Russell, to give one more example, writing in 1938 about this subject, saw no need to go into details of how to measure what he was writing about. He wrote of priestly power, kingly power, revolutionary power, naked power, but none of these needed to be measured.[34]

As late as 1954 the historian A.J.P. Taylor wrote about the nineteenth century that "the test of a Great Power is then the test of strength for war". And that test was to be decided by the infantry, "infantry determined the outcome of battle". But he did make his contribution in a vague way to the ranking of powers "the difference between the Great Powers was much less than that between any of them and the strength of the small states."[35]

In general, before 1945, that is, before the IR component of the modernity story started getting properly established, the elements that gave one nation greater or lesser power did not need to be debated. There was some research and writing on measurement but this was not considered to be a central problem. Since it was war that actually decided who was more powerful such measurement was only useful to try and anticipate which of the powers had an edge over which other in the event of war. The world of international relations was confined to Europe, with the USA and Japan as necessary appendages, the measure of each player's power was thought to be known and actually was roughly known, and far more attention was given to the things that had mattered in history, such as the policies of leaders, the way balance could be achieved, or the impact of revolution.

## ENDNOTES

[1] Michael Howard, Military Power and International Order, in John Garnett, ed., *Theories of Peace and Security, A Reader in Contemporary Strategic Thought*, Macmillan, London, 1970, p. 42.

[2] Michael Howard, War and Nations, in John Hutchinson and Anthony Smith, eds., *Nationalism*, OUP, Oxford, 1994, p. 256.

[3] Thus generating a phrase often used by IR scholars in the post-1945 world, *bellum omnium pater.* The second quotation is from Bertrand Russell, *History of Western Philosophy*, George Allen and Unwin, London, 1947, pp.61, 63.

[4] Thucydides, *History of the Peloponnesian War*, Penguin Books, London, 1972, pp. 145, and 402-403.

[5] This includes the *Bhagavadgita*, which extols going to war as the highest duty, as the opening of the gates of heaven for a Kshatriya; and dilates on the dishonour, disrepute worse than death and shame of a Kshatriya who refuses to go to war.

[6] Actually he didn't, despite the interpretation given by Ainslee Embree in the reference cited here below; he thought of it as the first resort; see the text further on in the chapter for quotations from Kautilya. He was adviser to Chandragupta Maurya, and helped him in establishing a great empire in the fourth century BC, and which extended over the greater part of India and all the way to the Hindu Kush.

[7] Ainslee T. Embree, ed. *Sources of Indian Tradition, Vol. I, From the Beginning to 1800*, Penguin Books, New Delhi, 1992, p. 87.

[8] According to the Indian epic, *The Mahabharata*, Manu was imbued with great wisdom and devoted to virtue. And he became the progenitor of a line. And in Manu's race have been born all human beings, Brahmanas, Kshatriyas and others, who have, therefore, been called Manavas.

[9] See Manu's Code of Law, *Manava-Dharmasastra,* transl. Patrick Olivelle, OUP, New Delhi, 2006, pp. 159-164.

[10] Kautilya's *Arthashastra*, translated by R. Shamasastry, Mysore Printing and Publishing House, Mysore, 1967, pp. 295, 347 and 292, respectively.

[11] The Chief Qadi of Egypt, in the ninth century, quoted by Saleem M.M. Qureshi, Pakistan: Islamic Ideology and the Failed State, in Veena Kukreja and M.P. Singh, *Pakistan, Democracy, Development and Security Issues*, Sage Publications, New Delhi, 2005, p. 99.

[12] Bernard Lewis, *The Political Language of Islam*, The University of Chicago Press, Chicago, 1988, p. 73.

[13] Niccolo Machiavelli, *The Prince,* Wilco Publishing House, Mumbai, 2004, pp. 57, 75, 143, 146, and 35 respectively.

[14] Thomas Hobbes, *Leviathan*, Penguin Books, London, 1985, pp. 185-187.

[15] The cases in this and the last paragraph are cited in Major-General J.F.C. Fuller, The Conduct of War, 1789-1961, Natraj Publishers, Dehra Dun, 2003: a quotation by Sir Charles Oman cited on p. 16; the next one is from p. 30, then one from p. 23.

[16] Adam Smith, *The Wealth of Nations*, Bantam Books, New York, 2003, p.886.

[17] Note that he was also a proponent of perpetual peace, see Chapter 2.

[18] Jean-Jacques Rousseau, *The Social Contract and Discourse on the Origin of Inequality*, ed. Lester G. Crocker, Pocket Books, New York, 1967, Ch. 3, p. 10.

[19] This has had a longish history. For centuries the Christian just war tradition flourished, peaking during the Crusades, but then, especially after the Peace of Westphalia, secular claims to decide about war eclipsed those of the Church. Now after 1945 there is a revival of the tradition; and a debate. Catholic Bishops in the US, as one example, put out in 1983 a pastoral letter, 'The Challenge of Peace: God's Promise and Our Response', in which the tradition was reasserted; and then Noam Chomsky wrote that this kind of revival was just a method of legitimizing the pursuit of American political and economic hegemony in *Hegemony or Survival, America's Quest for Global Dominance*, Metropolitan Books, New York, 2003. The real point is that if the revival of such a tradition is needed for the exercise of the power of war, whoever needs it is strapped to the modernity war concept in which morality, institutions or traditions have to be cited to wage war; they are precursor, not sequel, to war.

[20] Edward Gibbon, *The Decline and Fall of the Roman Empire,* The Modern Library, New York, undated, Vol. III, p. 426.

[21] Jeremy Bentham, A Plan for an Universal and Perpetual Peace, in Jeremy Bentham, *The Principles of International Law*, Essay 4, MHTML document on the internet.

[22] Quoted in Alfred Vagts, *A History of Militarism, Civilian and Military*, The Free Press, New York, 1959, p. 131. The 'happy goal' was marriage to his fiancée, attainable only once he had been promoted, which would happen with service in the war.

[23] Carl von Clausewitz, *On War*, Penguin Books, London, 1982, p. 345.

[24] Introduction to Carl von Clausewitz, op. cit., p. 21; and the text of the book, pp. 119 and 402.

[25]Alfred Vagts, op. cit., p. 208.

[26] See Alfred Vagts, op. cit., pp. 222 and 233.

[27] Charles Darwin, *The Origin of Species by Means of Natural Selection*, John Murray, London, 1884, p. 429.

[28] Alfred Vagts, op. cit., p. 390

[29] Quoted in Barbara Tuchman, *August 1914*, Macmillan, London, 1981, p.22

[30] Alfred Vagts, op. cit., p.389.

[31] Niall Ferguson, *Empire, How Britain Made the Modern World,* Penguin Books, London, 2004, p. 264.

[32] Quincy Wright, *A Study of War*, University of Chicago Press, 1942, pp. 848-9.

[33] Quincy Wright, *A Study of War*, abridged version by Louise Leonard Wright, University of Chicago Press, Chicago, 1970, p. 121.

[34] Bertrand Russell, *Power, A New Social Analysis*, George Allen and Unwin, London, 1938.

[35] A.J.P. Taylor, *The Struggle for Mastery in Europe, 1848-1918,* Oxford University Press, 1954, p. xxiv.

# 2

# Peace Plans

The ever lengthening list of just causes for war led to peace plans, for if these just causes were removed by negotiation which brought all sides together peace might be assured.

That war and peace could thus be separated from the other parts of human existence was an ideal to which, until the first half of the twentieth century, only priests and philosophers subscribed, while Kings, other rulers and military leaders did not believe it had any relevance, as pointed out in chapter 1. But the ideal brought forth the concept of a Perpetual Peace which later became an integral part of the modernity story.

Some of the most notable of the peace plans are discussed in what follows.

## Peace Plans: A European Peace

A general European or a world peace had been suggested even before the Peace of Westphalia. Dante Alighieri pleaded in the early fourteenth century for world government in *De Monarchia*. This is the one pre-Westphalian peace plan that corresponds most closely to the truth canons of the modernity story.

Of all things that are ordered to secure blessings to men, according to Dante, peace is the best; by quiet the individual man grows perfect in wisdom; and society is best fitted for its proper work, which may be called divine. The detailed argument follows Euclidean logic. Man's chief aim, wrote Dante, is "to actualise continually the entire capacity of the possible intellect, primarily in speculation, then, ... secondarily, in action" Seated quietly, man "grows perfect in knowledge and wisdom". Hence it is only amid the calm and tranquillity of peace that he can attain to the maximum his powers of intellect and understanding. This world of peace means a unified world; put the whole earth under a monarchy, under one prince who, possessing everything, would desire nothing further, and you have universal peace. In that world the sole ruler would wield power only for the sake of the world's benefit, not his own; he would keep all kings content in their kingdoms, so that peace reigns among them; and this would be strictly a government of law. There are, of course, no details on how this is to be attained, but we do know that Dante was defending the Holy Roman Empire against the claims of the Papacy to the supremacy of Church over temporal power, so perhaps he meant that Empire should rule the world.[1]

Proposals for European peace were made by Pierre Dubois, Antoine Marini and Henry IV of France, among others, all made in response to Turkish military pressure in the East.

Pierre Dubois, more or less in the same period as Dante, was a French publicist and adviser to the French King who suggested the establishment of a state of peace among the Christian nations to be enforced by a Council which would, of course, be led by France. The Council would arbitrate disputes as part of the maintenance of peace but its main function would be to enable the carrying out of successful crusades for the recovery of Jerusalem, the making of peace to serve the ends of war. The Christians had lost Jerusalem to the Sultan of Egypt in 1244, hence the title of his 1305 essay, *De Recuperation Terre Sante.*

Antoine Marini was Chancellor to the King of Bohemia, George of Podebrady, in the fifteenth century. The latter had a grand design to create a league of European rulers for a common front against the Turks with himself at the head of it; an alliance with Hungary in 1462 was a start. Then he sent Marini off to Poland, Venice and France to follow up on the grand design. He, in turn, during the following two years, proposed a scheme to negotiate with other Christian courts the creation of a federation with a permanent Congress in order to do battle with the Turks, again making peace for war. It was not a great success.

Henry IV of France, in the late sixteenth century, proposed a Grand Design, which seems to have been written by his Minister,

Duc de Sully. The Design was to divide Europe into fifteen states of nearly equal size so that rivalry among them could be reduced to a minimum; they would get together to form a Christian Republic with a General Council, comprising representatives from each of the states, to oversee it. Of course, Henry IV would oversee the entire process; while, what was left unsaid, French military strength would ensure that it would be the dominant power.

Other so-called peace plans of a similar kind were proposed at the time; they were all in response to the expansion of the Muslim power westwards. They were not peace plans, in fact, they were war plans, and they are included here only because peace plans concern the story of modernity and these have been generally (but wrongly) part of that story in the existing literature.

The plan of Desiderius Erasmus, Dutch, humanist and Catholic theologian, was a little bit earlier and of a rather different nature. It is still discussed among the interesting peace plans of the centuries, but its interest is not its feasibility. It was actually not so much a plan as an appeal for peace, and its interest is in its complete harmony with the renaissance episteme. As such, though it does not really belong to this chapter and the modernity episteme, some of its flavour deserves to be reproduced here.

This is the complaint made by peace speaking in person against the warlike nature of man. In the course of the complaint all the elements of the universe are brought together. The celestial bodies move, and have ever moved, in perfect harmony; the very elements preserve eternal peace; animals destitute of reason live with their own kind in amity, elephants herd together, storks have public meetings, dolphins defend each other, even the vine embraces the elm, and among insensible substances the loadstone attracts iron. The 'accursed spirits', who destroyed the concord between man and the heavens, even they hold union with one another. So man, who is still in discord with other men, must follow the way of nature.

## The Peace Plans of Modernity

It was with the start of modernity, after the mid-seventeenth century, the Peace of Westphalia, that the really elaborate peace plans were proposed. So from the viewpoint of IR, both historically and in their nature, these plans are (now rightly) an integral part of modernity; they are one of the products of the Thirty Years' War. But note again that these are the plans of philosophers and intellectuals, not those of Kings, rulers and other statesmen.

There are too many of these peace plans for a detailed discussion of each; even the phrase 'perpetual peace' had become so fashionable by the early eighteenth century that a succession of them appeared only to take advantage of this fact, leading eventually to its use more in sarcasm than from conviction. Five of them, which are still discussed today and best illustrate the episteme of modernity, are outlined in what follows. In each of them the structure of truths is built upon the advantages of peace; then the causes of war are identified leading logically to their elimination by a series of specific steps.

The English Quaker William Penn wrote one of the earliest plans of this period, an *Essay Towards the Present and Future Peace of Europe* in1693, which appears to have been influenced by Henry IV's Grand Design. Section I of the essay covers the advantages of peace: 'it preserves our possessions; we are in no danger of invasions; our trade is free and safe; and we rise and lye down without anxiety'. That is only a small part of the list and at the end of the essay another list of nine advantages is given, the ninth being the 'Manifest Privilege' that the princes of Europe 'may choose wives for themselves, such as they love, and not by proxy', that is not for promoting alliances to augment their strength.

Then come the causes of war. 'Men seek their wills by War rather than Peace'; they are moved by ambition, pride of conquest, greatness of dominions, and then there are the three basic causes: the desire to keep what you have; to recover what you have lost; and to add to what you have by taking what belongs to your neighbour.[2] Justice will, in the face of all these motivations for war, procure peace and preserve it. Government is the means of justice, and for a more general peace the princes of Europe representing their governments should meet regularly, and establish rules of justice which they will observe in their mutual relations. Thus 'Europe would quietly obtain the so much desired and needed peace'.[3]

Penn includes some technical details, no doubt, for the use of the protocol officers and diplomats of the time. The meetings of princes should take place in a circular room with many entrances to avoid disputes about precedence; the idea presumably being that all should enter at the same time. Voting will be weighted by the value of the territory of the concerned Prince: Germany gets twelve;

France and Spain ten each; Italy eight; England six and so on. The conclusion is that as parents govern their families, magistrates their cities, estates their republics and kings their kingdoms, all by rules of justice, so by the same rules Europe may obtain and preserve peace.

The Abbe Charles-Irene Castel de Saint Pierre published in 1713 a *Project for Making Peace Perpetual in Europe,* the first of the many to appear under the 'perpetual peace' title; and the first to use the logical process taught by Descartes in his discourse on method. Saint Pierre's starting point was the argument of Thomas Hobbes that it is in the very nature of man to be in a war of every man against every man. Men, therefore, strive for peace for fear of death and the desire of such things as are necessary for commodious living. To secure this they "conferre all their power and strength upon one man or upon one Assembly of men, that may reduce all their Wills, by plurality of voices, unto one Will."[4] But this does not happen between kings and sovereigns because with the posture of war between them, they uphold the industry of their subjects; war does not entail misery. Saint Pierre moved the Hobbesian argument the required step further by applying it to the world of states: the advantages of peace are the same; the causes of war lie in the nature of things – states are in a war of every state against every state; they must, therefore, agree to confer their power to a federation by treaty in order to eliminate the basic cause of war.

The treaty suggested contained twelve 'fundamental articles', then a more detailed section on 'important articles' supplemented by 'useful articles'. The fundamental articles envisage that the twenty-four sovereign powers of Europe should form a permanent confederation for peace and security. Once fourteen of them have agreed to join such a confederation, the others will be compelled to do so, if necessary, by making war upon them (so much for perpetual peace). Members of the confederation shall not take up arms except against a declared enemy of European society; disputes will be mediated; there shall be no interference in each other's governments except to help them deal with rebellion. All decisions will be taken by a three-fourths majority.

Jean Jacques Rousseau developed Saint Pierre's peace plan. He took the latter's two-volume work, abbreviated and edited it, put in ideas of his own, and then published it in 1761 as yet another project for Perpetual Peace. Rousseau was, of course, an admirer of

Sparta and believed that victory in war established rightfulness, ideas which he elaborated in a 1749 essay on whether the progress of the arts and sciences has contributed more to the corruption or purification of morals. But that was an earlier phase. Here he outlined the advantages of peace in poetic style: "I see in my mind's eye all men joined in the bonds of love. I call before my thoughts a gentle and peaceful brotherhood, all living in unbroken harmony, all guided by the same principles, all finding their happiness in the happiness of all."[5]

The second pillar of the structure of truths comprises the causes of war, of which there are six. Rousseau says man made war to make conquests, to protect himself from aggression, to weaken a too powerful neighbour, maintain their rights against attack, to settle a difference which has defied friendly negotiation, or to fulfil some treaty obligation. This leads to the final truth about how war is to be eliminated. Essentially it consists in the application to the Europe of nations of the principles he had advocated for the nation of man: that they associate together and hand over all their powers to the association or body so formed, a sovereign body that expresses the General Will; this leads to real freedom for the individual within the nation; if any refuses to join he shall be forced to do so, in Rousseau's well-known phrase, 'he will be forced to be free'. Applying this to Europe there must be a federal government to bring the nations of Europe together. In this federation every major power must participate; they will all be forced to be free and no one is to be allowed to pull out; all its laws are binding on all members and coercive power will be available to ensure this. This would be, as in the case of Saint Pierre's plan, war to make peace; note the contrast with the pre-Westphalian plans which were about peace to make war.

Then he gets to the five articles of the treaty to implement this. They specify the creation of a congress of the federation; voting within it; how the presidency will pass from one to the other member; the contributions to be made; and how violators will be punished and compelled to comply with the provisions of the treaty.

## Kant's Abiding Influence

The best known and certainly most admired proposal for perpetual peace is that of Immanuel Kant, published in 1795. This is because his ideas in general are central to the episteme of modernity, since in them pure logic leads to certain knowledge about the world.

Kant has a good claim to be thought a model of the great philosophers that the modern West has produced; hence he has had the strongest influence, even at this distance of two centuries, on liberal thinking about matters of peace and war. Today's liberal peace proponents most frequently cite his essay, with the title *Perpetual Peace: A Philosophical Sketch*.

The British philosopher Bertrand Russell, who is understandably suspicious of German philosophy, nevertheless admits that he "is generally considered the greatest of modern philosophers."[6] But he was a philosopher and cannot from that viewpoint be directly compared to military and strategic and purely political thinkers. In any case the key ideas of peace and liberal thinking today can be traced back to his writing even where this is not explicitly acknowledged.

His starting point is that reason altogether condemns war, but only an international government can actually prevent it. In *The Science of Right* he gives one set of reasons for peace. "The universal and lasting establishment of peace constitutes not merely a part but the whole final purpose and end of the science of right as viewed within the limits of reason". So it is that "the morally practical reason utters within us its irrevocable veto: There shall be no war."[7] And in the *Perpetual Peace* essay he notes that reason, "from its throne of supreme moral legislating authority, absolutely condemns war as a legal resource and makes a state of peace a direct duty."

The causes of war are first of all nature. "The state of peace among men living side by side is not the natural state; the natural state is one of war". But then in the text of his proposal there are six preliminary articles which are really a coverage of why states go to war against others, hence what to avoid. For instance, when peace comes and the parties to it have "tacitly reserved matter for a future war"; or if a state, large or small, comes under the dominion of another state; or standing armies continue in existence, "which incessantly menace other states by their readiness to appear at all times prepared for war"; or there is forcible interference in the internal affairs of another; all these are causes for war and specifically forbidden by the preliminary articles.[8]

At this point, in elaboration of what was stated in the introduction to this book, a comment on the central part of his philosophy is necessary, in order to do justice to his line of thinking as well as to further develop the picture of modernity. Kant proposed two distinctions, the first between statements which are analytic, which he also calls explicative and those which are synthetic, which he also calls augmentative. An analytic statement is one where the predicate is part of the statement as in 'the people rule in a democracy' wherein democracy means people's rule. Analytical statements can always be recognised by means of the principle of contradiction meaning that no subject can have a predicate that contradicts it. A synthetic statement is one where this is not so and separate things are brought together as in 'democracies are more peaceful than other forms of government' wherein only experience can tell us whether this is true; the statement itself does not do so. The second distinction is between empirical knowledge and *a priori* knowledge. Empirical knowledge is like a synthetic statement based on experience. But *a priori* knowledge is known, as soon as it is seen, to be a general truth; it is true regardless of experience, like, for instance, the axioms of pure mathematics. It is "not such as is independent of this or that kind of experience, but such as is absolutely so of all experience."[9] Kant's central philosophical problem was to bring together synthetic statements and *a priori* knowledge: in the example given above, to demonstrate as a general truth that, regardless of experience, democracies are more peaceful than other forms of government.

This fusion of synthetic statements with *a priori* knowledge assumes considerable interest when it is applied to ethical judgments in international relations. If the fusion leads to general truths which require no other validation, as Kant had intended, then there must be actions which are ethical regardless of their causes and consequences. Such is the well-known 'categorical imperative' for which "the Law contains no condition by which it is limited, nothing remains over but the generality of the law in general, to which the maxim of the action is to be conformable."[10] This fusion, in other words, leads to irrefutably certain knowledge about ethical questions.

Peace is evidently regarded by Kant as a categorical imperative, and the three main propositions of 'Perpetual Peace', given in the form of definitive articles, need to be seen against the background of the categorical imperative. These deal, respectively, with the domestic, the international and the person-to-person aspects.

The first proposition is that if the citizens must give their consent before war is declared, there will be great hesitation in doing so. If the state is not a republic, in other words if the citizens have no rights, then the state is owned, so to speak by its head, who will not suffer at all in case of a war, and will be all the more prepared to declare it. The constitution of every state should, therefore, be republican. Some two centuries later this was generally interpreted as 'democratic', leading to a flood of academic literature citing Kant as the originator of the theory that democracies do not go to war with each other.[11]

Within the academic community the most prominent advocate and populariser of Kant's lead was Michael W. Doyle. Doyle revived the Kantian argument or rather what the academic literature believed was the Kantian argument. In a celebrated 1986 article on '*Liberalism and World Politics*'[12] he put the democratic peace idea at the centre. Democratic representation, ideological commitment to uphold human rights and transnational interdependence explain why certain states are 'peace prone'. The absence of these characteristics makes states 'war prone'. Not only are democratic states peaceful, but such states have to forge alliances among themselves. Such alliances, he argued in later writings, would defend the democratic peace zone; they would also act, the categorical imperative, to expand that zone by providing inspiration, giving help to those struggling for a democratic polity and the use of even military intervention if other means do not succeed. Such intervention would be cheaper than to have to deal with authoritarian and non-democratic regimes. With that argument ingurgitated modernity acquired one more justification for making war.

The second definitive article, which follows, is that therefore states can and should demand of other states that they enter into agreements based upon each state respecting the rights of others. This will lead to a federation of free states, a league of peace in which there is no dominion of one over any other. This will happen "if fortune directs that a powerful and enlightened people can make itself a republic, which by its nature must be inclined to perpetual peace, this gives a fulcrum to the federation" and more and more of them will join it. Once this happens there will be no need for any member of the federation to submit to any kind of compulsion by the federation, and all will adjust themselves to the constraints of public law. Ultimately the federation will include all the nations of the world, so here Kant is not confining himself to Europe.

The third definitive article is on universal hospitality, meaning giving an outsider, by right, the ability to become a fellow inhabitant in your land at any time. This would correspond, roughly, to what is known as track II or people-to-people friendship in our time. By showing hospitality to people from far away, "distant parts of the world can come into peaceable relations with each other, and these are finally publicly established by law" and will lead eventually to world citizenship.

Then comes Jeremy Bentham, who famously founded the principle of the greatest happiness of the greatest number for decision-taking, and who wrote *A Plan for Universal and Perpetual Peace* in 1789, though it was published after he died.[13]

His starting point, why have peace, is "the extreme folly, the madness of war ... mark well the contrast. All trade is in its essence advantageous ... all war is in its essence ruinous." So there can be no disputing the utility of a plan for universal and lasting peace; the only possible objection being that such a plan would be hopeless, visionary. Then come the causes for war. There is unjust ambition, "jealousy, sincere and honest jealousy", vulgar prejudice, ignorance, weakness and so on. The curable causes are two: colonies and alliances. "Distant dependencies increase the chances of war", so Britain and France should give up their colonies and decide not to acquire any more. In case of war England could make an attack on France only in the colonies. If that cannot be done, because there are no colonies, would Britain attack the territory of France? "Such madness does not belong to our age." Similarly the giving up of alliances would save the danger of war resulting from those alliances.

From this analysis emerges a fourteen-point programme setting out further details about why it would be of advantage, and of no disadvantage, for Britain to give up the colonies and found no new ones; have no treaty or alliance with any other power whatever; nor a treaty for exclusive trade; have no naval force beyond that needed to deal with pirates; nor augment it. The same points are applied to France, followed by the proposition that if Britain and France agreed, the principal difficulties would be removed to the establishment of general and permanent pacification of Europe, a pacification which could be maintained by limiting the number of troops. Then comes the establishment of a common court of judicature, but with no coercive powers, for since war is ruled out the contending parties to any dispute will accept the court's decision, whether just or unjust. "Just or unjust, the decision of the arbiters will save the credit, the honour of the contending party."

So here we see how visionary the votaries of the modernity story can be.[14]

## ENDNOTES

[1] Quotations from the *De Monarchia* of Dante Alighieri, edited with translation and notes by Aurelia Henry, Houghton, Mifflin and Company, Boston and New York, 1904, Book I, chapter IV.

[2] Compare the law giver Manu, cited in chapter 1, who has a very similar list of causes for war, the King acquiring things which are not his and so on; of course Manu recommends war, consonant with the traditional episteme.

[3] See William Penn, in the *Online Library of Liberty*, An Essay Towards the Present and Future Peace of Europe by the Establishment of an European Dyet, Parliament, or Estates (1693), available on the internet.

[4] Thomas Hobbes, *Leviathan*, Penguin Books, London, 1985, p. 227

[5] Cited from the internet, Sanderson Beck, *Peace Plans of Rousseau, Bentham, and Kant* in rousseaustudies.free.fr/ArticleBeck.htm. See also Jean-Jacques Rousseau and Charles Irene Castel de Saint-Pierre, *A Project for Perpetual Peace*, J.Johnson and T.Davenport, London, 1767.

[6] Bertrand Russell, *History of Western Philosophy*, George Allen and Unwin, London, 1946, p. 731.

[7] As quoted by Sanderson Beck, op. cit. on the internet.

[8] Immanuel Kant, *Perpetual Peace*, text accessed from the internet. It is also in Immanuel Kant, *Towards Perpetual Peace and other writings on politics, peace, and history*, edited and with an introduction by Pauline Kleingeld, and which includes essays by, inter alia, Michael W. Doyle, Yale University Press, 2006.

[9] Immanuel Kant, *Critique of Pure Reason*, J.M.Dent and Sons, London, 1942, p. 26.

[10] Cited by Bertrand Russell, op. cit., p. 737.

[11] Kant didn't, in fact, say democracies will be peacefully inclined, but that republics will be. And he thought democracy is, properly speaking, necessarily a despotism, since once all decide, no one can disagree. What he did was separate who has the power, a one person autocracy, a few in an aristocracy, or all the people in a democracy, from how is it exercised, by the separation of the legislature from the executive or not. If not, you get despotism, if yes you get republicanism. But he was definitely not in favour of democracies.

[12] *American Political Science Review*, Vol. 80, No. 4, pp. 1151-69.

[13] The Jeremy Bentham text was published in *The Works of Jeremy Bentham*, Vol. II, under the superintendence of John Bowring, Tait, Edinburgh, 1843.

[14] Quotations from Jeremy Bentham, A Plan for a Universal and Perpetual Peace, in *The Principles of International Law*, Essay 4, MHTML document on the internet.

# 3

# War, Power and Making Empires

The making and unmaking of empires can be told according to the traditional world-view or story, or that of modernity. Each continues into that of the so-called Cold War, told according to the same story. In one story war and power are linked with empire; agency depends on how well you did in war; and there is doubt about whether there was ever any such thing as the Cold War. The story of modernity is different. Where empire-making or the Cold War is concerned,[1] war and power are separated, while agency is only in the hands of the so-called great powers. This leads to the Cold War story that we are familiar with.

The stories are not, however, mutually altogether exclusive. Most historians and commentators incorporate elements of both stories into their narratives of the period in question, so we should not be surprised to find that inexplicable contradictions enter the texts from time to time, nor that the same authors, the same books and once or twice the same page[2] are occasionally quoted in support of one story, and then in support of its opposite, in what follows.

This chapter looks at empire-making from the viewpoint of the traditional story; the next chapter looks at the same from that of modernity. In this one we first look at the empire-makers, then we look at those who resisted them as also the evolution of nationalism through violent resistance to the empire-makers.

**The Empire-Makers: Empire, Power, War**

Eleven countries made empires of one sort or another in Asia and Africa during the years after 1800: eight of them were European, in order of their arrival on the scene: Portugal and Spain; Holland; England; France; Belgium, Germany and Italy; two were the US and Russia; one was Asian, Japan. There were others who tried, like Sweden which had a piece of territory in the eastern US in the seventeenth century which was taken from them by the Dutch; and Denmark which had some slave trading areas in West Africa for supply to an *entrepot* in the West Indies; but in these other cases an empire did not actually get to be made.[3]

Since empire is discussed here to illustrate a particular theme the focus of this and the next chapter will be on Asia and Africa. Within those geographical bounds two empire-makers will get most attention in this chapter, the Portuguese and, less so, the English, though there are references to some others when needed to further illuminate a point. Two others, the Dutch and French, are discussed in the chapters on Indonesia, Algeria and Vietnam, chapters 5, 6 and 10 respectively.

The connection of empire with power may be illustrated in detail by the case of Portugal, since it was the first on the scene. At first this connection was only in the minds of the more imaginative authors, the sea captains of their imaginations and, of course, the imaginations of actual sea captains. Thus the author of the imperial saga and national epic of Portugal, Luis Vaz de Camoens, who wrote the *Lusiads* in the 1560s, started it with an incantation to his Great King, "whose far-flung dominions greet the sun's gaze alike when it rises, when half-way through its course, and when it sinks to rest". He also compared those who had established this empire to all the great figures in history, the Greeks, the Romans and so on, and found the latter coming off second best. By way of incidental comparison, we will come across many quotations in other nationally important texts about the other likenesses to Rome: including the British Empire in the nineteenth century and America in the post-Cold War world.[4]

Continuing with Camoens, "let us hear no more then of Ulysses and Aeneas and their long journeying, no more of Alexander and Trajan and their famous victories". With the daring and renown of the Portuguese "another and loftier conception of valour has arisen."

Very much in accord with the traditional story, Camoens then proceeds to picture the Gods assembled together as Vasco da Gama sets sail for India. "Up on Olympus, the Gods were assembling in council to consider further happenings in the East. Jupiter had sent his summons out by Mercury ..." And, sure enough, those on Olympus came to the aid of da Gama. Sailing from Malindi on the East Coast of Africa to Calicut on the West Coast of India he was met by a violent storm; Venus herself came down "to soften by amorous beguilement this troublesome confederacy of the winds...".[5]

Albuquerque, da Gama's most illustrious successor, had the same experience of divine help. Attacking Hormuz by sea early in the sixteenth century, he found that of the great number of Muslims who had been killed and whose bodies were in the water, "most of them had many arrows sticking in their bodies ... although I had brought with me neither arrows nor archers." And there were other experiences like that which he had in Muscat, when a large mosque was razed to the ground and three of his men were under it, in a place where "a thousand men would have died" ... but they came out, alive and well, upright and standing and with no wounds or bruises.[6]

Despite such extra-terrestrial assistance, however, the Portuguese were never able to make an empire, notwithstanding their claims; or at least nothing that anyone today would recognize as one. Actually, there was a wide gap between what the Portuguese did and what they claimed to have done. The history books record the latter as the former, largely because they rely on Portuguese records, there being a serious paucity of others. So "one has to wade through long, self-congratulatory, turgid hyperbole about Portuguese activities to pick up a few nuggets of information ..."; and what information there is includes "copious detail on their military triumphs, though less on their defeats."[7]

Let us see what actually happened. Albuquerque thought he should be able to control the sea by capturing Malacca, Hormuz, and Aden, the three 'keys' to the Indian Ocean. He did capture the first in 1511, the second in 1514, but was never able to take the third. Anyway, at its largest, the empire he built consisted of a few trading posts, some fortified coastal points and, so far as claims go, the vast expanse of sea in between. For Albuquerque himself claimed that it consisted of these trading posts/forts and the vast expanse of sea in between. This reflected the reality that they were not strong enough to make territorial gains. Albuquerque's principles were that "Portugal must hold only key fortresses and trading factories. She must rely on naval power to defend them. Territorial empire was beyond her power…"[8]

Actually they had little enough success even with naval power, and that little success was due to the European custom of arming their merchant men. In the Indian Ocean, merchantmen were normally never armed since the security of passage and control of piracy was assured by the major coastal powers, which had naval vessels for the purpose. Given their attacks on unarmed pilgrim ships and merchant men the Portuguese were seen to be what they were, pirates and not very effective ones at that. The standard Portuguese vessel used by Vasco da Gama and his successors was the 200-ton armed caravel. Today a vessel of that size would not be considered ocean-going; in the open sea its pitch and roll was so violent that its guns would point sometimes at the sky, sometimes down into the water. The most you could hope for was to hit the masts and sails of the opponent, thus slowing him down so that you could ram and board, the standard tactic of war at sea until well into the nineteenth century. So it was, for example, that when Albuquerque's flagship, and that was a 400-ton ship, attacked a merchantman in the straits of Malacca in 1510 there was no effect. Then the entire Portuguese fleet closed in and started shooting at her, "but this did not affect her in the least, and she went on sailing … The Portuguese then shot at her masts … and she dropped her sails …our artillery did not hurt her at all…"[9] At a later date, along the coastline of India, through the sixteenth century and till 1595 when the great Calicut admiral Kunjali III died, the Zamorin's fleets under him continuously challenged the Portuguese armed vessels for the control of the seas. K.M. Panikkar describes the way Kunjali repeatedly attacked their fleets, destroyed their ships in one naval engagement after another, and laid siege to their trading factories.[10]

And in 1538, when the Portuguese had been around for something less than four decades, the Ottomans sent a large fleet into Aden, captured several Portuguese ships and more or less put an end to any little influence they might have had over trade through the Red Sea and Gulf routes. On this rather flimsy basis they later claimed that they had once held the keys to the Indian Ocean, and that they had an empire in that ocean, that they were the Lords of the Sea.

Leaving aside empire, trade was the major purpose of the Portuguese excursion into the Indian Ocean; they even declared a monopoly on the trade in spices. But that monopoly remained an empty declaration, for even in this they made no impact.

Trade between Western India and Europe goes back to pre-Alexandrian times and even if we discount those early reports since they have so much of the fabulous and miraculous, the *Periplus of the Erithraean Sea*, written around 70 AD, is neither; it is a factual account giving lists of ports on the Red Sea and the Arabian Sea, their imports and exports, the kind of trade they did with Indian ports, particularly Bharuch. The Greeks and the Romans certainly traded extensively with India, going down the Red Sea and then using the monsoon to navigate to Indian ports. And it was a complex trade, with cloth made in Egypt; ivory, tortoise shell and rhino horn from Eritrean ports; Italian wine; textiles, iron and steel from India, as well as that item most in demand – war elephants; all being exchanged in complex markets and ports like Berenike and Myos Hormos along the trade routes. Before the year 1500 trade in the Indian Ocean area had been largely in the hands of Asians: Muslims from the Persian Gulf and the Red Sea regions; Indians from Gujarat and Kerala; Malaccans and others. The bulk of it was intra-Asian trade; a small part of the total amount of goods that entered this trade was sent to Europe through the Red Sea, Alexandria and Venice.

The Portuguese were late-comers to this established pattern of trade. There was no hope at all that they could make much impact on trading patterns which had been established over millennia.

Furthermore, the Turks controlled the Red Sea, so the trade within Asia continued and even the passage of spices to Europe continued to be largely outside Portuguese hands. In spite of the monopoly they had declared every one else carried on trading and more spices reached Europe from other shippers and by overland routes than the Portuguese themselves were able to carry. Asked by Lisbon how this could happen, Albuquerque replied that he had not enough ships, nor enough men, nor enough discipline among the men he did have.

In the year 1600, meaning more than a century after the entry of the Portuguese, the pattern was the same, but the Portuguese had joined it. They used Gujarati merchants and their capital, usually sent goods on non-Portuguese bottoms and, in short, as a Dutch Governor, Anthony van Dieman, put it "look upon this region as their fatherland, and think no more about Portugal. They drive little or no trade thither, but content themselves with the port-to-port trade of Asia, just as if they were natives thereof and had no other country." In summary "to see the Portuguese as having a powerful impact on the Indian Ocean in the sixteenth century is to distort the facts of the matter."[11]

So the bulk of the Indian Ocean trade was and remained always outside the control of the Portuguese, whether they had the ships *in situ* or not; and the *Estado da India* was, throughout, like those of the Dutch and the English that followed them during the next two and a half centuries, "a trading network concerned with the distribution of goods rather than their production."[12] One estimate is that one-tenth of the total pepper trade between the Indian Ocean and Europe actually found its way to Lisbon and that estimate is probably too high.

In any case the King of Portugal was inclined to be cautious; he knew how weak the Portuguese really were. To Pedro Alvares de Cabral, one of Albuqueque's predecessors, he specified that if he met any Muslim ships "you are not to come to close quarters with them if you can avoid it, but you are to compel them with your artillery alone to strike sail so that this war may be waged with greater safety and ... less loss."[13] And he was not convinced that Albuquerque should get all the help he said he needed, so the latter's letters are full of pleas for more, an apt precursor to modern-day diplomats setting themselves aims which headquarters think are too high and then asking for the resources to achieve them. After taking Malacca in 1511 he wrote to King Manuel complaining about having been ordered to avoid war. "Your Highness thinks you can keep these fellows under control with fair words and offers of peace and protection ... you do not send me arms or men or any military equipment ... the captains who come out of Portugal and do as they please ... pay scant attention to my decisions and orders." Then he asks for money to "keep three thousand well-armed troops here" for if goods and merchandise one to be obtained "then we must fight the Muslims for them."[14]

In fact, while Portuguese captains were trying to create an empire in the Indian Ocean (while their Spanish counterparts tried the same in the Americas) their governments at home in general were cautious; they did like the prestige of having an empire and the King of Portugal took for himself the title "Lord of the conquest, navigation and commerce of India, Ethiopia, Arabia and Persia".

But they were also anxious that money should not be spent on this distant venture; indeed that it should earn money.

The arrival in Asia of the Portuguese, to sum up, "does not mark the beginning of a new epoch in the commercial and political history of the area."[15] This was not another era of history starting. And the so-called Portuguese empire was not a territorial empire but a network of small fortresses and factories along the littoral of the Indian Ocean. By the middle of the seventeenth century, in any case, Sultan Ibn Saif of Oman had captured their fortified port in Muscat; and by 1698 the Oman fleet was able to capture the main Portuguese base in Fort Jesus. And by 1700 even the network of fortresses and trading stations had ceased to exist; since all that remained was a handful of them.

Now for the British, whose effort to acquire an empire was important; but there is more on this in later chapters, so here we can give a small selection of quotes by way of illustrating the way they thought about these matters.

The equation of war with power rewritten as empire equals power equals war is well put by Francis Bacon (1561-1626, meaning well before the Peace of Westphalia) in his essay *Of True Greatness of Kingdoms and Estates;* "but above all, for empire and greatness, it importeth most, that a nation do profess arms, as their principal honour, study and occupation". He goes on the cite Romulus, who told the Romans "that, above all, they should intend arms" and Sparta, which "was wholly (though not wisely) framed and composed to that scope and end." The thought is identical to that of Kautilya and Machiavelli, with the addition of empire making.

When Francis Drake set out in 1577 to annex the *Terra Australis* in the South Sea, the scholar Dr. John Dee wrote that the exploit would establish a true *Imperium Britannicum* and invoked the memory of Alexander. Even in the 1760s it could be said that, "in the present state of Europe it is colonies, trade and, in consequence, sea-power which must determine the balance of power upon the continent."[16] This was true even of revolutionary France, when it was announced that it should be called *l'Empire des Francais,* instead of Royal France.[17] Later sea captains had similar ideas, and here is the Governor of the English East India Company, whose aim, as he defined it in 1687, was "to establish such a polities of civil and military power, and create and secure such a large revenue to maintain both ... as may be the foundation of a large, well-grounded, sure English dominion for all time to come."[18] By then the English company "had the legal right and the military will to wage war in aggressive ways..."[19]

In the same style the British Empire soon came to be compared to Rome; but it was better. In 1774 the Rev. John Entick and others published a pamphlet, *The Present State of the British Empire*. Here it was asserted that that Empire "is arrived at that height of power and glory, to which none of the states and monarchies upon earth could ever lay the like claim. Rome, in all her grandeur, did not equal Great Britain, either in constitution, dominion, commerce, riches or strength."

But to sum up, the English launched their ventures early in the seventeenth century along with the Dutch, the French in 1664. They all had experiences similar to the Portuguese. In the early eighteenth century the Maratha admiral Kanhoji Angre built a fleet at Vijayadoorg which was able to challenge the British who had by then become the senior partner in the colonial enterprise. He levied a 'chauth' or 25% tax on ships sailing the Arabian Sea in a direct challenge to the permit system imposed by the British, a system under which they claimed the exclusive right to impose taxes on shipping. The British governor of Bombay equipped a fleet which attacked Kanhoji Angre's headquarters in 1717, but fell back, defeated. In November 1718 another fleet was sent to try and subdue him, but when they attempted a landing "the Maratha guns mowed the party down. Only a very few survived the attempt" and the British withdrew. Then they asked for Portuguese's help and a much bigger combined force attacked the Marathas, which "ended in an inglorious failure. The Portuguese fled on attack; the English lost most of their guns and all their ammunition."[20] A couple of years later Dutch help was sought; the latter sent out a fleet from Holland along with a body of troops, but the attack which then materialised did not fare any better. Kanhoji died in 1729, but his successors continued to contest the European supremacy of the sea lanes. Here we also have a typical example of the empire makers at work: with the emergence of a serious threat, the British, the Portuguese and the Dutch pooled their resources and strengths in the attempt to defeat him.

But with the passage of the centuries the size of empire was increasingly the measure of the power of a nation, and by the late nineteenth century, as we shall see, the power and prestige of

European great powers had come to depend on the acquisition of an empire and the size of that empire.

As for the link between empire-making and war, three quotations may usefully be given. One says that beneath the assertions of the missionaries, the traders, the nationalists, the strategists with their chokepoint theories, "imperialism boiled down to a military phenomenon."[21] Another is that "thanks above all to their superiority, founded upon the military revolution of the sixteenth and seventeenth centuries, the Western nations had managed to create the first global hegemony in History."[22] Yet another has it that Europe "imposed its will on Africa at the point of a gun. It was a lesson that would be remembered, fifty year later, when Africa came to win its independence."[23]

## The Struggle for Freedom: Nationalism

This brings up the other side of the imperial experience: nationalism as the foundation of resistance against the empire-makers. There are many sources for the origins of nationalism and many forces that play a role in the growth of nationalism.

It is probably easiest to envisage this subject by looking at a parallel from biological evolution. Biologists picture the origin of life as large numbers of molecules in a complex chemical 'soup' interacting until they reach the point of autocatalysis. A "living organism is a system of chemicals that has the capacity to catalyse its own reproduction"; and in this next stage the molecules autocatalyse themselves to speed up the process by which they themselves are formed.[24] Then the molecules acquire increasing complexity until they reach the stage of living cells. This introduction of order into the chaos of the originally inert chemical soup is, after a certain threshold is crossed, almost inevitable; it is not a matter of chance. The resulting living cells develop, in the further course of evolution, the ability to replicate themselves, then the ability of replication with cell differentiation, then the ability to coordinate themselves into tissues, organs, and so on, called morphogenesis. Diverse cells have diverse functions, but each exists by means of and for the benefit of the whole organism or body, which is a given, like the geographical boundaries of a nation; and the whole exists by means of and for the benefit of each. The individual cells and the whole organism evolve from internal changes such as by mutation, as well as from alterations in the external environment; they need to adapt to their surroundings. But this whole process is an incompressible algorithm, meaning it cannot be described in a space shorter than it takes to happen; there are no laws by which generalisations about its behaviour can be obtained. Here is a dilemma: since the process is inevitable there should be some laws governing the way it moves from one stage to the next; but it is also incompressible, meaning there are no such laws. The dilemma is resolved by recourse to a division between the broad generalisation, which can reasonably be made, and the detailed prediction, which cannot.

Nationalism, similarly, can be seen as evolving by autocatalysis. The central driving force, to come together, to continue together, to achieve independence, to reproduce itself, comes from those who live within the boundaries of the nation state. And we can make the broad generalisation that sometime in the middle of the seventeenth century the political, economic and social forces were such that the emergence of the nation was inevitable, while being unable to predict precisely how or where they would evolve.

Many ingredients or resources go to make the 'soup' that autocatalyses into the nation and to make nationalism more cohesive: personal factors, family ties, local traditions are among them for there is, within every society, a number of feelings and emotions among individuals that they belong to this or that collectivity beyond the family, a group sharing a language or dialect, a religion or sect, ethnicity or blood, class or guild, among many other possibilities; then there are the sources imposed from above, so to speak, including again religion, ethnicity, language and culture, geography and a common history with pride in achievements made during that history, a name that has endured, all these may be used by national leaders in making and strengthening the nation; technology, the communications revolution, industrialisation, modernity in general as well as other forces such as globalisation are all forces that can be used and are relevant, though that relevance is to be discovered by the use that is made of these forces by individuals and groups of people.[25] Diverse combinations of these ingredients make for diverse kinds of nationalism; the greater the variety of ingredients, the more resilient will be the nation.

In the making of nationalism some ingredients are difficult to change: geographical boundaries, ethnicity or language. Attempts to change these, as many a national leader in Asia and Africa has found, may put the whole nation-building exercise into jeopardy. Others can be invented or moulded: the legacy of a common history or a national mythology. There is, in any case, a continuous recreation of the nation by force or persuasion, such as you cannot describe by laws. It is for those engaged in making or strengthening the nation to choose the right ingredients out of all those which are available, and best use those ingredients or resources in a way that makes autocatalysis most effective, most generative of an ever strengthening nationalism. And this is an exercise in constant inventiveness. The process of mutation by which one or other of the resources of nationalism is emphasised more or less, new resources are created or old ones discarded is never ending.

In brief, the phenomena associated with the nation – nationalism, the nation-state, national symbols and so on – "all these rest on exercises in social engineering which are often deliberate and always innovative."[26] No matter that the claim of nationalists is usually to great antiquity in such matters, but standard national languages, ethnicities, common memories and histories, ancient cultures, all those primordial factors which are supposed to explain nationalism, are often actually of very recent and deliberate creation by rulers, ruling groups, interested parties and the like.

So the question to ask about this process is never of the static order, do these criteria make a nation, as Eric Hobsbawm did. It is also never of the dynamic order, what was or what can be done to create the imagined community and thereby the nation, as Benedict Anderson did.[27] Both those kinds of questions refuse to accept the inevitability of the worldwide emergence of the nation; they are the wrong questions because there is no way of locating some inherent criterion or quality, some essential or unchanging reality, some primordial factor, some blood relationship or common memory or history, which can account for nationalism as a general phenomenon. So the proper question is of the order, how much skill in nation-building has been shown by the leaders, those who wish to build a better or a stronger nation, out of the ingredients or resources that are available or can be invented for people living within certain geographic boundaries?

## The Creation of Nationalism in Europe and Turkey

It would be as well to give some specific examples to illustrate the above generalisations regarding nationalism being constructed in many ways. We can start with the European example, since this is well studied but, more important, usually said to be quite different to that of Asian and African countries: in Europe there is alleged to have been cultural uniformity, which "eased the way to state making and nation formation". That, as Eric Wolf points out[28] and the following examples show, is not true; the making of nationalism in Europe followed exactly the same trajectory as everywhere else.

It may be made largely by a ruler. In the twelfth century the Song of Roland glorified the Emperor Charlemagne's stand against the Arab forces in the Pyrenees, a wholly invented story; but it made that Emperor, in the twentieth century, an important and oft-quoted symbol for European unity and the idea that Europe is a nation. It may be made by a hero. The poem of El Cid established a Spanish hero, again a more or less invented character, who had much to do with the later growth of nationalism.

Or nationalism could be created in some part by a national patron saint. When in the fourteenth century the St. George's Red Cross on a white background became the uniform for English soldiers, a long step had been taken in creating a sense of nationalism in a geographical region of quite mixed culture and ethnic composition. It may be made by one or a few groups of people with special interests in terms of language, ethnicity, money, power. There were not very many people who led the French Revolution, but they brought popular sovereignty and nationalism together for the first time. The Napoleonic conquest of large swathes of Europe gave a tremendous boost to the urge in other countries to adopt this combination. Over the years public ceremonies were invented to promote this. Bastille Day, for example, was invented in 1880, a hundred years after it was actually supposed to have happened, and it was "an annual assertion of France as the nation of 1789, in which every French man, woman and child could take part."[29] And they did take part, showing the skill with which French leaders used this resource for nation-building. In post-revolutionary France the educational system, starting from primary level, was impregnated with secular revolutionary content. The institutionalisation of the Revolution as event, which resulted, became an essential input for converting peasants without identity into Frenchmen and Frenchmen into Republicans, which blossomed into the growth of French nationalism.

Staying for the moment with Europe, the invoking of highly

specific pasts is one example of a way of promoting nationalism. In the late twentieth century legendary pasts were again brought alive in several European countries that faced ethnic dilution and multi-cultural diversity through immigration and the rise of different cultures. The attempt was, say, in the case of England, "to rediscover, by a virulent form of regressive modernisation (an attempt to capture the future by a determined long detour through the past), those discursive forms of manly and entrepreneurial 'greatness' which could restore 'Englishness' as a beleaguered national identity." Thus interested groups, commercial or otherwise, revive vanishing crafts, establish heritage sites where the sights and sounds, even the lives of an imagined past are recreated, and 'recreate' literature trails based on fictional works.[30]

From the above we get a distillate: two things take this whole autocatalysis process forward more rapidly: firstly, war; and, secondly, the direction given by the state.

As for war, this is incorporated directly or by suggestion into almost all the above examples; it has in fact always been the chief instrument by which the nation was built. Taking random examples, for the USA it was the War of Independence that made the nation, the Civil War that united it; and the battle of Gettysburg, always commemorated, that became the icon of the latter. For Britain, "nationalist history is the history of its battles … wars fought for the most part by a monarchy which … became a focus for national sentiment." For France it was the wars after the Revolution: Marengo; Austerlitz; Jena. And, as could be expected, the imperial wars put the crown of success on this violent story. So "war has been a principal determinant in the shaping of nation-states."[31]

In regard to the state and nationalism, nation-building is a "process initiated by the state, within the state, and for the state" and David Hume said this aptly: " 'Where a very extensive government has been established for many centuries it spreads a national character over the whole empire and communicates to every part a similitude of manners…' In France and Britain monarchs who were not nationalists had built nations. The nation-state was the result of their policies without this ever having been their objective."[32] That this process could take many years is seen in the case of France. The historian Marc Bloch asserted that French national consciousness was already highly developed by about the year 1100. Others think French and British nationalism was of ancient, if not quite so ancient, vintage, the fourteenth century at the latest according to Sydney Herbert. But then Eugen Weber researched the matter more carefully and documented that the French did not consider themselves as French till around 1870, and, maybe, not till 1914. There is "ample evidence that Europe's currently recognised nations emerged only very recently, in many cases centuries later than the dates customarily assigned for their emergence."[33]

In England, too, the process took many years. Geoffrey of Monmouth blessed it with a common name and a myth of origin in the late fourteenth century. A Saxon mythology of ancient liberties gave it more body in the sixteenth and seventeenth centuries.

Turkey is an example which deserves to be mentioned, since a multi-ethnic empire that had once stretched hundreds of kilometres east and west suddenly became a small nation; nationalism had to be created at virtually one stroke and again it was war and the state that did it.

Kemal Ataturk created a specifically Kemalist Turkish nationalism based on descent from the Oguz Turkish tribe, on pre-Ottoman history and on language and culture, which were promoted and eventually written into the February 1937 constitution as one of the six foundational principles of the Republic. This asserted that the Turks were the direct descendants of the world's greatest conquering race, that they had played a leading role in the origins and development of world civilisation, and that it was the Turks who had contributed most to what had been great in all of Turkish history. The attempt was totally to obliterate the idea that being multi-cultural, multi-ethnic or multi-lingual had any significance.

The ideological basis written into the 1937 constitution was sought to be spread and consolidated by cutting off, from historiography, the Ottoman Empire. Under the influence of Ziya Gokalp and other nationalists, Turanism or Turkism was defined as the source of Turkey's greatness. Gokalp's favoured instrument was the newspaper, which, in Turkey "has given a common consciousness to those who speak the same language by uniting them into a 'public' ... has consequently aroused a consciousness of national traditions and of cherished ideals. The sentiment of nationality once it arises amongst the masses spreads easily over neighbouring peoples ... leads to revivals in moral life, in language, in literature, and in economic and political life ..."[34]

Revival of Turkish identity and self-esteem, a necessary antidote to the recent setbacks, was founded on a portrayal of Turkey's past which started with epic history based on the geographic spread of the Turkish people from the Pacific to the Aegean; and took in the archaeological evidence from Anatolia. Thereafter, there was Kemal Ataturk and the revolution, and Anatolia became the heartland, the source of the tradition and culture of a Turkey which would confine its ambitions to its modern borders. The Ottoman period was virtually deleted. This mono-ethnic picture was reinforced by changing the language: the script to Latin, and the replacement of Arabic or Persian words by Turkish. But there was no irredentism, no claim to any kind of role among the Turkic people of Central and Western Asia.

This particular experiment was not fully successful as Nobel laureate Orhan Pamuk explains. Ataturk instituted an ambitious programme of reforms, changing from the Arabic to the Latin alphabet, from the Islamic to the Christian calendar, including Sunday instead of Friday as rest day, improvements in women's rights. But "he identifies Europe with civilisation; it follows that that which is not European is humiliatingly uncivilised. This humiliation is closely bound up with nationalism. Westernisation and nationalism come from the same source." In other words, there was an ancient and essential element in Turkish nationalism, according to Ataturk, but traditional customs, dress and so on misrepresented it and that misrepresentation had become part of the reality, so it had to be erased. "Ataturk believed that Turkish apparel misrepresented the nation". So he changed it by decree, along with a whole lot of other elements of tradition. So here we have the essentialist story of modernity overlaid with the making of nationalism according to the traditional story. But, adds Pamuk, and here we suspect he is talking about himself as much as anybody, the Turkish westerniser is ashamed of not being European; ashamed of what he does in his struggle to become European, losing his identity in this struggle, and thus "ashamed of who he is and ashamed of who he is not."[35] Such a comment reflects that the skill with which Ataturk sought to build the nation was not enough to carry conviction with at least some of Turkey's intellectuals.

However, in its more recent aspect, in the 1930s and 1940s the idea that the state should generate the nation came somewhat into disrepute because of the German and Japanese examples. Their nationalism and particularly the ruthless way their governments of the time promoted it in a fanatic and extreme form came to characterise the depictions of nationalism, including the scholarly depictions, in the debate. It is easy, since then, to assume that totalitarianism, or the total identification of the individual with the state, or fascism, the absolute subservience of the individual to the state, is what nationalism should mean.

## The Creation of Nationalism: Asia and Africa

When the colonies achieved independence after 1945, therefore, it was with this background that they had to cope. After the achievement of independence, it had to be the state that further built and reinforced nationalism. But because of its more recent aspect the question whether nations form states or states, nations, was thus presented in its starkest form to the dozens of states that came into being after the post-World War retreat of colonial empires. They had borders, an administrative apparatus, a law enforcement machinery and a structure of institutions set up by the colonial power. But few had national solidarity in the sense of ethnic, religious, linguistic or other essentialist unity or even homogeneity. This was not new, for no state has ever had the kind of national solidarity that theory demands. But these new states had to reckon with far more powerful states led by the USA and the USSR who wished to ensure the failure of their nation building by insisting it was a negative exercise, and a route to fascism. This entire subject is considered in more detail in chapters 7 and 8, the so-called Cold War according to the traditional story.

In Asia and Africa, to return to the main theme in the perspective of the traditional story, all the nationalist forces were united against imperialism. The nationalists had an inborn drive for independence; they were able to use the history of the nation as well as other resources to develop this drive; and, as was the case everywhere else war, here the war of liberation against foreign rule, has often been the chief instrument in doing this; while in more recent times the state has always initiated and pushed it forward.

As for the drive for sovereign independence, Jawaharlal Nehru, India's first Prime Minister, who did more, and more consciously than any other leader of modern India, to build nationalism, put it thus: "For any subject country national freedom must be the first and dominant urge; for India, with her intense sense of individuality and a past heritage, it was doubly so." He has a great deal to say about that heritage, the unique cultural tradition and the five thousand years of history, but the argument is not that without such a heritage the urge to be free would be weaker. It could not be, since it was European archaeologists and historians who had delved into and recreated large sections of that heritage and their main aim was to show that only fragmentation and internal divisions had characterised that past. It is again Jawaharlal Nehru's writings on the subject that are typical and the best known, as in this extract, about how "the long panorama of India's history unfolded itself before me, with its ups and downs, its triumphs and defeats. There seemed to me something unique about the continuity of a cultural tradition through five thousand years of history, of invasion and upheaval ... the hundred and eighty years of British rule in India were just one of the unhappy interludes in her long story."[36]

For further illustration we can take the Indian nationalist leader Surendranath Banerjee who recommends that "we should seriously set ourselves to the task of studying the history of our own country" in order to build patriotism, strengthen the national spirit and if "you seriously wish to regenerate your country, wish to see her great and prosperous."[37]

And there is Chaudhary Rahmat Ali, one of the originators of the idea of Pakistan, who claimed the same. First of all, "Pakistan was the birthplace of human culture and civilisation. The second is that it was the earliest centre of the communal aggregation of human society. And the third – the most dynamic of all – is that, ever since the dawn of recorded history, it is the first and strongest citadel of Islam in the Continent of Dinia and its Dependencies ... there are not many countries that can claim to have maintained their national sovereignty for a unbroken period of 1,145 years as can Pakistan from 712 to 1857."[38]

But mention may also be made here, by way of example, of African leaders all of whom faced this question and decided to place the state at the centre of nation-building after independence. When Sekou Toure said that the state is the grouping together of the organic structures of the nation, or Leopold Senghor of Senegal said that "the state is the expression of the nation, it is primarily a means to achieve the nation", they were not so much voicing an opinion as urging their own people to accept a nationhood coterminous with the existing state. African leaders in general, after their countries had achieved independence from colonial rule, saw that they must proceed from the state, which was given and delineated by the colonial power, to the nation.

Other examples can be given. Zambia's President Kaunda has been quoted as saying "our aim has been to create genuine nations from the sprawling artefacts the colonialists carved out"; and similarly others: "Cameroun's President Ahidjo sees the institutions of the state as a means to achieve nationhood ... Yakubo Gowon also compares African and European nation building. He sees the process but not the pace as essentially the same in Africa and Western Europe: A newly independent African state struggles against great odds of history, geography, ethnography and evil effects of imperialism to build a nation in less than a fiftieth of the time it took European states to build theirs."[39] Tom Mboya asserted that "a nationalist movement should mean the mobilisation of all the available groups of people in the country for the single struggle"; and you have to simplify the struggle into a single idea: independence; thus nationalism meant first of all the struggle for independence, then came everything else.

## The Empire-Makers Cooperate

So we have the encounter between these two forces, the empire-makers and their opponents the nationalists and two aspects of the encounter need to be noted.

Firstly that as early as the sixteenth century the empire-makers realised that they must cooperate with each other if they are to succeed in building their empires. One of the roots of such cooperation lies in the long-standing fear of an onslaught by the barbarian hordes on the Christian peoples of Europe. Over the centuries Europe has been invaded from the East: by the Moors in the seventh century, who overran Spain and ruled it for seven hundred years, longer than the whole of Spanish history since then; by Genghis Khan and Timur Lane and the Mongol hordes in the thirteenth and fourteenth centuries; by the Ottomans who almost annexed Vienna in the seventeenth. By the late nineteenth century, historians were warning of another invasion by a flood of yellow faced barbarians and, according to Oxford historian Charles Pearson, "we shall wake up to find ourselves ... thrust aside by peoples who we looked down upon as servile." Before the 1914-

1918 European war Kaiser William II of Germany drew a sketch which was elaborated into an oil painting, 'The Yellow Peril' depicting, according to the note he penned to go with the painting, the powers of Europe called together by the Archangel Michael, "to unite in resisting the inroad of Buddhism, heathenism and barbarism for the Defence of the Cross. Stress is specially laid on the *united* resistance of *all* European powers."[40]

It seems contradictory that such an announcement was followed by two of the bloodiest wars ever experienced by the human race, the source of both the wars lying in the differences among the Europeans. But from a longer historical viewpoint it is nevertheless true that this fear gave reality to the very concept of Europe, converting it into the beginnings of an identity for its inhabitants, one outcrop of which was that outside Europe they must work together, cooperate in building their empires.

In any event what we see happening on the ground is that when it came to expanding the empire, whether the problem was of strong local resistance or of the possibility of a clash between differing European interests, there was cooperation.

Minor skirmishes between one empire-builder and another were purely local initiatives by enthusiastic sea captains and adventurers, never approved by their head offices. Such was the story of Mahe' la Bourdonnais, appointed Governor of French Mauritius in 1735, who tried to intercept English shipping in the Bay of Bengal but failed for lack of support from headquarters; or of Admiral de Suffren, Commander of the French fleet in the Indian Ocean from 1782, called by one well-known authority a comet in the sky on the stage of history.[41] He, too, challenged English shipping, but had no bases, too few ships, no support from France and little discipline among his officers, who seem to have known which way the wind was blowing, for they regularly engaged in trade for their private profit, buying goods in India and the East, shipping them on English bottoms which were widely seen as the safest and then keeping the profits in English bank accounts.

Such also was the British French confrontation at Fashoda, on the upper Nile, in July, 1898. There a small French force under Jean Baptiste Marchand confronted a much larger British force under Horatio Kitchener. The accepted version is that neither being prepared to yield, "war between the two countries was a real possibility."[42] But the best qualified commentators agree that by the evening both were seen on the deck of Kitchener's flagship, glasses of whisky and soda in their hands, "swapping anecdotes about beating the Dervishes." And this so-called confrontation led to the Entente Cordiale between the two countries in 1904.

Two examples, out of the many available, will suffice to show that whatever may be the situation, the empire-builders of Europe cooperated.

The first: in 1879 an international body was set up to control the affairs of Egypt. The ruler, the Khedive Ismail, had been taking loans from European banks which he found, by that year, he could not repay. So a European consortium led by Britain and France, deposed the Khedive, and began to run the country in such a way as to collect their debts. This led to a nationalist uprising led by Arabi Pasha (or Ahmed Orabi), a coup in September, 1881 followed by establishment of control over most of the country by forces loyal to Arabi Pasha who fought to secure Egypt's independence from foreign domination with the slogan "Egypt for the Egyptians." At a later time Arabi Pasha went into Egypt's history as the first of the nationalists and was an inspiration, three quarters of a century later, for Gamal Abdel Nasser, who regarded him as a national hero.

The European response was to act together to oust Arabi Pasha, and so they agreed. But only the British and French had the military wherewithal *in situ* to do so. Then the French Parliament refused to give money for the proposed expedition. Though the British and French navies had together appeared before Alexandria in a show of strength, it was left to Britain alone to carry out enforcement measures against the Egyptian nationalists.

The second: in and opposite the island of Zanzibar the Germans were in 1887 attempting to establish one of their first imperial ventures. This sector had been allotted to them by the Berlin conference of 1884-85. As they did this they met with resistance from Abushiri ibn Salim al-Harthi, "leader of this first uprising against German imperialism in Africa". By late 1888 Abushiri's militia started offensive action against the Germans. "Up and down the coast the Germans were hunted down like rats." So they called for British help. A joint naval blockade was mounted so that Abushiri was cut off from his weapons supply and from his bases on either side of the Zanzibar channel. Thus protected German reinforcements went in and defeated Abushiri. But here again, the African resistance to imperial encroachment and conquest became the inspiration for a later struggle for total independence.[43]

The showpiece of this cooperative endeavour was the Berlin conference, November, 1884 to February, 1885. Fourteen representatives of Europe's greater and lesser powers, those in the business of making empires as well as those not, met to divide up Africa. The German Chancellor, Otto von Bismarck (1815-1898), made the speech welcoming the delegates with the declaration that they had met in a common endeavour to spread the 'three C's', commerce, Christianity and civilisation, to Africa by opening up the interior of that continent. By the end of that conference King Leopold of Belgium showed adroitness in getting the Congo allotted to him, far more than his tiny country could handle; the French extended their claims against the British and others while their people in the field, so to speak, were busy planting the flag up and down central Africa as evidence of having taken possession;[44] so as to get allocation of territory, bits and pieces here were exchanged for bits and pieces there. As one historian put it, "here was a true thieves' compact: a charter for the partition of Africa."[45]

The Berlin conference was followed by the Brussels Treaty of 1890 (followed by further agreements of 1892 and 1899) by which the Europeans agreed that in the parts of Africa between the twentieth parallel North and the twenty-second parallel South there will be an embargo on the supply of arms to native or local buyers. This was the territory that was yet to come under effective rule, and one of the major problems faced by the Europeans was that the Africans who resisted their advances seemed to be able to get arms almost as good as theirs.

This leads to a conclusion. The compact arrived in Berlin precisely presaged what happened from 1945 to 1990. Berlin had several participants that carried weight, the latter period had just two; Berlin was about Africa, the latter period was about the whole world; Berlin was fronted by the three 'C's, working in tandem; the latter period by only two, capitalism and communism, also working in tandem. But, looked at, in the context of the traditional story, the difference between the two ends just about there.

## A Violent Confrontation

The second aspect of the encounter is the continuous violence with which it took place. This has also been explained by a number of writers from the colonies. Here is one example. The very act of acquiring colonies was one of violence, for "to the non-European, the expansion of Europe is experienced as the unabashed dawn of systematic and organised global violence. This is a violence that closes off the different and differing cultural and historical totalities within which the non-European exists." Once empire is established it sets up, all over the different colonies, little Europes in each of which Europe itself is recreated within the geographical spaces of the colonies; within this geographic space the coloniser lives the life of normality, in the word chosen by Edward Said. This life of normality, the continuation of this life, is the sign that the colony is being managed successfully, that there is no anticipation of resistance. It is obvious, then, that "the first act of freedom that the colonised engages in is the attempt to violently disrupt the normality which European colonial society presupposes."[46]

The classic on this theme is by Frantz Fanon. Between the coloniser and the colonised the "first encounter was marked by violence and their existence together – that is to say the exploitation of the native by the settler – was carried on by dint of a great array of bayonets and cannons."[47] And violence is needed to overthrow it. This violence comes up slowly with the continuation of colonial rule until it is just under the skin of the masses. Here and there it explodes; then there are repressions which, "far from calling a halt to the forward rush of national consciousness, urge it on". The nationalist political parties, those who are known as the mainstream leadership, says Fanon, have not called for armed insurrection except in very few cases. But they are the only ones who can control it, the colonisers know that they cannot deprive the masses of their leaders since then the latter would let violence take unbridled hold of their actions. Finally it is these mainstream leaders that the coloniser welcomes "with open arms" and "in two minutes endows them with independence", because "it is the intuition of the colonised masses that their liberation must, and can only, be achieved by force"; so there is this uncontrolled violence of which the threat is hanging at all times in the air. And this violence is not disruptive of national unity; on the contrary, it is all-inclusive and national; it contributes to the liquidation of regionalism and tribalism and the promotion of the unity of the nation. It is a positive force.

But we are familiar with this and for our purposes it is the other side which is more important: the resistance of the people colonised to the imperial or colonising power, and the role of that resistance, the anti-colonial war, in building the independent nations of Asia and Africa. The resistance was ceaseless, widespread, violent and very effective, leading finally to victory in the war against the empire-makers. And for every nation subjected to empire this war served to inspire one generation after another, leading to the most important elements in the nationalist ideology of the independent state. Several examples of this are given in the next section of this chapter.

But this point needs elaboration; this is done below.

Nationalism and nation-building were not, as the UNESCO General History of Africa points out, primitive or the work of a blood thirsty minority, nor savage. Resistance to foreign rule, which lay at the heart of nation-building in Asia and Africa, was based on recouping sovereignty. "The idea of sovereignty clearly did provide an ideology for resistance."[48] Other matters have been linked to the urge to be free of colonial rule. One is that, as the spirit of emancipation rose, "the driving inspiration was not that all men should be divided by becoming nationals, but that all men should be united by becoming free"; and equal, for in Africa it was directed at "the abolition of all those artificial barriers against equality, and, therefore, against freedom, that racism and imperialism had imposed."[49] But these do not in any way qualify the urge to freedom, which was just there as an integral component of nationalism: it was ceaseless and boundless in its striving to be free from colonial rule; it was violence that actually achieved freedom even if it did happen that at independence power was handed over to a non-violent stream; it was aimed at the eventual creation of or continuation of a functioning state; and that state would create or complete the process of the consolidation of the nation.

The resistance was there when the Europeans started to move into the lands that were to become parts of their empires; the UNESCO General History of Africa cited above points out that "virtually every sort of African society resisted, and there was resistance in virtually every region of European advance."[50] It continued to be there when they tried to consolidate their rule; it was there, and it grew in vigour and strength, with the burgeoning of the movements that led eventually to independence; from one point of view the "resistance to invasion, revolts against colonial rule and the rise of nationalist movements during the 1950's should be seen as part of a continuing theme of self-defence and self-realisation among a wide range of African people... ."[51] And it contributed thereafter to further consolidate the unity of each of the independent nation states that emerged.

Furthermore the two sides, coloniser and colonised, were more evenly balanced than is apparent for much of the period. The colonial powers had to fight one battle after another as they moved inland from their trading stations along the coast: guerilla war, set piece battles, insurgency, met their efforts to consolidate or stabilise their rule. Within the movements that led to independence the militant elements played a key role, even though this was usually denied by the colonial powers and often by other streams of the nationalist movement; and in the post-independence commemorations it is those who took the path of war and violence against the colonisers who were acclaimed. The heroes of the nation were the heroes of the armed resistance.

In short, the colonial powers were forced out of the colonies by military defeat or the prospect or certainty of defeat for "no imperialist country ever parted with power as a result of discussions and debates" but only by mass struggle and direct action.[52]

This can be illustrated by the story of the way India achieved independence, about which there has been some debate.

Ranajit Guha highlights the contrast between two historiographies. There is the elitist historiography, which depicts this story "as a sort of 'learning process' through which the native elite became involved in politics" getting involved in the institutions put in place by the colonisers, wanting not independence but the rewards which the colonisers had themselves deliberately built into the construction of those institutions. So Indian nationalism is represented as the indigenous elite leading the people from subjugation to freedom. In this the "parameters of Indian politics are assumed to be or enunciated as exclusively or primarily those of the institutions introduced by the British for the government of the country"; it is, in Guha's words, one-sided, blinkered, bankrupt. For our purposes it would be called the historiography of modernity, or better, the story of modernity, which is covered in more detail in chapter 4. On the other hand, there is the traditional story, in which the people *on their own*, quite independently of the elite, make and develop nationalism. Here we return to the violent opposition, for nationalism "was an autonomous domain" in which the principal actors were "the subaltern classes and groups" mobilised horizontally, more spontaneously and more violently; and it was militant demonstrations of opposition to imperial rule that characterised this story of nationalism.[53]

It was, in any case, the moment when the British realised that they could no longer trust the Indian army to carry out their orders that they decided that they would have to quit, be forced out or leave before that happened. The nationalist leader Netaji Subhas Chandra Bose had organised during World War II with help from Japan, an Indian National Army, the idea being that this armed force comprising Indians, professional soldiers taken prisoner by the Japanese during their advance into Southeast Asia, labourers from the plantations in Malaysia, traders and shop-keepers from Burma and other civilian recruits, should advance to Delhi and drive out the British. After the war three of the military personnel who had joined the INA were brought to trial; there was so much agitation, led this time also by the Congress party, the 'mainstream leaders' in the vocabulary of Frantz Fanon, that they had to be released. Nationalist emotions were overwhelming the disciplinary loyalties of the armed forces and in March 1946 Premier Attlee of Britain told Parliament that "today I think the national idea has spread right through and not least, perhaps, among the soldiers who have given such wonderful service in the war."[54] There had been the naval mutiny by three thousand sailors aboard their ships and in barracks ashore, in February 1946, and rumblings of discontent among the Indian officers in the Air Force. The British Indian armed forces, the kernel of British imperial power, was no longer to be relied on, and the British decided to leave before they were forced out.

It would be useful to examine in a little more detail just a few of the many episodes in the story of resistance, for this resistance greatly reduced the number of years for which the Europeans were able to rule their empires. These are a small selection of examples, not intended to give anything like a comprehensive picture of the effectiveness of resistance to colonial ventures; some more, and in more detail, are given in the chapters on Indonesia, Algeria, Vietnam and Afghanistan (chapters 5, 6, 9 and 10 respectively).

Some of resistance wars in Africa were by African empires that were powerful, such as that of Samori Toure in West Africa.

Born in 1830, Samori Toure had been accepted as Keletigui or war chief by his people by the time he was forty-one. He built the Wassoulou Empire comprising major portions of what are today Guinea, Mali, Sierra Leone and the Ivory Coast. By 1878 he was strong enough to take on the French, who were expanding inland from the coast. By then he had 30,000 armed men under him, all of whom were well trained, since he himself was a military strategist of genius, and equipped with guns bought from the British. He even sent blacksmiths for training and started the production of weapons, copies of Gras-Kropatcheks, though they were not very good copies since he did not have the machine tools and quality steel needed. And his empire lay in the area that the French wanted; so in April, 1883 they attacked the army led by his brother Fabou. They were driven back with few survivors within a few hours, and "the white soldiers were so exhausted that they had to cling to the tails of their mules to stand up."[55]

The French pulled back and did not attempt another advance till 1885. In that year an expedition under Col. A.V.A. Combes tried to advance to the Bure goldfields. Samori's forces, divided into three mobile columns, encircled the French positions, cutting them off from communications and inflicted another defeat on them. In fact it was not till 1898 that, with British help, the French were able finally to defeat and capture him.

After they achieved independence Guinea (October, 1958) and Mali (September, 1960) continued to celebrate his achievements in written history and oral tradition. Sekou Toure, the first President of Guinea, a direct descendant of Samori, followed his tradition of militancy in the final struggle. When French President de Gaulle, forced to grant independence, offered the French West African countries the choice between membership of the French community with all the financial, trade and economic advantages but, of course, with curbed independence, or full and immediate independence, Sekou Toure alone chose full independence in 1958. So he attracted de Gaulle's vindictiveness; when the French left they took every administrative record with them, cut all political and economic ties. But Sekou Toure had pointed the way for others and by 1960 they all followed suit.

Then there was the empire of the Asante nation. The empire that they built was started in what is now Ghana in the early eighteenth century by Opoke Ware (1700-1750). By the nineteenth century it was the most powerful state in West Africa, with a centralised administrative system, a well trained and equipped army, advanced educational facilities, and extended trading interests which reached the Europeans who were just arriving along the coast. Here it was the British who were trying to push inland. In 1806, then again (since the British tried again) in 1814-15 and in 1823-26 the Asanti attacked, defeated and drove back the British. In the 1823-26 war they killed the British Governor and used his skull as a drinking cup. The British tried to cultivate the Fanti, rivals to the Asante. The year 1863 saw another war in which the Asante attacked both the British forces and those of their allies. By now British public opinion had turned against further involvement in Ghana but those in the field persisted. Finally, in 1873 they were able to win a victory, penetrating through to the Asante capital of Kumasi, burning it down, getting besieged there for four months before they were able to withdraw. It was only in 1894, with the Berlin compact in force so that the British were assured of European support if needed, and with the general arms embargo, that they were able to feel strong enough to try again. This time the Asante empire came to an end; and in 1896 its territories were annexed.

But Asanti resistance was not yet completely broken. In 1900 the Queen Mother of the Asante state of Ejusu, Yaa Asantewa, led an Asante army against the British, surrounded their fort, and cut off those inside for six months. Yaa Asantewa continued as a source of inspiration to the people of Ghana, as seen for instance in the celebration of the anniversary of her struggle in 2000. She was depicted, sitting on a horse in front of the fort, a rifle in one hand, a dagger in the other, defying the cowardly soldiers within to come out and fight like men. A Yaa Asantewa museum was opened; Jerry Rawlings and his wife Nana Konadu strongly backed the celebration and even named their daughter Yaa Asantewa. An Asante Congress was convened with the theme "Celebrating the Vision and Heroism of Yaa Asantewa"; and a mock battle held at the fort, a replica of what happened a century earlier. All this was part of the effort to strengthen the structures of nationalism in the post-independence years.

Another example. The Zulu empire was located in KwaZulu Natal. Under Shaka (c. 1787-1828) it became the most powerful in the whole of South Africa, subduing or allying with most of the neighbouring tribes like the Sithole, the Qwabe, the Thuli. Shaka developed an effective military organisation with frequent drilling of troops, the introduction of new weapons and tactics like the famous buffalo horn formation: flanking right and left wing attacks being the horns; a central attack as the chest; and the loins, reserves kept for later use. He changed the nature of war in Southern Africa and after him the Zulu impis were feared by all his rivals. So when the British came up against the Zulu empire in 1879, now led by King Cetshwayo, the latter had had half a century to internalise Shaka's legacy.

In January of that year the British invaded Zululand. They had an army of 18,000, well equipped with artillery and firearms and they pitched camp at a place called Isandlwana, a name which would go down in history. On the other side were 20,000 Zulu warriors picked by Cetshwayo; they attacked and in that offensive, as the historian Thomas Pakenham put it, the centre of the buffalo horn formation swamped the forward defence lines of the British; the flanking right and left wings flooded down into the British positions and the latter "broke and fled ... soon the track was blocked by panic-stricken men, many of them wounded, screaming for help".

The impact was, for the British, traumatic. Their dreams of a new British empire from the Cape to the Zambezi "died on the battlefield of Isandlwana". Britain was humiliated in the eyes of every other power, her influence declined; for the government of Disraeli it was a mortal blow.[56]

Isandlwana also went into history as one of the biggest triumphs of African nationalism and an inspiration to all succeeding movements for independence and rejuvenation. When, for instance, the Premier of KwaZulu Natal spoke on the legacy of King Cetshwayo in Durban on 22 January, 2007, he described Isandlwana as part of the continental wars of resistance against colonialism and imperialism as well as apartheid. Then he recalled the resistance of Samori Toure, of the Asante. These and others, the war of the Maji Maji from 1905-07, the Bhambatha uprising of 1906,[57] the Algerian war of independence from 1954-62, the war waged by the Mau Mau against the British in Kenya by which they won independence, the creation in 1961 of a modern guerilla army (Umkhonto We Sizwe) in South Africa to fight the forces of the state of South Africa and in support of the ANC; all these were seen by him as links in an unbroken chain of violent and effective resistance to the empire builders.

So it was that "the Baole of Cote d'Ivoire fought the French village by village until 1911; the Igbo of Nigeria were not fully defeated till 1919; the Jola of Senegal not until the 1920s; the Dinka of southern Sudan not until 1927 ...the 'Mad Mullah' in Somaliland led Dervish warriors in a holy war against the British for twenty years until his death in 1920. Bedouin resistance against Italian rule in Libya ended only in 1931 after nine years of guerilla warfare."[58]

Many of the wars of resistance were one-sided. In 1905 several tribal groups in East Africa, the Ngoni, the Ngindo, the Pogoro, the Matumbi, among others, combined to push back the German advance. This was led by Kinjikitile Ngwale and called the Maji Maji war or rebellion. At first they were able to drive the Germans off their tribal land, but reinforcements came from Germany, and by 1907 the war was at an end having claimed 75,000 African lives. But the name of Kinjikitile is still honoured in Tanzania, heir to German East Africa, and it is honoured as a revolutionary, a nationalist and an inspiration to the movement that brought freedom.

One African war ended in the defeat of the would-be imperial power. Massawa, the Eritrean port on the Red Sea, is where the Italian attempt at making an African empire began. The British had been there but evacuated it in 1885; Gladstone, with Isandlwana still enlivening his nightmares, wanted to be rid of it, and a secret deal was made for the Italians to take over. They started pushing south and met their first reverse in January, 1887 in Dogali, where the forces of Emperor Yohannes of Ethiopia routed their column. By March 1889 Yohannes was dead; Menelik II succeeded him. Meanwhile the Italians, undiscouraged by Dogali, pushed on, supplying arms to Menelik in exchange for territory, avoiding a confrontation. Soon they had a small piece of Eritrea, their only overseas empire. But they wanted a proper empire like the other Europeans had and that could not be done without a fight.

So in September 1895 the Governor of Eritrea, General Oreste Baratieri, arrived in Massawa determined to take on Menelik, who had meanwhile been building up his strength: breach loaders and ammunition from the Italians; 100,000 rifles and ammunition for them from the French, smuggled in because there was, since 1890, an embargo; machine guns and artillery. And he had trained his army in the use of these weapons. So when Baratieri's army of 17,000 men advanced into Ethiopia, the army facing it was as well armed and probably better trained.

The battle of Adowa took place on the first of March 1896. By nine in the morning of that day the Italians had been routed. Out of Baratieri's army 10,000 were killed, captured or missing. There were street riots in Italy; Premier Crispi lost his job; Baratieri was sacked and tried before a court in Asmara, the capital of Eritrea; the Italian army did not get over the humiliation for forty years, and perhaps not even then: in 1935 Italy under Mussolini once again attacked Ethiopia with better results, but even this did not quite restore Italian army morale, as their performance in World War II showed.

Menelik used his triumph to expand his empire. The French and British now looked on him as a potential and powerful ally. He promised them support and in exchange took a chunk of French Somaliland as well as a chunk of British Somaliland. His empire was now twice the size of that which Yohannes had had.

### The Course of Empire

In summary, empire-making, from the viewpoint of this story, was actually an unceasing war waged by several European countries acting in concert against almost all the African and Asian nations. It was a long war, compared to wars in general, which led in a number of cases to varying but always temporary periods of pacification through military occupation. In every case the eventual outcome of the war was the defeat, forcible or under threat of force, of the imperial power and eviction of that occupation.

Take the year 1800, often said to be a watershed of sorts.

On land, with one exception, the empire still, in 1800, consisted only of trading posts and fortified ports. The big exception was in India, where the British gained the right to tax collection, the Diwani, after the battle of Plassey in 1757. This was still only partly empire, since that right was as vassals to the throne in Delhi; their seal had the imperial titles and their mint struck the imperial coin, i.e. that of the throne at Delhi. In writing this story, therefore, the European presence in Asia and Africa till the late eighteenth century needs to be reduced to the somewhat fugitive presence it actually was, contested continually, one of several other presences, and not particularly noteworthy. So "until the nineteenth century, the Europeans remained largely confined to their numerous forts around the coasts."[59]

In the traditional story the change ascribed to the year 1800 actually took several decades to complete. It started in the last quarter of the eighteenth century and continued to happen through the first quarter of the next. Thereafter, the rate of change accelerated through the nineteenth century, of which the last quarter saw a new factor which again changed the nature of empire. A broad description suggests three kinds of change that happened after 1800.

The first was that, starting with the end of the eighteenth century and through the first quarter of the next the European empires in the Americas were lost. These had largely been established by Spain and Portugal, with Britain (in North America) and France (in Canada and the Caribbean) in second place. The Spanish and Portuguese empires went back to the early sixteenth century and had been gradually expanding since then, but outside the Americas there was no imperial territory, only, as pointed out above, with a few exceptions, coastal settlements, trading posts, fortified ports. This was about the size of empire established by Albuquerque. When the empires of Spain and Portugal came to an end, therefore, and during "the first quarter of the nineteenth century the colonial empires were in retreat ... they were smaller than at any time since 1700."[60] Or, equally accurately, since 1500.

The second kind of change was the gradual, very gradual, expansion of territorial possessions in Asia and Africa after 1825.

The third kind of change was the introduction, under the driving force of Social Darwinism and its emulators, of imperialism of a new kind after about 1875 leading to an accelerated expansion of this territory. Hence, while the European empires expanded by about six and a half million square miles from 1800 to 1878, they then grew by another eight and a half million square miles from then till 1914, that is about three times as fast.

These kinds of changes are not to be confused with the periods of time described as eras. Eras in the history of empire are the device used by historians devoted to the modernity story to essentialise the relations between the empire-makers and the nations of Asia and Africa. So it was that very roughly the changes might be associated with different periods of time, but the key operational factor here is not the growth of the empire but the resistance that growth encountered, a resistance which was very varied in strength and effectiveness; some succumbed as early as the eighteenth century; some, such as Afghanistan, never succumbed. There is so much variation in time and space, so many players to consider, that it becomes impossible to generalise.

The imperial ventures, on this reckoning, were short footnotes in the history of the regions where empires were supposed to have been established, footnotes which endured for between fifty and a hundred years, unless we move into the world of modernity. This is done in the next chapter.

## ENDNOTES

[1] During the decades when empires were being made, roughly the last half of the nineteenth century, war and power continued, as always, to be closely connected in the relations between the great powers of Europe. This applies also to the story of modernity; but in this chapter we are concerned with the underdog story, of the relations between the great powers, on the one hand, and the smaller ones, most of which were colonised, on the other.

[2] But not the same lines, as far as I know!

[3] In what follows 'colony' is used for territorial acquisitions by the western powers in Asia, Africa and Latin America; and 'empire' for a more general expansion of territory on the Macedonian or Roman pattern and which may also include colonial expansion.

[4] The emotive significance of Imperium for the western or generally modernity civilisation, and of all the expressions derived from it like *Imperium Orbis Terrae* or *Imperium Populi Romani*, which meant a world wide dominion built in the course of a long and great history, was based on the inspiration of Rome. Polybius set out to prove that the dominance of Rome was the goal of history. Hence also, of course, the frequency with which kings in Europe assumed the title *Kaiser*.

[5] Luis Vaz de Camoens, *The Lusiads*, transl. William C. Atkinson, Penguin Books, Middlesex, 1980, pp. 39-40, 42 and 157 respectively.

[6] *Albuquerque, Caesar of the East*, Selected texts by Afonso de Albuquerque and his son, ed. and translated T.F.Earle and John Villiers, Aris and Phillips, Warminster, 1990, pp. 57, 61.

[7] M.N. Pearson, India and the Indian Ocean in the Sixteenth Century, in Ashin Das Gupta and M.N. Pearson, eds. *India and the Indian Ocean, 1500-1800*, OUP Calcutta, 1987, p. 72.

[8] D.K. Fieldhouse, *The Colonial Empires, A Comparative Survey from the Eighteenth Century*, A Delta Book, Dell, New York, 1966, p.139.

[9] A Portuguese source quoted by Geoffrey Parker, *The Military Revolution, Military innovation and the rise of the West, 1500-1800*, Cambridge University Press, 1988, p.105.

[10] K.M.Panikkar, *India and the Indian Ocean*, George Allen and Unwin, London, 1951, pp.47-8.

[11] Quoted by M.N.Pearson, op. cit., in Ashin Das Gupta and M.N.Pearson, eds. *India and the Indian Ocean, 1500-1800*, pp. 78 and 71-72, respectively.

[12] Kenneth McPherson, *The Indian Ocean, A History of People and The Sea*, Oxford University Press, Delhi, 1993, p. 141.

[13] Geoffrey Parker, op. cit. p. 94.

[14] Albuquerque op. cit. pp. 103, 111.

[15] Kenneth McPherson, op. cit., p. 138.

[16] Quoted by Geoffrey Parker, op. cit. p. 82.

[17] For several references on this see Richard Koebner, *Empire,* Cambridge University Press, 1961.

[18] D.K.Fieldhouse, op. cit., p. 151.

[19] Nicholas B. Dirks, *The Scandal of Empire, India and the Creation of Imperial Britain*, Permanent Black, Delhi, 2006, p.170.

[20] K.M.Panikkar, op. cit., p. 61.

[21] Douglas Porch, *Wars of Empire*, Cassell and Co., London, 2001, p.59.

[22] Geoffrey Parker, op. cit., p.154.

[23] Thomas Pakenham, *The Scramble for Africa*, Avon Books, New York, 1992, p. xxiii.

[24] Stuart Kauffman, *At Home in the Universe, The Search for Laws of Self-Organization and Complexity,* Oxford University Press, 1995, p. 49.

[25] The modernity story asserts the reverse: that technology, the communications revolution and so on impact on individuals and groups.

[26] Eric Hobsbawm, The Nation as Invented Tradition, in John Hutchinson and Anthony Smith, eds., *Nationalism*, OUP, Oxford, 1994, p. 76.

[27] See chapter 4 for further details of what Hobsbawm and Anderson had to say on the subject, and which fits into the modernity story.

[28] Eric Wolf, *Europe and the People Without History*, University of California Press, Berkeley, 1982, p. 379. Wolfe asserts that European societies were not homogeneous; 'it is not true that cultural uniformity eased the way to state making and nation formation in Europe'.

[29] Eric Hobsbawm, op. cit. above, p. 77.

[30] Stuart Hall, Culture, Community, Nation, in David Boswell and Jessica Evans, eds., *Representing the Nation*, A Reader, Routledge, London, 1999, p.39.

[31] Michael Howard, War and Nations, in John Hutchinson and Anthony Smith, op. cit. above, pp. 254-7.

[32] Benjamin Neuberger, State and Nation in African Thought, in John Hutchinson and Anthony Smith, op. cit. above, p. 233.

[33] References and citations in this paragraph from Walker Connor, When is a Nation?, in John Hutchinson and Anthony Smith, op. cit., above, pp.154-9.

[34] Zia Gokalp, *Turkish Nationalism and Western Civilization*, trans. and ed. N.Baker, George Allen and Unwin, New York, 1959, pp. 71-85.

[35] Orhan Pamuk, *Other Colours, Essays and a Story*, Faber and Faber, London, 2007, pp.212-3.

[36] Jawaharlal Nehru, *The Discovery of India*, Meridian Books, London, 1956, p.40 and 39, respectively. Note that the hundred and eighty years belongs to the modernity story; the traditional one has only about ninety.

[37] Surendranath Banerjee, The Study of Indian History, in Elie Kedourie, ed. *Nationalism in Asia and Africa*, Weidenfeld and Nicolson, London, 1971, p.230.

[38] Chaudhary Rahmat Ali, The Idea of Pakistan, in Elie Kedourie, ed. op. cit. pp. 245-6.

[39] The quotes in this paragraph are from Benjamin Neuberger, op. cit. above, p.232, 235.

[40] Niall Ferguson, *The War of the World, History's Age of Hatred*, Penguin Books,

London, 2007, pp. 43 and 46 (italics in original).

[41] By K.M.Pannikar, in *India and the Indian Ocean*, George Allen and Unwin, London, 1951, p. 68.

[42] See D.K.Fieldhouse, op. cit. p. 224.

[43] Thomas Pakenham, op. cit. pp. 548, 346 and 348, respectively, from Fashoda onwards.

[44] Article 34 of the General Act which emerged from the conference legalised by European recognition, acts by 'any power which henceforth takes possession of a tract of land on the coasts of the African Continent outside of its present possessions, or which, being hitherto without such possession, shall acquire them and assume a protectorate ..."

[45] Niall Fergusson, *Empire*, Penguin Books, London, 2004, p. 236.

[46] Tsenay Serequeberhan, Colonialism and the Colonised: Violence and Counter-violence, in Emmanuel Chukwudi Eze, *African Philosophy, An Anthology*, Blackwell, Oxford, 1998, p.238 and 235 respectively. Serequeberhan has used modern and even post-modern philosophy – phenomenology and hermeneutics for example- to articulate a post-colonial African philosophy rooted in the 'lived experience' of liberation struggles.

[47] Frantz Fanon, Concerning Violence, in Emmanuel Chukwudi Eze, ed. op. cit., n. 7 above, p. 142.

[48] A.Adu Boahen, ed. *The UNESCO General History of Africa*, Abridged edition, Vol. VII, Africa under Colonial Domination, 1880-1935, James Currey Publishers, London, 1990, p.27. The UNESCO General History is acknowledged to be a major breakthrough in the recognition of Africa's cultural heritage.

[49] Basil Davidson, *Africa in History, Themes and Outlines*, Phoenix, London, 2001, pp.325-6.

[50] A.Adu Boahen, op. cit., p. 26.

[51] Basil Davidson, op. cit., p. 300.

[52] The quotations in this section are from Frantz Fanon, *The Wretched of the Earth*, in Emmanuel Chukwudi Eze, op. cit. pp. 231-2. This, Fanon's book, is the classic on violence and liberation struggles, described as the most important book on colonialism yet written. Contrast the take of Mahatma Gandhi on the use of violent revolutionary activity in achieving independence. He asserted that this would be "suicidal at this stage of the country's life, if not for all times in a country so vast, so hopelessly divided, and with the masses so deeply sunk in pauperism ..." Cited by B.R.Nanda, *The Making of a Nation, India's Road to Independence*, Harper Collins, New Delhi, 1998, p.197.

[53] Ranajit Guha, On Some Aspects of the Historiography of Colonial India, in Ranajit Guha, ed., *Subaltern Studies I, Writings on South Asian History and Society*, OUP Delhi, 1982. The quotations are from pp. 2-4. Guha's two stories are very close to modernity, on the one hand, and traditionalism on the other – and have been so identified here, but actually his first historiography stops short of asserting (as modernity does) that nationalism was entirely the creation of the colonisers; while his second stops short of saying (as the traditional story does) that without the use or tremendous latent threat of violence colonial rule would not have ended.

[54] Quotes taken from S.C.Sen Gupta, *India Wrests Freedom,* Sahitya Samsad, Calcutta, 1982, pp. x, and 308-10.

[55] Thomas Pakenham, op. cit., p. 174.

[56] See Thomas Pakenham, op. cit., pp. 67-71. Of course the dreams were resurrected soon thereafter.

[57] The Zulu fighter Inkosi Bhambatha went to King Cetshwayo's royal kraal at Usutu to pay homage and then rose against British rule in 1906, a rebellion considered to be the fore-runner of freedom. At the centenary celebrations for the occasion South African President Tabo Mbeki said, "today we are free because of what leaders like him did and must never forget what we owe them."

[58] Martin Meredith, *The State of Africa, A History of Fifty Years of Independence*, Free Press, London, 2005, p.4.

[59] Geoffrey Parker, op. cit. p. 120.

[60] D.K. Fieldhouse, op. cit., p. 177.

# 4

# Modernity in the Colonial Era

The four central arguments of this story or episteme are, firstly, that in the acquisition of the colonies, the role played by war and power was insignificant; whatever wars were fought were against primitive peoples who could offer only token resistance. Actually they welcomed the civilizing influence of the empire-makers. Secondly, there were many causes for empire. Indeed the empire-makers did not really want to make empires; these were acquired more or less by accident, the wholly unexpected outcome of a well-meaning desire by the Europeans to trade in peace, to find Christians, to civilize backward people, among many other things; or perhaps they emerged because nature had so decreed.

As for the other side, and this is the third argument, nationalism was quite different in Africa and Asia from the European experience; in the colonies it was largely the creation of the empire-makers, who taught the people there the essential lessons about ethnic, religious or linguistic and other homogeneity.

Fourthly, as for the encounter between these two sides, there was really no encounter worth the name; the empires were lost because of rivalries among the empire-makers, the high cost of maintaining the empires or other causes that had nothing to do with the colonised people.

In every aspect, thus, this story is the polar opposite of the traditional story.

These four central arguments are elaborated as follows:

## War and the Empire-Makers

The empire-makers, so the modernity story goes, were so much better armed, and had such a superiority of tactics and strategy that whatever military engagements took place could only be called 'little wars' by the use of hyperbole; they were all trivial affairs, quite inconsequential compared to those within Europe. At some point in the argument Social Darwinism appears, to make it clear that whatever happened in these little wars, as for instance, the destruction of African peoples and races, was decreed by the rule of the survival of the fittest.

Thus it is that the general histories of warfare written in the countries that made empires, meaning most by far of those that were ever written, make little or no mention of wars fought in the making of empires. *The Cambridge History of Warfare*, edited by Geoffrey Parker, has not included a single chapter on such wars; while the website *historyofwaronline.com* does include the Zulu war of 1879, including the signal defeat of British forces at Isandlwana, but no other imperial war is mentioned, none, in a history that purports to cover all of warfare since the earliest times. General J.F.C.Fuller, writing about *The Conduct of War*, does mention three imperial wars, but none of those which the African or Asian nations fought to keep out the empire builders; indeed he believes the expansion of empire in the nineteenth century was "bloodless".[1] And a survey by Larry H. Addington on *The Patterns of War Since the Eighteenth Century*, purported to be a synthesis of the many changes in war that happened in the period, has just three pages on the wars fought to gain control of empires, and those, too, largely about the first and second Boer wars. There is hardly any mention of all the other wars fought by the British, the French and the Germans, nothing on the Italian defeat at Adowa, nor mention of the wars fought in Afghanistan, or in India or Southeast Asia. In *A History of Warfare* by John Keegan, described by *Time* magazine as one of the century's most distinguished military historians, you will not find any mention of Samori Toure and his Wassoulou Empire, nor of Opoke Ware and the Asante nation or Cetshwayo and Isandlwana. These are examples of a general trend. It is to the histories devoted to the specific subject of empires that we have to go to find out about these wars; and even there the mentions are brief.

The modernity story is clear in asserting that for short periods colonial war may have had some little importance in the making of empire, but it had no connection with other aspects of life, politics, economics, culture and above all civilisation, the *mission civilisatrice* of the empire-makers; in the long run all these other factors were of greater significance. The colonisers did, of course, resort to war, but this was largely against savages, those un-civilised peoples who were quite unable to understand the benefits of being subject to alien rule by a civilised nation. "Wars and rebellions have always been the stuff of which traditional histories have been written", but the anti-colonial resistance movements and their leaders "figure as momentary interruptions of the grand sagas of colonial conquest ... simply 'disturbances', sometimes 'aberrations', their perpetrators reduced to the status of dacoits or fanatics often led by crazed monks, popes, and prophets."[2]

The wars of this kind that were fought were short, one-sided and insignificant because "European forces were able to conquer large parts of Asia and Africa – empires of truly Napoleonic proportions – at an astonishingly low cost. What made this possible was the crushing superiority of European firepower ..."

The better weapons of the empire-makers were the result of a series of innovations through the centuries. The musket came in the sixteenth century and by the early seventeenth had replaced every other gun. For two centuries after that there were no major changes. The Brown Bess, still used in 1853, was very similar to the guns used at Blenheim in 1704. It took a minute to load, misfired half the time, didn't fire at all in rain or damp weather, and was inaccurate, "soldiers commonly shot away their weight in lead for every man they killed." Improvements came: in 1807 a new and more reliable firing mechanism; then came the rifling of the barrel which made the gun far more accurate; then in the 1860's muzzle loading was replaced by breech loading, meaning a tremendous increase in the rate of fire, which led to the Maxim gun (and others like the Gatling) and a shift which "dramatically widened the power gap between European and non-Western peoples and led directly to the outburst of imperialism at the end of the century."[3]

The Maxim, which became the preferred weapon of the coloniser, fired eleven rounds a second; it was the perfect weapon for the purpose.

The little available literature is bursting with stories about how effective were these guns. A British historian reproduces an eyewitness account of one battle against the Matabele of what came later to be called Rhodesia. The battle was at the Shangani River in 1893. "The Matabele never got nearer than 100 yards ... for the Maxims far exceeded all expectations and mowed them down literally like grass." Four of the seven hundred invaders died, while 1,500 of the Matabele were killed. Then the historian adds that to the Matabele it seemed that the white man came with weapons that spat bullets as sometimes the heavens spit hail.[4]

The instances of small European forces annihilating large native armies multiplied. In "1891, near Porto Novo, a French detachment of 300 men, firing 25,000 rounds of ammunition in 2 ½ hour battle, defeated the entire Fon army. In 1897 a Royal Niger Co. force composed of 32 Europeans and 507 African soldiers armed with cannon, Maxim guns, and Snider rifles defeated the 31,000-man army of the Nupe Emirate of Sokoto... in Chad a French force of 320, most of whom were Senegalese tirailleurs, in 1899 defeated Rabah, reputedly the fiercest of the slave traders, with his 12,000 men and 2,500 guns."

Perhaps the most celebrated of all these one-sided engagements was the 1898 battle of Omdurman, where General Kitchener defeated a large Dervish force of the Khalifa Abdallah Abdallahi of the Sudan, the heir to the Mahdi who had in 1885 decisively defeated the British under General Gordon, killing and decapitating the General himself.

Winston Churchill, later to be British Prime Minister, was there and wrote of it in words designed to uplift Social Darwinist hearts, of the cool Britishers, firing "without hurry or excitement ... the soldiers were interested in the work and took great pains ... while on the other side bullets were shearing through flesh, smashing and splintering bone; blood spouted from terrible wounds ... and it was the most signal triumph ever gained by the arms of science over barbarians." Five hours, wrote Churchill, and the strongest and best armed savage army yet arrayed against a modern European Power had been destroyed and dispersed without difficulty, at small risk and with insignificant loss to the victors.[5]

Years later, post-Cold War era language is combined with Social Darwinism in this description of the event, written in the year 2003: "It was at Omdurman on the banks of the Nile that the two civilisations clashed: on the one side, a horde of desert dwelling Islamic fundamentalists; and on the other, the well-drilled Christian soldiers of Greater Britain ..." The Dervish army of 52,000 was routed by Kitchener's force of 20,000; a quarter of the former were killed and the total of casualties there, killed and wounded, was 95 per cent; just forty-eight British soldiers and a few of their Egyptian allies were killed. Kitchener then ordered all the wounded Dervishes killed and he also carried off the Mahdi's head in a kerosene can as a trophy after desecrating his tomb to get it out.[6]

Apart from the quality of the weapons, and to add to the evidence that the colonisers completely dominated the military scene, it is asserted that tactics were important. Since it was the Europeans who invented the weapons and had the manufacturing capacity to make them, it was also they who first perfected the tactics to go with them. War strategy was even more important. European commanders in the field were accustomed to attaching importance to the capture of urban centres, while in Asia and Africa this was relatively unimportant, for the opposition just melted into the jungles and countryside, able to live off the land and to continue their resistance from there. Such strategic problems, too, were solved with innovative approaches such as the confining of whole populations to enclosures where the resistance could not enter.

### Empire-Making: *modus operandi*

Just as the histories of warfare make no, or virtually no mention of imperial wars, so the histories of how colonial empires were made make very little mention that war was important in the effort.

This second neglect is associated with three factors, apart from the sheer triviality of colonial wars mentioned above.

Firstly, the Portuguese, the Dutch, the French, the British were there really only to explore, to spread Christianity and to trade; they had actually no intention to make an empire. For the purposes for which they were there, they had to ensure that their explorers were able to carry out their work in a secure environment, hence native opposition must be eliminated. As for Christianity, the Europeans "worked to realise a policy ... that should finish off the slave trade and 'civilise the Africans'", or whoever else was in the way.[7] Furthermore, they tried to trade, but the seas were infested with pirates; on land their trading posts were attacked. They had to resort to a little bit of war in order to trade. Through the seventeenth and eighteenth centuries the profits of the trading companies fell as the volume of their trade expanded, and partly as a consequence of this expansion. So many spices were being shipped West that prices and even demand fell; the market was satiated. So they could not pay their employees adequately and allowed the latter to trade on their own account which, of course, led to a further fall in profits – the employees engaged most of their energy in the private trade, even using the companies shipping for this purpose.

As debts mounted and share prices fell the companies were obliged, so the story goes, to go in for plantations so that they could directly control the supply and prices. This meant war against those who owned the territory to be used for plantations. And slave labour had to be used on the plantations, which meant further minor military operations to get hold of the slaves. The Dutch conquest of Banda in 1620-21 is often cited in this context: this was the home of nutmeg trees; it had to be depopulated to ensure control of the supply of nutmeg; then the land was handed over to Dutch settlers who brought in slaves; from then on the supply of nutmeg was under control. This brought in the question of territorial revenue and in 1686 Josiah Child, the East India Company Governor in India, wrote that without territorial revenue "it is impossible to make the English nation's station sure and firm in India upon a sound political basis."[8] So though "in general the use of force remained an integral part of the commercial presence in Asia,"[9] this was a low level use of force, since the Europeans were not there to make empires.

But, secondly, and in general, the empires were acquired by accident. The British expansion in India, for example, was said to be "a classic example of unplanned expansion" after 1815. The expansion of British power in that period was a response to and "the result of Indian interests and policies rather than of British policy." But this was never, according to the version of the story told most often, the result of a desire to conquer; "in no case was expansion the outcome of a deliberate plan in a European capital to acquire new possessions"; and, what is more, "no colony was acquired during this period primarily as a result of calculated desire for it in Europe."[10]

One explanation for this is that the empire was acquired by those in the field despite the real wishes of those at home, "a classic case of the metropolitan dog being wagged by its colonial tail."[11] Another, better known, is that it was actually acquired without anyone wanting to acquire it, in a fit of absent-mindedness. One day the Western democracies woke up to freedom and "discovered themselves 'imperial' and were considerably embarrassed by the discovery."[12] Or, as one British historian of the nineteenth century put it of the empire, "it should be held without any effort. As it was acquired without much effort on the part of the English state, it must be retained the same way."[13]

Thirdly, during the course of the nineteenth century another, a much broader and deeper, reason for making empire in Asia and Africa emerged. This was what nature had decreed; it was not war that mattered but the more profound processes of nature. In November 1869 was published Charles Darwin's *Origin of Species by Means of Natural Selection or the Preservation of the Favoured Races in the Struggle for Life,* which seemed to provide scientific support for the idea that the white races were superior, the master race, and destined to prevail in the war of nature. The others, the subject or backward races, were destined for conquest or even elimination. This was quite openly advocated by the Social Darwinists.

A young Cambridge graduate, Charles Dilks, inspired by Charles Darwin's voyage on the 'Beagle', made a voyage around the English-speaking world in 1866-67 and in his account of the voyage surveyed the varied people of the British Empire, showing that there was a bitter racial struggle being waged in the English-speaking world. The struggle was caused, he believed, by the inferior races impeding the progress of the English people to universal dominion. The book became popular in Britain as well as on the Continent, and led to the growth of empire sentiment. In March 1869 a 'United Empire' society was launched with well-known members of Parliament in it; the new Prime Minister, Gladstone, was present at its inaugural dinner. In another ten years everybody was an imperialist and a Social Darwinist.

The citations are most often about the Germans, but Social Darwinism was a widespread belief in some form in Europe and the US at the time. One author tells us how in Africa the Germans dealt with a rebellious nation, the Hereros of Southwest Africa, who, the German general in charge of operations in the first decade of the twentieth century, said "must disappear", be exterminated. Five years later only twenty per cent of the population remained.[14]

Yet another tells us how, as far as the populations of the British Empire were concerned, "there was no shortage of jolly little wars to be waged against racially inferior opponents"; and such theories made it "gratifying to think that in massacring them with their Maxim guns, the British were contributing to the progress of mankind."[15]

The turning point here was that with Social Darwinism the colonial powers acquired a sense of destiny, of the evolution of the human race, which made it far more difficult even than before for Asians and Africans to counter them on the battlefield.

## Nature of Nationalism

Here the starting point of the modernity argument is that in Africa and Asia nationalism took a very different trajectory to that of Europe. Nationalism cannot, in this argument, be looked at as the product of spontaneous processes like autocatalysis; it is there or it is not, present in the essential characteristics of a people; it cannot be created, but has to be discovered and in Asia and Africa this discovery is done by the Europeans.

The loyalty of individuals to national entities has, in the literature of modernity, been associated with a number of things which those individuals have in common, as givens. These include ethnicity; a geographically compact territory, in which they have lived historically; shared myths and/or a shared memory, of cosmological origins, of battles lost and won, of Kings and revolutions; a culture, language and religion that is lived in by the masses; a common economic space; duties and rights which all those individuals have in common. Other things can be, and have been, included, since the literature is substantial. In opposition to the traditional story, which tells us that all these are fortuitous or incidental resources to be used flexibly for building up and strengthening nationalism, modernity tells us that all these components of nationalism are essential, primordial, unchanging, inherent in a people, just like the laws that govern the universe of modernity are timeless, immutable, impersonal.

So nationalism can be defined; it can be measured and described with precision. One common definition is by race. The word itself suggests this. 'Nation' is of Latin origin and conveys the common ties of blood that unite the members of a nation. The verb 'nasci' means to be born; the noun 'nation' means race or breed, and when the word first came into the English language in the thirteenth century, it was thus used. So this is the basis for primordialism, one of the grand narratives of the subject which begins with family and kin group; they expand over the years to become an ethnic or nation. The emotional bonds of kinship are transformed into loyalty to and the readiness to sacrifice for, the nation. The nation then, in the final phase of its evolution, becomes a state. One of the best known exponents of this narrative is Georg Wilhelm Friedrich Hegel, in whose philosophy of history the nation plays the central role, similar to that played by classes in Karl Marx. Nations are charged by destiny with the task of carrying out the dialectical process; and in every age of history there is one nation which is so charged. The final destiny, in all cases, is that the nation forms itself into a state, which embodies all that is most valuable in human life. As far as the individual is concerned the state is the "actually existing realised moral life...the Divine Idea as it exists on earth ... the embodiment of rational freedom ..."[16] And the worth of the individual, his objectivity, truth and morality, only exist insofar as he belongs to a state.

Max Weber offers another example, though not quite so categorical. He suggests that a nation need not necessarily or absolutely be based on common blood, but it is "apt to include the notions of common descent and of an essential, though frequently indefinite, homogeneity."[17] Clifford Geertz attaches greater importance to ties of blood; the sense of self of the peoples of the new states, those which recently acquired independence from the colonial powers, "remains bound up in the gross actualities of blood, race, language, locality, religion, or tradition". These primordial attachments "have an ineffable, and at times overpowering, coerciveness in and of themselves"; and they are the "preferred bases for the demarcation of autonomous political units."[18] So, of course, they threaten the integrity of the new states.

In the spring of 1859 the liberation of Italy was being fought for by Sardinia and France. Nationalism, Italian nationalism, seemed to have triumphed and along with it the essentialist idea of nationalism. The *Edinburgh Review* commented that nationalism meant "each political unity constituting a state is to be commensurate with one of those branches of the human family which have the same language, race, national character, and that the rule of any of these branches over fractions of another branch is to be regarded as an intolerable oppression." But the *Review* rejected this as the basis of state formation, writing that such a definition would "lead to the entire dissolution of the multifarious states which are properly called empires and in particular those of Russia, Austria and Great Britain."[19]

Ernest Renan has another kind of essentialist definition, that of memory, that a nation is a soul, a spiritual principle very similar, presumably, to the state in Hegel. "Only two things, actually, constitute this soul ... one is the possession in common of a rich legacy of remembrances; the other is the actual consent, the desire to live together ..."[20] A variant of this is that by its history and nature the nation is a kind of legitimate state. "...the nation-state, however governed, is the one sort of state which is by its nature both legitimate and internally cohesive. The fundamental premise of nationalist ideas is that nations are objective realities, existing through history."[21] This suggests that all those social entities that existed in history and had the potential to become nations have become nation-states by now. Only they are the true nations and all the others are not. Those secessionist movements that today claim to speak for nations do not actually represent nations, for if they did they would have been nation-states by now. So here we have an argument that legitimises the states of today and delegitimises all those minorities that claim to be nations on grounds of ethnicity or language and so on and seek statehood on that basis. Of course, the argument could be turned on its head to suggest that the making of states out of nations is not yet complete, hence any of those essentialist or primordial bonds could be taken as justification for secession.

Anthony Smith, one of the most important writers of today on nationalism, has the same argument, which again could be used both ways. He suggests that the traditions, symbols, values, myths and the like of the ethnic communities of the past made for incipient processes of nation formation. "These processes and the heritage they bequeathed are as much part of the modern nation as the technical, economic and political institutions required by a modern civilisation."[22] If, for instance, there was no identifiable territory with the distinctive features of a people in it, as was not the case in any of the colonies, then you had 'nationalism without nations', a nationalist movement among heterogeneous populations based upon the territorial unit in which they have been forcibly united by the colonial power.[23]

A classic essentialist definition citing a mix of factors is by Joseph Stalin. After listing all the separate features that should go into the definition and explaining them he summarises: "A nation is a historically constituted, stable community of people, formed on the basis of a common language, territory, economic life, and psychological make-up manifested in a common culture."[24] But, he further elaborated in *Marxism and the National Question*, published in 1913, the nation is a historical category "belonging to a definite epoch, the epoch of rising capitalism. The process of elimination of feudalism and development is at the same time a process of the constitution of peoples into nations."

## Modernity Made Nationalism

Yet another version of the essentialist argument is that modernity made the nation with the obvious corollary that since the empire-makers introduced modernity to the colonised, they were really the ones responsible for the generation of nationalism in Asia and Africa. Two of the most cited writers here are Ernest Gellner and Benedict Anderson, sometimes marked down as Gellner's successor. Gellner's theory has been called "the most cogent, powerful and influential of the modernist theories of nationalism."[25]

Gellner's starting point is that the nationalist principle as such "has very deep roots in our shared current condition, is not at all contingent, and will not easily be denied." This shared current condition can be explained by the imposition of high culture. During the early period of industrialisation the traditional structures of family, religion and community were weakened; villagers were driven into the cities from the countryside and in these urban conglomerations they became disoriented. In this situation, which is a specific one, general social conditions make for standardised, homogeneous, centrally sustained high cultures, so "well-defined educationally sanctioned and unified cultures constitute very nearly the only kind of unit with which men willingly and often ardently identify". There is "no need to assume any conscious long-term calculation of interest on anyone's part"; no conscious decision is needed. The high culture pervades the whole of society, defines it and needs to be sustained by the polity. This, and only this situation, called the "industrial variant of the human situation" makes for the birth of nationalism, and "it is nationalism which engenders nations, and not the other way round."[26] So modernisation makes for the changes which necessitate a form of high culture, that high culture pervades the whole of society and needs to be sustained by the polity, meaning that state and culture must now be linked. In other words, nation creates the state and not the other way round. "That is what nationalism is about, and why we live in an age of nationalism."[27]

Anderson has a somewhat different angle on what is essentially the same argument. Modernisation loosened the grip on men's minds of "three fundamental cultural conceptions, all of great antiquity". These were "the great transcontinental sodalities of Christendom, the Ummah of Islam, and the rest"; secondly, that the monarch rules by divine dispensation; and, thirdly, that cosmology and history were indistinguishable. Then modernisation, economic change, rapid communication and discoveries took place. So there was need for new ways of linking power and time. But it was print-capitalism that precipitated the coming of these new ways. The "development of print-as-commodity is the key to the generation of wholly new ideas..." And the primacy of capitalism ensured that of all the possible and different varieties of new community which modernisation could have generated, it was the nation that became so popular. So once the cultural conceptions of antiquity lost the hold they had exercised on men's minds, print-capitalism (which plays the role of high culture in Gellner, and Anderson emphasises, as does Gellner, that the process in which it was involved was "largely unself-conscious") became the trigger of modernity to ensure the people could relate to each other and to nature and the cosmos in new ways, all of which can be encapsulated in the nation. Specifically, it "created the possibility of a new form of imagined community, which in its basic morphology set the stage for the modern nation."[28]

Yet another version links nationalism to modernisation through the impact of globalisation, which, of course, brings it even closer to the version that it was really the creation of the empire-makers. Globalisation creates a world market for goods, services, capital, technology and people. Globalisation provokes resistance, which takes the form of nationalism. "In a world of globalisation, peoples began to demand not integration into larger states but secession, independence, and access to the world market on their own terms." By way of all-roundness globalisation also includes the opposite, national unification, as in Germany, Yemen, China, Korea.[29]

The modernity story has one consistent element: in the matter of nationalism, especially the matter of progress from nation to state, the West is different from the rest in a deeply fundamental way. The general thrust of the argument is that modernisation came late to the rest, so they got left behind in the development of nationalism. Charles Tilly put it best and most neatly. First a few national states were formed in Europe; then wars, alliances and "other manoeuvers" mapped out most of Europe into distinct national states; then Europe extended its political and economic domination to the rest of the world; and then the European client states and colonies, through rebellions and through international agreements, formed autonomous national states on the European pattern, thus "the extension of this state system to the entire world."[30]

The sometimes unspecified part of this evolutionary development is that, the rest having come late into nationalism, they continue today to feel the pangs of late entry in the form of secessionist movements, hence the "much greater frequency of secessionist movements in backward regions."[31] This, which legitimises secession, is in direct contradiction to the argument that all those several entities of the past that had the potential to become nation-states, have by now so become. But it is still part of the modernity story, for it bases itself on the impersonal forces at work at the source of nationalism.

It is this story that says Pakistan, as one example, "is not a nation-state"; and of post-colonial states in general that "commonly with short histories and contingent state boundaries, these states do not represent nations with an air of permanence." Jinnah himself, the founder of Pakistan as a nation, had no such doubts. He asserted that the Muslims of India had a "distinctive culture and civilisation, language and literature, art and architecture, names and nomenclature, sense of values and proportion, legal laws and moral codes, customs and calendar, history and tradition, aptitude and ambition."[32]

One depiction of Indian nationalism was even more damning; that in 1900 the notion of Indian nationhood "was constructed around the liberal concept of loyal subjects aspiring to be granted some self-rule, for example, the right of Indians to take part in the Civil Service."[33]

For the Cambridge historian, Percival Spear, an acknowledged authority on South Asian history, who for years held a lecturership in the subject at his university, and whose standard Penguin Books text on the history of India has gone into reprints and new editions every two years since it was first published in 1965, and, of course, been read the world over, there was no Indian nationalism. "...what we call Indian nationalism ... was by no means nationalism in the commonly accepted western sense, a common aspiration for self-government based on a common language, territory, or racial strain. Rather it was a mingling of old ideas with new ..." The old ideas included xenophobia, a system of castes - "inward looking and divisive", competing cults, tribalism, regionalism and a long list of similar factors. The new ones were brought in by the colonial power, like the "campaigns against suttee and infanticide stirred uneasy consciences" and brought change.[34]

Thirty years later the eminent historian Eric Hobsbawm published *The Age of Extremes*, which was, for a shorter period, equally or perhaps even more widely read. He is equally dismissive. Apart from China, Turkey and Iran, elsewhere in the colonial world, "the idea of the independent sovereign state, which we take for granted, was meaningless to people, at least (even in areas of permanent and fixed agriculture) above the village level."[35]

Hobsbawm is categorical in asserting that most of the dynamics, "of the greater part of the world's history in the Short Twentieth Century are derived, not original. They consist essentially in the attempts by the elites of non-bourgeois societies to imitate the model pioneered in the West ...the ideologies, the programmes, even the methods and forms of political organisation which inspired the emancipation of dependent countries from dependence, backward ones from backwardness, were Western."[36]

There is a strong case, writes another colonial historian, "for seeing the roots of nationalism in the impact of alien ideas and practices which, by infecting dependencies with European ideals of liberty and equality, made them resent subordination." The idea of western influence as a solvent has variants. It was the creation of an elite to serve the colonial administration that "was a solvent of stability for ... the educated elite were necessarily imbued with European ideas."[37]

One author finds that in Indonesia late colonial capitalism produced "new types of professionals ... editors and journalists, mechanics and accountants, school teachers and apothecaries, politicians and surveyors." These were the peoples who fostered nationalism.[38] Another, an American who spent years researching Indonesia, finds that the Dutch created nationalism there. "Dutch administration welded together peoples of various tongues and cultures into one political unit and ... joined the archipelago's many local patriotisms together into one all-embracing patriotism."[39]

It "was the assimilation by Asians and Africans of western ideas, techniques, and institutions, which could be turned against the occupying powers", which hastened the end of the imperial age. European and even American authors asserted that the European colonial intervention "acted as a solvent of the traditional social order ... brought about substantial economic changes ... led to the rise of western educated elites..." which led the nationalist movements.[40] As example, Vietnam, says another author, "was not, in the terminology of Karl W. Deutsch, a nationality, and the fragmentation of its politics reflected the divisiveness and parochialism of the Vietnamese people." So "nationalism in Vietnam was essentially an anti-French reaction rather than a defined positive force".[41]

Among the authors most frequently cited in this regard is Rupert Emerson, who affirmed that "the greater the disruption of the old society under the intruding impact of Western force ... the speedier and more complete the assertion of nationalism is likely to be"; and then he goes on to assert that a genuine nationalism has to await the creation and "the appearance of a Westernised elite ... which translates to the local scene the nationalist experience of the West and serves as the crystallising centre for the inchoate disaffections of the mass".[42]

The importance of education in this field of development cannot be over-rated. Citing the case of an early twentieth century nationalist, a British author asserts that "Aurobindo Ghose personified the nationalism that would soon manifest itself throughout the Empire precisely because he was the product of the ultimate English education."[43] Another refers to the French policy of assimilation, educating the colonised peoples so as to inject into them appropriately large doses of French culture. This was a policy which "had strangely different results from those it was intended to produce. It has been said that the bitterest opponents of the French were those who knew the language best." In Southeast Asia generally, the author of the most popular textbook of the 1960s and 1970s on its history writes of the locals who "imbibed the heady wine of Western political thought"; who learnt about Britain's constitutional struggles, about the American War of Independence and the French Revolution; and then "the flame of freedom scorched their souls"; and "thus the nationalist movements acquired both means of expression and technique through Western education."[44]

A version of this story also fits into W.W.Rostow's *Stages of Economic Growth* theory. This says that the policies of the imperial powers brought about "transformations in thought, knowledge and institutions – as well as in trade and in the supply of social overhead capital – which moved the colonial society along the path towards take-off" and that is what forced the withdrawal of imperial rule.[45]

It was not just Western authors that told this kind of story. Those from the colonies also did so. Ferhat Abbas, the prominent Algerian political activist, is quoted as saying, "if I had discovered an Algerian nation, I would be a nationalist and I would not blush for it as though it was a crime ...but such a homeland does not exist. I have not found it." Another, Obafemi Awolowo, a Yoruba leader who dominated Western Nigerian politics for thirty years, wrote that "Nigeria is not a nation. It is a mere geographical expression. There are no 'Nigerians'..."[46] In other words the idea of the nation was not based on any local facts, but had been implanted by the West. To quote just one more, this one an academic from India, "it is an irony of history that in the very process of consolidating their rule the British unleashed forces which were to strengthen Indian nationalism". Furthermore, it was transport and communication that made the Indian nation. With approval he gives a quotation, "Railways", said Edwin Arnold of *Light of Asia* fame, "may do for India what emperor Akbar could not, make India a nation." It was from the English educated class that the founding fathers of the Indian National Congress were drawn; it appeared to them that after centuries of stagnation and disunity "India had an opportunity of imbibing from the West the spirit of progress and reform ..."[47]

The direct consequence of asserting that the nationalist and freedom movements in the colonies originated in the socio-economic changes, educational advancement and the learning of Western ideas generated by the actions of the colonial powers was that the West should also be able to control this in such a way as to prevent decolonisation. For, faced with the challenge of independence movements, "it is wrong to assume that the imperial powers were necessarily unable to meet and reject the challenge."[48]

### The Empire Lost: *modus operandi*

But now we have to depict the encounter between these two forces, the empire-makers and the nationalists. In this encounter it was neither nationalism nor the so-called 'freedom fighters' nor any other form of local resistance that was the principal challenge Europeans faced, but a number of other causes and it was these that eventually brought down the empires. In brief it was hardly an encounter; the empire-makers themselves did the unmaking of empire.

The main cause was European rivalries; these were primarily responsible for bringing the imperial era to a close. Add to this Japanese aims in Asia, their conquests during the war, and US aims, and this set of propositions is complete.

At the onset of the colonial age rivalries had characterised the relations between the empire-makers: between the Portuguese and the Dutch in the East; then between the French and the English in the Americas and in India; between all these powers during the scramble for Africa; between the Americans and Spaniards in the Caribbean and in the Philippines.

The scramble for Africa, in particular, has been singled out to demonstrate how these rivalries worked to expand the empire. "It is impossible to understand the scramble for Africa without seeing that it had its antecedents in the perennial struggle between the great powers to maintain – or overthrow – the balance of power between them in Europe and the Near East." Now at the close of that age of empire it was again colonial rivalries that characterised their relations. The Empire was dismantled not because it had oppressed anyone but "because it took up arms for just a few years against far more oppressive empires." And for the British, if it was not more oppressive empires, then it was the Americans, whose aims during the Second World War "were in many ways more overtly hostile to the British Empire than anything Hitler had ever said." So, one way or the other, it was "rival empires more than indigenous nationalists who propelled the process of decolonisation forward."[49]

Again and again it is the same theme: "European imperialist rivalries and ambitions culminated in the 1880s"[50] scramble for Africa.

The rival Europeans themselves encouraged nationalism in the colonies, especially during the two great wars of the twentieth century: the Germans in the Maghreb; the British and the French in Syria; above all Japan in Southeast Asia during the years of its occupation. "A few years of Japanese invasion and occupation of parts of Indochina, Malaya, Burma, and Indonesia transformed these countries into more self-conscious, nationalistic, and psychologically detached peoples."[51] Put differently Asian nationalism was a guaranteed success "when the war flattened the card castle of European imperialism... The surrender ...at Singapore in 1942 had been the signal that European empire in Asia was doomed."[52]

Attached to the struggle against rival empires and US hostility, which might have derived from its own desire to establish a version of empire, was the cost of the struggle to keep the empire.

This was so quite early and we have seen above the views of the King of Portugal on Albuquerque's persistent demands for more arms, men and ships to make war. One of the major reasons for soaring costs was that the employees of the East India Companies, as one example, spent more time making money for themselves, on private trade than for the companies. By the eighteenth century this was a problem of growing dimensions for the English company in particular. "By 1772 its servants in India were making fortunes, but the company was financially embarrassed by high military costs in Bengal, unexpectedly low selling prices at home and a banking crisis."[53]

The argument here is not that having an empire was expensive; but that defending it against profiteering by your own employees and against rivals was. Every colonial power found, at the end of the 1914-18 war, that the cost was too burdensome. This argument had been anticipated by Adam Smith when he railed against "the expense of the peace establishment", which was a charge on the revenue of Great Britain, but only benefited those who held the monopoly of the trade with the colonies. He adds to this the expenses incurred on "colony quarrels" as he calls them, like the war with Spain which began in 1739, and whose expenses were in reality, whatever may have been the pretense, "a bounty which has been given in order to support a monopoly", and to which those who actually benefited contributed nothing.[54] This is also recognisably similar to the Leninist thesis on imperialism: the increasing concentration of production and capital leading to an ever larger role for monopolies; and then the defence or the acquisition of territory by the state to promote the interests of those monopolies.

Then came the 1929-33 economic crisis and the resulting depression when unemployment in Britain rose to unprecedented levels, three million by 1932, and the cost of the empire seemed even less affordable. According to this story, the 1939-45 war clinched the argument that the empire was simply unaffordable. At the end of that war Britain had a debt of US $ 40 billion, manufacturing output was steeply down, there had been a sharp depreciation of the pound against the dollar, and Britain had a rate of economic growth which was the lowest in Europe.

Apart from this, colonial interests in these areas had been strictly limited and these interests were now changing and narrowing: if the German or French threat to British colonies, for instance, was gone, clearly their strategic value had to be assessed very differently; if desert areas had blossomed into large oil producers, clearly strategic and commercial interests there had a very different shape, requiring different policies.

All this resulted in a weakening of the will to rule, self doubt, a realisation, as Leonard Woolf, husband of Virginia Woolf put it, of the absurdity of one civilisation and mode of life trying to impose its rule upon an entirely different one. So "the British seemed to have wearied of imperialism's responsibilities even as they shouldered them..." and for France, pursuing its *mission civilisatrice,* the growing agitation for political rights "cast a shadow over the future of empire."[55] In the case of many colonies there was the realisation that full occupation and governing them was not really something the colonial power wanted any more.

So it was that "all over the Empire, a generation was quietly cracking" in its faith in its ability and the rightness of governing the varied peoples of the empire; and at home a "collective attack of doubt" spread among the traditional elite that had always so strongly supported imperial aims.[56]

## Empire Making and the Empire Lost: Marxist Variant

The modernity story or episteme has a variant which needs to be outlined here. This is the Marxist-Leninist account of how and why colonial empires came to be made and unmade; it was taken up, with some modifications to suit the changing realities by Soviet authors and spokesmen after the 1917 revolution. Note, however, that this is only a variant of the same story; it is not a different story.

The Marxist-Leninist story is about the material conditions of society. It was not war or technology or the drive for power or the grandiloquent dreams of statesmen which took the history of empire forward; it was the mode of production and the relations of production which combine to form immanent laws that take the process forward. At a certain stage after industrialisation and the capitalist mode of production is reached there comes a time of heightened competitiveness, of falling rates of profit, the growth of monopoly and of the continued accumulation of capital, of finance capitalism. In this stage *laissez faire* capitalism has been replaced by monopoly capitalism; the monopolies hinder the free flow of capital since they wish to curb production to increase profits; so capital accumulates and needs outlets. Imperialism is then the inevitable outcome of this highest stage of monopoly capitalism, as the advanced capitalist countries seek new avenues for profitably investing their capital, new markets and new sources of raw material. So "the central *raison d'etre* of imperialism is the extraction of profit from the labour of the indigenous people by whites by virtue of their control over the machinery of the state." The Boer war of 1899 provoked John Atkinson Hobson's denunciation of imperialism by the use of this argument, since it "burst the dam of his moral indignation", and led him to write that it is the investor who gains from imperialism. He has money surplus to his needs because of the inequitable distribution of wealth and seeks outlets in the empire for this money.[57]

In Lenin's classic work of 1916, *Imperialism: The Highest Stage of Capitalism,* he sought to explain what had brought about the 1914-18 European war. It was the international rivalries and tensions associated with this search for avenues of investment which had led to the division of the world into empires and spheres of influence and had eventually produced the war. There were a handful of usurer states sucking the substance of all the rest; the policies of these usurer states were directed and controlled by finance capital.

This line of thinking had some unexpected or unintended proponents. Thus, as example, the British Colonial Secretary Edward Stanley said in Parliament in 1842 that it was the colonial trade "which more than any other employed our shipping, consumed the produce of our manufactures, and gave encouragement to native and to colonial industry and, more than all that, which kept entire that strong, that beneficial tie of nationality, that tie of mutual connection between the different parts of this great empire, which constituted its protection from war and its strength and glory in peace." Lord Salisbury agreed. At a Conservative Party banquet in July 1878, he said: "The commerce of a great commercial country like this will only flourish – history attests it again and again – under the shadow of empire." And Captain Lugard, wrote in 1895, "Let us admit that commercial enterprise in Africa is undertaken for our own benefit, as much as and more than for the benefit of the African, we have spoken already of the vital necessity of new markets for the old world." The increasing wants of a rising population forced Britain to expand.[58] Disraeli was even more categorical in adopting an argument which seems no different from the Marxist line, when he announced that London was the key to India, London, that is to say, the Stock Exchange, weaving a vast network of commercial and industrial interests.

Marxist theory is even less accommodating to any suggestion that the nationalists, those who were being ruled, may have played some role in the whole process. For the forces leading to the making of empires were exclusive to the advanced capitalist countries. The laws that take the process forward being inexorable, those that were colonised had no say in determining the pace of colonisation, its geographic location, or its precise nature.

This variant of the story is also quite categorical in explaining the how and why of the unmaking of empires. It was the Soviet Union that did it.

It was the Soviet Union's policy of unity with suppressed nations and support of their liberation movements that was of historic significance. "Any major decrease in the area of imperialist domination, the defeat of colonialism and the winning of independence by the enslaved nations would be unthinkable without this."[59] This can be elaborated in the following way. "The victory of the Great October Socialist Revolution put an end to the domination of capitalism on a global scale and split the world into two opposing socio-economic systems. It ushered in the general crisis of capitalism, with the collapse of imperialism's colonial system as one its characteristic features."[60] To give just one more quote on this subject, it was the "rise of the socialist world system" which "set off a tide of anti-imperialist and national liberation revolutions which swept the colonial system away."[61]

In all the elaborations of this variant of the story, it needs to be emphasised, nationalism has no positive role to play. At an early stage, in a tribal society, nationalism can play some kind of a role. But this is a narrow nationalism. Nationalism "plays a positive role when it is replacing tribalism, ethnic and religious separatism. But it is a symbol of backwardness in regard to the class consciousness of the working people." As far as the larger forces are concerned, such as the growth of working class consciousness or the increased power of the proletariat, the processes by which the highest stage of capitalism evolves, nationalism can only be an irrelevant or negative factor. Today "the essence of nationalism is to be found primarily in the opposition of national unity to class division and of national consciousness to class consciousness."[62] Nationalism directed towards national unity is, therefore, to be frowned on.

## And the Eras of History

So there was really no encounter between the empire-makers and the nationalists. It is just that for several centuries Europe has dominated the history of the world; and this history of the world can be divided into eras, in opposition to what was stated towards the end of chapter 3.

The new era of imperial history starts around 1500 AD, once the colonisers have established contact in Asia and Africa. "The change which came about in world history after 1500 is quite without precedent. Never before had one culture spread over the whole globe... and it was almost entirely a one-way process. Europeans went out into the world; it did not come to them."[63] The very opening sentences of the famous lecture titled *The Geographical Pivot of History* that Sir Halford Mackinder delivered to the Royal Geographical Society in London in January, 1904 asserted that future historians would describe "the last 400 years as the Columbian epoch ... a great historic epoch ... which saw the expansion of Europe against almost negligible resistances".

One author writes about "the five-hundred-year European conquest of the world – the history of aggression, subversion, terror and domination now termed the 'North-South' confrontation" and adds that the Cold War is only a particular phase in this history.[64] Note that this is decidedly anti-imperialist, but belongs still to the same episteme, the modernity story, as that of the imperialists.

The first time period within this new era has the Portuguese dominating; in the Indian Ocean "the Portuguese dominated this trade in the sixteenth century; their fire-power swept all before them and they rapidly built up a chain of bases and trading posts", a thalassocracy that had never yet been seen, but which the Dutch (in a small way) and then the British (gigantically), in subsequent time periods, were to inherit. "With Columbus's discovery of the Americas (1492) and Vasco da Gama's rounding of the Cape of Good Hope (1498) began the era of Colonialism, manifested in the advent and advance of Western Europe's political dominance over the whole world in the four following centuries".[65] Another take on the same argument is the following, "Da Gama's expedition opened the door to maritime trade between European and Asian people and helped to establish permanent links between various regions of the world".[66]

So it was first the Portuguese and then the English. As they voyaged the world, the Portuguese left records of their landfalls everywhere and "by doing so, they established both primacy and possession." They were the first around the Cape of Good Hope, the first around South America, the first in Japan and "it would be easy to multiply 'firsts' by Portuguese in terms of encounters with cultures hitherto unknown ..." Theirs was a 'World on the Move'[67] The English, too, in this portrait of history which the traditional story would not recognise, made the world. Theirs was the biggest empire ever, bar none. "No organisation in history has done more to promote the free movement of goods, capital and labour than the British Empire in the nineteenth and early twentieth centuries...and to impose Western norms of law, order and governance around the world."[68]

And it was truly the whole world that was involved in this exercise that dominated the history of those centuries. For in 1800 already Europe and its possessions "covered about 55 per cent of the land surface of the world; in 1878, 67 per cent; and in 1914, 84.4 per cent."[69] Expansion continued. And by 1939 there were only seven countries in the whole world and some of them only partially that had escaped colonial rule. The British Empire, "already formidable in 1800 with a land area of 1.5 million square miles and a population of twenty million, increased its land area seven-fold and its population twenty-fold in the following hundred years."[70] By 1922 it was 36.6 million square kilometres in size, larger than the previous largest ever, that of Kubla Khan, which in 1268 was only 33.2 million square kilometres.

## ENDNOTES

[1] Major-General J.F.C. Fuller, *The Conduct of War, 1789 -1961*, Natraj Publishers, Dehra Dun, 2003, p. 134.

[2] Reynaldo Ileto, Religion and Anti-Colonial Movements, in Nicholas Tarling, ed., *The Cambridge History of Southeast Asia, volume three, From c. 1800 to the 1930s*, Cambridge University Press, 1999, p. 193.

[3] For this and the previous paragraph see Daniel R. Headrick, *The Tools of Empire, Technology and European Imperialism in the Nineteenth Century*, OUP, New York, 1981, pp. 84 and 85

[4]Niall Ferguson, *Empire, How Britain Made the Modern World*, Penguin Books, London, 2004, p. 224. How the historian discovered what the Matabele thought is not explained.

[5] Quotations in this and two previous paragraphs from Daniel R. Headrick, op. cit. pp. 117-119.

[6] Niall Ferguson, op. cit., p. 270-1.

[7] Quote from Basil Davidson, *Africa in History, Themes and Outlines*, Phoenix, London, 1991, p. 281.

[8] Cited in Nicholas B. Dirks, *The Scandal of Empire, India and the Creation of Imperial Britain*, Permanent Black, Delhi, 2007, p. 170.

[9] K.N. Chaudhuri, *Trade and Civilisation in the Indian Ocean, An Economic History from the Rise of Islam to 1750*, Munshiram Manoharlal Publishers, New Delhi, 1985, p. 88.

[10] D.K.Fieldhouse, *The Colonial Empires, A Comparative Survey from the Eighteenth Century,* A Delta Book, Dell, New York, 1966, pp. 193, 190 and 178 respectively.

[11] In Daniel Headrick, op. cit. p. 6.

[12] H.G. Wells, *The Outline of History, Being a Plain History of Life and Mankind*, Garden City Publishing Inc., New York, 1931, p. 1033.

[13]J.R. Seeley quoted in B.R.Nanda, *The Making of a Nation, India's Road to Independence*, Harper Collins, New Delhi, 1998, p. 171. Seeley made the famous comment, in his best-selling book, *The Expansion of England,* that "we seem to have conquered and peopled half the world in a fit of absence of mind."

[14] Basil Davidson, op. cit., p. 299.

[15] Niall Ferguson, op.cit., p. 265.

[16] Quoted in Bertrand Russell, *History of Western Philosophy*, George Allen and Unwin, London, 1947, p. 767.

[17] Max Weber, The Nation, in John Hutchinson and Anthony D. Smith, eds., *Nationalism*, OUP, Oxford, 1994, p. 22.

[18] Clifford Geertz, Primordial and Civic Ties, in John Hutchinson and Anthony D. Smith, op. cit., pp. 30-31.

[19] Richard Koebner and Helmut Dan Schmidt, *Imperialism, The Story and Significance of a Political Word, 1840-1960*, Cambridge Univerity Press, 1964, p. 41.

[20] Ernest Renan, *Qu'est-ce qu'une nation*, trans. Ida Mae Snyder, Calmann Levy, Paris, 1882, p. 26.

[21] Susan Reynolds, *Kingdoms and Communities in Western Europe (900-1300)*, Clarendon Press, Oxford, 1984, p. 251.

[22] Anthony D. Smith, History and Modernity: Reflections on the Theory of Nationalism, in David Boswell and Jessica Evans, eds. *Representing the Nation*: A Reader, Routledge, London, 1999, p. 58.

[23] Paul Kratoska and Ben Batson, Nationalism and Modernist Reform, in Nicholas Tarling, ed., op. cit., p. 251.

[24] Joseph Stalin, The Nation, in John Hutchinson and Anthony D. Smith, op. cit. p. 20.

[25] Anthony D. Smith, op. cit., p. 49.

[26] Ernest Gellner, Nationalism and Modernisation, in John Hutchinson and Anthony D. Smith, op. cit. pp. 64-68.

[27] Ernest Gellner, *Nations and Nationalism,* Blackwell, Oxford, 1983, p. 38.

[28] Benedict Anderson, *Imagined Communities*, Verso, London, 1991, pp. 37-46.

[29] Fred Halliday, Nationalism, in John Baylis and Steve Smith, eds., *The Globalization of World Politics, An Introduction to International Relations*, OUP, New Delhi, 2005, p. 523.

[30] Charles Tilly, Europe and the International State System, in John Hutchinson and Anthony Smith, op. cit. p. 253.

[31] Donald Horowitz, The Logic of Secessions, in John Hutchinson and Anthony Smith, op. cit. p. 268.

[32] Athar Hussain, Peregrinations of Pakistani nationalism, in Michael Leifer, ed. *Asian Nationalism,* Routledge, London, 2000, pp. 127 and 133.

[33] Meghnad Desai, Communalism, secularism and dilemma of Indian nationhood, in Michael Leifer, op. cit. p. 97.

[34] Percival Spear, *A History of India*, Volume two, Penguin Books, Harmondsworth, 1975, pp. 158-161.

[35] Eric Hobsbawm, *The Age of Extremes, A History of the World, 1914-1991*, Pantheon Books, New York, 1994, p. 207.

[36] Eric Hobsbawm, op. cit., pp. 200, 202.

[37] D.K. Fieldhouse, op. cit., pp. 398 and 399.

[38] Benedict Anderson, *The Spectre of Comparisons, Nationalism, Southeast Asia and the World*, Verso, London, 1998, p. 130.

[39] George McTurnan Kahin, *Nationalism and Revolution in Indonesia*, Cornell University Press, New York, 1961, p. 37.

[40] Geoffrey Baraclough, *An Introduction to Contemporary History*, Penguin Books, Harmondsworth, 1983, pp. 160 and 171 respectively.

[41] John T. McAlister, Jr., *Vietnam, The Origins of Revolution,* The Penguin Press, London, 1969, pp. 100-101 and 291. Deutsch, by the way, had a strange mixture of class and nationality in his definition: "an alignment of large numbers of individuals from the middle and lower classes linked to regional centres and leading social groups by channels of social communication and economic intercourse..."quoted by John T. McAlister Jr. on p. 101.

[42] Rupert Emerson, *From Empire to Nation*, Beacon Press, Boston, 1960, p.44.

[43] Niall Ferguson, op. cit., p. 214. The same author also says exactly the opposite, that it was education that produced pro-British sentiment. "The key to the

emergence of a pro-British Indian elite was education". And he says it in the same book, on p. 189.

[44] D.G.E.Hall, *A History of South-East Asia*, Macmillan, London, 1964, pp. 689 and 717. Hall refers to the outburst of nationalistic assertiveness among the students when the University of Hanoi was opened in 1907, so much so that it had to be closed the following year.

[45] W.W. Rostow, *The Stages of Economic Growth*, Cambridge University Press, 1966, p. 112.

[46] Both quotations from Martin Meredith, *The State of Africa, A History of Fifty Years of Independence*, Free Press, London, 2005, pp. 7-8.

[47] B.R.Nanda, *The Making of a Nation*, op. cit. above, pp. xvii-xviii.

[48] D.K.Fieldhouse, op. cit. p. 400.

[49] All the quotations in this paragraph from Niall Ferguson, Empire, op. cit., pp. 230, 298, 351, 359.

[50] Basil Davidson, op. cit., p. 283.

[51] David Thomson, *Europe since Napoleon*, Penguin Books, Harmondsworth, 1966, p. 851.

[52] J.M.Roberts, *The Penguin History of the World*, Penguin Books, Harmondsworth, 1995, p. 941.

[53] D.K.Fieldhouse, op. cit., p. 170.

[54] Adam Smith, *The Wealth of Nations*, Bantam Books, New York, 2003, pp. 781-3.

[55] Douglas Porch, *Wars of Empire*, Cassell and Co., London, 2001, p. 206-7.

[56] Quotes from Niall Ferguson, op. cit., pp. 320, 323.

[57] See Elie Kedourie, ed. *Nationalism in Asia and Africa*, Weidenfeld and Nicolson, London, 1971, pp. 2, 5.

[58] Richard Koebner and Helmut Dan Schmidt, op. cit., pp. 60, 143 and 208.

[59] Karen Brutents, Introduction to the volume *Cooperation between the USSR and Developing Countries,* USSR Academy of Sciences, Institute of Oriental Studies, Social Sciences Today editorial board, Moscow, 1986, p. 6.

[60] Vladislav Dadayan, *The Orbits of the Global Economy*, Progress Publishers, Moscow, 1988, p. 106.

[61] Pyotr Manchkha, *Problems of Africa Today*, Progress Publishers, Moscow, 1979, p. 5.

[62] R.Ulyanovsky, ed., *The Revolutionary Process in the East: Past and Present,* Progress Publishers, Moscow, 1985, pp. 182, 185.

[63] J.M.Roberts, op. cit., p. 607.

[64] Noam Chomsky, *World Orders, Old and New*, OUP, Delhi, 1998, p.74.

[65] Irfan Habib, Colonialism, in Peter Burke and Halil Inalcik, eds, *History of Humanity, Scientific and Cultural Development, Vol. V, From the Sixteenth to the Eighteenth Century*, UNESCO/Routledge, London, 1999, p. 61.

[66] Jerry H.Bentley, Herbert F. Ziegler, *Traditions and Encounters*, McGraw Hill, 2000, p. 535.

[67] A.J.R.Russell-Wood, *A World on the Move, The Portuguese in Africa, Asia and America, 1415-1808,* Carcanet Press, Manchester, 1992; quotes are from p. 3.

[68] Niall Ferguson, op. cit., p. xxii.

[69] D.K.Fieldhouse, op. cit., p. 178.

[70] Daniel R. Headrick, op. cit., p. 3.

# 5

# Indonesia

What follows is based on the traditional story, with some references to that of modernity.

The Dutch occupation and colonisation of Indonesia, as much as any other empire-making experience, is marked and sign posted at the beginning, as at the end, by war and military operations. They were greeted by resistance and revolt when they entered Java and the other islands; they were evicted forcibly at the end as the Indonesians finally wrested independence.

## Making War and Empire

For the Netherlands, war and empire defined and were coterminous with the emergence of nationhood. In 1568 they were part of the Spanish Habsburg Empire; in that year a revolt against the empire led by William the Prince of Orange had been easily crushed. Their only assets were a substantial share of the Baltic seaborne trade, acquired by thrift, better ships and above all the need for a country of dunes, bogs, lakes and the constant threat of the sea, to trade to make a living. Eighty years of war later they were free in a federation of seven republics, and had started the process of creating a nation based *inter alia* on past heroism, including an epic though mythical saga of resistance to the expansion of the Roman Empire. They had also, because of their maritime skills, acquired what passed in those days for an empire. Its contours were shaped by a compromise between the interests of three parties: the state called the States General or the two

Chambers of Parliament; the several commercial companies that had sprung up after the maiden Dutch trading expedition to the Indian Ocean; that had sailed in 1595, returned in 1597, and though it did not make much profit, it generated a tremendous enthusiasm. So the companies that had sprung up were brought together to form the East India Company (VOC) in 1602. The third interest was that of successive Governors-General of the VOC who were on the spot and often able to decide policy without waiting for instructions from headquarters.

The state wanted an empire. The Charter given by the States General to the VOC empowered it to conclude treaties of peace and alliance, to wage defensive war, to build fortresses and strongholds, and to enlist naval and military personnel who would have to take an oath of loyalty to the Company as well as to the States General. The commercial companies wanted profits; their leading investors saw that war would increase expenditure and when they saw the authorisation given to the VOC many of them sold their shares in it. Indeed the Heeren XVII, the seventeen-member Board of Directors of the newly formed VOC, responding to this view, constantly emphasised to their agents in the field the need to send cargoes home rather than to wage costly wars, much as the Portuguese King had done a hundred years earlier. The successive Governors-General certainly wanted empire and they saw that war was the necessary instrument to achieve this, but they had to keep the commercial interests at home contented by arguing that without war trade would be impossible. So it was that the equation empire equals power equals war was adopted by the Dutch and in succeeding years, around Europe, Holland was known to be the school of war. A Portuguese chronicler wrote in the eighteenth century, "It seems that Mars, after wandering around the globe, had finally fixed his headquarters in Holland".[1]

In the early years Jan Pieterszoon Coen, who became Governor-General in June 1618, stated Dutch aims best. He had already, four years earlier, given a policy brief to the directors recommending "a programme of vast territorial expansion and colonisation".[2]

This programme, like that of Albuquerque, was to establish a Dutch oceanic or seaborne empire without large territorial holdings, an imperium with Indonesia as the nucleus. This meant control over small pieces of land along the Indian Ocean littoral islands, fortified trading settlements and the like, and control of the sea in between.

As in the case of Albuquerque, you could claim to have such an empire, like virtue, even if what you had bore little relation to what is generally understood by the term. What he wrote in 1614 was: "You gentlemen ought to know from experience that trade in Asia should be conducted and maintained under the protection and with the aid of your own weapons, and that those weapons must be wielded with the profits gained from trade. So trade cannot be maintained without war, nor war without trade."[3]

So there we have, from the person who has been called "a conscious empire-builder like Albuquerque, Dupleix and Clive" and the founder of the Dutch East Indies Empire, another take on the equation between empire and war, this time between trade and war. In May 1619 he took the small Javanese port of Jakarta and soon claimed almost the whole island of Java, and included in his claims the offshore islands to the north; and the Indian Ocean to the south, a claim which "remained a paper one for a long time". Nearly half a century later Anthony van Diemen, the Governor-General, argued in support of the conquest of territory when his directors wanted trade and criticised the heavy casualties and expenses of his repeated expeditions in search of territorial gain. "We are taught by daily experience that the Company's trade in Asia cannot subsist without territorial conquests."[4]

## Indonesian Nationalism: Resources

In the case of Indonesia, as in other cases, it has not been religion, or language, or ethnicity, or a common history, or geography that have defined the entity called nationalism or the contours followed by that entity. It is nationalism, as propagated by those who fought for freedom and, later, more specifically those tasked with building the nation that has defined the role to be played by religion, or language and so on, in accomplishing that task. So religion, language, ethnicity, are not the specified particularities from which the nation emerges; the nation is the specified particularity from which religion, language, and ethnicity emerge. They are also, of course, resources from which the further building and consolidation of the nation can be achieved. So when we come across an argument like that of Benedict Anderson that "it is generally recognised that the intelligentsia were central to the rise of nationalism in the colonial territories ..."[5], and that in the specific case of Indonesia it was the colonial school system that promoted nationalism, it is necessary to reverse that argument to correspond to the traditional story; for Benedict Anderson has an assumption based on the modernity story which for obvious reasons he cannot state: that the Indonesians could, like putty, be shaped, made to become intellectuals or not, made to go to school or not. The reality is that nationalism in the colonies created the intelligentsia; and it was equally nationalism that made parents send their children to school to learn.

It would be useful to mention the very varied resources for the building and consolidation of the nation in Indonesia.

The Buddhist and Hindu empires of Indonesia have played an important role as resources. Strengthening this role is the presumption of the antiquity of these empires. A Hindu kingdom was recorded in Yavadvipa (Java) in 132 AD when its King, Devavarman, sent an embassy to China. It was a well established Kingdom, leading to the likelihood that Hinduism could have come to Indonesia before the first century AD. By the seventh century there was an extensive Buddhist empire based in Palembang, Sumatra, the Srivijaya Empire. Chinese records indicate it was a growing, aggressive power, mounting military expeditions against neighbouring Java. "Thus does Srivijaya emerge to view as an expanding power, stretching out her tentacles towards the Straits of Malacca on the one side and those of Sunda on the other."[6] The religious inspiration was from India. George Coedes, who discovered and established the importance of the Srivijaya empire and also first drew attention to the Indian influences in Southeast Asia in a major work of synthesis, '*Les Etats hinduise d'Indochine et d'Indonesie*', quotes the Chinese pilgrim I-Ching that "there are more than a thousand Buddhist priests" in Srivijaya whose studies are patterned on those of India; if a Chinese priest wished to 'go West' for studies he would do well to spend a year or two in Srivijaya before going on to India.[7]

Another and perhaps even greater Buddhist empire was that of the Sailendras based in Java from the eighth century. The Sailendras brought most of Indonesia under their authority, and according to an Arab source of the time, their empire "was so large that even the fastest vessels could not complete a round trip of it in two years."[8] They were not only a major naval power, but advanced the culture of the country. The famous stupa-cum-Buddhist temple of Borobodur, housing 400 statues of the Buddha and thousands of bas reliefs illustrating the Buddhist texts, was built in their time; they also introduced a new script, Devanagari.

There were others, more Hindu than Buddhist. Towards the end of the first millennium a powerful Kingdom of Singasari under Dharmawangsa established its rule over East Java. He got the Mahabharata translated into Javanese and ordered twelve translations of the Gita. But the Majapahit Kingdom, with its base in Central Java from the thirteenth century, is better known. It was certainly the most powerful kingdom in the history of Indonesia, maintained by overwhelming sea power. Indeed, its founder, known as Kertarajasa Jayavardhana, is credited with defeating the Mongol armada that Kublai Khan sent out to conquer Java at the end of the thirteenth century. At its peak, it included not only the whole archipelago but most of the Malay peninsula, parts of present-day Vietnam and Cambodia as well as the Philippines.

And then, in time to offer resistance to the Dutch empire-builders, came Mataram, an Islamic empire[9] which by the middle of the seventeenth century, under Sultan Agung, ruled most of Java. He repeatedly attacked Batavia, where the Dutch were trying to consolidate their trading position; the Dutch Governor-General there regularly sent him tribute and it was not till the middle of the eighteenth century that they were able to defeat Mataram and divide it into two: Surakarta and Jogjakarta.

In order to assess how Indonesian history was used to reinforce and consolidate nationalism it is necessary to recall that religions were not brought to Indonesia by conquering armies and enforcement measures. Buddhism, Hinduism, and Islam all came to the country gently, used persuasive methods to convert rulers and people. Coedes quotes Gabriel Ferrand that during the Indianisation of Southeast Asia as a whole the penetration of Buddhist and Hindu cultures into these regions started when Indian trading vessels arrived in Java. The newly arrived traders established friendly relations with the local chiefs, giving them presents, amulets, treating their illnesses; they learnt the local language, married the daughters of the chiefs, and "only then were the strangers able to use their civilising and religious influences with any chance of success."[10]

Islam came the same way, slowly and peacefully. Muslim traders from Gujarat and Persia began visiting Indonesia starting in the thirteenth century. Much of the trade between Malacca and Java was in Javanese hands and as they moved back and forth between the two they brought Islamic influences with them; the coastal towns, asserting their independence from Majapahit, came under this influence first. As they propagated Islam, its influence spread. The ruler of Demak converted, founded an Islamic centre, and started expanding his empire. But as Islam spread it accommodated and even integrated the local beliefs and customs; the Gods and heroes of the Hindu epics, though they could no longer be worshipped, were used for naming children and places. In general, despite the overwhelming Muslim majority in Indonesia today, religious beliefs tend to be syncretic. So the consolidation of nationalism and political life "has been directly and indirectly affected by animism, Hinduism, Buddhism, and Islam. Srivijaya and Majapahit are even today symbols of national glory".[11]

The life of Sukarno, who led the Indonesian struggle for independence and then became its first President, illustrates this well. He was brought up, his biographer writes, on the precepts of *kedjawen*, which is "a basically tolerant, syncretic, mystical and pantheistic view of life, which draws its main inspiration from a mixture of the original Javanese animist beliefs, Hinduism, Buddhism, and Islam, and which is practised by the majority of Javanese." And in his autobiography he recalls how he was named after a hero in the Mahabharata, "Father was a devotee of Mahabharata, the ancient Hindu classics... and said 'we shall name you Karna'. Karna is one of the greatest heroes in Mahabharata ... you shall be a second Karna."[12]

While still very young he attended, as large numbers of Indonesians have done through the centuries, the wayang or shadow plays depicting scenes from the Hindu epics, the Ramayana and the Mahabharata. As he consolidated nationalism he used verses from the Gita to describe the concept, the spirit of the nation: "fire cannot burn it, nor water engulf it, nor the hot winds scorch it. Impervious, unassailable, unconquerable and free, immortal ..."[13] And when the time came to declare independence in 1945 he needed arguments to convince Indonesians to unite in one nation so he went back to the theme of the ancient empires. He "explained that Indonesian nationalism meant the establishment of a state, which should contain the territories that in the distant past had been part of the great empires of Srivijaya and Majapahit."[14] Those were the only two occasions, he suggested, when Indonesia had experienced a national state.

When Sukarno set out to build nationalism in Indonesia he did it through the mechanism of the state, though it was a state taken from ancient history. The "Indonesian Nation is not only a group of individuals who, having *le desire d'etre ensemble*, live in a small area like Menangkabau or Madura, or Jogja ... the Indonesian people are all the human beings who, according to geopolitics ordained by God Almighty, live throughout the entire archipelago of Indonesia from the northern tip of Sumatra to Papua ... only twice have we experienced a national state; that was in the time of Sriwijaya and in the time of Madjopahit."[15] And here is a comment on the way Indonesia set about doing this. "Indonesian nationalism in challenging Dutch rule consciously repudiated an ethnic rationale defining itself exclusively with reference to the colonial territorial legacy." It was during the rule of President Sukarno that this kind of nationalism was built up; thereafter, under President Suharto, this policy "was set aside and replaced by a concentration on economic development through an engagement with the internationalist capitalist economy".[16] The change, the decision to abandon the project of building nationalism before it had been properly constructed, was a major reason for the successful separation of East Timor from Indonesia.

## The Creation of Nationalism: Depo Negoro

Returning to the story of resistance to the Dutch efforts to make an empire, the effectiveness on the ground, so to speak, of Indonesian nationalism can only be seen on the battlefield, for violent opposition to the Dutch occupation of Indonesia was unceasing. A few examples have to serve as illustration.

In 1825, as the Dutch tried to move into and consolidate their hold on Jogjakarta, Prince Depo Negoro, the best-known of the nationalists, resolved to evict them. He attacked Jogjakarta with a strong force and expelled the Dutch from there as well as other parts of Java. Thereafter he conducted guerilla operations against them. Thus began the Java war which continued until he was captured in 1830.

Years after that Depo Negoro continues to be depicted in two ways.

According to the story of modernity he was "a religious fanatic, given to solitary meditation in sacred caves."[17] He rebelled against the Dutch not because he was a nationalist but, and this is the endlessly told story of the conflict between progress and religious regression, between the lexus and the olive tree, because the Dutch wanted to build a road over some land on which a sacred tomb was located. He "spent much time wandering about the hills in the environs of Yogyakarta, visiting shrines, caves and other holy places"; and when, after his defeat, there were many more uprisings against Dutch rule, these were religious, and it was the ulema that played a "crucial role in unrest and resistance."[18] His revolt "was a kind of blind instinctive protest against the disintegration of a traditional society".[19] Other reasons have been given: he was unhappy because the Dutch refused to recognise him as the religious head of Java; he had problems of succession to the throne, despite being the eldest prince in the royal family.

For the Indonesians, and here we come to the traditional story, he is a nationalist, hailed as the hero of the liberty of the Indonesian people. At meetings of the nationalist party, the Pendidikan Nasional Indonesia, held during the struggle against the Dutch and after, his portrait is prominently displayed there, duly garlanded. A film, *November, 1828*, regarded as a classic and which swept all the major awards at the 1979 national film festival, is about Depo Negoro's life and struggle against the Dutch. It is about a village occupied by the Dutch and then liberated by Indonesian nationalists; it connotes both the birth of a nation into the modern world and the unity of all the diverse patriotic forces. When the attack of 1 March, 1949 was launched, the first of March all-out attack, as it was to be known, the key event that brought independence quickly to Indonesia, it was, appropriately enough, the Third Division of the forces of the Republic, known as the Diponegoro Division, which took the lead in it.

In the Moluccas the Pattimura war against Dutch occupation started in 1817; the Muslims united with the Christians in the effort to evict the colonisers. Then there was Tuanku Imam Bonjol of Sumatra who launched a war against them in the early 1820s, and which continued till he was defeated in August 1837.

It was Aceh that offered the most effective resistance to the Dutch empire making effort, so effective that the whole region was never brought into that empire. An Islamic Kingdom, Peureulak, had been established in Northwestern Sumatra early in the ninth century. In subsequent centuries, as the Buddhist and Hindu kingdoms grew weaker, the successors of that kingdom came to control the Malacca straits, their ports became important trading centres and entrepots in the trade across those straits, and those kingdoms regularly tried to extend their control to the Malay peninsula. When the Portuguese came to the region in the early sixteenth century they built a fortress in Pasai on the Sumatran coast, but were soon evicted by Sultan Ali Mugayat Shah (1511-1530); and their military commander, Horge de Brito, was killed. Several later Portuguese efforts to establish a foothold were also foiled.

So when the Dutch came they were understandably wary. Step one was to work with the British, whose help they would need against Aceh. Under an Anglo-Dutch Treaty of 1824 the Dutch surrendered all their possessions in India, gave up their claims to Singapore and the British recognised their primacy in Sumatra. Thirty years passed; they still didn't feel strong enough to take on Aceh, and it was not till 1856 that they began moving into Batak district, Bencoolen and Palembang, constantly facing resistance, including sea battles, which drained their resources in lives and material. Then in 1871 they struck a bargain with the British: the latter would give active help in Aceh, while the Dutch would surrender whatever they had on the Gold Coast.

In April 1873 the Dutch invaded Aceh; their forces were decisively defeated. In December of that year they sent in a larger force and this time were able to retain a foothold. But they faced a generalised resistance from the local chiefs and religious leaders. By 1885 they had, for the time being, abandoned the idea of bringing Aceh into the empire. Instead a series of fortified strong points were established from East to West on the northern-most tip of Sumatra and covering Kutaraja (now Banda Aceh), connected by rail. It was the sign of a soft approach; the Dutch wanted to negotiate. But the chiefs took it as a sign of weakness and increased their attacks. One Governor followed another. Van Teijn (1886-91) tried leniency; Pompe van Meerdervoort (1891-92) tried a tough line; Colonel Deykerhoff (1893-96) tried leniency and one of the chiefs, Teuku Umar, came over to the Dutch side in 1893; they let him form a legion. But it was only a tactic; he and his legion went over to the offensive against the Dutch in 1896 and he became one of the heroes of the resistance, joining forces with Panglima Polem to wage a war that lasted nearly ten years. And then others took the lead; so despite the claim that the Aceh war ended in the first decade of the twentieth century, a claim based on the surrender of the Sultan of Aceh Darussalam, guerilla war continued and that war was never really won.

Other wars too continued into the twentieth century, like the one waged by the people of South Sulawesi till they were overcome in 1910; or by the ruler of Bali who, outgunned by a large Dutch force in1908, refused to surrender and fought to a certain death; thereafter Dutch rule over the island was a military occupation undiluted by any pretense to civil control.

Thus it was that the so-called 300 years of the Dutch empire really meant partial control, established slowly and spasmodically which was never completed and, in any case, lasted only four decades.

The inexplicable ability of the Indonesians to resist Dutch colonialism found its best expression, as far as literature is concerned, in Louis Couperus' *The Hidden Force.* Largely written during an extended stay in Java in 1899, by one of the great classic novelists of Holland, this is a major contribution to the colonial literature of the world. It was 'the unutterable' that opposed the Dutch in Indonesia, according to Couperus. The story is of a Dutch official posted to Indonesia, a Resident called Van Oudijk who struggles unsuccessfully against the secret forces of darkness representing Asia and personified in the Hadji. At the very end Van Oudijk comes face to face with a trainload of Hadjis and he "felt it, the unutterable, that lurks in the ground, that hisses under the volcanoes, that slowly draws near with the far-travelled winds, that rushes onward with the rain, that rattles by in the heavy, rolling thunder, that is wafted from the far horizon of the boundless sea, that flashes from the black mysterious gaze of the secretive native ... that gnaws like a poison and a hostile force at the body, soul, and life of the European, that silently attacks the conqueror and saps his energies ... the unutterable."

## Mainstream Nationalism

All this resistance comprises examples of what Frantz Fanon calls the violent response to colonialism which is just under the skin of the masses and explodes here and there. There are also, continuing his conceptual framework, the nationalist political parties or mainstream leadership, the only ones who can control that violence and the ones to whom independence is eventually bestowed by the colonial power.

A number of these emerged, starting with the Boedi Oetomo (noble endeavour), founded in May 1908 by a small group of Javanese students. The founding day, May 20, is now a day of national celebration, the Day of National Awakening. It was led by nineteen-year-old Soetomo, who went on to become a prominent national leader. But its aim was not independence; it was non-political, to promote education, advance agriculture, industry and commerce and, for the Indonesians, everything that will guarantee them the life of a dignified people. Government regulation number 111 absolutely forbade any organisation or meeting of a political character. Boedi Oetomo was to be the motor driven by the young to propel their elders forward, while they played the role of steersmen "who with dexterous hand knew how to avoid dangerous rocks in order to bring the boat to safe harbour." Sukarno was a member of its youth organisation and known even then for his uncompromisingly radical views; he was called Bhima, after the uncompromising Mahabharata warrior. But as months passed the older generation did come forward; by late 1909 Boedi Oetomo had some 10,000 members.

But soon more overtly political organisations came up despite the ban and its members moved to them. The first of these was Sarekat Islam (SI), founded in 1912 and led by H.O.S.Tjokroaminoto, who quickly became Sukarno's mentor. By 1916 it had almost half a million members and had adopted self-government as its aim; by 1919 there were two and a half million members and the aim became complete independence. Government pressure on it increased; its branches were recognised but not the central organisation; the hold of the central leadership consequently weakened. In a parallel move, and it could not have done better if it had been coordinated with the Dutch authorities (though there is no clear evidence that there was any such coordination), the communists began to infiltrate it, using those branches that were weakest. "The government's legislation forcing Sarekat Islam's organisational disintegration made the conditions for infiltration ideal."[20]

But they were unable to get control of the centre and in May 1920 decided to set up the Communist Party of the Indies, PKI, which, of course, immediately came under the disciplinary regime of the Comintern. Its subsequent actions need to be seen in the light of the fact that, for the Soviet Union, controlling nationalist movements was more important than letting them achieve their main aim, independence. Indeed, to the extent achievement of that aim might lead to the assertion of views independent of the Comintern and internationalism, meaning the directions issued by the Communist Party of the Soviet Union, "this road is fraught with the danger of nationalism absorbing the elements of internationalism ... the opposition of national unity to class division and of national consciousness to class consciousness ...national exclusiveness."[21] This effectively put international communism on the same side as Dutch colonialism, both together facing the movement for Indonesian independence, an alliance that movements for independence all over the world have had to withstand throughout the third, fourth and later decades of the twentieth century.

The PKI spent the next half decade trying, with considerable success, to get control of the SI branches. But then Moscow stepped in. The SI branches were dependent on the support of the peasantry and to Moscow this looked too much like an alliance with the freedom struggle, for that too was based on peasant support. So Stalin announced in May 1925 that the PKI was "overrating the revolutionary potential of the liberation movement and underrating the importance of an alliance between the working class and the revolutionary bourgeoisie against imperialism". This was left deviation.[22] Then followed some flip flops by the Comintern, which accused the PKI of not devoting enough attention to a united front, or the opposite, not devoting enough attention to the peasants. In any case, the leadership of the party split and, seemingly under directions from Moscow, the more radical branch launched a revolution in November 1926. It was obviously going to fail and perhaps destroy the party, but Moscow's purpose seems to have been to weaken the freedom struggle; and this is what happened. Dutch forces crushed the revolution; the entire leadership of the party, including large numbers of the rank and file, were arrested, some 13,000 in all. Most were soon released but 5,000 were imprisoned and a thousand exiled. Along with this, and this seems to have been the expectation of Moscow, the government interned a large number of national leaders who were known not to be any part of the PKI.

The resulting disarray of the nationalist movement was, however, temporary. By 1927 Sukarno was ready to take on its leadership.

In July of that year he and others established the Perserikatan Nasional Indonesia, a name later changed to Partai Nasional Indonesia or PNI, dedicated to the achievement of complete political and economic independence based on national unity and self-reliance and through a programme of non-cooperation inspired by the freedom struggle in India. The PNI grew rapidly, largely because of Sukarno's leadership and political abilities and within two years was the core of the nationalist movement. So the Dutch arrested Sukarno and several of his colleagues in December 1929 and kept them under detention for two years. Their problem was that the upsurge of the national movement could not be stopped; if he was kept under detention it would go further underground, the sporadic incidents of violence that were regularly taking place would multiply. If he was released he would be a hero. And when they released him in December 1931 it became immediately apparent that he was a national hero. Going to Surabaya by train "at every station where the train stopped crowds of jubilant Indonesians were standing and waving", special Sukarno editions were run by the national newspapers, he was overwhelmed with garlands, hugged and kissed wherever he went.

So in August 1933 he was again arrested, sent into exile and this time not allowed back to Java till the Japanese came into Indonesia in 1942 and released him.

During his years in and out of prison Sukarno had fine-tuned his political thinking. He rejected both the Western and Soviet models for the evolution of the Indonesian nation. Instead he suggested Marhaenism, after the name of a poor peasant who he had met while cycling around Bandung. Marhaenism was essentially about the unity of all Indonesians, whichever class or group they belonged to, whichever island they came from, whatever their language or ethnicity. In 1926 he had published three articles suggesting that Marxists, Muslims and Nationalists should work together. Two decades later he continued to emphasise this theme. "I always urge: unity, unity, unity, and again unity. And we must understand that our revolution can only exert its maximum power when it is truly a national revolution." That unity would bring success to the national revolution. Then came the tasks of constructing the state, occupy government positions, "regulate the Indonesian finances, unify all the islands of Indonesia within one independent state, make Indonesia strong ..."

So the path was clear: first comes unity, a precondition for the national revolution and one which was important in a nation of such ethnic, cultural, linguistic and geographic diversity, scattered over hundreds of islands; then comes the state; and then comes the task of coordinating "all these millions of Indonesians into a state and a national consciousness ..."[23]

Many years later, in 1961, he gave a speech in which he elaborated this. "Yes, we in Indonesia have already passed through the gruelling process of forming our national ideology and we have now reached our synthesis, i.e. Indonesian socialism ... yes our Indonesian socialism developed through turmoil. In the course of that turmoil we have learnt many things ... we have learnt that the basic ingredient of any national ideology must be the national inheritance of that nation itself, its heritage from the past, the traditions which bind its people together and set the pattern of their life. In Indonesia this is *kerakjatan, gotong royong, musjawarah* and *mufakat* – the people as source, collective effort for a common goal, discussion and deliberation, consensus of opinion."[24]

## Post-1945: The Return of the Dutch, with a Lot of Help

During the years 1945-49 the Dutch struggled to re-establish colonial control over Indonesia. They had been driven out by the Japanese in March, 1942, who occupied the islands until August 1945.

While one military occupation had replaced another during those years, the Indonesian movement for independence continued roughly on course. The Japanese released Sukarno who went back to Java, established contact with the other nationalist leaders, and planned how best to negotiate the road to independence. The anger of the people against the foreign ruler continued to grow, now directed against the Japanese. Sporadic violent insurrections broke out. In March 1943 the Japanese agreed to set up an Indonesian organisation, Poetera (Centre of People's Power) as a move towards greater self-government, hoping to use it to prosecute the war effort. By the end of 1943, however, "it was clear to the Japanese that the Poetera was accomplishing considerably more for the Indonesian nationalist movement than it was for the Japanese war effort,"[25] so they dissolved it. Meanwhile, underground nationalist organisations were growing, many in touch with the mainstream leadership, and others not. In any case it was clear after three years of Japanese occupation that the nationalist movement was far stronger and now more confident of its ability to take over the reigns of government; this was not, by the way, because of anything the Japanese did or did not do, but because of the action of the processes of autocatalysm.

When it became clear to the Indonesian leaders, Hatta, Sukarno and others, that Japan had lost the war and would soon surrender they decided to declare the independence of the Republic of Indonesia, which was done immediately after the surrender, on August 17, 1945 and they then adopted a constitution for the newly formed Republic of Indonesia.. A volunteer army, known as Peta, which was formed by the Japanese to help defend Indonesia from the expected attack by the Allies, and which numbered by then 120,000 armed men, was to be the backbone of Indonesia's national military effort to defend the Republic.

With the war at an end the Dutch frantically dispatched reinforcements in the bid to take control back from the Indonesians, to re-establish their rule. Everybody helped. The British helped, of course; they were the major colonial power; and they were the first on the scene after the Japanese surrender. British and Dutch troops, under the guise of disarming the Japanese troops on the islands and repatriating allied prisoners of war and detainees, attacked the forces of the Republic.

The Americans helped; the Dutch were important to the security system they were building up in Europe. American ships were used to transport Dutch reinforcements who were, of course, equipped with American weapons, given on lend lease. On 24 October 1945 Sukarno appealed to the United States not to do this; it had no effect.[26]

The Japanese helped; in early September they had been instructed to retain control until Allied troops arrived and they, therefore, tried to disarm the Peta, without much success; then the British, who started landing in Jakarta from September, 29, 1945, with the alleged task of disarming the Japanese and taking them into custody as prisoners of war, rearmed them instead of disarming them and told them to 'restore law and order', specifically to take back from the control of the Republic cities such as Bandung. So they started systematically attacking the forces of the Republic.

Louis Mountbatten, head of South-East Asia Command, had one directive: restore Dutch rule; for the rest, like the surrender of

Japanese forces, the freeing of Allied prisoners and the collection of information on war crimes, he had been instructed that they were secondary. Soon, therefore, the British themselves went into action. The 49$^{th}$ Brigade of the 23$^{rd}$ Indian Division of the British Army had landed in Surabaya on 25 October 1945. The Government of the Republic had already told the British that they would not be opposed but should make no attempt to bring in Dutch troops or any Dutch agencies. Lieutenant-General Christison, who was in overall command, agreed; and then immediately went back on this by bringing in Dutch officials in an effort to establish the nucleus of a Dutch armed presence. And they started confiscating Republican transport, calling for the Indonesians to surrender arms. In Surabaya a major battle developed on October 28; it was a disaster for the British whose Commander A.W.S.Mallaby was killed along with hundreds of his troops. In panic the British appealed to President Sukarno, who personally came, arranged a ceasefire and, on 30 October, signed an agreement with the British Commander that the latter would acknowledge the Indonesian army and occupy only two small areas. And now the British went back on their word again; this time they brought in aircraft, warships and heavy guns to displace the Indonesian youth organisations which had taken over the city. So here on one side were the reinforced British, with 15,000 troops, veterans with a plentiful supply of Sherman tanks, machine guns, mortars, a squadron of tanks, 25 pounder cannons, howitzers, the naval guns of the Cruiser HMS Sussex, four destroyers in harbour and units of the Royal Air Force; and there on the other side were the Indonesians with small arms and some mortars, a lot of Japanese equipment which they had never used so they had to keep referring to field manuals to learn its use. It took a month's heavy fighting for the British to take Surabaya back; and that fighting made Indonesian independence an international issue but, more important, gave the Indonesian people the confidence that they could achieve independence even if they had to fight for it.[27]

By then the administration of the Republic was fully functional and as Allied troops continued to land through October, and tried to insist that Netherlands law would be applied and the 'lawful government of the Netherlands East Indies' would soon take control, the first of the Dutch troops started to land and it was clear that a major confrontation would develop.

But the Dutch faced a problem. The battle of Surabaya had shown the strength of the forces behind the movement for independence; what the Dutch now needed was breathing space in which they could build up their forces without the constant attacks that they and the British faced. This was even more necessary because the British had had enough; this was not really their war; their troops were largely Indian, now susceptible to nationalist urgings from India; they decided that they would start pulling out by late 1946. The Dutch needed a ceasefire. So they proposed an agreement and the leaders of the Republic, anxious, as have been other leaders in other colonies facing similar situations, that the militant nationalist elements not get stronger, agreed. The result was the Linggadjati Agreement of November, 1946, under which, apart from ending hostilities, the Netherlands Government recognised the Republic as the de facto authority in Java and Sumatra and agreed that the two sides would cooperate in setting up a democratic, sovereign, and federal United States of Indonesia.

In fairness it should be mentioned here that within the spectrum of Dutch political opinion on the subject there were those who really thought it a good idea to abide by this agreement, to help set up a sovereign United States of Indonesia. Here is where the Americans stepped in. By early 1947 the Dutch economy was in parlous circumstances; in April they assessed that within two months they would go bankrupt as a nation; they were desperate for financial help. So in May the Prime Minister, C.J.M.Beel, asked two financial experts, Hirschfeld and Albarda, to go out to Indonesia and find out if something could be made of Dutch assets there. Recall that this was the time the US had Marshall Plan aid under active consideration. When Hirschfeld and Albarda got to Batavia they met the American consul there, Foote, who told them categorically the Dutch would have to reconquer Indonesia as the only way to establish their credit-worthiness. Otherwise there would be no Marshall Plan aid for the Netherlands.[28]

Anyway, by mid-July, 1947, Dutch military preparations were ready and they launched a major offensive against the forces of the Republic, backed by tanks, other armoured vehicles and with strong air support. They managed to take territory and to control some of the urban centres, but made hardly any impact on the forces of the Republic, which, following Depo Negoro, abandoned the flat country for the jungles and hills, from where guerilla war continued.

And there was stalemate.

US military and logistic help had, in the meanwhile, continued, and now there was also diplomatic support. On 28 July 1947 India and Australia had referred the Indonesian question to the United Nations Security Council (UNSC) under Article 39 of the charter, threats to the peace. The US refused to support the Indonesians and suggested a ceasefire between the two sides followed by a settlement of their dispute by arbitration or other peaceful means. On 1 August 1947 the UNSC called upon both sides to ceasefire immediately and to settle the dispute by arbitration or other peaceful means.

But the stalemate made the Dutch realise that the Republican forces were stronger than they had anticipated. Despite heavy armour and aerial support they were able to advance little beyond the coastal areas in Sumatra or Madura, though progress in Java was better. Everywhere the forces of the Republic withdrew in good order to the mountains, taking with them their weapons, transport equipment, machinery and food supplies. No Republican forces had surrendered, they were no weaker than before. The Dutch needed another ceasefire, another breather. So they agreed to observe the ceasefire called for by the UNSC, which took effect at midnight on 4-5 August 1947. Here was a further opportunity for US diplomacy to support the Dutch while feigning neutrality. After the ceasefire, while negotiations began again, the Dutch military buildup continued. There were also skirmishes; the Dutch were able to make significant gains, saying these were mopping up operations; in fact these operations created ever new ceasefire lines which increasingly favoured the Dutch. The negotiations went through the medium of a three-member UNSC Good Offices Committee, in which the Dutch selected one, the Republic one, and by agreement the US was the third. The Republic told the Committee about the Dutch post-ceasefire mopping up operations and requested that the original ceasefire line be restored, in reply to which the US representative said "unless the terms demanded by the Committee were accepted by the Republic, the American Government would probably not be inclined to oppose further Dutch attempts to impose a settlement by force".[29]

In the meanwhile, in the accepted tradition of all empire-makers facing defeat, the Dutch tried to divide Indonesia into smaller pieces. On 29 December, 1947 Governor-General Van Mook announced the creation of a new 'state' of East Sumatra, one of the richest parts of Indonesia. Three weeks later, on 21 January 1948, he announced another 'state', Madura and that the Dutch had extended recognition to it; two months later elections to a Madura Parliament were held, but three-quarters of those elected were pro-Republican. A little later, 25 February another 'state', West Java, was recognised.

## The Renewed Nationalist Upsurge

It was like holding back the tide, for the national upsurge among the people had now surfaced across the whole of the country. Local leaders emerged. Immediately after the Republic had been proclaimed they had sent couriers to Jakarta who returned with texts of the proclamation; these were printed and distributed widely. Posters were put up. The message was painted on goods trains so that rural Indonesia would know. In some cases, like Sumatra, telegraph and telephone offices received the text of the proclamation and their employees had it printed and distributed. And in the absence of clear directions from Jakarta, a heterogeneous local leadership sprang up. In central Java they "made leadership changes by organising elections to find local candidates acceptable to all groups."[30] In Aceh reformist Ulema emerged to take the lead in carrying forward the momentum of independence. In East Sumatra there was a mix of former members of the colonial establishment, radical and moderate nationalist who had been active before the war, younger nationalists who had worked with the Japanese, and leaders of the local militias preparing to fight the Dutch. The youth organisations or Pemuda played an important role in every region; they were, like Boedi Oetomo had been, "the spur and spearhead of the struggle, both urging their more cautious elders on to decisive, irrevocable action and being their instruments in carrying out such action."[31] In West Sumatra their struggle ensured that the Dutch were confined to the coastal areas. In Sulawesi dozens of youth groups came up spontaneously in response to the proclamation of independence and to do battle against the Dutch.

All these groups and leaders repeatedly proclaimed their loyalty to the Republic, whose "very weakness during this period served to strengthen the loyalty of the local revolutionaries to its leadership". For it was the "idea of an independent Indonesia that had gained strength and force over the previous three decades."[32] They all wanted to be part of a united and independent Indonesia.

At the level of the central leadership of the Republic, meanwhile, the diplomatic exercise continued. In all this diplomacy the US continued to back the Dutch. An agreement of sorts was reached, the Renville agreement of 17 January, 1948, which called for a truce, and which the leaders of the Republic, who could see that time was on their side, agreed only after intense pressure that if they did not, then the US support for the Dutch would become even stronger. Under the agreement for a ceasefire line, the van Mook line was established to separate the two armed forces. The Renville agreement also provided for a plebiscite to decide whether the people wished to be part of the Republic or of a Dutch-sponsored federal United States of Indonesia.

The next eleven months were spent by the Dutch in further building up their armed strength on the islands. During this critical period, when a final showdown between the two sides was obviously only waiting to happen, the Soviet Union entered the picture in support of the Dutch.

In September 1947 a political line had been adopted by Moscow, according to which the world was divided into two blocs, irreconcilably opposed to one another; it was the duty of communist parties everywhere to rise up against the lackeys of imperialism, namely, the newly independent governments. The so-called Cold War was, incidentally, fully under way by then from the other side too. Winston Churchill's 'Iron Curtain' speech was made in March, 1946, while President Truman's Doctrine was announced in March, 1947.

The radical Indonesian communist leader, Musso, who had been in Moscow, was sent back to Indonesia in August 1948 and in September, with the outcome of the struggle between the Dutch and the Indonesians uncertain, the Soviet Union ordered the Indonesian Communist Party to launch an insurrection against the Republic in Madiun, eastern Java, which was the third largest town in the territory controlled by the Republic. On 18 September, 1948, the Communist Party of Indonesia (PKI) seized the government offices, telephone exchange and army headquarters in Madiun, and formed a Soviet government there, announcing that this was a signal for people everywhere in Indonesia to take control of state power. A few hours later Moscow radio pitched in, backing the Madiun action as "a popular uprising against the Government of the Fascist Japanese Quislings, Sukarno and Hatta."

The aim of this uprising was not, of course, a general revolution. The Republic was known to be far too strong and its leaders far too popular for that. The aim was two-fold. Firstly, with the bulk of the Republic's troops facing the Dutch across the van Mook line in the ceasefire which had been agreed in January, 1948, this put an additional burden on the Republic; indeed, Madiun was a major distraction for the Republic, and throughout the course of the uprising "the Republican government was never certain enough of Dutch intentions to risk pulling more than a small part of its troops back from the van Mook line to fight the rebels."[33] Secondly, this action would ensure that US support to the Dutch, which always had to face a strong anti-colonial domestic lobby, continued; if communism were the threat, and if that is what the Dutch were fighting to stave off (in the inverted logic of the story of modernity, since it was not the Dutch but the Republic that was fighting the communists), they would have to be helped. And US support to the Dutch did, in fact, continue. When the Republic's representatives asked, in early December, 1948, what the US position would be in case the Dutch attacked and made territorial gains, the State Department replied that it depends on the situation. And US military supplies to the Dutch, which actually served to encourage them to break the Renville truce, continued.

## The Dutch Lose the War

So within weeks, in the early morning of 19th December, 1948, with the forces of the Republic distracted by the communist uprising, and with assurances of US support, the Dutch launched their second military action, starting with Jogjakarta, which was quickly taken. This time they intended to wipe out any claim to legitimacy that the Republic had. American Mitchel bombers attacked Jogjakarta, the city was surrounded and within hours the leaders of the Republic, Sukarno, Hatta, Sjahrir, were captured and flown to Sumatra. The unilateral abrogation of the Renville agreement which this entailed was announced, of course, only by the onset of the attack itself.

In all this the fact of US support was crucial. As the influential commentator Arthur Crock wrote in the *New York Times* of 25 December, 1948, the US did believe that "the Dutch are the very keystone of the military and economic security system in Western Europe that is vital to the United States ... the delicate fabric of Western security against Russian communism woven with such difficulty and still far from complete, could easily be shattered by an American attempt to isolate Holland..."

So the Dutch announced that the Republic was no more.

And one commentator quoted the comment of van Mook, the Dutch Governor-General, that "if we play our cards right, we can stay here for another hundred years."[34]

But the Republic rejected this story; they believed the last stage in the struggle was just beginning and that the Dutch attack was the signal for the final end of Dutch rule. And, indeed, the story told by the Republic turned out to be the true one; by the end of that year, 1949, and after lengthy negotiations, Indonesia was independent.

For, in fact, after they launched the attack the Dutch position was much weaker. By now they had 150,000 troops in Indonesia, but all of them were on the defensive. The countryside was fully controlled by Republican forces and their guerilla attacks increased in frequency and effectiveness as the weeks passed. Dutch settlers were abandoning their plantations and moving to the cities. Within the cities the population was increasingly and openly hostile. Typewritten copies of the speeches of Sukarno and Hatta exhorting the people to continue the struggle, which had been written as soon as they knew of the Dutch action, but not broadcast since they were captured too quickly, circulated from hand to hand in the cities and in the countryside. The Indonesian currency, the Rupiah, rose in value against the Dutch guilder; the Indonesian peasant supplying rice to the towns as much as the Chinese shopkeeper selling stores had more confidence in the picture of Sukarno on the Indonesian currency than in the Dutch guilder.

The Dutch, of course, desperate for as much diplomatic support as they could get, not to mention the money which the Americans were giving them and which would stop if the reality ever got out, painted a very different picture, that they were fully in control, that the Republic didn't exist any more. An American academic, visiting Jogjakarta in early January, 1949, saw how much the situation conformed to what the representatives of the Republic had been saying and how different it was from the picture painted by the Dutch. In the city itself control by the Dutch was only partial; and the inhabitants there were only women, children and old men, for "the young men had gone to the countryside to fight the Dutch from there."[35]

For a while, in the first few weeks of 1949, however, the West went along with the Dutch story. Then on 1 March, 1949 came the Republican offensive which became known, in the records of Indonesian history, as 'the first of March all-out attack'. Detailed planning for the attack was done by a relatively junior officer of the Republic's forces, a Lt.-Col. Suharto, whose reputation derived from it, and which was a major input into his acceptability as President, which he became in 1967, remaining in that position till 1998.

Suharto spent time researching the city and working out details, area by area, of how his forces, used to operating in the platoon size operations which guerilla warfare necessitated, would coalesce into the much larger groups required for urban warfare. Troops of the Republic were infiltrated into the city for two weeks before the attack began; units were detailed for each sector of an attack that came from all sides, with one battalion placed inside the city centre to organise the people.

So on the chosen day troops of the Republic moved out into the open in every part of Jogjakarta and occupied it for several hours, keeping the Dutch largely confined to their barracks. Suharto himself led his troops in the attack from the West. The Royal Netherlands Indies Army units in the city handed over arms and ammunition to the Republic's forces, and the whole city seemed suddenly full of them. People left food and drink outside their doors for them; the red and white colours of the flag of the Republic flew all over the city. Suharto later claimed "we were able to show that TNI was still intact as an army and could go out and enter a city any time we wanted to"; he thought the attack was extremely influential, causing the UN Security Council to place pressure on the Dutch to cease operations and re-embark upon negotiations with the Republic.[36]

A more objective viewpoint would accept that the Dutch had already lost the war; the 1 March attack merely showed the world that this was so. In doing so, it no doubt also showed the truth of this to the many Dutch leaders who were not yet convinced. The Dutch now had a stark choice: negotiate and leave or be expelled and leave. They had, in fact, lost the will to continue the fight. In

May, 1949, a ceasefire was agreed; negotiations under UN auspices began some three months later and on 27 December the Federal Republic of Indonesia became sovereign and independent.[37]

The Republic, as it came into being in December 1949, had a federal structure; it was the Republic of the United States of Indonesia comprising what was formerly the Republic and fifteen other political entities which the Dutch had set up, each of which had considerable autonomy. The final phase of the independence movement was, therefore, to bring all those entities under one political roof. This was completed by 15 August 1950, when Sukarno, by then President, signed into law a Unitarian Constitution for the now renamed Republic of Indonesia.

## ENDNOTES

[1] Quoted in C.R. Boxer, *The Dutch Seaborne Empire, 1600-1800*, Penguins Books, London, 1990, p. 95.

[2] D.G.E. Hall, *A History of Southeast Asia*, Macmillan and Co. London, 1964, p. 282

[3] Quoted by Geoffrey Parker, *The Military Revolution, Military Innovation and the Rise of the West, 1500-1800*, Cambridge University Press, 1988, p. 132

[4] C.R.Boxer, op. cit., pp. 211, 212 and 107 respectively.

[5] Benedict Anderson, *Imagined Communities, Reflections on the Origin and Spread of Nationalism*, Verso, London, 1995, p. 116.

[6] D.G.E. Hall, op. cit. p. 43.

[7] G.Coedes, *The Indianized States of Southeast Asia*, ed. Walter F. Vella, East-West Center Press, Honolulu, 1968, p.81. To 'go west' means, of course, to go to India.

[8] Quoted in D.P. Singhal, *India and World Civilisation*, Rupa, Calcutta, 1993, Part II, p. 141.

[9] To quote C.R. Boxer, op. cit., p. 213, this was 'an Oriental despotism of the traditional kind.'

[10] G. Coedes, op. cit., p. 22.

[11] Ram Dev Bhardwaj citing an interview with a former Indonesian Prime Minister, in *Sukarno and Indonesian Nationalism*, Rahul Publishing House, Delhi, 1997, p. 27.

[12] C.L.M. Penders, *The Life and Times of Sukarno*, Sidgwick and Jackson, London, 1974, pp. 4-5.

[13] Ram Dev Bhardwaj, op. cit. p. 112.

[14] C.L.M. Penders, op. cit. p. 87.

[15] Quoted by George McTurnan Kahin, *Nationalism and Revolution in Indonesia*, Cornell University Press, Ithaca, 1952, p. 123.

[16] Michael Leifer, The changing temper of Indonesian nationalism, in Michael Leifer, ed. *Asian Nationalism*, Routledge, London, 2000, pp. 167, 158.

[17] D.G.E. Hall, op. cit. p. 514.

[18] Reynaldo Ileto, Religion and Anti-Colonial Movements, in Nicholas Tarling, ed., *The Cambridge History of Southeast Asia, volume three, From c. 1800 to the 1930s,*

Cambridge University Press, 1999, pp. 204-5.

[19] Brian Harrison, *South-East Asia, A Short History*, Macmillan, London, 1963, p. 185.

[20] George McTurnan Kahin, op. cit., pp. 65 and 71 for this and the previous paragraph.

[21] O.V. Martyshin, Nationalism in the East, in Professor R. Ulyanovsky, ed. *The Revolutionary Process in the East: Past and Present,* Progress Publishers, Moscow, 1985, p. 185.

[22] Quoted by George McTurnan Kahin, pp. 78-9.

[23] Quotes from this and the four previous paragraphs from C.L.M. Penders, op. cit. pp. 45 and 110-111.

[24] Quoted by Peter Lyon, *Neutralism*, Leicester University Press, 1963, p. 188. This is from Sukarno's speech at the Non-aligned Summit in Belgrade, 1961.

[25] George McTurnan Kahin, p. 110.

[26] Jayashri Deshpande, Indonesia, *The Impossible Dream, United States and 1958 Rebellion*, Prachi Prakashan, New Delhi, 1981, p. 6.

[27] See, on this, Brig. Gen. Nugroho Notosusanto, *The National Struggle and the Armed Forces in Indonesia,* Centre for Armed Forces History, Djakarta, 1980.

[28] The incident has been cited by H. Baudet, M. Fennema et al., *Het Netherlands belang bij Indies*, Het Spectrum, Utrecht, 1983, pp. 93-94.

[29] George McTurnan Kahin, p. 228.

[30] Anton Lucas, The Tiga Daerah Affair: Social Revolution of Rebellion? In Audrey R. Kahin, ed., *Regional Dynamics of the Indonesian Revolution, Unity from Diversity*, University of Hawaii Press, Honolulu, 1985, p. 32.

[31] Audrey R. Kahin, West Sumatra, Outpost of the Republic, in Audrey R. Kahin, ed., op. cit., p. 151

[32] Audrey R.Kahin, Overview in Audrey R. Kahin, ed., op. cit., p. 281.

[33] George McTurnan Kahin, op. cit. pp. 294 and 295 for this and the previous paragraph.

[34] Quoted by Jayashri Deshpande, p. 17.

[35] George McTurnan Kahin, op. cit., p. 395.

[36] Quoted in R.E.Elson, *Suharto, A Political Biography*, Cambridge University Press, 2001, pp.37-8. TNI is the Indonesian National Army.

[37] A very different version of what happened, and this corresponds to the modernity story, is that it was the US which acted to make the Dutch lose the war! C.L.M.Penders says in op. cit., p. 133, that the Dutch Foreign Minister Stikker visited Washington in March, 1949 and he was told there by the American authorities that the US "might consider economic sanctions" against the Netherlands; "this threat by the United States caused the Dutch position to erode rapidly."

# 6

# Algeria

How the French established an empire in Algeria, tried to set up a *toute-presence* colony, meaning by totally eliminating the Arab population, and then lost it all in war, is told here on the basis of the traditional story, with some references to that of modernity. Once the French lost the Algerian War they lost not only the last of their empire, but also their global position, their claim to be a great power, which till 1962 didn't look absurd, and centuries of French greatness came to a close.

## Making War for Empire

France's empire in Algeria is among the examples of a relatively rare form of empire. If we take a spectrum of such forms, arranged according to the methods of control over the colonised people which were adopted by colonisers, and the number of people sent out by the imperial power to exercise that control, we could at one end place the very indirect control exercised, for example, by the British in the princely states of India. A British resident, and in later years it was often an Indian resident, accompanied by a small guard, represented the entire British presence. At the other end is the direct control involving a much larger imperial presence, in which every military and civil functionary is sent out by the imperial power. The rare form of this is where settlers go out in large numbers to populate the country, where the natives become so marginal or irrelevant that colonisation is complete, despite the continued existence of a substantial majority native population, used now only for the most menial tasks. South Africa is one of the best examples of this; Zimbabwe is another; and Algeria is the median case; it was French policy there, at least at the start of the empire making venture, to drive all those Algerians not required for menial tasks into the desert, there presumably to be extinguished, and to replace them entirely with the French.

The urge in France to acquire the prestige and demonstrate the power that comes with the possession of an empire was strong by 1830. Its diminished status in Europe after being defeated in 1815 played a role. The French King, Charles X, was unpopular at home and wanted to boost his popularity, another factor. Apologists refer to the feeble story about the Dey of Algiers insulting the French consul, which makes the French invasion a punitive expedition, except that it took place three years after the insult. But, within the framework of the traditional story, it is the equation war equals empire equals power, or just empire equals power and for acquiring it war is necessary, which is most relevant. So when the French wished to show that their power mattered, having an empire was the way to do it. And, as with all empire-makers, Rome entered the picture at an early stage, for to populate both sides of the Mediterranean with the Latin civilisation was a trade-marked Roman idea or myth.

One quotation should suffice to illustrate the point: "Louis Bertrand, an important colonial novelist at the turn of the century and one of the major proponents of the myth, was to note later that 'we have come here to recapture the work of the Romans in this country, that its geographic constitution, neighbourhood, and past places it naturally under Latin hegemony'".[1] It was one of the reasons that at a subsequent stage they decided that this empire should be populated entirely by the French; the Arabs should be eliminated or at best relocated far into the desert.

So when the French went into Algiers in June 1830 it was not for punitive purposes, nor for trade, nor were their intentions to do with the promoting the *mission civilisatrice*. There was little doubting the military nature of the expedition. The expeditionary force of 37,000 men and some 600 ships which sailed from Toulon was equipped not only with muskets, but some thirty 24 pounder guns, another twenty 16 pounders along with dozens of smaller cannon, howitzers and mortars. After occupying Algiers their intention was clearly to go further inland and set up colonies and an empire.

In keeping with the presumption of the modernity story that the acquisition of empire does not require much in the way of war, the French expedition had a festive air about it, a carnival-like atmosphere. Parisian ladies had rented space on a special ship which would accompany the expedition so that they could watch the assault. A French newspaper advertised that a "new enterprise will be established on the occasion of the war against Algiers". A ship would be fitted out as a hotel, and "persons wishing to witness the bombardment of Algiers and the landing of our troops will be lodged and fed for 15 francs a day", and the ships would be kept at a "respectful distance to avoid enemy fire."[2]

The confidence seemed justified. The Dey had a total of just under 9,000 troops, Turkish janissaries in an all-infantry corps, of whom only 5,000 were stationed in Algiers. They were defeated on 19 June. There was no other military engagement and the French entered Algiers on 5 July. They had had only four hundred casualties and had captured a treasure that more than paid for the entire expedition. Then resistance began and the confidence was seen to have been hubris.

And talk of war came to the surface. General Thomas Robert Bugeaud, appointed to command French forces in Algeria in May 1836, recalled years later that "they (the pacifists) did not even want us to go to war but we did it in spite of them. They wanted us to colonise the flower pots on the terraces of Algiers." And then he elaborated the way it should actually be done. "To conquer them their livelihood must be attacked ... the territory of each tribe must be attacked; the villages destroyed, the fruit trees cut down, the harvests burned or dug up, the granaries emptied, the ravines, rocks and caves scoured to seize their women, children, old men, cattle and possessions." Others were equally explicit. One of the commanders, a General Rovigo, has been quoted to say that since the Algerians could not be civilised, they must be dispersed "like wild animals who keep away from the vicinity of inhabited places, they must recede to the desert as we progress with our settlements; they must stay forever in the sands of the Sahara." Years later a Henry de Sarrauton wrote in 1891 that the Algerians would never accept European values; their religion forbids them from adopting French civil and political institutions because the Koran is "at the same time their religious code, their civil code and their political code" hence this people "must be driven back, step by step, and be replaced gradually and systematically by a French population. That is the only way for Algeria to become truly French".

This policy was defended by the French war minister Girard who said "we must decide to drive them far back, even to exterminate the indigenous population. Devastation, fire, spoiling of agriculture is perhaps the only means of solidly establishing our domination." The French liberal political philosopher Alexis de Tocqueville praised this policy almost as enthusiastically as he praised democracy in America. An empire in Algeria was needed, he thought, for to abandon it "would be, in the world's eyes, a declaration of French decline."

As for the means to be used in this war de Tocqueville bemoaned that some "dislike the burning of harvests, the emptying of silos and the seizing of unarmed men, women and children. In my opinion they are necessary evils to which everybody wanting to make war with the Arabs must submit."[3]

De Tocqueville praised the methods suggested by Bugeaud; war in Africa, he wrote, endorsing the brutal methods being followed, "is a science. Everyone is familiar with its rules and everyone can apply those rules with almost complete certainty of success. One of the greatest services that Field Marshall Bugeaud has rendered his country is to have spread, perfected and made everyone aware of this new science."[4]

So with the approval of their most eminent liberal political philosopher, their government in Paris and their high command, the French armed forces in Algeria set about cleansing, driving back or annihilating the Arab population of the country with a brutality that was not seen again till Nazi Germany after 1933. Here we can give only a few examples of the ways in which the French tried to translate their vision of empire into reality.

## The *Toute-presence* Colony

In April 1832, in order to clear the areas around the capital, the French commander de Rovigo ordered an army detachment to the El Oufia tribal settlement near Algiers. The tribe was unarmed. The French soldiers killed 12,000 men, women and children, while in subsequent days the markets had for sale, heads on spikes, bracelets still attached to severed hands and earrings with pieces of flesh clinging to them. Three years later, Abdel Kader having established himself as Amir, the French forces attacked his capital at Mascara, a town of 10,000 people. All were killed, except 1,000 Jews, and the town burned to the ground. In Constantine, which was attacked in 1837, several of the inhabitants escaped to the nearby mountains and hid in caves. They were smoked to death by the lighting of fires in the entrances; only ten survived. When there was protest in France at this brutality, the Army learnt its lesson; two months later there was another atrocity, the burning of another city; the garrison commander Saint Arnaud "suffocated fifteen hundred Moslems in another cave, carefully left no survivors to tell the story, and in a confidential message reported to Bugeaud: 'No one went into the cave; not a soul ... but myself'", and the government agreed that it was not important to give too many details to the press about such matters.[5] Reporters were banned and the officers told to ensure that in all future encounters, as a matter of standard practice, there were no survivors.

It happened again and again through the 1830s and 1840s. A town was attacked; the women and children sought shelter in caves in the surrounding mountains; they were asphyxiated by smoke from fires lit at the entrance (or sometimes immured, the entrances sealed) as did a certain Colonel Pelissier in June 1845 to over 700 members of the Ouled Riah tribe; guards were left there to ensure there were no survivors. Entire tribes, entire villages, were massacred, razed: the Zatcha tribe; the Ben Saada; the Ouled Sidi Sheikh tribe from the Oran region; the Zouagla from Constantine; the Amouche village, burnt down in 1842; the Ben Salem village in 1844; the Bel Kassem ou Kassi, the same year. And, over the decades, the same instructions were repeated. A Colonel Montagnac writes in *Letter of a Soldier*, 1885, "A severed head produces a terror stronger than the death of fifty people ... this is the way one should wage war against Arabs. Kill all males who are more than fifteen years old ... annihilate anything that does not crawl at our feet like dogs."

The policy was, to some extent, effective, though it fell short of its main aim of annihilating the entire native population; the Algerian resistance was too strong for that. The main towns were depopulated except those needed for menial work. By 1838 the population of Oran came down from 60,000 to 10,000; other towns were smaller and some were completely depopulated. The total population of Algeria, 3 million in 1830, was down to just over 2 million by 1856. Given a modest rate of growth of one per cent a year this means a total of one and half million Algerians had been annihilated. In those years the French settler population had reached 150,000. The settlers were given land generously. In 1833 all religious or waqf land had been confiscated; in 1845 all village land held in common, community land was taken over. The authorities "offered French settlers free transportation, land, seed, and livestock" and their produce was allowed duty free entry into France.[6]

In terms of the French colonial narrative, 1830 was the starting point of an era in history. Before colonisation Algeria had been an empty space devoid of civilisation "... the French settlers transformed this ... made the desert bloom ... they, and not the local population, had a right to own the land."

In opposition to the French was the Algerian nation. There has been a good deal of debate about whether Algeria was a nation; this is echoed in almost every part of the European empires. The French were sure they were not and remained sure of this till they lost the war and had to leave. Even French communists were quite clear in their view that it was not a nation. In a speech of March 1939 Maurice Thorez, general secretary of the French Communist Party, stated the official policy that Algeria was a nation in formation; "Algeria was not yet a fully fledged nation, but a melting pot of some twenty races which were in the process of creating a nation ... the Algerian Communist Party was ... the only party which was uniting all the various races into one political organisation". His conclusion was that France under the Third Republic was moulding the Algerian nation and it would, therefore, be "in the best interests of Algeria to remain under the protective wing of the Third Republic".[7]

Another and an even better starting point for getting into this debate would be the Algerian nationalist leader Ferhat Abbas's famous 1936 declaration, which has already been quoted in chapter 4: "Had I discovered the Algerian nation, I would be a nationalist and I would not blush as if I had committed a crime. ... However, I will not die for the Algerian nation because it does not exist. I have not found it. I have examined History, I have questioned the living and the dead ...".[8]

This line of argument, which is entirely in accordance with the story of modernity, assumes that a nation is an entity fixed for all time, or at most that it evolves according to some fixed rules, which are generally to be discovered only by the European ruler. When Eric Hobsbawm writes about proto-nationalism based on "feelings of collective belonging which already existed and which could operate, as it were, potentially on the macro-political scale,"[9] he is assuming the same thing; he goes on to examine whether language, or ethnicity or religion and culture or belonging to a lasting political entity are sufficient to generate such feelings and finds, treating each of them in a static manner, that none of them are.

## Algerian Nationalism: Resources

But we need to give up the assumption about fixed entity or fixed evolutionary path for nationhood, and look for the many resources which can be used to ensure and strengthen even disparate people's loyalty to the nation.

The inhabitants of the Atlas Mountains, that run east to west and are located just south of the Algerian coastal plain, have contributed a great deal to those resources. The people of the mountain, as Fernand Braudel and others have pointed out, have certain common characteristics, no matter which part of the world the mountains are located. In the first place they are refugees. "For the mountains are a refuge from soldiers and pirates." In the case of Algeria, it was the Berbers, the oldest inhabitants of the country, who sought refuge in the mountains of Kabyle and the Aures from the depredations of Carthage and Rome, but who also resisted those empires. Secondly, they are inured to a life of hardship, to the harsh climatic conditions and to the hard work of eking out a living from rocky and infertile land. And so, thirdly, they are mobile. Often they are herdsmen moving from one pasture to another, nomads who spend the summer along the mountainous stretch and the winter in the lower altitudes of the coastal belt. There were at least five different categories of Algerian nomads, including the camel breeding Saharan nomads; others who summered up in the mountains; cattle breeding nomads; and those who were semi-sedentary. And they made raids into the coastal plain for booty.

Living in hamlets rather than the village communities preferred by the plainsmen, the people of the mountain have everywhere developed, over the centuries, an intense sense of independence, of the supreme importance of personal liberty, the rejection of any form of government control. They have been the most important home of rebellion against established authority. Violence comes easily to them; and through the histories of the mountain regions of the world violence and cruelty abound, and the vendetta is the most common form of justice.

But also, and as a consequence, their social structures are egalitarian; there are no hierarchies, no caste, class or social layers; groupings are based on family and tribe; no poor man will bow to a rich one. So also they do not accept religion without an admixture of their own tradition, meaning that "magic practices and superstition abounded in daily life ... sorcerers, witchcraft, primitive magic, and black masses were the flowerings of an ancient cultural consciousness" which found refuge in the mountains.[10]

In Algeria the people of the mountain, the Berbers, were the first to bring centralised rule. A Berber King, Massinissa, brought the various tribes of the country under his rule, in what was then called Numidia, from 201 BC to 148 BC, with his capital in Cirta, today's Constantine. His aim was to build a strong, prosperous and unified state, forcing the turbulent tribesmen of the time to settle as farmers. He fought against Carthage, which attempted to subjugate his Kingdom, and thereby earned the gratitude of Rome. His grandson Jugurtha, however, incurred the anger of Rome and fought the Roman armies heroically for eight years (112-104 BC). In twentieth century Algeria his memory has been resurrected as a symbol of struggle against foreign domination, a resource for nationalism. And during the war of independence a nationalist author, Kateb Yacine, wrote a novel, *Nedjma*, in which he "invoked Jugurtha as one of the ancestors of the Algerian nation, incarnating the spirit of resistance at the heart of Algerian history."[11]

Then there is St Augustine in the fifth century, son of a Berber mother, who has also been claimed not only as one of the founders of the Algerian nation, but to underline how deep are the roots of Christianity there and how firm the foundations of a multi-religious society.

## The Creation of Nationalism: to be Arab and Muslim

The most potent resource for nationalism was to be an Arab and to be, at the same time, part of the Muslim Umma. During the Umayyad Caliphate, the reign of Muawiyah, 660-680, his general Uqbah ibn-Nafi brought Egypt under his rule and then by 670 continued westward through all the lands of North Africa "until the waves of the Atlantic stopped his horse."[12] His tomb near Biskra has become a national shrine. To be Arab is to have in some measure a share in one of the greatest empires ever seen, which once extended from the shores of the Atlantic to the approaches to China, one which was certainly larger than that of Rome at its zenith. It is to share in a language and culture that are among the richest in history, unrivalled advances in science that laid the foundations of the revolution in science and technology that created our contemporary world. Islam was the dominant religion of the Arab nation, but Christians and others were included. "When the great Crusades came, Muslims and Christians alike rose up in all parts of the Arab world to fight and defend one idea – that of Arab nationalism ... the Christian Arabs were not deceived by the pretensions of the Crusades."[13]

As for being Muslim, the largest number of Muslims worldwide is non-Arab, but by virtue of having founded the faith, of spreading it from one end to the other of the Afro-Asian landmass, of owning the language in which the only authentic text of the Koran is written, the Arabs have claimed, with some justice, a special place in it.

In Algeria, as elsewhere in the Muslim world, there was no conflict between promoting the idea of Muslims as a nation and that nationalism which arose within the boundaries of the political entities established by the colonial powers. Even before Westphalia nationalist states had been established in conjunction with Islam, such as by the Safavis in Iran in 1500. Centuries thereafter, Shah Waliyullah (1703-1762) in Delhi wanted a purified Islam as the basis for the restoration of a state structure on the Moghul pattern, a nationalism focused on a part of the Muslim world. And the great reformer Jamaluddin Afghani could inspire both local or restricted nationalism and pan-Islamic sentiments. In fact nationalists looked to the purification of Islam and to a wider Umma as a force to strengthen the nationalism advocated within their own countries, which, of course, had elements other than Islam also. It has been pointed out, in regard to nationalism in the Muslim world, that each nationalism is distinctive, "with its own geographic, historical, economic and other particularities, individual characteristics that it is the nature of nationalism to stress."[14]

The nationalism of Indonesia and that of Egypt, for instance, will be quite different from each other, but each will have its component of Islam, and each will have a different kind of that component. That Islam which fits into Turkish nationalism is different to that which fits into Iranian nationalism.

Two Berber dynasties, the Almoravids and Almohads, ruled North Africa, including Algeria, from 1054-1212. The Almoravids originated from a brotherhood established in a fortified monastery (or ribat, hence their early name, Murbits ) in Senegal. They started as warrior monks and spread over an empire extending from Spain to the Senegal and Mali in the South, and halfway across Algeria to the East. Yusuf ibn-Tashfin (1061-1106), one of the founders, laid the foundations for the city of Marrakesh, which became their capital. So Morocco uses this period more than the Algerians as a resource for nationalist aspirations. Yusuf, after some correspondence with the Abbasid Caliph in Baghdad, assumed the title Amir ul Muslimin (Commander of the Muslims) while acknowledging the Caliph as Amir ul Muminin (Commander of the Faithful), another example of reconciling local with nationalist aspirations. The Almohads (from al-Muwahiddin, or Unitarians) emphasised the restoration of the original purity of Islam and "carried fire and sword throughout Morocco and adjacent lands"[15] in a holy war that extended their empire from Spain to all of North Africa including Libya, again with Marrakesh as the capital. The Islamisation and Arabisation of North Africa was completed by the Almohads; many of the scattered tribes who had so far resisted it were brought into the fold. And this was a purer, more orthodox version of Islam than the region had so far seen.

In the next phase, starting 1518, Khairuddin Barbarossa and his brother, having conquered Egypt, and brought it under Ottoman rule, spread westwards across the coastal plains of North Africa. The system instituted for North Africa by the Ottoman Empire was to place a Pasha or Dey at the head of the local administration. Each Dey was supported by a corps of Janissaries (from Yenicheri, Turkish for new troops) and tried to secure the loyalty of as many tribes as possible. But it was for privateering that the Algerian coastal towns, of the Barbary coast, came to be known best. Algiers itself was the headquarters; Fernand Braudel calls the years 1560 to 1570 the first brilliant age of Algiers; the years 1580 to 1620 are called its second brilliant age, in which command of the sea was the road to prosperity, "as spectacular as the first and certainly more far-reaching... In Algiers, all life depended, needless to say, on the volume and success of pirate shipping, down to the pittance of the poorest muleteer in the city."[16]

When the French arrived in 1830 it was the Ottoman appointed Dey and his janissaries who offered the first, somewhat ineffective, resistance.

## The Creation of Nationalism: Abdel Kader

The real resistance to the French empire came from Abdel Kader, later known as the Amir of Mascara, whose towering achievement put him among the greatest nationalists to oppose the European imperial endeavour.

He did not have a state or an army when the French landed, and started the task of national reconstruction two and a half years later. And then he built, against all the efforts of the French at imperial expansion, a state that included two-thirds of Algeria, an efficient administration and a pugnacious army that kept the French confined for fifteen years to three small coastal enclaves. His state was a source of unity among the diverse Algerian tribes and an inspiration to those who, in later decades, resisted the French. And he did this on his own; the Ottomans could have helped him, after all it was a piece of their empire that the French invasion had taken over, but they didn't. When he asked for help they replied that they appreciated he was resisting the French, could not give any help and would he please in future communicate only in cipher. He made overtures to the British, who were France's imperial rivals, by offering them an Algerian port for exclusive use; and to the Americans, who were just then in the middle of a diplomatic dispute with the French over claims going back to the Napoleonic wars, possession of the port. Neither was interested. As always, in the face of a serious threat, the colonial powers cooperated.

Before he started his resistance movement Abdul Kader had been taken by his father on pilgrimage to Mecca and Medina; and then to Baghdad, to the tomb of his namesake Abdel Kader al-Jalili (1077-1166) founder of the Qadirite fraternity, the first Islamic fraternity, which, "one of the most tolerant and charitable, now claims followers throughout the whole Muslim world."[17] It is said that these pilgrimages were a source of inspiration to him throughout his life, although he was above all a political and military, not a religious leader.

On 22 November 1832 a large gathering of tribal and religious chiefs at Mascara, his hometown, pledged allegiance to him and he was proclaimed Amir ul Muminin. With this authority he proceeded to gather the forces and build the state that was to resist the French imperial effort. The Emir of Mascara, later to be known in fuller form as the Emir Abdel Kader El Jezairi (or Emir of Algeria), was also well armed; he was to set up the facilities to manufacture his own rifles and cannon. In the interior of the country he had built a nation by the age of 25, with a well-run administration, banks, schools, hospitals. And he decided to expel the invaders. He started by bringing the different rulers of Western Algeria together under his flag.

Right from the outset he inflicted a series of defeats on the French which forced them to reconsider their expansion plans. At the end of June 1835 his forces defeated the French at Macta, a mountain pass located just east of Arzew in western Algeria. The battle went into French history as 'the disaster of Macta', "one of the worst military defeats sustained by the French during their occupation of Algeria." He did the same at Constantine a year later. His was a form of guerilla war; the French found it difficult to cope with this.

There was one engagement after another. In April 1836 he attacked a French camp at the mouth of the Tafna river, north of Tlemcen, and scattered their forces. After a series of such engagements, all small scale but disastrous for the invaders, the French Minister of War wrote on 22 May 1837 of the "desperate and ruinous war" which "would impose sacrifices out of all proportion to the advantages that success could procure..."[18] The French wanted only, he continued, a maritime establishment, the security of her trade and the growth of influence in the littoral. Eight days later they concluded with Abdel Kader the Treaty of Tafna; in this the French recognised his rule over two-thirds of Algeria, while he accepted French sovereignty over the two coastal enclaves held by them, one around Oran and the second around Algiers. The French agreed to sell guns and gunpowder to him, while he agreed to give wheat, barley and 5,000 head of cattle to them.

But French imperial ambitions continued to expand, and to attain them they built up the strength of their forces on the ground. By 1840 they had over 58,000; by 1846 they had 106,000, a third of the entire French army, and were continuing to build up their strength as fast as they could, as against Abdel Kader's 80,000, most of whom were irregulars.

In the initial years after the Treaty of Tafna, and as the fighting resumed, he concentrated on forcing the French onto the defensive in their coastal enclaves, even as they built up their strength, and on attacking their forward camps with large contingents of troops. As the French build-up continued and they were able to defend such outposts, he began avoiding frontal clashes, switching to cutting their lines of communication, harassing the flanks of mobile columns, concentrating on inflicting the maximum of casualties rather than on winning set piece engagements, although on occasion, as at Sidi Ibrahim in September 1845 against a force commanded by a Colonel de Montagnac, he could still emerge victorious from such a battle, having there killed 300 and taken 100 prisoner.

But these were well trained troops, equipped for battlefield engagements and as they went into the offensive, Abdel Kader was obliged to resort once again to guerilla war.

It was not until 1847, when close to 200,000 French troops were needed to do so, that Abdel Kader was increasingly forced into the defensive; the tribes which had allied with him went over to the enemy and on 21 December 1847 he himself surrendered to them.[19]

Abdel Kader's state was a "kind of federal government based on tribal equality, with regular troops, assisted by locally enrolled militiamen."[20] It was initially divided into eight provinces; after the Treaty of Tafna, in which he gained additional territory, four more were added. Each province was divided into districts, which in turn were divided into qabilas or tribal zones. One assessment by a Dr. Warnier, who was in the French consulate in Mascara, 1837-39 suggests a "league of provinces, with their distinctive chiefs, governments, and resources, recognising the supremacy of the central government's chief in order to fight the common enemy." But the tribes, as always, retained a good deal of independence and their commitment to the cause contributed much to his success, so in the early years, as one military success followed another, tribe after tribe rallied to his leadership. Over the years many of them were to leave his banner, then rejoin it as his political and military fortunes fell and rose. And his repeated call to the Algerian people was to unite "for only unity means power, division produces weakness. Let us, therefore, efface all the racial differences among the true Muslims", as he urged in a letter to Qaid Ibrahim.

In later years Abdel Kader was to be an inspiration not only for the Algerian resistance to the French, but also for movements everywhere that fought against European imperial expansion. The Algerian nationalist writer Katib Yacine wrote a biography published in 1953, one stimulator for the fight for independence that began in 1954 and ended in victory. In the Algerian military manual written in 1957 he is described as a "legendary hero ... among the greatest figures of our history ... the incarnation of pure patriotism, but also the authentic leader, the builder, the thinker, the statesman."[21] And when his remains were brought from Syria to Algeria in 1967 this was clearly a state occasion of enormous importance.

Even during the time of Abdel Kader others, and in increasing numbers, had emerged to fight the French all over Algeria. Ahmed Bey ruled the Constantine province even as Abdel Kader was expanding the area under his control. French troops under General Clauzel attacked Constantine in 1836 and were "thoroughly defeated ... the supply system broke down and troops were constantly harassed by guerillas."[22] Such a one was also Bu Maza who emerged east of Oran and led a group of Berber troops into Orleansville. This was the occasion for the French, once they had recaptured Orleansville, to hunt the Berbers, and when Colonel Pelissier, leading the French forces, in the 1845 incident mentioned above, lit fires at the entrance of caves in Dahra and smoked to death over 700 members of the Ouled Riah tribe, mainly women and children.

A few more examples will suffice to illustrate that during the nineteenth century Algeria was never fully under French control. As the French moved into the Kabyle mountains in 1846 Lalla Fatma N'Soumer led the resistance. At the battle of Oued Sebaou, 1854, in the Northern Djurdjura region she was part of the forces of Bou Baghla as Mohamed El Amdjed Ibn Abdelmalik was called; she took control of the battle and led her forces to a decisive victory that was celebrated throughout the Kabyle mountain region. Further battles during the course of that year, including at Icherridene and Tachkent, were also won by her. It took the French three years and the dispatch of considerable reinforcements finally to defeat her.

Then there were the uprisings, at Oued el Kabir in the Aures mountains in 1858-1859; a year later in Beleznaa in the east, and then in Ben Suassar near Oran.

Another was Sheikh Mohamed El Mokrani, who initiated the

Great Kabyle uprising of 1871, along with his brother, Boumezrag, who also went into the history books. They were fighting under the banner of Sheikh Mahieddine, the son of Abdel Kader. The uprising spread to the whole of Constantine province, to the South, into the desert region of Ouled Sidi Sheikh, as far west as Oran, as "eight hundred thousand Muslims answered his call."[23] It was a nation-wide uprising which, though Mokrani was killed in May 1871, continued for another year. Then in 1881 Sheikh Bou Amma led an uprising from Saida south of Oran, which saw another one in 1914 by the Beni Chougrane, several more in the Aures, and one by the Touaregs led by Si Mohamed El Abed in the Hoggar region.

## Mainstream Nationalism

This brings us to the nationalist political parties, the so-called mainstream leadership, which emerged in stages. Conceptually it is convenient to look at the three parts of it as different organs of the body called nationalism.

You will have guessed that this excludes the Communists. The French Communist Party had established a branch in Algeria in the 1920s and this was converted in 1936 into the Algerian Communist Party (PCA) which was totally subservient to Moscow. Its effort in Algeria was to undermine by infiltration and taking over its apparatus wherever possible, one of the parts of the nationalist movement, the Star of North Africa (ENA) which was leftist in its economic policy and committed to full independence. The French Communist Party did not believe Algeria was a nation, as indicated above; the party believed it should remain part of France. Further the PCA had a largely French Algerian membership; when the revolutionary war began in November 1954 it issued a communiqué condemning it as adventurism; during the war of independence, and whenever there were clashes between the French and the Algerian nationalists, which was often, they openly sided with the French.

The first of these nationalist organs was assimilationist, wanting equal rights for the Algerians in an Algeria that would remain French. The Young Algerians formed in 1908, took up the issue when the French introduced conscription in February 1912. They were from a liberal elite of well-to-do, well-educated Algerians and they sent a letter to French Prime Minister Georges Clemenceau saying they opposed conscription for Algerians; but if they were granted the full rights of French citizenship this opposition would be dropped. Abdel Kader's grandson, Khaled Ibn Hashim, known as Emir Khaled, who had graduated from the French military academy at St. Cyr and been a captain in the French army, was one of the Young Algerians and demanded an end of discrimination against Algerians in the armed forces selection and promotion systems. In 1919 he wrote to US President Woodrow Wilson suggesting the representation of Algeria at the Versailles Conference and also wanted the Algerian question to be placed before the League of Nations.

Some reforms followed these demands, including an expansion of the Algerian voters' list and of the list of public offices which they could hold. Some of the Young Algerians took advantage of these reforms. They and others also formed a new organisation in 1926, the Federation of Elected Natives. This asked for the assimilation of those who had made social, economic and educational headway, meaning the grant of full citizenship rights without jeopardising their Muslim identity, equal pay for equal work, the abolition of restrictions on their travel between Algeria and France. The eventual aim was the integration of Algeria as a full province of France, hardly a nationalist aim, but the mainstream leadership has many purposes to serve.

One of the best known of this group was Ferhat Abbas, "the proponent of assimilation par excellence", who once reportedly told a French communist that "the greatest danger facing those of us who want to collaborate with the French people is the revolt of the peasants, who are ready to take up arms."[24] His personal life reflects his political; his father wanted all his children to be raised as Europeans and so he was raised as one; he was educated in a French lycee, did his military service, read about Islam not in Arabic but in French translation, divorced an Algerian wife whom he had married early and married a French woman, became a leading member of urban society (in Setif) and in 1934 was elected Municipal Councillor there. He had by then fully defined his views; he wanted emancipation on the basis that Algeria's future lay firmly with France. It was people like Ferhat Abbas that he had in mind, when the French Governor-General Maurice Violette said in the National Assembly about the Muslims of Algeria, "Gentlemen, these men have no political country of their own. They do not even claim their religious country. They crave to be admitted to your country."[25]

But by 1943 Abbas moved to advocating independence more than assimilation. In February that year he and fifty-five nationalist leaders presented the French authorities with a *Manifeste du Peuple Algerien* demanding self-determination, a separate Algerian constitution guaranteeing liberty and the equality of all the inhabitants of Algeria as also the recognition of Arabic as an official language on par with French. From there it was only a short step to demanding complete independence.

The second organ of nationalism was the movement for religious revival under the leadership of Sheikh Abdul Hamid Ben Badis. He had his religious education in Tunisia and Egypt and was recognised for his deep learning. In 1931 he brought a number of Ulema together to form the Association of Algerian Muslim Ulema (AUMA). When Ferhat Abbas declared in 1936 that the Algerian nation did not exist, Ben Badis replied in the well-known formulation, "Islam is my religion, Arabic is my language and Algeria is my country ... this Algeria is not France ... it does not want to become part of France. It could not become part of France if it wanted to ... it is far removed from France and does not want to integrate."[26] A Ben Badis institute in Constantine, a network of madrasas throughout Algeria, a paper, Al Shihab and the exemplary though puritanical conduct by him and of those who were close to him soon attracted tens of thousands of followers; Islamic fervour in post-independence Algeria is to a great extent due to his influence.

The third and most important organ, the heart of the nationalist movement, began to be formed when Ahmed Messali Hadj joined the ENA; this was an association of Algerian workers in Paris, started in 1926; as mentioned above it was generally leftist. In 1927 he became its President. On 10 February 1927, at the 'Congress of Eastern Peoples' held in Brussels under the aegis of the Third International, he demanded total independence for Algeria from France, the first time this demand had been made. From this it has been asserted that it was the radical nationalism of Algerian migrant workers in France that drove the call for independence; and that the call for independence cited above became a sort of historical founding event and was the first enunciation of modern Algerian nationalism, which is in line with modernity in suggesting that an external influence was at work. At the end of this chapter there are other arguments of modernity on this subject.

The ENA programme also demanded freedom of the press, the creation of a separate Algerian National Assembly and the withdrawal of all French forces from Algeria. So it was banned in 1929, but continued to work underground, especially among Algerian migrant workers in France. Messali Hadj returned to Algeria and in 1937 founded the Algerian People's Party (PPA). This too was banned in 1939 and Messali Hadj put into detention. But the PPA continued its work underground, creating political cells in the urban areas and training paramilitary groups in the Kabyle and Constantine regions.

It was in March 1944 that the two organs, one led by Ferhat Abbas and the liberals, the other by Messali Hadj, came together in the Association of Friends of the Manifesto and Liberty (AML). This demanded independence, but as a Republic federated with an anti-colonialist France. It quickly gathered a mass following and its newspaper *Egalite* had a readership of half a million within months. When the AML was banned in 1945 Messali Hadj formed the Movement for the Triumph of Democratic Liberties (MTLD) in 1946 and this took an even more radical stance, opposed federation, any formal links with France and demanded total independence based on separation. Within it some of the younger members led by Hocine Ait Ahmed and after him Ahmed Ben Bella created a special organisation in 1947 with the specific purpose of conducting military operations, the OS or Secret Organisation.

This was in the wake of one of the crucial inputs to the freedom struggle, the 1945 massacre at Setif.

On 1 May 1945, Labour Day, Algerian nationalists resolved to organise demonstrations across the country demanding independence. There was some violence, including in Algiers and Oran, but it was limited. Then came 8 May, VE Day and they decided to organise even larger demonstrations; the authorities told them they could do so, but only in Setif and only if no Algerian national flags or nationalist banners were displayed. These conditions were ignored, the marchers shouted nationalist slogans and a clash with the police ensued, which became the signal for a wider national uprising. This was immediately condemned by the Algerian Communist Party as the work of Nazi agents, but the French official response was, as it always had been, to launch an indiscriminate massacre of Algerians which, of course, the members of the Communist Party joined.

Martial law was declared; every Muslim had to wear an armband; those without were shot without warning. It was the policy of General Thomas Robert Bugeaud all over again. Foreign Legion units roamed the countryside killing and pillaging. Three naval frigates shelled the coastal villages while bombers and fighter planes attacked the villages further inland from the air. The French set up vigilante groups that 'took out' whole villages, on the nineteenth-century pattern, leaving no one alive. Mass graves were opened for the dead, or the bodies burned in lime kilns. The general massacre continued week after week and the final death toll of Algerians, without doubt a gross underestimate, was 45,000.

Setif and the massacres elsewhere were not, as it has sometimes been described, the beginning of the war of independence; they were not the end of the negotiation phase; all this was not "a line in the sand, a point of no return."[27] All the above descriptions belong to the modernity story. As far as the traditional story is concerned, it was just one incident, more important than many others, more brutal than some but less brutal than others, in a struggle to evict the French which the Algerians had begun in 1830 and never given up. It was more important because some Algerians, who had still toyed with assimilationist ideas, now became convinced that full independence was the only course open; because they and others who thought negotiation might provide a way towards independence, came to believe that the only possible end of French rule was a violent one; and because the view spread that the sooner this happened the better. So from now on the story of Algerian independence, which was always about the violent expulsion of the French, was better focused on that clear aim.

## Nationalism: The War Begins

After its launch in 1947 the OS gradually built up its military and political cadres. The size of its army reached 500 men who were given intensive training; they even launched some attacks on French interests. But by 1950 French intelligence had tracked them down. Ben Bella himself was arrested; several caches of arms and explosives were unearthed and the OS was, in effect, no more, though several of its leaders, including Ben Bella, escaped to Cairo.

The next step had to be taken with greater secrecy and, therefore, on a smaller scale; training hundreds of militants in advance of any action had only added to the risk of exposure; what was now needed was a handful of leaders who would train the cadres as the actions got going; and the actions themselves would lead to a flood of applicants so there would be no shortage. Through most of 1954 a small group of young leaders led by nine men who were later to be known as the Club des Neuf met in Berne, Switzerland, to plan the struggle. Initially the larger group was called the Revolutionary Council for Unity and Action (CRUA); this was later, as soon as the struggle was actually launched, changed to National Liberation Front (FLN). The struggle itself was, of course, inspired by the guerilla tactics of Abdel Kader who, the leaders of the struggle believed, was the founder of modern Algeria

Algeria was divided into six zones, commanders selected for each and they were given full powers to decide on organisation, who to recruit, how to train them and what actions to launch. The struggle was to start on 1 November 1954. On that day some seventy attacks were launched throughout the country, many of them in the Aures region. In Batna, in the northern Aures, two French soldiers were killed; east of that in Kenchela, another two were killed. There were incidents of bomb throwing, of arson, attacks on police stations. They were all small scale; seven Frenchmen were killed in all, a dozen wounded; but they were countrywide; and the organisation behind them remained secret. The French thought at first this was done by bands of Tunisian nationalists from across the eastern border; the military command in Algiers thought it was a tribal revolt, of which they had seen so many over the years; the Mayor of Algiers toured the Aures region and concluded this was a general insurrection. Some 200 supporters of Messali Hadj who knew nothing of the FLN or of the actions were arrested. Army columns rushed to the Aures; an airlift of paratroops from France began; helicopters patrolled the skies. No one who had had anything to do with the actions was caught.

But a tract was distributed the same day telling its readers that the FLN had launched a national struggle aimed at national independence through the 'restoration of the Algerian state, sovereign, democratic, and social, within the principles of Islam'.

That was the beginning. Then came the spread of the struggle and, as the French realised what was happening, a repression of such savage brutality as had, in fact, only recently been seen in Nazi Germany. It was Setif multiplied many times over. Muslims were shot at random; the local French settlers, the so-called *pieds noirs*, formed vigilante groups which went from house to house, dragging women and children out, butchering them without quarter. "Thus Algeria descended into an inferno of violence, an endless cycle of repression and revenge that was eventually to destroy the Fourth Republic."[28]

By early 1956 it had become clear to all but a few Algerians that the FLN would get them independence. Ferhat Abbas, for instance, had, after 1 November 1954, condemned the insurgents publicly; then he blamed the French for not letting Algerians manage their own affairs; by April 1956 he had openly gone over to the FLN. So did the Association of Algerian Ulema, as did individual members of the Communist Party, since FLN policy throughout was that they would have to give up their party allegiance first. "The FLN's predominance was almost total,"[29] specially "with the bulk of the Muslim people on its side, with more arms coming from Egypt, with more recruits coming forward and a new enthusiasm for the insurrection sweeping through the country."[30]

In the field the FLN' military wing, the National Liberation Army (ALN), launched ambushes, attacks on post offices and police stations, blew up railway lines. There was debate about the exact tactical line that should be followed. Zone I, the Aures Mountains led by Ben Boulaid, was one of the most active; he was able to lead attacks on police posts, army patrols and on French farms. Zone III, under Belkacem Krim, was also active; French farmers from both zones began leaving their farms and moving into the cities. But other zones were less active.

Despite this the struggle was gathering strength as a newly appointed French Governor-General, Jacques Soustelle, saw on arrival in January 1955; he saw how little the French intelligence knew about the FLN; how little they could do against it. Repression, widespread and general seemed to be the answer.

On 1 April 1955 the French National Assembly passed the first of the Algerian state of emergency bills, which were then extended periodically throughout the independence struggle. The bill provided for control of the press and radio, arrest on suspicion, restriction of movement and special powers to the administration. Special powers, suspending the citizen's recourse to law, were acquired. With time French army officers were placed in administrative posts so that Algeria came, in effect, to be under martial rule; since special military cells were set up to try all offences, regardless of their nature, this was also martial law. And that was the time French military strength was built up rapidly. Units were diverted from Germany and French West Africa. By 1956 the number of French forces in Algeria had been increased to half a million, ten times as large as the most generous figure for the total ALN strength and almost the same number that the US required in Vietnam ten years later. Reservists were called up; conscripts were deployed. Military service was extended in time. This was total war.

As the year 1955 advanced and it became clear that none of this was enough, Philippeville, August 1955 provided an early sign of what more was to come. In response to ALN attacks the military and French civilians launched a campaign of indiscriminate killing. As an officer of the 18$^{th}$ parachute regiment was quoted saying, when they came to a group of Algerians, "we opened fire into the thick of them, at random. Then as we moved on and found more bodies, our company commanders finally gave us the order to shoot down every Arab we met. You should have seen the result ... at midday, fresh orders: take prisoners. That complicated everything. It was easy when it was merely a matter of killing ..."[31]

By mid-1956 it was time for the FLN to take stock. A lot had been achieved. The struggle had grown and spread; the people were with it and it was the only one they supported, despite the continued existence of others like Messali Hadj's Algerian National Front (MNA). The ALN now controlled large parts of the Aures and Nementcha mountain regions, as the Djurdjura and Constantine countryside. In those mountain villages FLN cadres no longer bothered to hide; they drilled and trained openly, even playing football with the villagers. It was well on the way to becoming a mass movement, if only it could show equal confidence in the cities.

It had consistently received moral and material support from President Nasser of Egypt and from the Arab League; it had represented Algeria at the Conference of Afro-Asian nations Heads of Government convened at Bandung, Indonesia, in April/May 1955 (not as observers but as members of the Iraqi delegation). They were able there to lobby the various delegations for wider international support. In New York, later that year African and Asian delegations to the UN General Assembly proposed a resolution stressing the need for self-determination and an end to colonial rule and negotiations between the French government and the 'true representatives of the Algerian people'. The item became an annual feature on the agenda of the UNGA.

The two great powers were, expectedly, in general opposed to the FLN, while on specifics keeping their bets open. For the Soviet Union the relationship with France, the possibility of being able to weaken its links with NATO, was incentive enough to be critical, especially as it quickly became clear that this was a national, not an ideological struggle. There was also the reality mentioned above, that the members of the Algerian Communist Party were largely French settlers or *pieds noirs*; they were unambiguous in their support for the latter. The FLN, in turn, were suspicious of the Communists; some of the latter wanted to join up and were allowed to do so as Maquis Rouge squads, who were then systematically sent into the front line of fire fights against the French forces so that few survived. However, towards the end of the struggle, as it became increasingly clear that the FLN would win, the Soviet leaders became more friendly, and Nikita Krushchev even met Belkacem Krim during the 1960 session of the UNGA. The US, anxious to win over the support of the Arabs, as was apparent during the 1956 Suez war and after, was less supportive of France. One Senator John F. Kennedy even made a lengthy intervention in July 1957 in the Senate calling on the Republican administration to work for a solution that would recognise Algeria's independent personality, and thereafter the US abstained on the UNGA resolutions.

Taking stock was done at the FLN's Soummam (in Kabyle) conference of August 1956. As many as 250 delegates from all over Algeria attended; some zones were under represented due to the secrecy about the venue; the external delegation based in Cairo was unable to attend at all. But the decisions taken there guided the remainder of the struggle.

Among other things it was decided that the political leadership would supervise military matters; that the internal leadership would take precedence over the external; and that there would be collective leadership through frequent meetings of the Committee of Coordination and Execution, a five-member executive body which would be all powerful, ensure liaison among different zones, decide on promotions and appointments of officers. It was also decided to move the focus from actions concentrated in the rural areas to those in the towns. And among the towns Algiers was to be the focus.

## The Battle of Algiers

Through the latter half of 1956 there were daily actions mounted in Algiers, bombings in cafes, in the streets, in the sports stadium, in a dance hall. In December 1956 alone there were 120 actions, so that "the FLN rebellion had emerged, at the end of 1956, immeasurably stronger than at the beginning of the year."[32]

The Casbah in Algiers was the operating centre for most of the FLN cadres involved. And now came another great wave of repression. In January 1957 all police and security responsibilities were handed over to the army. They were given carte blanche; there was to be no enquiry, no questioning of any actions taken by them. General Jacques Massu's 10th Paratroop division moved into Algiers by the end of January and into the Casbah on 27 January. The FLN had called a strike and all the shops were shuttered. French armoured cars and tanks arrived, attached hawsers to the shutters and dragged them off their moorings; in one case a shell was fired into the shop to get it open; as looting began the soldiers joined in. In some places loudspeakers announced that all owners should return to their shops; or they were hunted down in their places of residence and dragged out; resisters were shot.

That was the beginning. In succeeding weeks paratroop groups went through the narrow alleys, searching houses, taking a random selection of the residents out for questioning which invariably involved extensive torture. Half the 80,000 residents of the Casbah, men, women and children, were so 'questioned'. Thousands of others were reported killed trying to escape, the usual euphemism for those, including women and children, caught on suspicion and shot in the back of the head. Reports appeared in the French press, despite the censorship. For months French public opinion refused to believe them, until leftists among them started reporting how they had also been tortured, and many of them disappeared.

The pressure on the FLN leadership was intense and most of them left for Tunisia. In the Casbah the leadership was taken up by Yacef Saadi, who, as the battle for the Casbah progressed, surrendered to the French; later (1965) he was to make an epic film, *The Battle of Algiers*,[33] based on the actual story, in which he played himself with the *nom de guerre* Jaffar. He was succeeded by Ali Amar, better known as Ali la Pointe, who was more dangerous, and who is the real hero of the film. When French troops surrounded his house on 8 October 1957 they dared not go inside and launched enough explosives into it to bring it, and all the neighbouring houses, down, in the process killing twenty-five people including eight children.

That was the battle of Algiers and in the following months it became clear that the French had already lost the war by then. Colonial wars have that characteristic that the colonial power has lost before it can be convinced that it has; and the nationalist is only negotiating because he knows that this is necessary to minimize the extent of atrocities that the colonial power can carry out because of his heavier guns. Franz Fanon explained this when he wrote in 1959 that "the form and content of national existence already exists in Algeria and ... there can be no turning back. While in many colonial countries it is the independence acquired by a party that progressively informs the diffused national consciousness of the people, in Algeria it is the national consciousness, the collective sufferings and terrors that make it inevitable that the people must take its destiny into its own hands ... Colonialism has definitely lost out in Algeria, while the Algerians have definitely won." By late 1957 the FLN had already become a mass movement and now during 1958 it received support in the war against the French from a base that had further unified and become hardened and more determined. The rising generation, as Frantz Fanon wrote in 1959, "is neither more flexible nor more tired than those who launched the struggle". For them, having a gun, being able to fight the French, had become the only chance of giving meaning to life.[34]

So now an increasing number of Algerians who had been pro-French or neutral went over to the FLN. The French tried to raise anti-FLN armed groups from among the Kabyles, on the theory that there must be some age-old hatred between Kabyles and Arabs, as their anthropologists and sociologists said there was. A Force K comprising a thousand Kabyles was armed and trained for the purpose in total secrecy. But as pointed out above, it was the people of the mountain like the Kabyles that contributed the most to Algeria's resources of nationalism. For months Force K passed on their weapons to the FLN, while generating fake encounters after which they were reported lost or captured by the FLN. Then the French found out that it had been with the FLN from the beginning so they had to terminate it. There were others with whom the same thing happened. And there was Bellounis, an MNA leader who had gone over to the French, and "had been extensively and expensively equipped by them." At one point he had two thousand men under him and had given himself the rank of general. In the early months of 1958 his followers started leaving for the FLN, he himself became megalomaniac and the French executed him. So "ended disastrously yet another private army enterprise."[35]

This meant the FLN had no shortage of recruits. Every Algerian, so hardened was the anti-French resolve by 1958, wanted to join the war for independence. So the total strength of the FLN was rising; by early 1958 it had 40,000 trained and uniformed fighters; the battalion size was enlarged to 400 to cope with the increase; if the regional and village militias are included the strength was 130,000. Moreover, money and weapons were available in plenty. Money was being collected in Algeria; and from Algerian workers in France; and the Arab League members were now channeling ever increasing amounts into the coffers of the FLN. As for arms the most important international arms dealers were almost queuing up to supply them. From the US, the UK and especially from Germany, the arms flowed liberally. A group of ex-Nazis who had moved into Cairo used their contacts in Germany for the purpose. The weapons were also more modern: 81 mm mortars; 30 mm and 50 mm machine guns; Brownings. And French casualties mounted. In August 1957, 76 French soldiers were killed in four days fighting; then another ten in an ambush; then another seven. "This was the deadly pattern, as month followed month."[36] And the desertion rate among the Muslim troops of the French continued to rise. The morale of the French army fell and kept falling; recruits failed to show up for transport to Algeria, or dodged the draft.

## The French Lose the War

The French had only two options: win the war by mass genocide of the Algerian population; or accept defeat and leave. The first was unthinkable, even though a great deal of what they had done thus far might have suggested that it was not. They didn't do the second. And faced the situation Albert Camus had so vividly portrayed a dozen years before the war in Algeria started, of the *Outsider* trapped by the Algerian sun, "the same red glare as far as the eye could reach, and small waves were lapping the hot sand in little flurried gasps ...". and he tried to key up "every nerve to fend off the sun and the dark befuddlement it was pouring into me" and, unable to leave, unable to take control of himself, he ends up on the guillotine.

An early sign of what was to come was the reception accorded in Algiers to the French Premier Guy Mollet on 6 February 1956. He was a socialist and had taken over just the month before. The French in Algeria suspected he was ready to negotiate with the FLN. In Algiers he went to lay a wreath at the war memorial and was pelted with clods of earth and tomatoes provided to the crowds around by a local French restauranteur, while the police stood and watched. Fifteen months and more passed. The situation in Algeria continued to worsen. On 21 May 1957 Mollet was voted out on a question relating to his economic policy, but as always the main reason, sitting in the background, was Algeria. Thereafter, there was no government at all for three weeks. Then Maurice Bourges-Maunoury formed one, which lasted till the end of September. Other governments came and went until it was decided to give Pierre Pflimlin a chance. The French in Algeria with the support of a demoralised army were quite anxious since they were convinced that all this instability could only herald the start of negotiations with the FLN and that Pflimlin would in any case decide to negotiate.

They took control over Algeria on 13 May 1958. Mobs took control of the Government General building and called on General Massu, who had conducted the Casbah operation, to take charge. In response Massu put himself at the head of a Committee of Safety and made it clear he would no longer take orders from Paris. The call from Algeria was now for General De Gaulle to take over the government in Paris.

On 1 June he did and now it was the turn of the French army to begin mutilating itself. But if it had not been for De Gaulle that army would in all probability have mutilated France. Since its poor showing against Germany in 1940 this was an army that had never won a war. In March 1947 poorly armed nationalist forces in Madagascar fighting against that army had taken over a third of the country; reinforcements were rushed from France and 100,000 Malagasy died in the subsequent repression. At Dien Bien Phu the army lost a battle that was extensively pre-advertised and followed by the whole world as representatives sat in Geneva for negotiations which were crucially dependent on the outcome of that battle. In Morocco and Tunisia nationalist movements, of which the thrust was the violent eviction of colonial rule, forced France to grant independence in early 1956. Then, later the same year, the French joined Britain to invade Egypt and were again defeated; much of the huge quantity of arms captured by the Egyptians there was diverted to the FLN.

In 1959 General Maurice Challe, then commander of French forces in Algeria, raised the level of operations against the Algerian freedom fighters led by the FLN; their units were hunted down and eliminated or captured; they were pursued into the countryside; wired fences and minefields restricted their movements; they were, to all appearances, steadily weakening. By the time he left in 1960 Challe declared that the rebel was no longer king of the djebel; and that the military phase of the rebellion had been terminated. Even the head of their provisional government, Ferhat Abbas declared gloomily that the underground forces would not be able to live for a long time let alone achieve victory. But already by 1959 the FLN had actually won the war, as Franz Fanon wrote.

And despite their declarations the French seemed to know it too. And now they were really determined not to lose Algeria. Whatever greatness remained for France, and it had the tradition of a long and noble history to uphold, now depended on its ability to retain its empire in Algeria. "The most powerful politicians in France were firmly committed to the idea of preserving French Algeria" and this was across all political parties; there was a "national consensus over the need to fight and win in Algeria and, for the army in particular, "Algeria became the touchstone for the army's ability to perform its duty."[37] And nearly became that army's tombstone. They had been given 500,000 men against the FLN's 20,000,[38] full control there in Algeria was in their hands; all administrative and police power had been handed over by the government; they had a doctrine for the exercise of that power – that of permanent war waged by world communism sponsored by the Soviet Union – and that war had to be won no matter what the methods used; it was "a doctrine forged from years of warfare in Indo-China which, if carried to its logical conclusion, would have led to fascism not only in Algeria but France as well."[39] And they had a scapegoat, their previous defeats were due to political interference and they would not allow that to happen again.

## And Nearly Mutilate Themselves

Only de Gaulle, who had built up groups of loyal officers which expanded as the 1939-45 war drew to an end, could have controlled this.

De Gaulle's policy seemed no different to that of his predecessors. This was typified by what Premier Mendes-France had said to the National Assembly soon after the war of independence began, on 12 November 1954, "The Algerian departments are part of the French Republic. They have been French for a long time, and they are irrevocably French ... Between them and metropolitan France there can be no conceivable secession ... this must be clear once and for all", and added that France would never yield on this "fundamental principle." Premier Mollet, years later, was equally uncompromising. "France without Algeria would no longer be France".[40]

And so was de Gaulle, at first. On his first tour of Algeria in early June 1958 he declared at Mostaganem (though not elsewhere, and later dismissed even that as superficial) "Vive L'Algerie Francaise" to an enthusiastic response from the crowds of *pieds noirs*. As he realised that France was losing the war, he changed his views. He emphasised the need for change; he praised the FLN, calling in October 1958, in a phrase that was to become well known, for the 'peace of the brave' and by 16 September 1959 he made his famous nationwide radio and television address announcing self-determination for Algeria. Taking all factors into account, the Algerian, the national and the international situation, "I deem it necessary that recourse to self-determination be here and now proclaimed."[41]

The reaction to this in the army and among the French in Algeria built up slowly. General Massu told a German newspaper in January 1960 that most French officers in Algeria probably would not obey de Gaulle, upon which he was recalled and large groups of French, rallying to his support, set up barricades all over Algeria in what came to be known as 'Barricades Week'. This was brought under control but not the discontent in the army, especially as negotiations began between de Gaulle's government and the FLN.

In April 1961 came the General's revolt. General Challe who until the end of 1959 had been the French Commander-in-Chief in Algeria, along with other senior officers took rebel paratroopers to seize the radio station, the post office and other key buildings like the military headquarters and the Prefecture in Algiers. Then the rebels announced over the radio that the army had taken over Algeria, and that this had been done, in the words of Challe, "in order to keep our solemn promise, the promise of the army to hold

Algeria, so that our dead shall not have died for nothing."[42]

But there were too many senior officers who remained loyal to de Gaulle and too much support for him within France, for such a revolt to succeed. Within five days it had collapsed and the senior generals leading it had surrendered.

Parallel to this the negotiations between the French and the FLN continued. They had begun in France in mid-1960 and the final phase was concluded in Evian, Switzerland in March 1962. The positions taken by the two sides showed who was winning the war. The French tried to press for an immediate cease-fire; the FLN refused, saying a ceasefire would follow a full agreement on all outstanding issues. The French tried to separate the Sahara for it was now known to be rich in oil; the FLN refused even to consider this. The French suggested that European enclaves could be established within Algeria; the FLN replied that no kind of partition would be acceptable. The French said at least there could be prior agreement about the kind of association France and Algeria would have after independence; the FLN replied this could be decided after independence. The French had lost the war; they had no bargaining position left.

And so, on 8 March 1962 the negotiations ended with the decision to grant full independence to Algeria; a referendum in France approved the decision on 8 April with 90 per cent in favour; on 1 July a referendum was held in Algeria which also voted 90 per cent in favour (with 10 per cent being the *pieds noirs* abstaining) and on 3 July 1962 France formally handed power to the FLN. Algeria gained independence with its national unity intact.

## Interpretations of Modernity

Algerian independence does not require an explanation. The Algerians wanted independence; every nation does. They fought a war for it; they won the war and achieved it. So much for the traditional story.

However, as has been customary, a large number of explanations have been put forward, all of them starting with the sometimes unstated assumption based on the modernity story that they did not win the war.

One by a leftist historian of Africa is that the war ended "not when one side or the other had gained an obvious victory – the military position at the end was much nearer to one of stalemate

…" but because French metropolitan interests were shown to be in conflict with those of the settlers.[43]

One cites multiple factors. President John F. Kennedy was "leaning heavily on de Gaulle", while the Soviet Union was giving more and more support to the FLN; plus de Gaulle was in a much weaker position and had "no option but to negotiate purposefully to end the war" after the General's revolt of April 1961, since that had broken and demoralised the army in Algeria.[44]

Another is more categorical, that "from a military point of view the war in Algeria was lost by the insurgents, but that they won it by political and diplomatic means."[45] This explanation, that the war was won by politics and diplomacy, has some elaborate variations, among the most important being a book by Matthew Connelly who writes that "the French won the battle of Algiers, 1957, effectively sealed off the borders in 1958, and had reduced the mujahideen remaining in Algeria to scattered and increasingly desperate bands by 1960. Yet all along they gave ground on the Algeria's future status and finally accepted the inevitability of its secession when the insurgency was at its weakest" This "supreme paradox" is explained by the Algerian's use of the weapons of human rights reports, press conferences, youth congresses, world opinion and international law more than conventional military objectives.[46] The abandonment by France of Tunisia and Morocco in 1956, later having to give up its African empire, the end of European influence in the Arab world because of the Suez war of 1956 and its withdrawal from NATO are all factors which, in Connelly's opinion, go to shape the post-cold war world, hence the title of the book.

This brings us, in the next chapter, to what is generally known as the Cold War.

## ENDNOTES

[1] See Leonard Koos, Colonial Culture as Francophone? The Case of Nineteenth Century Algeria, in Kamal Salhi, ed., *Franco-phone Post-colonial Cultures,* Lexington Books, Lanham, 2003, p. 19.

[2] Cited in Rachid Tlemcani, *State and Revolution in Algeria*, Zed Books, London, 1986, p. 31.

[3] Quoted by A.Aroua, *Reading Notes on French Colonial Massacres in Algeria,* on the internet site, www.hoggar.org/books/massacres - pdf, pp. 8, 15, 9, 14, 11 and 37 respectively for this and the previous two paragraphs.

[4] See the Wikipedia article on *French Algeria*, Conquest of Algeria.

[5] Edward Behr, *The Algerian Problem*, Penguin Books, Middlesex, 1961, p. 21.

[6] Hisham Sharabi, *Nationalism and Revolution in the Arab World,* D. Van Nostrand Co., New Jersey, 1966, p. 27.

[7] Martin Evans and John Phillips, *Anger of the Dispossessed*, Yale University Press, New Haven, 2007, pp. 4 and 46-7 for this and the previous paragraph.

[8] Alistair Horne, *A Savage War of Peace, Algeria, 1954-1962*, Macmillan, London, 1977, p. 40.

[9] Eric Hobsbawm, *Nations and Nationalism since 1780*, Cambridge University Press, 1995, p. 46. This particular quote supports the argument of modernity; but note that in chapter 3 I have quoted the same author in support of the traditional story!

[10] Fernand Braudel, *The Mediterranean and the Mediterranean World in the Age of Philip II,* Fontana Press, Glasgow, 1986, pp. 31 and 37 for this and the previous paragraph.

[11] Martin Evans and John Phillips, op. cit., p. 15.

[12] Philip K. Hitti, *History of the Arabs, From the Earliest Times to the Present,* Macmillan, Hampshire, 1985, p. 213.

[13] Rafiq Asha, Arab Nationalism in William Sands, ed., *The Arab Nation, Paths and Obstacles to Fulfillment*, The Middle East Institute, Washington, 1961, p. 27.

[14] Wilfred Cantwell Smith, *Islam in Modern History*, Princeton University Press, 1957, p. 74.

[15] Philip K. Hitti, op. cit., p. 546

[16] Fernand Braudel, op. cit., pp. 880-886.

[17] Philip K. Hitti, op. cit., p. 437.

[18] Raphael Danziger, *Abd al-Qadir and the Algerians, Resistance to the French and Internal Consolidation,* Holmes and Meier, New York, 1977, pp. 117 and 137, for this and the previous paragraph.

[19] Vide Thomas Pakenham, *The Scramble for Africa*, Avon Books, New York, 1992, p. 166.

[20] Edward Behr, op. cit., p. 16.

[21] See Raphael Danziger, op. cit., pp. 186, 79 and 217-8 respectively for the quotes in this and the previous paragraph..

[22] Edward Behr, op. cit., p. 18.

[23] Martin Evans and John Philips, op. cit., p. 31.

[24] Rachid Tlemcani, op. cit., p. 59.

[25] Quoted in Edward Behr, op. cit., p. 45.

[26] Martin Evans and John Philips, op. cit., p. 44.

[27] The words used by Martin Evans and John Philips, op. cit., p. 52.

[28] Martin Meredith, *The State of Africa, A History of Fifty Years of Independence*, Free Press, London, 2005, p. 49.

[29] Martin Evans and John Philips,op. cit., p. 59.

[30] Edgar O'Balance, *The Algerian Insurrection, 1954-62*, Faber and Faber, London, 1967, p. 63.

[31] Cited by Alistair Horne, op. cit., p. 121.

[32] Edward Behr, op. cit., p. 82.

[33] Directed by Gillo Pontecorvo; it won the Golden Lion at the 1966 Venice Film Festival. The last scene in the film is the most graphic. With the FLN cadres in the Casbah killed or having escaped there is quiet there, but then in 1960 the whole of Algiers erupts; the entire people now demand independence and the scene shows

close-ups of faces, crowd shots, aerial shots of masses of people. It is clear that every one of them is a potential FLN recruit; the French have lost the war.

[34] Frantz Fanon, *Studies in a Dying Colonialism*, Monthly Review Press, New York, 1959, pp. 28, 31 and 26-7

[35] Alistair Horne, op. cit., p. 258

[36] Edgar O'Balance, op. cit., p. 91.

[37] Gil Merom, *How Democracies Lose Small Wars*, Cambridge University Press, 2003, pp. 89-92.

[38] For purposes of comparison and as illustration of the changing times, note that at the height of the French campaign against Abdul Kader, in the mid-1840s, they had 200,000 compared to his 80,000.

[39] Edward Behr, op. cit., p. 132.

[40] Quoted in Alistair Horne, op. cit., pp. 98, 545.

[41] Edward Behr, op. cit., p. 156.

[42] Alistair Horne, op. cit., p. 450.

[43] Basil Davidson, *Africa in History, Themes and Outlines*, Phoenix, London, 1991, p. 338.

[44] Alistair Horne, op. cit., p. 463.

[45] Edgar O'Balance, op. cit., p. 220.

[46] Matthew Connelly, *A Diplomatic Revolution: Algeria's Fight for Independence and the Origins of the Post-Cold War Era*, Oxford University Press, 2002, pp. 3-6.

# 7

# The 'Cold War' that wasn't—I

During the forty-five-year period after 1945, according to the traditional story, the postulate that war equals power equals war, supplemented during the previous century by the equation empire equals power equals war continued with modifications.

This chapter considers the events that led to those modifications and then points out the consequences. Then it examines in further detail what happened to the empires of France and Britain; the next chapter examines how fared the two 'super powers', according to the same story.

## The Universal Hunger for Peace

It was the horrifying and seemingly purposeless slaughter in the trenches of the 1914-18 European war, the resumption of that slaughter during the 1939-45 World War, and the emotions that had to be generated among whole populations which were now at war that brought the Kantian peace argument to the fore. That was the biggest modification.

Wars of massive casualties were not unknown before 1914. There are historians who claim that the An Lushan revolts in eighth-century China had cost some 30 million lives; that in the thirteenth century Genghis Khan cost the populations of the areas he conquered 35 million lives with his indiscriminate killing of whole towns and villages; and that even the Manchu conquest of China cost 25 million lives. But those conflicts were far away from Europe. Within Europe the tradition before the seventeenth century was to have rather genteel wars. The Thirty Years' War changed that, the subsequent wars of the eighteenth and nineteenth centuries reaffirmed that change and though none of those matched the twentieth century wars, the ground for what to come had been prepared.

Furthermore, in all those earlier wars, within as well as outside Europe, the bulk of the casualties was from disease and hunger; five per cent or less were killed by the direct violence of battle. What happened in the 1914-18 war took these trends forward with unprecedented rapidity, for it was of an entirely different order to anything that had gone before.

Disease took its toll, but improvements in medical science during the nineteenth century ensured that that toll was small; it was the direct violence of battle which claimed a much higher percentage of all the lives taken than ever before. This was trench warfare combined with the killing power of the machine gun, where advances of a few yards could claim thousands of lives. In just one battle, that of the Somme, the British army took 60,000 casualties on the first day; the whole battle, from July to November, 1916 claimed six hundred thousand British and French casualties and half a million German lives. But that battle was a draw. The other major battles of that war, at Ypres, Verdun, the Marne, had similar orders of casualties. Direct military action claimed ten million lives in that entire war. If one includes the wounded and taken prisoner, the total comes to nearly 33 million. As Raymond Aron put it, "total war, as it took place in 1914-18, with problems of supply, strategy of attrition, stable fronts, and field fortifications, left the public with a horrifying memory of tens of thousands of soldiers sacrificed to conquer a few square miles, the inhuman life of the trenches, the crushing and startling technical superiority of arms, organisation and production over personal qualities" and this nourished the revolt against war.[1]

There were three principal reasons for the exceptionally high casualties.

Firstly, continuing the historical trend mentioned in chapter 1, the major powers had been steadily acquiring the ability to put ever larger armies into the field. The natural increase of population in Europe had been much higher in the nineteenth century than ever before. Then, as mentioned, "conscription changed the basis of warfare. Hitherto soldiers had been costly, now they were cheap;

battles had been avoided, now they were sought, and however heavy were the losses ..."[2] Moreover the manpower of the European colonies was available by the end of the nineteenth century; over 2 million Africans served in the 1914-18 war; as that war began, one-third of British troops in France were from India and by the time it ended over a million troops from India had been conscripted to the war effort.

The second reason was the advance of technology: small bore rifles firing smokeless powder; the machine gun which had by then been almost perfected; quick firing artillery. Not only were the men available, but now the means to kill them rapidly and in large numbers were also available.

Thirdly, the wealth of the Europeans nations had grown exponentially during the nineteenth century. The wars of the eighteenth century and earlier were often brought to a close because one or more of the combatants simply could not afford to keep paid and well supplied men any longer in the field; some experts like Norman Angell had assumed that this would also be true of a twentieth-century war. But actually economics was no longer a constraint. The economic growth which was fuelled by the industrial revolution and the endless surge in productivity that followed, combined with the assets of the colonies, ensured that.

So the war went on and on as each side tried to exhaust the other in terms of war dead and wounded.

The numbers killed and wounded during the 1939-45 war, for the same reasons, were even higher. It is estimated that 25 million Soviet citizens died violently in that war, over one in ten of the total prewar population; in Poland, Germany and Yugoslavia the mortality rate was about the same, around ten per cent of the prewar population. There were 61 cities in Germany with more than 100,000 people in each; half a million tons of bombs were dropped on them and seventy per cent of the total number of dwellings in them destroyed. There was no more distinction between combatant and non-combatant. In other countries the mortality rate as a percentage of total population was much lower, less than one per cent for Italy, France and the United Kingdom, around 0.2 per cent for the United States.

But to compound the effects of the mortality rates, these two wars were accompanied by a massive outpouring of intolerance and hatred. Nations had to resort to ideology to maintain morale at home and among the troops, to keep the soldiers fighting a war which they believed was serving no purpose, so it became a war of liberation, or a crusade for democracy, or the promotion of a particular way of life. The opponent had to be described as a demon who would have to be totally crushed; "the demand for total victory was ... a reflex reaction to total war."[3] The racial theories, of which the holocaust was just one apocalyptic outcome, were paralleled by hate on the battlefield. The British, the French, and the Germans took prisoners and then slaughtered them, killed those they found in the trenches they overran in the most horrible way possible.

Both wars represented extreme cases of the cause coming first and then the war, a trend which, as we saw, was initiated by the Thirty Years' War.

After the wars, and particularly after the 1914-18 war, analyses about the futility of it all began. Typical of these analyses was the tendency to lay the blame on profiteers, the so-called military industrial complex, on editors, on other members of the elite. A war correspondent wrote that "the fires of hate were stoked up at patriotic banquets and in editorial chairs"; that the hatreds displayed by those who took part were "lighted and inflamed by their governors, their philosophers, and their newspapers."[4] The wars, in brief, were described as avoidable, started and kept going by evil men for malevolent purposes; they were not a normal part of the human condition.[5]

All this led to what H.G.Wells described the "universal hunger for peace";[6] eventually, this hunger was converted into the urgent necessity to abolish or at least curb the possibility that war could recur.

It was now, as a consequence, widely and generally believed "that peace was the normal condition between states and war, if it came, was an aberration resulting from the irrational acts of evil or psychotic men."[7]

So when Quincy Wright initiated a study of the causes of war in 1926, which was completed at the start of World War II, his starting point was "that the problem of preventing war is one of increasing importance in our civilisation" and that, indeed, war should and could be made obsolete as an instrument of national policy. Wright himself points out the change of paradigm. Throughout the nineteenth century, he writes, war was regarded as justified by its success in achieving its objectives; recourse to it was not regarded as subject to a legal or ethical judgment. However, after the 1914-18 war in particular, a "state was never justified in initiating a state of war ... from being a right and then a fact, war had become a crime".[8]

Other major thinkers on relations between states, cultures and civilisations also adopted the line that war was to be condemned as a component of human existence or means of intercourse between nations. Arnold Toynbee is among the most eminent. In his path-breaking ' A Study of History' in twelve volumes, of which the first six were published shortly before World War II, he writes that the "single art of war makes progress at the expense of the divers arts of peace", a deadly ritual that might complete the destruction of all its votaries. It is militarism and the militarist, Toynbee's words for those liking to wage war and those who do so that cause the breakdown and disintegration of civilisations. He writes of "the militarist who is so intemperate in waging wars of annihilation against his neighbours that he deals unintended destruction to himself" and of "militarism, a common feature of breakdown and disintegration ... in the downward course of a broken-down civilisation's career".[9]

Another authoritative comment describes war as nemesis and the twentieth century as the century of war; so "in both Europe and Asia, wars have been the single most important catalyst of the great political and ideological transformations that have characterised the century, and they remain humanity's principal nemesis both today and in the future."[10]

Here and there we come across writings that suggest the traditional ways of thinking about the links between war and power still commanded some allegiance. Here are some examples.

About the empirical part of the link *The Economist* asked in March, 1944, "What is a Great Power?" Then the answer was given, "a Great Power is a country capable of waging active and autonomous war against another Great Power ... and for a country to be beyond question a Great Power it must be able to fight with its own resources..." So, then, war "provided a rough-and-ready yardstick for ranking nations in a hierarchy of power."[11] Put slightly differently, a great power is a state "which cannot be defeated in war by any other state or coalition of states without it exacting comparable cost from its opponents."[12] While a "small state is a state which is unable to contend in war with the great powers on anything like equal terms."[13]

As for the normative part of the link, one author writes about power, the desire for it and the acquisition and exercise of it. This is "the raw material of politics, national and international, and violence may sometimes prove an effective means to secure or retain it" ... an accepted instrument for the extension or protection of power; for the aversion to war "there was little historical precedent".[14]

There were also comments about the link being self-contained. One exponent of the traditional story explains war as a "basic determinant of the shape the system assumes at any one time. It is war and the threat of war that help to determine whether particular states survive or are eliminated, whether they rise or decline, whether their frontiers remain the same or are changed ... even the terms we use to describe the system are scarcely intelligible except in relation to war and the threat of war."[15]

Another author who wrote a classic on the Art of War gave it the kind of importance Heraclitus had given. The influence of war, he explains, extends from the fate of nations down to the fate of the humblest individual. "It spreads into literature, music, painting, sculpture, architecture, science, medicine, and surgery. War pervades languages, so that speech and writing are reinforced by a host of bellicose terms, phrases and metaphors."[16]

As one more example, it has been pointed out, "major wars critically impact domestic politics by producing durable social changes and by redistributing political power among groups. An established literature explains how major wars may make as well as break states."[17] That last quote was about the Soviet war on Afghanistan, arguing (rightly) that it was the war that caused the collapse of the Soviet empire. Details about this are in chapter 11.

But these comments are neither typical nor representative. War had in fact come generally to be regarded as evil. You could not now in general advocate war without an ever longer list of just causes and compelling arguments suggesting that it was being waged to destroy a greater evil.

To this labeling of war as evil add the advent of nuclear weapons from 1945 on. This seemed to render war between the major powers, those that possessed the new weapons, impossible for all time. President Truman, who had ordered the use of these weapons against Japan in August, 1945, thereafter turned against their use ever again; and Joseph Stalin seemed to agree. There were some who did advocate their use. During the Korean War, for example, the United States considered the use of atomic artillery shells against Chinese troops; and General Macarthur was known to have favoured the use of nuclear bombs, if necessary, against the Chinese mainland during that war. There were other occasions such as the Cuban missile crisis when a nuclear war seemed to have come close.

But the possibility of their future use was generally regarded with abhorrence. Hans J. Morgenthau, who virtually created the paradigm by which we think about international relations in the post-1945 world, put this succinctly, "when universal destruction is the result of victory and defeat alike, war itself is no longer a matter of rational choice but becomes an instrument of suicidal despair." Another influential American commentator, C.L. Sulzberger, contemplated the arguments of those who still thought that war between the US and the USSR could be considered, and said that once the latter had acquired missiles and hydrogen explosives, "war as a contemplated policy became replaced by suicide as a contemplated policy. This is acceptable to no one."[18]

All this has had two effects, as far as the traditional story is concerned.

Firstly, and more crucially, the old equation of war and power was still valid for relations between the great powers, on the one hand, and the smaller states, on the other. But while wars against smaller states, those who didn't have the new weapons, were still very possible, you couldn't talk too much about this. You also had to find or manufacture that long list of just causes to go for such a war and you had to try getting it over with quickly.

We may refer here to the study of war by Quincy Wright who devotes a long chapter to 'Causation and War', listing scientific causes, historical causes, practical causes. Over the years a voluminous literature has grown setting forth causes of war other than those which might be connected to the search for power: ideology, religion, ethnicity, greed, population increase, among others. This meant that if any of the above stated causes of war was just cause which, of course, included such as the defence of freedom or the victory of socialism and communism, or others like the self-determination of a people, then and only then was there sufficient reason to go to war, over-riding the normative objections. It may be illustrative here to contrast Clausewitz, who had nothing on the causes of war, since for him it was a rational instrument of policy. Nor on consequences; whereas post-1918 studies of the consequences of war are devoted to the number of casualties and the damage wrought. And in the years after 1945 it became for the media almost a competition as to who could show the most hideous consequences in terms of the dead, the wounded and the destruction wrought, in the case of Clausewitz these consequences are, for the victor, pursuit of the defeated enemy, and for the latter, incessant resistance and a slow retreat; no other consequences are mentioned.

Secondly, with the advent of nuclear weapons, so far as relations among the great powers are concerned, power as we have known it till now goes into the textbooks, into cold storage; nothing of any significance happened in the mutual relations of the great powers themselves and their allies; nothing changed; there was no conflict of any kind, not even the smallest scale clash of arms. War between them, it came to be realised gradually, was now quite unthinkable and could not now or ever again be the criterion to judge power. The so-called combatants confronted each other from time to time; "they have shouted threats and abuse at each other, they have flexed their military muscles to intimidate each other, but they have not struck at each other."[19]

The US was now in 1945, having fought two wars for control of Europe, a part of that continent. With its allies, who were the most powerful countries there, it controlled most of West Europe. A line running roughly from Lubeck on the Baltic Sea southwards to the Adriatic divided the continent; east of it was controlled by the Soviet Union. Towards the northern part of the line some countries were not controlled by either, such as Finland and Sweden; and towards the southern part of that line there were others like Greece and Yugoslavia, that were also not controlled by either. But apart from these and a few other exceptions like Switzerland the lines were clearly drawn. Although, therefore, there was a centuries-old tradition that the great powers of Europe were rivals, this was now only true in the simulatory sense that the US and the Soviet Union could be described as rivals. None of the shifting alliances and pacts that characterised the 19th and earlier centuries was relevant. There was no question of gain or loss of territory, of resources or of any of the other issues of earlier centuries. For, there could be no war. Within a few years both sides had enough nuclear weapons to destroy each other many times over, no matter how the war started.

There were some tensions, such as over Poland in 1945; over Iran in 1946; over Greece and Turkey in 1947; that was also the year the Marshall Plan for massive American aid to West Europe was announced, further hardening the divisions in Europe; in February 1948 there was a communist coup in Czechoslovakia, and then in June of that year the Soviet Union blockaded Berlin. Other tensions came as the years passed. A large number of words were spoken and written; there were some movements of naval forces, an airlift. Nothing at all changed. The Soviet and American forces continued to make faces at each other across the line that divided Europe. For the entire four and half decades that followed, no Soviet soldier killed an American nor vice versa. Europe ceased to matter for IR.

This meant, by the way, not only that the great powers were able to focus more sharply on their relations with the smaller countries, to the detriment of the latter, but that cooperation between them in tackling those smaller countries became easier.

So this chapter and the next are based on the traditional story, the presumption that the old equation, war equals power equals war, held good empirically for the relations between the great powers and the smaller states in the years after 1945; that it was self-contained; and, though no longer normatively acceptable in the open way it was in past centuries, it was still applied normatively. In other words, when the great powers considered how to tackle situations in places like Asia, Africa or Latin America, war was one of the things to which, in their view quite normally, resort could be had. So here we ignore the framework built around what is called the 'Cold War'.

In consequence, just as war, during the colonial era, played the most important part in gaining and losing empires, so now it was violent military confrontations that generated the major changes in relative power during the so-called 'Cold War' era, and hence were the first and always the most decisive factor that settled the political shape of Asia and Africa as that era proceeded. We can, indeed, go further and state that the global balance, the hierarchy of world power, was decided by these violent confrontations.

We start with the way the underdogs ended the older empires.

## The Empires of France and Britain

There were four main victors of World War II: France, Britain, the Soviet Union and the United States. As one historian of the time writes, these victors of the war "had the opportunity to remake the world ... for a while the board of world affairs was as clear as it was ever likely to be. It was a time of hope and opportunity ..."[20] So a great deal of what follows will be concerned with how they handled this opportunity. The French, within seventeen years, were forced to abandon any hope they may have had of retaining great-power status. How that happened is described in chapter 6 on Algeria and the first part of chapter 10 on Vietnam. The British were forced to do the same five years later, and that is described in this chapter. The US had increasing difficulties exercising the presumed prerogatives of great power, some of which are recounted in the next chapter, others in the chapter on Vietnam. While the Soviet Union, attempting to exercise the same, went into collapse in Afghanistan, also the subject of another chapter.

But let us start with the first two. They ruled over extensive empires which they had no intention of relinquishing; they thought that, having won the war and liberated those parts of their empires occupied by Germany and Japan, they had a right to continue there. In any case the possession of an empire was virtually the only thing that gave them the right to sit at the high table, so to speak, to be evaluated as great powers. They had no assets comparable to the US or the Soviet Union. So only a liberation war or the likelihood of one could change the situation.

Such a war was conducted by Vietnam and resulted in the eviction of France from there in 1954, but it was yet not the end of France as an imperial and, therefore, a great power. Two years later, the liberation war in Algeria having begun, its two neighbours, Morocco and Tunisia, fought for and obtained independence. That liberation war meant France was over committed in Algeria, facing defeat by 1959. Because of the war in Algeria it did not have the resources to deal with armed opposition anywhere, and this was likely on past experience to arise or intensify in Madagascar; perhaps also in Niger; certainly in Guinea, where Sekou Toure, descendant of Samori Toure, led the freedom struggle; in Mali where Modibo Keita led a militant movement against the French. They decided to give independence to all their African colonies in 1960. By 1962 all that remained of an empire that once stretched from the Mediterranean through the whole of North Africa to the borders of the Congo, and east to the borders of the Sudan were some islands like Guadalupe, Reunion, French Polynesia, a few thousand square miles in the Horn of Africa – the Afars and Issas – and other coastal strips like French Guiana. France had overtly accepted what had been known since 1945, what she had spent a decade and a half resisting, that she was no longer a great power.

If we are to put it in a nutshell, France was defeated by the Algerians and, as a result, lost the status of great power. That was the first change in the post-1945 global power hierarchy.

Britain's imperial and world role ended because it lost the South Yemen war; that was the second change.

India's independence in 1947 was a blow; Lord Curzon's 1907 declaration was taken as truth by some: "When India has gone and the great Colonies have gone, do you suppose that we can stop there? Your ports and coaling stations, your fortresses and dockyards, your Crown Colonies and protectorates will go too …the toll gates and barbicans of an empire that has vanished."[21]

Britain also lost the use of the Indian army, which had been chiefly responsible for acquiring and defending the empire. But in India, according to the accepted modernity story, there had been a peaceful transfer of power; the British, therefore, continued to believe that their position and responsibilities as a great power, which, of course, meant imperial power, continued. In May 1947, with India's independence three months away, Foreign Secretary Ernest Bevin was able to say that so far as foreign policy was concerned Britain had not altered her commitments in the slightest, that Her Majesty's government did not accept the view that Britain had ceased to be a great power or had ceased to play that role; Britain still had a historic role to play. As far as the Indian army was concerned, the loss had to be made up, so conscription was introduced in 1946, the period of which was increased to two years in 1950; and there was a major increase in the number of colonial troops recruited. When everybody else was demobilising Britain was getting ready to play a renewed imperial role. The blow from the loss of India had not been fatal.

## Britain's Egyptian Adventure

The Suez war of 1956 was another blow. Under a 1936 agreement Britain had the right to station a 10,000-man force to protect the

Suez Canal for twenty years. That agreement was denounced by Egypt in 1951; another agreement was signed under which the British would leave the Canal Zone in early 1956. Soon after they had left President Nasser nationalised the Suez Canal Company on 26 July 1956. Britain and France decided to take military action to re-establish their control over it, so recently lost.

They wanted to act within a week but couldn't because they simply were not ready militarily. So while they got ready negotiations began.

US President Eisenhower got involved; so did Secretary of State John Foster Dulles; both were opposed to the use of force. A conference of canal users was convened; a canal users' association was proposed by the US; the UN Security Council met to consider the matter. Meanwhile, the British and French tried to get the US on board by persuading Eisenhower that Nasser was Hitler incarnate. French Foreign Minister Pineau "compared Nasser's action to the seizure of the Rhineland two decades earlier."[22]

Nasser had written a book, *Egypt's Liberation, The Philosophy of the Revolution,* in which he described the Arab circle surrounding Egypt, of which it was a part, its history inextricably linked up with that of the Arabs. The British thought this was Arab expansionism; Foreign Secretary Selwyn Lloyd denounced its ambitions while the French Premier called it the new *Mein Kampf* of an oriental Hitler. The British Premier, Anthony Eden, wrote to Eisenhower comparing Nasser's expansion plans to those of Hitler and his tactics to those of the Soviets; he would hold the Western world to ransom if he were not stopped.

In this they were partly right; Nasser was no Hitler, but he dreamed of Arab unity. Michael Aflaq, the philosopher of the Baath Party, wrote and spoke extensively on Arab unity, the natural unity of one race, one language, one culture, one history within an Arab homeland stretching from the Taurus to the Pusht-i-Kuh Mountains to the Gulf of Basra, the Arabian Sea, and Abyssinia. Every Arab sensed, in the early 1950's, the depth of the surge among all Arabs in favour of Arab unity. Many governments were against it, chiefly those of Lebanon, Jordan and the other monarchies like Iraq and those in the Gulf; they calculated rightly that this groundswell of public feeling would threaten their thrones unless it was suppressed. The communist parties of the region were even more opposed to it; under Soviet guidance, they didn't want nationalism to grow in strength; much as during the colonial period, they wanted it to be weak and under their control. The Soviet Union, like Britain and France, didn't like the idea of Arab unity at all. A great and charismatic leader and a great movement were needed to promote Arab unity by removing all these objections and Nasser clearly saw himself in that role. And he could have fitted it.

Egypt had led the view that the Arabs should make their own future; in 1951, before Nasser, it had rejected a US-British-French plan for a Middle East defence organisation, MEDO. When the British initiated the Baghdad Pact in 1955 they were hoping the Arabs other than Iraq would also join, apart from Turkey and Pakistan. Nasser's opposition frustrated that hope.

First Syria rejected it. They were still hoping Jordan would accept. General John Bagot Glubb, the British commander of Jordan's Arab Legion, reputedly one of the most powerful fighting forces in the Arab world, was highly regarded by King Hussein and had strongly advocated that Jordan join the pact. The British were certain the advice of 'Glubb Pasha' would be taken. Then on 2 March, 1956 Glubb was called to the Prime Minister's office and told that his services had been terminated, along with those of two other senior British officers of the Arab Legion, Intelligence Chief Colonel Coghill and Chief Staff Officer Brigadier William Hutton. Even worse, this piece of news arrived in Cairo just as the British Foreign Secretary Selwyn Lloyd was coming out of a dinner with Nasser, and he naturally thought it was done deliberately as an insult to him. "No event ...stirred the Western World as much", as one commentator wrote, and the British were so shocked that Premier Anthony Eden immediately called his Cabinet and heads of the Armed Services into emergency session. But King Hussein was cheered as he drove through the streets of Amman; clearly Nasserism was becoming an increasingly powerful force, one that had to be resisted. So the British and French were partly right: Nasser did have the potential to stir the Arab people while beyond that lay the dream and even the possibility of Arab unity.

Finally, the British and French were ready for action by the end of October, 1956. In a coordinated move Israel led by attacking Egypt on 29 October; on 31 October afternoon British and French aircraft started bombing Egyptian airfields and other targets in preparation for the invasion; this went on for five days. Then from early morning of 5 November British and French commandos were air dropped around Port Said. Following a naval bombardment amphibious landings were also made. Expectedly the Soviet Union joined in; Premier Bulganin "dispatched identical notes to Prime Ministers Eden, Mollet and Ben-Gurion, warning them to stop hostilities or face the possibility of Russian intervention ... 'We are fully determined to crush the aggressors and restore peace in the Middle East through the use of force'".[23] The Soviet intention clearly was to weaken Egypt by making this into an East-West matter, but on this occasion it didn't work.

The British and French expectation was that there would be no serious resistance, that the entire Canal Zone would be occupied within two days. But Egyptian resistance proved to be stubborn. Although his cabinet was undecided Nasser had decided that "Egypt must resist force with force ... Egypt would fight, and fight to the end. If the army was defeated and Cairo occupied he would organise and lead a guerilla resistance movement."[24] The Americans anticipated this and Eisenhower writes of his assessment that in this situation "local unrest would soon grow into guerilla resistance, then open revolt, and possibly, wide-scale conflict."[25]

And this, more or less, was what happened. Once the British and French forces found resistance building up in Port Said, as their forces were forced to fight street by street for control of the town, and when it became clear that even if, in a prolonged operation, they managed to occupy the Canal Zone, the resistance would not stop, they would then have to go on to occupy Cairo and then the whole of Egypt, they accepted defeat (not in public, of course) and announced a ceasefire, less than 48 hours after the operation had begun.

## And Egypt's 'Cold War' Adventure

There was worse to come, for both sides in this war. Let us leave the British for a moment to see how the story continued in the case of Egypt.

Egypt's victory created a strong groundswell of popular support for Arab unity under Nasser's leadership. In February 1958 Egypt and Syria came together in the United Arab Republic (UAR), this was greeted with tumultuous enthusiasm all over the Arab world, and many thought this could be the core which other Arab nations would eventually join. In Iraq, July 1958, a revolution removed the Royal family and brought General Abdul Karim Kassim to power.

It was a revolution inspired by Nasser's leadership of the Arab world, and post-revolutionary Iraq certainly wished to join the UAR. But Nasser was unable to capitalise on this popular groundswell to visualise that he would have to resist both the Americans and the Soviet Union.

Both had claimed the victory of Egypt as their own, and over the years its historiography became part of that of the 'Cold War'. The Americans were responsible, said the British, for they "used financial pressure to force a British acceptance of a cease-fire ..."[26] Apart from the Soviet letter to the British and French and Israeli Premiers, Bulganin had also written to President Eisenhower during the war suggesting that a joint US-Soviet force should march into Egypt to end the fighting, and a Soviet Foreign Ministry official told the Egyptian Ambassador in Moscow, 'we shall stand beside you'. And on this basis the Soviet Union also took the credit for the ceasefire, and started handing out advice on what to do next. Bulganin called the Egyptian Ambassador and advised him that Egypt should now consolidate; that one Suez had changed the balance of power in the world. Eisenhower, meanwhile, launched the doctrine known after his name. "The existing vacuum in the Middle East must be filled by the United States before it is filled by Russia", he told leaders of both parties on New Year's day, 1957 and clarified that he proposed to cooperate with and assist any nation or group of nations which so requested to develop their economic strength and to resist armed aggression from any Communist nation.[27]

However, for the moment Nasser was much too strong for all this to carry any conviction. In order to ensure that Egypt and its friends in the Arab world fitted into the 'Cold War' framework it was necessary for both the US and the Soviet Union that Nasser be weakened from within and defeated in war.

The communists in Egypt, Syria and Iraq did the first. When the UAR happened the Syrian communist party called for its dissolution and Khaled Bakhdash, its leader, left the country while the Egyptian communists were working the same way. Then, after the July 1958 revolution in Iraq, when it seemed natural that it would join the UAR, this worried the Soviet Union; by December 1958 the Iraqi communist party was openly agitating against it and this pressure led to the ejection from government in February, 1959 of all those who supported Arab unity. And when Nasser attacked the communists the Soviet Union responded, singling out the UAR for criticism; in his January 1959 report to the 21st Congress of the Communist Party of the Soviet Union party General Secretary Khrushchev said the Soviet Union cannot remain silent in the face of the campaign being conducted in some countries against progressive people, and pointedly referred to statements made in the UAR accusing the communists wrongly of helping to divide and undermine the national effort against imperialism. "Since there have recently been statements against communism in the UAR, and accusations have been levelled at communists, I, as a communist, think it necessary to declare that it is wrong to accuse communists of helping to undermine and divide the national effort in the struggle against imperialism".

Nasser replied in Damascus, one year after the creation of the UAR, that "we didn't start a crusade against the communists – we tried to stop communists from sabotaging the union of Egypt and Syria".

But as the years passed, Egypt had come to depend increasingly on Soviet military equipment and this dependence sucked it into the virtual 'Cold War' vortex. Nobody else gave Egypt military equipment; it was unable to diversify. And it was the policy of both the US and the Soviet Union that Israel should retain a comfortable military advantage over all the Arabs ranged against her.

So the time came to defeat Egypt in war. In the six-day war of June 1967 Egypt, Syria, Jordan, which also allowed Iraqi troops in for the purpose, and Lebanon, were defeated quickly and decisively by Israel. Thereafter neither Egypt nor the possibility of Arab unity was taken seriously by the great powers and, step by step, they assumed full control over the West Asian situation. The rest is the story of what happens when a smaller state, convinced that the two great powers are working against each other, succumbs to the modernity story, the virtual reality of the 'Cold War' while both the latter work jointly to undermine its autonomy.

Step one was taken quicky. Soviet President Podgorny, accompanied by Chief of Staff of the Soviet Army Marshal Zakharov arrived in Egypt immediately after the war in June 1967 and in return for continued military aid asked for a command post in Alexandria for Soviet ships in the Mediterranean. This "fitted in with Nasser's thinking because he had come to the conclusion it was to the advantage of the whole non-aligned world for Russia's naval presence in the Mediterranean to be strengthened." Then he met Nasser again and wanted a command post, a repair shop and Soviet marines to guard these; then he wanted the whole area to be given over to Soviet control and permission to raise their flag over it. Nasser "was trying to make the Russians see Egypt's defeat as their defeat", meaning he was moving straight into the 'Cold War' vortex. But at that time Nasser's popularity among the Arab people was still immense; he, and Arab unity, could still make a comeback.

So Israeli deep penetration air raids into Egypt continued in the post-June 1967 months. Egypt had no defence against these; they had not been given any. Finally, in January 1970 Nasser paid a secret visit to Moscow and asked the Soviet leaders to give him an effective anti-aircraft missile. They agreed; they also agreed to provide the crews. By April 1970 the missiles were in position and the raids stopped. So much for the Soviets, their role now more or less played out.

Then the Americans came. Nasser died at the end of September 1970 and Anwar Sadat took over as President. Having been given suitable hints, he made the approach to the US during the next couple of years, getting rid of those in his cabinet who were seen to be pro-Soviet and in July 1972 deciding to get rid of all Soviet military personnel in Egypt, by then numbering 21,000.

Even the French had at one time tried to play a hand, one indication of how low exactly Arab esteem in the world had reached after the 1967 war. In February 1968 President Aref of Iraq was in Paris and, as he was saying farewell to de Gaulle on the steps of the Elysee Palace, the latter told him, meaning the Arabs, "you know that we are backing you, even if you want the French Army." We are not told what Aref, who had certainly read the history of the Algerian War, thought of this offer.

By assuming that the two great powers were rivals, that they could be played off against one another, the Egyptians were going against the forces of history. Behind that assumption lay the assessment that the two of them alone had the initiative; whereas the initiative was passing into the hands of those smaller powers that could take advantage of the change in the balance of forces. So "by 1973 Egypt had almost become the laughing stock of the Arab world ... each day that passed was a day of humiliation for Egypt."[28]

## The South Yemen War

And now back to the British.

The blow of 1956 had not been fatal for them; a great empire is not brought to an end by one defeat, especially if you can argue, as they did, that it wasn't really a defeat; they had won the war and lost the diplomacy thereafter. It was finally brought to an end in 1967 when the people of South Yemen decisively won a war against them.

The 1956 war was not totally without effect. Along with violent resistance elsewhere in the empire, including Malaya and Kenya, Cyprus and the Gulf, the British had to retreat. First Malaya and Ghana, then East Africa, Nigeria, Cyprus had to be surrendered. But the British self-image of an imperial, now called world role, remained.

In 1958, for instance, Britain maintained force levels of over 100,000 men in the region east of Suez and this was not reduced as the years passed. New and major military equipment depots were added at Singapore, Aden and Kenya; air mobility exercises in the general region of the Indian Ocean were increased. Sea-borne task forces were readied. The army developed a handbook, *Keeping the Peace*, on countering guerilla war. By 1961 Britain had more operational ships east of Suez than west; by 1962, with all the African empire gone or going, there was a Chiefs of Staff paper which asserted that the main threat to British interests had shifted from Europe to Asia and Africa; dealing with that threat would be the main role for the British armed forces for the next ten years. So Britain was firmly set on an expanded world role. She had, according to official statements, a special responsibility for maintaining the peace in some parts of the world, more so east of Suez. The 1964 White Paper on Defence focused particularly on the world role. When Prime Minister Harold Wilson spoke that year in the Guildhall, on the occasion of the Lord Mayor's banquet on 26 November, he said, "We are a world power and a world influence or we are nothing."[29] This was reiterated in June 1966 when the government made it clear that they had neither the wish nor the intention to abandon the world East of Suez. Anybody who doubted that role was firmly told off. When US Secretary of State Dean Acheson suggested at West Point in December 1962 that 'Great Britain has lost an empire and has not yet found a role ... the attempt to play a separate role ... is about played out', he got a terse response from Prime Minister Macmillan that 'Mr. Acheson has fallen into an error which has been made by quite a lot of people in the last 400 years, including Philip of Spain, Louis XIV, the Kaiser and Hitler ...'.

Then the war came in South Yemen, at the end of which the world role was abandoned, immediately, completely and for good.

In 1962 Britain had decided to make Aden the heart of its world role. A separate military command structure had already been placed there in 1957. Now the Defence White Paper, 1962, titled *The Next Five Years*, clarified that Aden was to be in the future a base, meaning a place where troop ships, aircraft and heavy equipment for use in the role would be stationed; and a garrison, to help maintain law and order in the empire and Commonwealth. Land forces would be permanently stationed there and to enable a vivid picturisation of all this an 'Aden Forces Week' was organised that year with a programme of flag showing visits by British aircraft carriers, HMS' Centaur and Ark Royal along with their three escorts, a two-hour flying display by scimitars and sea-vixen jet fighters and an awed crowd of 50,000. Aden and Singapore, along with Britain itself, were to be the three key points of Britain's world role

When the Portuguese arrived in the Indian Ocean Aden was a major centre of trade: ivory, coffee and slaves came there from Abyssinia; the finest Arabian horses, in demand particularly in India, from the North; pepper, cloves, nutmeg from the East. All the big ships trading into the Red Sea called there. Albuquerque tried to conquer it in 1513; he was defeated and the Portuguese could never bring it into their empire, though without it they could hardly impose the trade embargo on the ships of other nations on which their profits depended. Not having Aden was one of the reasons their empire in the Indian Ocean, such as it was, crumbled. But by the nineteenth century Aden had fallen on bad times; the Cape route dominated trade; ships stopped calling; people moved elsewhere; when the British attacked and took it in 1839 the total population was only 1,000. Even so they gave the British a hard time; reinforcements were rushed in from India before the conquest could be completed.

Violent resistance continued from the different Yemeni tribes but it was not till 1957 that, following the boost given to Arab nationalism by the Suez victory, it intensified. Then in late 1962 several of the militant groups formed the National Liberation Front

(NLF). The first NLF attack took place in October 1963 in the mountains of the Radfan, just east of the road from Aden to the border town of Qatabah. In the weeks and months that followed the NLF showed just how adept it was at guerilla warfare. They were, according to British military sources, "accustomed to carrying out lightning raids and ambushes, they could move far and fast across the mountains and were thus an elusive enemy ... extremely courageous, as was shown by their capacity to fight on in the face of heavy artillery and air attack."

As the NLF extended their control over the villages the British declared a state of emergency in December 1963 and brought in reinforcements; they used helicopters for tactical attack as the French had first done in Algeria; they brought in Centurion tanks, they drove populations out of the valleys where the NLF was thought to be so that these could be swept; they dropped leaflets telling the people to clear out and then came in with heavy artillery and air power to blast the area. But the NLF was better; by 1964 they had extended their operations into Aden town.

The British tried other tactics. There were three distinct administrative units: Aden colony; the Western Protectorate; and the Eastern Protectorate. The two Protectorates were ruled by Amirs, tribal rulers who had entered into treaty relations with the British. In the late 1950s and early 1960s all these had been brought together in the Federation of South Arabia, a creation that the British hoped would be moderate and representative. So now they tried to get collaborators among the rulers. The NLF assassinated those who agreed to collaborate. They held elections to a Legislative Council in October 1964 and appointed a Chief Minister; then the Chief Minister called for a British withdrawal, so they sacked him and dissolved the Council. Finally, having by 1965 realised that they had lost the war, the British tried to find moderates with whom they could negotiate an orderly withdrawal, retaining at least some facilities. They found there were no moderates. And, as the days passed, they were more surely losing the war.

But they had to have some kind of face-saving device. By mid-1967, in desperation they tried to put together a caretaker government to which they could hand over power; the effort failed. And in this atmosphere of twice daily searches of the bedrooms, fluoroscopic examination of all incoming parcels, alarm bells behind every bed, British casualties mounted and the NLF stayed in the shadows; there was no one for the British to talk to. And then the Amirs who had been their interlocutors and representatives, the ones on whom they had been depending for the face saving, started surrendering to the NLF one by one.

The British position had actually collapsed by mid-1967 and they still didn't know who their opponents were. The unspoken message from the NLF was straightforward: leave or be thrown out. By August 1967 they found that all the structures of power they had so laboriously built up "had been simply swept away."[30] There was nothing for it but to leave. The NLF did them the final courtesy of a few days of negotiations in Geneva at the end of November 1967, so that they could say they had handed over power; nothing was negotiated except that diplomatic relations would be established.

And so the British left. During the last stages aircraft from the carriers *Victorious* and *Hermes* staged demonstrations of force over Aden; Wessex helicopters fitted with search lights and guns patrolled the airspace over Khormaksar airfield from where the last troops departed. But these were the death spasms of a sinking empire, as one historian suggested. And by 29 November they had all gone. There were no ceremonies, no leave taking; they just left. And a few weeks later, on 16 January 1968, "the last shudder" of those death spasms,[31] Premier Harold Wilson announced in the House of Commons drastic cuts in government expenditure, an about turn in the assumptions that had so far guided Britain's world policy including the acceleration of the withdrawal of British forces from East of Suez and, in effect, the end of Britain's world role. And even the US didn't sound happy; Dean Rusk, Secretary of State, said, "this represented a major withdrawal of the UK from world affairs, and it was a catastrophic loss to human society."[32]

## ENDNOTES

[1] Raymond Aron, *The Century of Total War*, Greenwood Press, Westport, Connecticut, 1954, p. 22.

[2] Major-General J.F.C.Fuller, *The Conduct of War, 1789-1961*, Natraj Publishers, Dehra Dun, 2003, p. 35.

[3] Raymond Aron, op. cit., p. 28.

[4] Philip Gibbs, cited in Niall Ferguson, The Pity of War, 1914-1918, Penguin Books, London, 1999, Introduction, p. xxviii

[5] The 1939-45 war, of course, does not quite fall into the same category, since many agreed that it had been necessary to defeat Hitler, who started it. But even in this debate, there were those, like the well known historian A.J.P.Taylor, who argued

that he was not solely responsible for it.

[6] H.G.Wells, *The New and Revised Outline of History*, Garden City Publishing Co., New York, 1931, p. 1102.

[7] Stephen E. Ambrose, *Rise to Globalism, American Foreign Policy since 1938*, Penguin Books, Harmondsworth, 1984, p. 14.

[8] Quincy Wright, *A Study of War*, abridged, University of Chicago Press, 1970, p. ix, author's note, and p. 370.

[9] Arnold J. Toynbee, *A Study of History*, abridgement of volumes I-VI by D.C.Somervell, OUP, London, 1949, pp. 190, 342, and 364.

[10] Gabriel Kolko, *Century of War, Politics, Conflict and Society since 1914*, The New Press, New York, 1994, p. x.

[11] Harold and Margaret Sprout, *Foundations of International Politics*, D. Van Nostrand, Princeton, New Jersey, 1962, p. 137.

[12] David Vital, *The Survival of Small States: Studies in Small Power/Great Power Conflict*, Oxford University Press, London, 1971, p. 5.

[13] Michael Handel, quoting Amry Vandenbosch in *Weak States in the International System*, Frank Cass, London, 1981, p. 36.

[14] Michael Howard, Military Power and International Order, in John Garnett, ed. *Theories of Peace and Security, A Reader in Contemporary Strategic Thought*, Macmillan, London, 1970, p. 42.

[15] Hedley Bull, *The Anarchical Society*, Macmillan, London, 1977, p. 186.

[16] Cyril Falls, *The Art of War, From the Age of Napoleon to the Present Day*, Oxford University Press, London, 1961, p. 2.

[17] Rafael Reuveny and Aseem Prakash, The Afghanistan war and the breakdown of the Soviet Union, *Review of International Studies*, 1999, Vol. 25, p. 696.

[18] Harold and Margaret Sprout, op. cit., pp. 146 & 103.

[19] Louis J. Halle, *The Cold War as History*, Chatto and Windus, London, 1967, p. 8.

[20] P. M.H. Bell, *The World Since 1945, An International History*, Arnold, London, 2001, p. 33.

[21] Quoted in Paul M. Kennedy, *The Rise and Fall of British Naval Mastery*, Macmillan, London, 1983, pp. 325-6.

[22] Cited by Dwight D. Eisenhower, *Waging Peace, 1956-61*, Heinemann, London, 1966, p. 36. Eisenhower thought the British were being emotional about the whole thing and the French 'even more emotional'.

[23] Alfred M. Lilienthal, *There Goes the Middle East*, The Bookmailer, Inc., New York, 1958, pp. 160 and 192 for this and the previous paragraph.

[24] Mohamed H. Heikal, *Cutting the Lion's Tail, Suez through Egyptian Eyes*, Andre Deutsch, London, 1986, p. 180. Heikal was editor of *Al Ahram*, the most influential of the newspapers in the Arab world; he was also a close confidant of Nasser.

[25] Dwight D.Eisenhower, op. cit., p. 40.

[26] J.M. Roberts, *The Penguin History of the World*, Penguin Books, London, p. 1023.

[27] Dwight D. Eisenhower, op. cit., pp. 177-183.

[28] Mohamed Heikal, *Road to Ramadan*, Natraj Publishers, Dehra Dun, 1981, pp. 47-48, 59 and 205 for this and the previous four paragraphs.

Heikal was editor of *Al Ahram*, the most influential of the newspapers in the Arab world; he was also a close confidant of Nasser.

[29] Joseph Frankel, *British Foreign Policy, 1945-1973*, Oxford University Press, London, 1975, p. 156.

[30] Fred Halliday, *Arabia Without Sultans*, Penguin Books, Harmondsworth, 1979, pp. 196, 198 and 218, for this and the previous four paragraphs.

[31] Paul Kennedy, op. cit., p. 326.

[32] Memorandum of Conversation, 11 January, 1968, *Foreign Relations of the United States, 1964-1968, Vol. XII*, p. 608.

# 8

# The 'Cold War' that wasn't—II

That brings us to the US and the Soviet Union.

They found themselves in a world in which the balance of strength between two great powers and their allies, on the one hand, and the so-called third world, had changed. During the first three quarters of the $19^{th}$ century there had been a certain balance, weighted only slightly in favour of the so-called great powers; so the colonial empires had grown very slowly, hardly quicker than during the $17^{th}$ and $18^{th}$ centuries. Indeed, apart from India there was almost no growth, though much was claimed, and this was due to the resistance of the nations of Asia and Africa against whom the colonial powers were fighting; the latter were not strong enough. Then around 1875 the imperial powers strength relative to their Asian and African opponents grew phenomenally and the empire grew with corresponding rapidity. Then after 1918 the balance shifted in the opposite direction and the great powers' hold on the colonies weakened. By 1945 the so-called third-world nations definitely had the edge over the great powers. So there was no question of the latter attempting the kind of control over the former that Britain and France or even Belgium and Portugal had over their empires fifty years earlier.

While this reinforced the arguments against going to war in the exercise of power, one of the alternatives was that they could to resort to ideology and other indirect methods. Ideology meant each of the third world nations had the choice, if at all they wanted great power control, over which one would control them and how much they could control. Other indirect methods were such as working together to ensure that the smaller countries didn't get the most powerful weapons or missiles; keeping them weak would be an encouragement to choose one side or other, as we saw in the case of Egypt in the last chapter. If that didn't work either the great powers could also simply assert that they had power even if it wasn't available; this would be by simulation. Finally, of course, as described by the traditional episteme or story, the two great powers did occasionally resort to war to extend their power.

So, first, ideology served as the starting point. The third-world nations would indicate their choice by the ideology adopted by them, though the great powers did put in a lot of effort, as we have seen in the case of Egypt, to influence that choice. Then, secondly, if no such choice was indicated, comes the simulacrum, the generation of the hyper real of power to conceal that there is none. And lastly war comes.

These three alternatives are covered below.

## Ideology and Super Power Endeavour

Where ideology was concerned the great powers endeavour comprised two stages.

In the first stage the third-world nation concerned would have to accept that its nationalism, its ideology, political and economic system would count for nothing if they were not aligned with one side or the other. The American diplomat and academic George Kennan gave voice to this in 1931, when he was in a diplomatic assignment in Latvia, "the present system of Soviet Russia is unalterably opposed to our traditional system, that there can be no middle ground between the two."[1] And thereafter it was reiterated often by President Truman for instance in March 1947, one of the passages quoted most often by historians "at the present moment in world history nearly every nation must choose between alternative ways of life"; one way has "free institutions, representative government, free elections, guarantees of individual liberty, freedom of speech and religion", while the other has "the will of a minority forcibly imposed upon the majority. It relies upon terror and oppression, a controlled press and radio, fixed elections and the suppression of personal freedoms."[2] And by the document called National Security Council paper 68 of April, 1950, the first comprehensive statement of an American national strategy, and which "came close to saying that all change was directed by the

Communists", meaning it was either them or us, and everyone would have to choose one or the other. Eisenhower was equally categorical, saying in his 1952 campaign for President, "we can never rest until the enslaved nations of the world have in the fullness of freedom the right to choose their own path."[3]

As for those who did not wish to join either side, who wished to remain neutral, Secretary of State John Foster Dulles made it clear during an address to Iowa State University in June 1956 that unless there were exceptional circumstances neutralism was "an immoral and shortsighted conception." At the heart of the US policy in this respect lay the concept of freedom in the shape given to it by President Roosevelt in his four freedoms speech of 6 January 1941, of speech, of religion, freedom from want and from fear. Then Secretary of State Dean Acheson elaborated it during the Korean war in a so-called 'strategy of freedom' speech of November 1950, setting out exactly what the US and the world have to do to ensure the safeguarding of peace and freedom. So there was freedom on the one hand and communism on the other. And communism, "no matter how it may be described or disguised, requires dictatorship as a condition of its existence ... the total destruction of individual liberty ... of freedom of choice."[4]

On the other side (the same side really) there is the thought process of socialism or scientific socialism. "In our modern system of international relations", wrote one author who was then a member of the prestigious Soviet Academy of Sciences and later went on to become Russian Foreign Minister and Prime Minister, "the contradiction between socialism and capitalism is the main and the decisive contradiction."[5] Put another way there are today just two new categories (that is, excluding relations among or between the socialists and the capitalists, which had been there since 1917) of international relations – "relations between the socialist and the developing countries, and relations between these countries and the imperialist states." It is meaningless, in other words, to talk of relations among the developing countries themselves. So the developing countries have to choose between one or the other; it is recognised that certain circles among them "are not averse to walking the nationalist tightrope" and though this may "produce ephemeral (and often illusory) advantages, the basic, long-term interests of the developing countries are damaged" by walking on that tightrope or by trying to "put together some kind of third force."[6] The same thing is true of ideas like Arab unity, which aroused as much opposition from the Soviet Union as from the US and the West. "Individual Arab peoples are evolving or have evolved, and even in some cases separate Arab nationalities ... peoples with some very pronounced differences."[7] Arab unity is, therefore, to be discouraged. And the communist parties in the Arab world did, indeed, discourage it, as we have seen in chapter 7 earlier.

In sum, so far as ideology was concerned "the Cold War presented itself as a worldwide contest between liberal democracy and communism. Each side looked forward to the eventual supremacy of its system all over the earth". There was no third course, because the essence of the global situation and, "according to this image, the essence of life, is the struggle between good and evil so represented."[8]

The second stage is to get the people and above all the leaders to act in such a way that their own nationalism, their ideologies and so on would be submerged and would stay submerged by the ideological framework of one or the other of the great powers.

We may consider three aspects of this stage: the political; the economic; and foreign policy.

The Soviet way was to put economics in the lead; then politics; and foreign policy would follow automatically. In other words, once an uncommitted nation implemented specific economic policies, a long step would have already been taken towards the door leading to the socialist camp. Politics would get you right to the door and foreign policy through it.

The economic part is set out, as one good example, in the report of the Central Committee to the 26th Congress of the CPSU. To show that the socialist orientation has been chosen there should be "the gradual elimination of the positions of imperialist monopoly, of the local big bourgeoisie and the feudal elements, and restrictions on foreign capital ... the securing by the people's state of commanding heights in the economy and transition to planned development of the productive forces ... enhancing the role of the working masses in social life ..."[9] The expansion of the public sector through large projects would create an increasing working class, concentrated in a few areas for propagation among them of the socialist ideology. This is to be done through nationalisation, which would herald "a major breach in the system of neo-colonialist exploitation",[10] but also nationalisation of indigenous corporations if any, in order to ensure the dominant controlling role of the state in the economy.

Then follows the political, first the coming to office of anti-imperialist and pro-left-nationalist petty-bourgeois strata supported by the urban and rural working people, a sort of intermediary step, and then the creation of a Vanguard Party, in which the now greatly strengthened working class would play an increasing role, and which will at a later or third stage evolve into a full-fledged Marxist-Leninist Party, meaning one controlled from the Soviet Union. Unless this third stage was accomplished, that is, unless the Soviet Union was given the rod, the Vanguard Party could reject Marxism-Leninism, and even turn away from the socialist path. But one author wrote happily in December 1979 that "the convergence of revolutionary democracy with the theory and practice of scientific socialism has become noticeably stronger. This is manifested particularly in the creation of vanguard parties of a new type in a number of countries (Angola, Mozambique, Benin, and South Yemen) which base their programmes on principles of scientific socialism."[11]

Finally there has to be the proclamation of socialism as the ultimate aim of the country's social development and all the other signals of the foreign policy path chosen: an anti-imperialist foreign policy; solidarity with others of socialist orientation; comprehensive cooperation and close friendly relations with the socialist countries as the principal international support of socialist orientation.[12]

For the US, on the other hand, the starting point was the political. The Eisenhower administration's defence budget was intended to help create and promote, as one example, "a system of freedom of choice for individuals, democratic procedures for government, and a private enterprise economy." For Kennedy it was "the preservation of 'Freedom under God'" and spreading individual liberty. For America it was necessary to ensure a demonstration effect; as President Reagan announced in 1983, "the undeniable truth that America remains the greatest force for peace anywhere in the world today ... the American dream lives – not only in the hearts and minds of our countrymen but in the hearts and minds of millions of the world's people ... who look to us for leadership."

President Kennedy was quite specific about the enemy. "The enemy is the Communist system itself – implacable, unceasing in its drive for world domination. For this is not a struggle for the supremacy of arms alone – it is also a struggle for supremacy between two conflicting ideologies: Freedom under God versus ruthless, godless tyranny."[13]

And then that "the great battleground for the defence and expansion of freedom today is the whole southern half of the globe ... the lands of the rising people."[14]

So it was the first purpose of US policy to ensure that the governments in the uncommitted nations should promote liberal political values and respect human rights and, in general, move towards a western style domestic order.

The economic part was also important. Within these societies there were high income groups and others; US policy was to create economic inter-dependence so that capital can more easily flow to the multinationals and local industrialists so that exports increase; labour saving technology which would put more economic power into the hands of the elite; and an economic structure that serves as inducement to the inflow of capital from outside into both financial and industrial sectors.

Finally there was, as in the case of the Soviet Union, the foreign policy commitment, which would need to be put in place through a security relationship. During the 1950's bilateral and multilateral security treaties and agreements multiplied so that by the early 1960's there were forty countries tied in eighty such treaties and agreements to the US.

## Super Power Cooperation and Condominiums

Another concern was to ensure that none of the uncommitted nations, and in fact no one who didn't yet have them, would be able to develop or obtain the kind of weapon which could threaten either of the great powers, much as the imperial powers had done in the late 19th century. This offered a strong foundation for cooperation between the US and the Soviet Union.

This was done through control regimes initiated by the two of them, with assistance from China and the larger West European countries.

The earliest and most important such regime was the Nuclear Non-Proliferation Treaty (NPT). Under this five states, the US, the Soviet Union, China, Britain and France, which had developed and tested nuclear weapons by the time the treaty was agreed, 1 July,

1968, undertook under the first article 'not to transfer to any recipient whatsoever nuclear weapons or other nuclear explosive devices or control over such weapons ... directly or indirectly'. They also agreed (Article III(2)) to control the export of nuclear related material and equipment, though at this stage there was no detailed definition of what this might comprise. All the others who signed the Treaty pledged not to receive nuclear weapons or other nuclear explosive devices, and to ensure that no state which did not have nuclear weapons got on the road to making them. Each of them also had to accept safeguards, meaning they would have to sign an agreement with the International Atomic Energy Agency under which the latter would be able to verify and ensure that nuclear facilities for peaceful purposes would not be used for weapons development.

Somewhat later it was decided to put down in detail all the things whose export should be controlled; a Professor Zangger of Switzerland suggested that this be done and helped draw up such a list, which was finalised in 1974, became the basis thereafter for export control and came to be known as the Zangger list. Somewhere near the bottom of the NPT there was mention of nuclear disarmament, but this may have been inserted for consumption by the media. The Treaty was renewed in permanence in 1995.

The regime initiated by the NPT was reinforced in stages, first of all by setting up a nuclear suppliers group or NSG. This was set up in 1978 to coordinate the conditions for export of nuclear-related materials and equipment. It includes the US, the Soviet Union and all developed nations that have any capability for the export of nuclear material, equipment or technology, as listed in guidelines that were drawn up for the purpose. The guidelines became the 'London Guidelines' or NSG guidelines Part I, under which if any item under export control is exported to a non-nuclear weapon state the latter must give a formal assurance it will not be used for any nuclear explosive device; must have an agreement with the IAEA requiring the application of full scope safeguards; shall protect the item from any intrusion or outside contact; and shall receive the same assurances from any third state to which the item might be transferred.

Subsequently came the NSG guidelines Part II in 1992, essentially after it was known that Iraq had carried out clandestine efforts at nuclear weapon development, and these provided that dual use items, meaning non-nuclear things which could conceivably be useful to develop nuclear weapons, like lasers or software or even machine tools would also be subject to control (dual use items are not included in the Zangger list; and the NSG provides for full scope safeguards, the Zangger list only for the items actually exported). Essentially it overlaps with the NPT but its purpose was to cover gaps in the latter such as the possibility of diverting material imported for civilian purposes, towards the development of a nuclear weapon capability.

Then other regimes came. The Comprehensive Test Ban Treaty of 1996, which has now been signed by some 180 states, aims to ban the carrying out of any nuclear weapon test explosion or any other nuclear explosion; but it has not yet entered into force, not having been ratified by all 44 listed states who are supposed to ratify it before it can come into force. And there is the Fissile Material Cut-off Treaty, designed as a non-discriminatory, multilateral and internationally and effectively verifiable treaty to ban the production of fissile material which could be used for a nuclear explosive device. This was recommended by a UN General Assembly resolution of December 1993, but negotiations have not yet started to get it going.

The Missile Technology Control Regime was initiated in April 1987 by the G-7, meaning the US, Canada, some West European countries and Japan; the Russian Federation joined it in 1995. All those who have any worthwhile missile technology are members. The idea was to ensure that the member-countries cannot be targeted and to this end control the transfer of technology. Subsequently, in 2002, it was thought that since India, Pakistan, Iran and North Korea have conducted repeated missile tests, the regime should be strengthened; so it was supplemented by an International Code of Conduct against Ballistic Missile Proliferation, known as the Hague Code of Conduct which has by now 119 signatory nations on board and is designed to be wider in its coverage. For instance, the MTCR had fixed the payloads and ranges for missiles in respect of which technology is not to be transferred; these are Category I items, systems capable of delivering weapons of mass destruction, payloads of at least 500 kilogrammes, up to at least 300 kilometres, with a Category II which covers payloads of less than 500 kilogrammes as also propellants, structural materials, jet engines, gyroscopes and so on. The Hague Code says no technology should be transferred, regardless of payload or range. Apparently these arrangements have been successful in slowing down or even stopping several missile programmes, such as those of Argentina, Egypt, Iraq, Brazil and South Africa.

There are some others like the 'Wassenaar Arrangement on Export Controls for Conventional Arms and Dual-use Goods and Technologies', which was concluded in 1995 to prevent the excessive transfer and accumulation of conventional arms like warships and tanks as well as the dual-use goods and technology to make them and that might threaten regional stability, regional and international security through the accumulation of conventional arms and related dual use goods and technology by state or non-state actors like terrorist groups. There is a constant effort to update the lists of items which should be subject to control. After the US attack on Iraq in 2003 it was found that a number of US aircraft were brought down by Man-Portable Air Defence Systems, so the Arrangement decided to include additional controls on MAN-PADS from that year.

All these regimes are based on the assumption that the technology for making nuclear weapons, middle-to-long-range missiles and heavy conventional weapons like tanks or ships was so difficult that only a handful of countries could develop it; all the others would have to be given it, or the weapons. This was not a sound assumption and the US made a serious effort, some three and a half years into the new millennium, to convert the strength of international opinion on the general subject of non-proliferation of all this into a mandatory part of international law, that the violation of any of the regimes, here the specific case was Iraq, would justify military action. But that takes us into the post-1990 period.

## Ground Rules

Cooperation between the US and the Soviet Union also showed itself in talk about ground rules for dealing with the third world, again a resurrection of the 19th century conferences and meetings by which the major powers of Europe agreed to divide up Asia and Africa into spheres of influence, protectorates or colonies. This was primarily because they had consistently failed to impose their will on smaller and third-world states despite what they saw as their overwhelming power. This, as one expert wrote, was what "led both powers to the gradual realisation that they had more reason to cooperate in order to cut losses, reduce risks and protect perceived gains..." It was "shared frustration" that oriented them towards cooperation rather than collision.[15]

Academic circles indulged in speculation about the existence of such ground rules. One suggests that "events in the year following Sputnik (1957) had the effect of establishing ground rules for the Cold War", since the US sent troops into Lebanon but the Soviet Union stayed out.[16] Another wrote that "with the world organised as it is ground rules have to be established and maintained" without crises that come as close to war as the one of 1962 over the Cuban missiles; and that crisis itself helped establish some rules.[17] Yet another wrote of a United States-Soviet condominium in Africa, so that once an African leader chose which side he wished to be on, the other side would stop subsidising his enemies.[18]

Some leaders other than those of the US and the Soviet Union said the same thing. French Foreign Minister Michel Jobert had referred in 1973 to the super power condominium and now in May 1982 Andre Fontaine wrote of the end of the condominium; super power influence became less assertive, the governments of smaller states eluded their control and the general propensity for war increased. "This amounted to the loss of joint dominion which has seemed so irreversible in international relations."[19]

Egyptian leaders felt strongly that the condominium was real and effective; especially about the 1967 war with Israel, which was covered briefly in chapter 7. General Abdul Hakim Amer, the Egyptian Commander-in-Chief, "charged the Soviet Union with collusion with the U.S.A." and that it had failed to give an accurate picture of Israel's troop disposition; not given replacements for the Egyptian aircraft that were destroyed by the Israelis; and put pressure on Egypt not to make the first strike, so that Israel could take the initiative, for on the evening of 25 May Eugene Rostow, US Under Secretary for Political Affairs in the State Department, had told the Egyptian Ambassador in Washington that the Israelis had information Egypt was going to attack that night, while the Soviet Ambassador to Cairo rang up Nasser a little while later, 3 a.m. on 26 May to say the same and to implore Egypt to desist.

But there was no official confirmation about ground rules, condominium, joint dominion or any of the other similar concepts. In June 1961, thinking to answer a question on this the US Department of State prepared a paper for the forthcoming meeting between Kennedy and Khrushchev in Vienna specifying that the "only ground rules for co-existence which exist in a jointly agreed document are in the Charter (of the United Nations) itself", which binds signatories to refrain from the threat or use of force.[20]

Other events led to talk about some kind of understanding between the two. When Eisenhower met Khrushchev for a summit in Geneva on 18 July, 1955, a 'Spirit of Geneva' signifying a future of goodwill and good relations was born. This was taken to imply US acceptance of Soviet control over East Europe. This did not prevent the Hungarian people from demanding that Soviet troops pull out of their country, in October 1956, and the Hungarian government announcing that it was pulling out of the Warsaw Pact. Then radio broadcasts from West Europe promising military help, especially from a 'Radio Free Europe' came to the aid of the Soviet Union; from being an attempt at freedom from Soviet control the uprising became dependent on American help, or even just an American conspiracy. Radio messages from the leaders of the uprising became desperate messages for American help, making the task of crushing it that much easier. So perhaps there *was* some kind of understanding at Geneva.

As part of the détente which began once the US realised that it had lost the war in Vietnam the two great powers signed a document defining the 'Basic Principles of Relations', on 29 May, 1972. This specified that they would "proceed from the common determination that in the nuclear age there is no alternative to conducting their mutual relations on the basis of peaceful co-existence"; that they "attach major importance to preventing the development of situations capable of causing a dangerous exacerbation of their relations"; and so will exercise restraint in mutual relations, settle differences peacefully and do all this with mutual accommodation and mutual benefit; and neither may obtain unilateral advantage at the expense of the other.

Some years later, in December, 1975, there were reports of a closed door meeting of US diplomats during which Helmut Sonnenfeldt, an aide to Secretary of State Kissinger, made a presentation which came to be known as the Sonnenfeldt doctrine; it even found its way into the *New York Times* on 6 April, 1976. It was that henceforth US policy should be to encourage more organic relations between the Soviet Union and its East European satellites, meaning the latter should have close enough relations to be content to stay within the Soviet sphere of influence. Kissinger himself argued that these close relations would remove the need for Soviet forces in East Europe and allow more autonomy there. Speculation grew that the two great powers might have agreed to earmark many more regions of the world for 'organic' relations with one or the other. But the doctrine itself came under attack from the US Congress, there is no real evidence that it ever became US policy and it was, in any case, based on a giant false assumption, since it was not the US or the Soviet Union, but the others who were doing the choosing, or whether at all they wished for organic relations. Only a war could change that.

Even so, scholars continued to write things. "In the sense that such agreements set codes of behaviour, Marquis of Queensberry rules for international relations, they can, in conjunction with agreements on specifics, create a climate of trust and a mutual recognition of possibilities and limits of cooperation."[21]

The codes of behaviour or ground rules proved to be useful on occasion, as, for instance, in bringing Europe gradually under US leadership, or holding the threat of Arab unity at bay. For this to happen, the smaller countries had to accept, as had President Nasser eventually, that world politics consisted of two things only: the overwhelming primacy of the two super powers, dwarfing everyone else and their unceasing rivalry.

## The Turning Point that wasn't

Some illustrations will show how, in general, this happened.

The first is that of Greece and Yugoslavia, often taken as a decisive turning point in the so-called 'Cold War'.

During the German wartime occupation of Greece there were two resistance movements: one led by the National Liberation Front (EAM) which was sponsored by the Greek communist party (KKE) and the other sponsored by the British and led by the right wing, the National Republican Greek League (EDES). Towards the end of the war, as British forces moved in, the KKE was in control of Athens and large parts of Greece; several weeks of street fighting proved necessary to evict it by January 1945. A year of peace followed. Then in February 1946 the EAM decided to renew the armed struggle, this time with Soviet encouragement in order to establish a socialist order. The British soon found they could not afford the money to keep 40,000 troops in Greece, as they had done so far, or for a Greek army of 100,000, necessary to fight the EAM.

So on 21 February 1947 they told the Americans they could no longer afford the financial commitment to defend Greece (or Turkey).

This was, if we turn momentarily to the modernity story, a "turning point for the West."[22] It led to the Truman Doctrine; it led to the domino theory, since Truman had specified that the collapse of free institutions in Greece and Turkey "might well spread throughout the entire Middle East"; and it led to American military and civilian involvement in West Europe through economic aid and the deployment of manpower. Actually, coming back to the traditional story, US military and economic aid and the personnel sent to supervise its use made little difference to the outcome in Greece. "American aid strengthened the right and the military in Greek politics, but did little to defeat the insurgency. On the contrary, the Greek government flouted American prescriptions ...it won by brute force. And it was able to do so because of the weaknesses of the insurgent movement."[23] Three things happened. The KKE, under Soviet influence, got deeper into Marxist ideology, stressing the importance of the urban working class, whereas their support base was among the peasantry. They switched, again under Soviet directions, from guerilla warfare to positional warfare which led to military disasters. Then in June 1948 the Cominform passed a resolution expelling the 'Tito clique' from the world communist movement; the KKE was strongest in the North, with Yugoslavia (as also Albania and Bulgaria) providing support, sanctuary and supplies; now in July 1949, thinking he would get US support against the Soviet Union Tito closed the Yugoslav border with Greece. Stalin himself had decided even earlier to abandon the KKE and had authorised Bulgaria and Albania to resume diplomatic relations with Greece, a sign that there was going to be no more support. So in October 1949 Nikos Zachariadis, the KKE leader, proclaimed an end to armed struggle. And soon after all this happened (February 1952) Greece became a member of NATO, though Yugoslavia remained independent, becoming over the years one of the most prominent members of the non-aligned movement. It was not easy to assert, from all this, that the US was in control; it seemed rather that developments had taken a course quite independent of the two great powers. In brief, there was no turning point, no dramatic onset of the 'Cold War' as a result of the above events.

In 1950 there was war in Korea.

At the end of World War II, during which it had been under Japanese occupation, the US and the Soviet Union had decided that the latter would disarm Japanese troops north of the 38th parallel, the former south of it. The division of the country continued. Then on 25 June 1950 the North Koreans launched a massive attack on the South. Prior to this, US spokesmen had suggested that it was not part of US national interest to defend South Korea and that it was not "very greatly important."[24] Now, on 27 June 1950, subsequent to the attack, President Truman formally extended his doctrine to Asia and declared that he had "ordered United States air and sea forces to give the Korean Government troops cover and support." At the same time, he announced the strengthening of US forces in the Philippines, accelerated military assistance to that Government as also "acceleration in the furnishing of military assistance to the forces of France" for the war in Indochina.[25] US troops went into South Korea and by October they were at the northern border with China. Then the Chinese entered the war which went back and forth until, by mid-1951, the front was roughly along the 38th parallel. And so it stayed. Neither side won, showing that, pitted against a largely rural and under-developed country, hardly one which could be called a great power, the US found it difficult to win. This was said to be because "the Chinese found cheap ways to stalemate every move the US-led coalition mounted ... constantly constructed fortifications ... that effectively protected them against firepower"; and besides the great US superiority was in the air and by early 1952 all the targets of any possible military significance had already been destroyed. So what now? One answer seemed to be to target civilians, something every power had done since 1920. That didn't help win the war. "In Korea the U.S. had to confront the reality that its technology could not, regardless of the claims of its many advocates, produce victory."[26]

According to modernity the Chinese performance in this war was written off as due to Soviet support. But the war had the side effect, as had the European crises of the late 1940s, of getting a number of countries to choose. The result was a US military alliance of 1952 with Japan, a mutual security pact of 1953 with South Korea and a Treaty of September 1954, the South-East Asia Collective Defence Treaty which brought the Philippines and Thailand (and, somewhat of an outsider, Pakistan) onto the US side. So some lines of division in Asia had now also been drawn but there were still two problems.

First, these lines were not the borders of any realm of power, only the elaboration of a structure to determine ideological leanings, hence part of the great power cooperative endeavour. The fact that country X chose an ideological alignment liked by the US (or the Soviet Union) did not mean that either of the latter had any real power over it. These alignments did not, therefore, make an empire.

Secondly, there were still too many who didn't recognize these lines. In Europe several countries stayed out; in Asia most stayed out. The non-aligned movement developed and its members even dared to presume to tell the two great powers what they should be doing. At the Belgrade nonaligned conference, 1961 Jawaharlal Nehru drafted a peace appeal to Khrushchev and Kennedy and the final declaration of the conference said "the further extensions of the non-committed area of the world constitutes the only possible and indispensable alternative to the policy of total division of the world into blocs, and intensification of Cold War policies."[27]

So power had also to be applied by simulation; the role of power was that of simulacrum. This simulation, as Baudrillard explains, is the generation by models of a real without origin or reality, a hyper-real. The hyper-real is created by words and figures and more especially by images and in this creation the media, therefore, have a crucial role to play. Signs of the real are substituted for the real itself, signs which can be repeated, modified, refined in the attempt to bring them close to perfection. In this hyper-real world signs of power replace actual power, while "power is no longer present except to conceal that there is none", and "when it has totally disappeared, logically we will be under the total spell of power."[28] This means that the concept need no longer stand up to testing; it is no longer necessary to ensure ideological alignment or to win wars to show power, for it is no more a relation of force but an object of social demand; and if a great power is pulled into a war the hyper-real enables it to announce victory regardless of the outcome on the ground.

It is only within the world of simulacra that both the traditional and the modernist stories can co-exist, so this world is like that of the renaissance wars, that were not really wars at all, but everybody agreed to call them wars; hence a triumph can be claimed uncontested, the possession of real power can be asserted, and since all this is done within a hyper-real world, it need not reflect any reality; it is the vaulting that great powers need to keep their impotence in the shadows.

One specific case illustrates the argument of the above two paragraphs.

## Simulacra in the India-Pakistan Case

From 3 to 16 December 1971 India and Pakistan were at war.

At independence, August 1947, Pakistan comprised two wings, East and West, separated by nearly 2,000 kilometres of Indian territory. This need not have been a problem; the enthusiasm for the two-nation theory, that the Hindus and Muslims of the sub-continent are two separate nations, was most vociferous in the East, which was the heart of the struggle for the creation of Pakistan. The leaders needed only to develop a distinctive Islamic sub-continental culture and polity in which the people from both wings could take part. Instead the West wing, with less than half of the population, tried to impose its will on the East; its language, Urdu, at the expense of Bengali; its economic development at the expense of that of the East which saw its share of GNP fall from more than that of the West in 1949 to less than 70% of that twenty years later; its foreign exchange use, especially for arms purchases, at the expense of the East, which earned most of it. No effort was made to nurture a shared sense of nationalism. If we ask the question posed in chapter 3, about how much skill was shown by the leaders in using the available resources to build the nation, the answer has to be very little or none.

In short the East was treated as a territory and a people to be exploited. The threat from India was used as an umbrella to cover all this; and a military alliance was concluded with the US to cover the threat. Over the years the Awami League, a political party dedicated to ending the exploitation through the achievement of greater autonomy for the East, became more and more popular. Elections held on 7 December 1970 gave it all but two of the parliamentary seats in the East and an overall majority in the whole of Pakistan, 167 out of 313 in the National Assembly. The military government led by General Yahya Khan refused to implement the result of the election, imposed martial law, and the East erupted into insurrection in March 1971. India was involved: the leaders of the insurrection often sought shelter in India and conducted raids from there into East Pakistan; while the Pakistan army cracked down on the civilian population so that a flood of refugees, some ten million altogether, flowed into India. By December 1971 General Yahya Khan decided to go to war with India; East Pakistan's secession could only be prevented if India were defeated in a war.

US policy to Pakistan was to keep the military strong as a balance against India, and in power if possible; in pursuit of that to give it as much weaponry as possible; and economic aid to keep it afloat. The military alliance was, of course, welcome, since it put Pakistan firmly into the ranks of the 'free nations'. So when war began the first US aim was to keep the country united; a truncated Pakistan would not be able to do much balancing against India. Within days of war breaking out it was clear that aim could not be achieved. The second aim was to convince Pakistan that the US had tried its best to help and had actually helped, in order to keep up their dependence on the US, their suspicions of the Soviet Union and their hostility to India. A Pakistan halved should not break with its past foreign policy. This was achieved by simulation. In other words, without doing anything that could influence the outcome, without, really, being able to do anything like that, the US convinced itself (and some others) that its second aim had been achieved; in this way the hyper-real, the operational double of the real, kept the real at bay.

The first thing was to deal with Pakistan's request for help. On 2 December the Pakistani Ambassador in Washington delivered a letter from Yahya Khan to President Nixon invoking Article I of their treaty of 1959 under which the US had agreed, in case of aggression against Pakistan, to "take such appropriate action, including the use of armed forces, as may be mutually agreed upon ... to assist the Government of Pakistan at its request." But this help would only be provided if there was armed aggression from a country controlled by international communism. Secretary of State Kissinger asked the Washington Special Actions Group, a select group which had been set up for dealing with just such situations, whether it could be said that India's action amounted to armed aggression from a country controlled by international communism, and referred to the Treaty of Peace, Friendship and Cooperation India had signed with the Soviet Union on 9 August 1971; perhaps that could prove India was a Soviet satellite. Then he asked if it was possible that India attacked first and was told it was indeed possible.

There was the question whether Pakistan could be supplied with arms. An embargo on the supply of lethal arms imposed in 1965 meant this could not be done directly; so could it be done indirectly, say through Jordan? Could F-104's be sent through there? asked Kissinger. He was told Jordan could not be authorised to send anything that the US itself could not. Could the US hope the Chinese would step in to help Pakistan? "We had to be ready to back up the Chinese if at the last moment they came in after all."[29] Another possibility was to force the blockade that India had imposed on Pakistan. Kissinger was told the blockade was legitimate belligerent action; that Pakistan had also taken similar action. There is then, in the most authentic accounts of what happened, a great deal of pique with the advice that the WSAG is giving and Kissinger says the US does not want to be even handed; the President believes India is the attacker; a US ally cannot be allowed to go down; the Indians cannot be allowed to scare off the US from taking action.

Finally it was decided on 9 December to send in a naval task force, TF 74, into the Bay of Bengal. Its mission was "to form a contingency evacuation force capable of helicopter evacuation of civilians, of self protection, and of conducting naval, air and surface operations as directed by higher authority in order to support US interests in the Indian Ocean area."[30] That mission was a good example of the hyper-real, a simulacrum. The intention was not to do anything, only to convince the Pakistanis that the US had done its best to help, had actually helped. By the time TF 74 was deployed it was already too late for the Pakistani army in the East; and it moved much too slowly for any decisive intervention – it passed through the Straits of Malacca on 13 December; there was no real risk of US involvement before the ceasefire came into force there on the 15 December.

And the Soviet Union was at one with the US on this; they too deployed a naval task force and told India they would not allow TF 74 to intervene. The operational double of the real had, so to speak, been doubled; there were now two simulacra.

The Pakistanis were not convinced, and we can trace much of the roots of anti-American feeling there to 1971.

But Kissinger was triumphant, for though the Pakistan army in the East had surrendered, the West was saved. Of India's ceasefire in the West, declared on the 16 December, he writes "there is no doubt in my mind that it was a reluctant decision resulting from Soviet pressure, which in turn grew out of American insistence, including the fleet movement and the willingness to risk the summit. This knowledge stood us in good stead."[31]

We can now turn to the use of military means, giving first two examples outside the Americas.

## Lebanon

An early example was in the Lebanon.

By the beginning of the year 1957 the US was ready once again to flex its military muscles on the international stage. The great post-war economic boom which started in the late 1940s and was boosted by the Korean War continued well into the 1950s. The signs of economic prosperity were everywhere: families who never owned houses were buying them as the move to suburbia resumed; three-quarters of all families owned cars in contrast to half in 1946; almost every home had a television set by 1957.

The conventional instrument for any muscle flexing was now less overpowering. After the July 1953 armistice in Korea US armed forces had been reduced in size; and that war, against an undeveloped country, not really a great power, didn't prove much about potency. But Eisenhower saw two mitigating factors that made the problem disappear. First, US public opinion was firmly supportive of the idea that communism must be pushed back. As early as his 1952 campaign he had opposed containment as negative, futile, immoral. The Republicans wanted rollback, not containment, and this was a centrepiece of the election campaign; and the public was behind this, as the results of both the elections, 1952 and 1956, showed. Secondly, the New Look policy made up for the lack of conventional forces; that meant brinkmanship, threatening the use of nuclear weapons whenever a crisis demanded the application of force, not sending in the Marines. The idea was that nuclear weapons were becoming more and more like ordinary weapons. Eisenhower said, "where these things are used on strictly military targets ... I see no reason why they shouldn't be used just exactly as you would use a bullet or anything else." And his Secretary of State, Dulles, having only nuclear weapons for use "had to flash a nuclear bomb whenever he wanted to threaten the use of force."[32] And Dulles backed this up by citing instances where going to the brink had led to an American triumph: Korea; Vietnam, after the French had been defeated and left; the Formosa straits.

So now, in early 1957, the US was ready, and an opening presented itself in West Asia. Here the Eisenhower doctrine, filling the vacuum in the Middle East before the Russians did it, and which was enunciated by Eisenhower and Dulles to congressional leaders on New Year's Day, 1957, had been formally approved. On 9 March, 1957 the US Congress approved a presidential resolution stating that "the United States regards as vital to its national interest and world peace the preservation of the independence and integrity of the nations of the Middle East", and is "prepared to use armed forces to assist" any Middle East country requesting assistance against armed aggression from any country controlled by international communism.

There were two caveats here: the country concerned had to request US assistance; and it had to be facing armed aggression from a country controlled by communism. So the first problem was that no one in the region wanted American assistance. A special emissary was sent to persuade them. Almost all flatly rejected the idea; none of them felt threatened, nor were they prepared to say they felt threatened. King Saud of Saudi Arabia even asked Eisenhower for a commitment that he was not going to interfere in the internal affairs of any Arab state.

There was, however, a small possibility in Jordan. There, King Hussein lived in fear of an Arab pro-Nasser movement developing. His Prime Minister, Suleiman Nabulsi, was neutralist, rather pro-Soviet than pro-US, keen on strengthening relations with the former, sympathetic to the Nasserites who were growing in numbers within the country. Two successive chiefs of staff of the armed forces, General Ali Abu Nuwar and General Ali Hiyari, seemed to be with Nabulsi, all of them probably planning a coup. They were all three dismissed and promptly took off for Damascus, a centre of Nasserism. Radio Cairo and Radio Damascus started calling for the overthrow of the King and the latter, thinking to invoke the Eisenhower doctrine, did talk about a communist coup being plotted against him. Perhaps, thought the Americans, one could say that Syria was controlled by international communism, though that would require a huge imaginative leap.

In April, 1957 Eisenhower, suitably encouraged by all this, suggested to Hussein that he should now invoke the doctrine, and, as an encouragement, a *demonstratio ad oculo*, as it were, moved several ships from the US Sixth fleet, a super carrier, two cruisers, fifteen battleships, to the Eastern Mediterranean.

Anyway the first thing was that the King must invoke the doctrine, and this, finally, he refused to do. So that came to nothing.

In Lebanon there was more of a possibility. President Camille Chamoun declared that he accepted the doctrine and the Parliament was persuaded (with the US super carrier *Forrestal* largely visible in Beirut port) to vote in its support.

A political crisis was brewing here. Lebanese politics had been a balance of sectarian interests. Seventeen sects were officially recognised. Given the population balance a National Pact of 1943 specified that the President should always be a Maronite Christian, the Prime Minister a Sunni Muslim, the Speaker of Parliament a Shia Muslim, the Minister of Defense a Druze, and so on, so that the distribution of power among the different sects and groups should be as agreed. In the Parliament itself the ratio of Christians to Muslims was 6:5, based on an earlier census. But now the balance of population had changed, though no new census had been taken since 1932, given the sensitivities on this point; it was known that the number of Muslims was increasing and an influx of Palestinians had accentuated this; they were agitated; they wanted more power. And Camille Chamoun, who was elected in 1952, wanted another six-year term, though the constitution provided that he could only be re-elected after a six-year interval. So his political ambition, the urge to keep Muslim aspirations at bay and to support the interests of the Christians led him to the doctrine.

Then, on 1 February 1958 Syria and Egypt merged into the United Arab Republic; Arab nationalism got a boost. By March 1958 Muslim rebels in Lebanon had taken to violence and rioting; there was fighting in Beirut and along the border with Syria; many of the rebels had taken shelter in Syria and when the latter opened the border in early May they came across in large numbers.

On 11 May, the American Ambassador in Beirut was approached by Chamoun: if he asked for assistance, what would the Americans do? Of course, he was told, the US "would respond favourably and strongly."[33] Again the Sixth fleet was alerted, sailed east and by 18 May, began making plans for the defence of Lebanon. But then everyone paused. The US waited for the request; Chamoun appealed to the Arab League and to the UN; he didn't actually ask for US help, so none could be given.

Again the weeks passed. Nothing seemed to happen; and there were the Marines on board the Sixth fleet, all ready to go.

Then, on 14 July 1958, came the Iraqi revolution. The King and his family were massacred; Prime Minister Nuri Said, who was very popular in the West, tried to escape, was caught and brutally done to death.

Chamoun now asked for assistance and by 3 pm on 15 July US Marines began landing on the Beirut beaches, in full battle gear, each carrying forty kilos of equipment and arms, accompanied by amphibious armour equipped tractors that roared up the sands, and with the thunderous reverberations of naval aircraft flying low overhead. And all this watched by the usual crowds on the beaches, the soft drink salesmen standing by their Coca Cola stalls, small boys selling ice cream and several amazed bathers. It was a week day so there were not too many of those. The Lebanese army didn't want the intervention and its Commander-in-Chief, General Fuad Chehab, was actually willing to try and stop the 'invasion', as he called it and issue instructions to his forces to do so. So the US Ambassador rushed to the beach to prevent any incident and to prevail on Chehab not to create a crisis.

Within two weeks the strength of the US force had reached 15,000. But there was nothing for it to do; there was no fighting, no threat, nothing. By October they all left.

It was, altogether, not quite what Eisenhower and the Americans had in mind when they thought of providing military assistance against armed aggression from any country controlled by international communism.

Two comments sum up this exercise. "The US Marines had not landed in pursuance of a defined objective: their purpose was to hold the situation and gain time in which the United States government could decide what their objective should be."[34] Somewhat less charitably, one American historian commented that, at the end of the whole exercise, "what they had accomplished was as much a mystery as why they had been sent in, in the first place."[35]

So at best this was a harmless exercise in muscle flexing.

But time passes. Things change. A quarter century later a similar exercise in muscle flexing, again in Lebanon, proved not so harmless.

By 1982 two factors had further complicated the situation there, one which was already complicated enough because of the uneasy sectarian balance among the population and the difficulty of so distributing power that everyone was happy.

One was the Palestinians. In 1970 Jordan expelled the Palestine Liberation Organisation from there; so they moved to Lebanon, which was too weak to do anything about it. By 1975 the Palestinian population had so grown that there were 350,000, including some 20,000 well armed fighters. Of course, the Sunni Muslims turned to the Palestinians for support, which they were glad to give, further upsetting the sectarian balance. The Christians, who had seen their position eroded over the years, resisted, and by 1975 incidents of fighting had begun; over the weeks this developed into a full-scale civil war between the two. The Lebanese army disintegrated. And then the Syrian army came in to help the outgunned Christians. So now for some six years, 1976-1982, 30,000 Syrian troops were in Lebanon as invited peacekeepers. But all the groups, who had over the years acquired sophisticated arms, retained them, and this situation most resembled a powder keg into which one end of a lit fuse has been pushed, with Maronite, Greek Orthodox, Armenian, Druze, Shia and Sunni rival factions, many of them broken further into sub-factions, each with its own well armed militia in addition to the Syrians.

One thing that could really have aggravated matters, shortened the fuse, was Israeli interference. And then one of them, the Phalange, the largest of the Maronite sub-factions, decided to ask for Israeli military help against the PLO and Muslims. So that was the second factor. In response to the request Israel started sending military and economic aid to the Lebanese Forces Christian militia (LF). Then it began small-scale raids on Palestinian positions in Lebanon; by April and May, 1982 the raids had intensified; then on 8 June it launched a full-scale attack. Starting with preparatory air strikes and an artillery barrage, 70,000 Israel troops crossed into Southern Lebanon, aiming to destroy all Palestinian opposition forces there. Within four days they had reached Beirut, and still their numbers were growing; by July there were 100,000 Israeli troops in Lebanon. There was, of course, a possibility that they would clash with the Syrian troops that were already there, but the Americans arranged a truce so that that would not happen.

The Israelis were really after the PLO fighters, now bottled up in Beirut, though intact and still fully armed. They didn't want to go into the city for that would have meant too many casualties; so they blockaded Beirut, bombarded it, starved it, trying to get the PLO to come out. It didn't work; the PLO stayed, and they didn't seem to have lost their fighting abilities.

That was when the US stepped in with an offer of a multinational (not UN) peace-keeping force to move in and oversee the evacuation of the PLO from Beirut. France and Italy also agreed to provide forces for the job. This was agreed and late in August the Marines started arriving. The evacuation of PLO fighters and of the Israelis from West Beirut was quickly completed and the Marines left by 10 September. But then they were back, and that is when the trouble began.

Bashir Gemayel, a Maronite Christian and one of key persons in developing the Phalange, their armed militia, had been elected President in August 1982. On 14 September, he was assassinated and though his brother Amine Gemayel was unanimously elected President by the Parliament, the Israelis felt instability was around the corner and entered West Beirut again (one of the things they did this time around was to look the other way as their friends the Phalangists massacred 800 Palestinians in the Sabra and Shatila refugee camps).

So now the Marines were back to support Amine Gemayel. And they hung on, increasingly coming under attack from snipers and facing the hostility of the population.

On 18 April 1983 a bomber drove a delivery van containing about a ton of explosives into the portico in front of the US embassy building and blew it up, collapsing the entire façade of the horse shoe shaped building. As may as 63 persons were killed including seventeen Americans. The Americans hung on, though, and worse followed.

On 23 October 1983 a truck loaded with almost six tons of explosives drove around the perimeter of the airport where the Marine landing team headquarters were located; then it crashed through the fence around the airport, through several further barriers and hammered its way right into the building housing the headquarters, where it exploded. The building was a four-storey reinforced steel structure resting on thick, fifteen-foot diameter, concrete pillars encasing thick steel rods. It wasn't enough. The massive upward pressure of the explosion sheared the pillars and lifted the entire structure of four storeys, more or less intact, into the air; it became airborne for moments and then slammed down, disintegrating into rubble. About 241 Americans died, mostly crushed by the collapsing building as it fell. It was the deadliest one-day attack on US forces abroad since World War II.

Six kilometres away the French troops were headquartered. Hearing the explosion they came out and were looking at the dust cloud when another truck bomb hit their building. Frenchmen, numbering 56, mostly paratroopers, were killed. President Reagan could not, of course, retreat immediately. But he'd had enough; on 7 February 1984 he ordered the American pullout from Lebanon and by 26 February they were all gone.

The finale came in September 1984 when yet another suicide bomber hit the US embassy in Beirut, burying Ambassador Bartholomew in the rubble. He was evacuated and the embassy closed.

Only one example of a comment is needed. "Instead of bringing an end to the domestic violence in Lebanon, instead of ensuring the orderly and complete withdrawal of the opposing Israeli, Syrian and Palestinian forces, and instead of promoting a rapprochement between Israel and its neighbours, the application of U.S. force and diplomacy had succeeded only in pushing these objectives beyond all reach."[36]

## Somalia and Ethiopia, Especially Somalia

The Soviet experience in the Horn of Africa was of a somewhat different nature, but showed the operation of the hyper-real equally well. Then the Americans came in and actually used military power. So this is the second example.

In 1977 Somalia and Ethiopia were at war. Both had been supported by the Soviet Union, politically, ideologically and with economic and military aid.

Somalia took independence in 1960 and had followed a generally uncommitted foreign policy. Religion and language united the Somalians, though deeper divisions existed because of clan loyalties. It leaned slightly towards the Soviet Union and got Soviet arms for its armed forces, but economic aid largely from the West. On 21 October 1969 the armed forces seized power in the name of a Supreme Revolutionary Council led by General Mohamed Siad Barre, and then, over the following years, moved much closer to the Soviet Union. Large projects were launched with Soviet aid; a large number of Soviet advisers were taken into the government departments including the military; Soviet naval visits started and continued to increase as time went by; and a campaign of nationalisation was initiated. Closer relations were developed with all the socialist countries, meaning the Soviet Union and its allies and a Revolutionary Socialist Party was formed as a vanguard party according to the requirements of scientific socialism.

Ethiopia under the Emperors had always been independent except for five years (May 1936 to April 1941) of Italian rule. Then a military coup of September 1974 put into power a Provisional Military Administrative Council. On 20 December 1974 the PMAC declared it had adopted socialism as its policy; thereafter an extensive programme of nationalisation of both foreign and local large industries was launched; agrarian reform was initiated; exclusive government control over natural resources asserted; a state monopoly on foreign trade introduced; and close relations established with all the socialist countries. Soviet commentators noted with approval the adoption of a Programme of National Democratic Revolution in April 1976; and by December 1979 a Commission for Organising the Party of the Working People of Ethiopia or COPWE was formed, to, inter alia, "disseminate the ideas of scientific socialism among the masses", in short a vanguard party.[37]

The war had already started and got over by then.

Somalia had claims on the Ogaden region of Ethiopia which was inhabited largely by Somalis. By mid-1977, having by then got an army of 37,000, heavy artillery and jet fighters from the Soviet Union, it felt strong enough to do something about those claims. Somali insurgents in the Ogaden, the Western Somali Liberation Front or WSLF, had been operating there for some years; now Barre launched an attack in their support and within two months had occupied most of the Ogaden. For about two months the Soviet Union tried to sit on both horses; Barre wanted more arms and they allowed him to visit Moscow in pursuit of them. But the Ethiopians would have none of this, so at the end of September 1977 they decided to dump Somalia; within weeks the flow of arms to Ethiopia was accelerated; 15,000 of the best Cuban troops were airlifted there; and in January 1978 a counter-offensive was launched. By March the Somalians announced their withdrawal or were thrown out from the Ogaden.

The episode showed three things: that the compulsions of local rivalries or disputes would always over-ride ideology in the third world; the commitment to scientific socialism was based not on any socio-economic reality but on a desire for military equipment; and that the role of the Soviet Union was often restricted to saying yes or no in response to that desire.

And, as an addendum, the fallout of all this on Somalia brought, years later, another lesson.

When Somalia was dumped by the Soviet Union, the West, led by the US, after a decent interval, of course, came in. In November 1977 Barre, the Soviet Union having dumped him, he also declared that he had broken with the Soviet Union, hoping the West would rush in with arms supplies; but they didn't. But by the early 1980s, with the 'cooling off' period over, a massive US economic aid programme got going, as also a substantial flow of arms which effectively went into the hands of Barre and his clan, the Marehan of the Darod, who controlled almost all government positions. The chief result of the massive aid programme was that soon half of Somalia's GDP was foreign aid; massive food aid was diverted by clan members, and sold on the market. With this level of food aid the economy, as was to be expected, collapsed. Agriculture collapsed; since so much food was coming in for free, no one wanted to grow it; all other economic activity collapsed, since it was all geared to dealing with the foreign aid and that was controlled by one clan. And with that Barre's hold on power started collapsing. Even earlier, as a result of the 1978 defeat in the Ogaden, rebellion had begun; a Somali Salvation Democratic Front led by the Marteyn clan of the Darod had been formed in Ethiopia and engaged in insurgency; a Somali National Movement (SNM), led by another clan, the Isxaaq, started another guerilla war; one of the clans, the Hawiye, formed the United Somali Congress (USC).

In early 1988 the SNM tried to capture two towns, Hargeisa and Burao, but were driven back with massive losses. In order to regroup they were forced to resort to even more aggressive clan-based recruitment. Then in 1989 Muhammed Farah 'Aideed' joined the anti-Barre rebellion. He has been described as "a ferociously touchy character whose nickname meant 'one who does not take insults lying down'; those who displeased him ran the risk of summary execution."[38] And he, too, resorted to recruitment on a clan basis, the Habar Gidir sub-clan of the Hawiye. This proved effective, so

Barre came under pressure and he, too, had to recruit even more aggressively on a clan basis. A war to liberate Somalia from the hold of a particular regime had thus become a clan war, factions splitting into sub-factions, fighting no longer for control of the state, which ceased to exist, but for local gains, food stores, extortion from relief agencies, control of goods especially the trade in the narcotic *gat* leaf.

With economic collapse the insurgencies and clan loyalties grew stronger; the army broke up into clan groups; by 1990 Barre was in effect only the Mayor of Mogadishu. In January 1991 the USC led by Aideed drove Barre and whatever remained of his army out of Mogadishu. Then a struggle for power between Aideed and another USC leader, Ali Mahdi, who was also a Hawiye but from a different sub-clan, broke out; there were also other clans in Mogadishu: the Isxaaq and the Majerteen, for instance, and neither would accept the Hawiye, no matter their leader. So they fought against them. Mogadishu was reduced to rubble as armed militias belonging to one or other clan or sub-clan battled in the streets. Well armed youth belonging to one clan or the other, riding in armed land rovers or pickup trucks, roamed the streets extorting and killing. "By late 1992, due to the civil war, the entire infrastructure of the country was ruined, mass killing, starvation, and disease afflicted much of the population ... there was no state, no one to negotiate with, no safety even for aid workers."[39]

Meanwhile, Barre's remnant forces went about plundering the countryside, burning villages, murdering and raping. According to UN estimates 300,000 died and 700,000 became refugees in that year.

In 1992 the UN decided to step in, or rather, the US did. UN Secretary-General Boutros-Ghali had been thinking for some time of ways in which the organisation could get into a more dynamic role. The vetoes of the 1945-90 period were no more; new tasks like ensuring human security were to be seen on the horizon; and the UN should be prepared to intervene within states. He outlined an *Agenda for Peace, 1992*, including a number of innovative concepts: preventive diplomacy, to prevent conflict; peace-making and then peace enforcement, if preventive diplomacy didn't work; peace-keeping, once the peace enforcers had done their job; post-conflict peace-building, to ensure the peace is kept in the long term. So the UN moved into Somalia. In December 1990 it had evacuated its personnel from there and through 1991, as fighting spread in the towns and country, they sat comfortably in Kenya. Now they moved back in.

But it was the US that really took the lead, guiding the UN to where all these innovative concepts of the *Agenda for Peace* could be applied.

In March 1992 the UN had arranged a ceasefire between Aideed and Ali Mahdi, but that didn't come into force immediately, while, with all the fighting that had already happened, civil order had completely broken down, a drought had led to famine, food just could not be sent in through the disorder. So an immediate ceasefire was really needed.

Step one was taken in April 1992 when the UN Security Council established a UN operation in Somalia, UNOSOM, to supervise the ceasefire between the clans which the UN had itself helped to organise a month earlier. This would enable food and humanitarian relief to be sent in. But UNOSOM had hardly any budget, no staff and certainly no capability to control the hundreds of gunmen driving around unhindered in Mogadishu in the so-called 'technicals', heavily armed pickup trucks; they were in control of the ports and airport, hijacked relief supplies and raided godowns. The months passed. UNOSOM couldn't actually do anything. So it came under attack by the media, by politicians in and outside the US and, most important, by the aid agencies like ICRC and CARE, who urged the international community to go in and run the country; meaning, of course, that the US should do that. "The international community, backed by UN troops, should move in and run Somalia, because it has no government at all", said Philip Johnston, president of Care-US in September.[40] US President George Bush and Boutros-Ghali liked the idea.

President George Bush offered US troops to the UN at the end of November 1992; this led to the historic UNSC Resolution 794 of 3 December 1992, voted on unanimously, the first ever to establish a humanitarian operation using Chapter VII of the UN Charter, that is, treating a humanitarian problem, the "magnitude of the human tragedy" as constituting a threat to international peace and security. So it had voted unanimously for armed intervention to establish a secure environment for humanitarian relief operations and six days later US Marines began landing in Somalia. Bush called the exercise Operation Restore Hope, and when the first US troops landed on the beaches of Mogadishu on 9 December, to a rousing reception by the massed international media, but no one else, and immediately got busy explaining exactly what they were about to do, the enthusiasm in the US and elsewhere was almost palpable.

US Ambassador to the UN Madeleine Albright coined the phrase 'assertive multilateralism' to cover this. And Somalia was the test case. As Albright said at one point, "we will embark on the unprecedented enterprise aimed at nothing less than the restoration of an entire country as a proud, functioning and viable member of the community of nations."[41]

There were no discernible US interests in Somalia; no one in Somalia had asked for UN, US or any other kind of intervention, though arguably there was by late 1991, and certainly by 1992 no state or other authority left there to do so; and when US troops did go in there was no congressional approval.

In any case by February 1993 the US had 28,100 troops on the ground in Somalia, with another 5,550 from other countries; this was UNITAF, the United Task Force.

But Robert Oakley, the former US Ambassador to Somalia, now head of Operation Restore Hope, "became hostage to the order that the warlords could provide, as this order was the key to the humanitarian effort."[42] So the warlords, who had already controlled Somalia before the US came, continued to reign supreme; as Jennifer Parmelee wrote in the *Washington Post* on June 25 1993, they were the players, everybody had to play ball with them, so "the world danced with the warlords."

On the whole the operation did save thousands of lives; but it also told the warlords like Aideed that without them the US could do little. Then came UNOSOM II, established by UNSC Resolution 814 of 26 March 1993 and this was much more ambitious, an attempt by the UN, again a first ever, to rehabilitate political institutions and the economy, to advance political reconciliation; in short to establish a new government, and to do more, to construct schools and public utilities, rebuild the communications system and in fact the economy; the UN, meaning the US, would go in and make a whole nation from scratch. Meaning the warlords first had to be disarmed and disempowered, meaning Aideed.

The UN forces for this job went in from May 1993; on 5 June, as a group of Pakistani troops went in to inspect an arms storage site manned by Aideed's supporters they were attacked. A few kilometres away, as word spread, another UNOSOM II patrol was attacked, then another. Twenty-six Pakistani soldiers died in all and the UNSC instantly passed resolution 837 authorising the arrest and detention of those responsible, meaning again, Aideed. There was no inquiry, no one troubled to go into the details of the incident. It was taken for granted that Aideed was responsible and under the directions of retired US Admiral Jonathan Howe, commander of UNOSOM II, UN troops now went on a manhunt, wild west bounty hunting style, and in fact Howe put a bounty on Aideed's head, US $ 25,000; he also put 'Wanted' posters all over Mogadishu; while combat aircraft and helicopter gunships were called in to attack all his known hideouts; with shoot-at-sight orders. The carnage was immense. In one attack on a residential building the best of the best, the elite "Delta Force commandos, dressed in black, abseiled from helicopters, burst through closed doors, firing from the hip, and arrested nine people", including the resident representative of the UNDP and a senior UN staff member, an Egyptian lady dressed in a pink negligee.[43] Civilian casualties rose. This could have gone on.

But on 3 October 1993, Aideed lured a US force into his stronghold in the Black Sea district of Mogadishu. Sixteen helicopters including eight Black Hawk troop carrying helicopters, along with ground forces, went in. As it entered the Black Sea district the entire force immediately came under attack by Aideed's men. The ground force convoy was surrounded and pulverised by gunfire as they tried to negotiate the maze of allies to escape. One Black Hawk helicopter was shot down, then another, then another two were badly damaged by ground fire and barely managed to get back to base. Altogether eighteen American soldiers died and seventy-five were seriously injured; two of the battered corpses were dragged through the streets as trophies while Somalis danced in the streets and CNN cameras whirred, scenes shown again and again in the US.

The US didn't have the stomach for any more of this. Within 48 hours President Clinton decided that all US forces would be pulled out of Somalia by 31 March 1994. He declared that it was not the task of the US to rebuild Somali society, thus repudiating not only the UN resolutions on the subject but also what his cabinet members had been saying. Ambassador Robert Oakley, who understood how to deal with recalcitrant Somali warlords, was sent in and met

Aideed, who was now *persona grata*, so to speak, quite openly. All US forces ceased patrolling the streets immediately. Everyone else contributing to UNOSOM II arranged to go even sooner than the Americans. The operation was abandoned; all UN staff left; a heavily reinforced UN compound which once had a shopping mall, movie theatres, street lighting, state of the art communications equipment, was abandoned to looters; soon nothing was left of it; even its foundations were gone. A UN resolution of 16 November 1993 suspended all action against Aideed who, having by then acquired something of an international reputation as an oppressed national hero struggling against overwhelming imperial forces, arrived on 2 December triumphantly in Addis Ababa to attend a UN sponsored peace conference.

All that was left was the 'Mogadishu Syndrome' and, of course, the warlords, now in full control.

It is most appropriate to mention at this stage the modernity version of the same story and even more appropriate that a precise rendition of that version is readily available in the film directed by Ridley Scott, *Black Hawk Down*.[44] The film tells the story of what happened in October 1993 in the Black Sea district of Mogadishu. Its very opening takes the audience back to the 'Darkest Africa' of Joseph Conrad; in dark greenish colours, with predominating images of deprivation it "produces little more than a sense of alienation for the viewer." The Americans in the film are individuals, playing chess and scrabble, watching TV, listening to Elvis Presley. The Somalis, on the other hand, "appear as a mob, as an uncontrollable raging mass of people ... their movements and appearance increasingly resembling that of rodents ... the fight against them becomes an extermination campaign." As for the war, entirely in accordance with the modernity story, it is divorced from any other part of life; "the purpose of the mission becomes completely self-referential. All that is left for the soldiers to accomplish is to survive the battle."[45]

## The US and Latin America

The change in the balance of military power between the great powers and the smaller ones after 1945 is well illustrated by the relations between the US and Latin America. Given below are some random examples: three in brief; and then two in more detail.

The US had the Monroe doctrine of 2 December, 1823, that, as for the European powers, "we should consider any attempt on their part to extend their system to any portion of this hemisphere as dangerous to our peace and safety."

In December 1904 and December 1905 came the Roosevelt corollary to the Monroe doctrine. The International Court of Justice had ruled that if a country owes a debt to another, the latter is justified in launching military operations to collect the debt. In the instant case the debtor was Venezuela, the creditors Britain, Germany and Italy, all quite capable of trying to push their way through the Monroe doctrine. So the US said in effect that it could not allow any breach of that doctrine but would exercise "an international police power" where there were chronic cases of wrongdoing in the hemisphere, requiring intervention by a civilised nation.[46] In other words, the collection of debts was OK, but the US would do it.

From time to time there had been portents of change. In December 1936 a Buenos Aires Convention had adopted a 'Special Protocol Relative to Non-Intervention', in which the US and the Latin Americans agreed to 'declare inadmissible the intervention of any one of them' ... 'and for whatever reasons, in the internal or external affairs of any other.'

But the US had got all this straightened out when the State Department announced in 1950 that if communism was extended to any part of the hemisphere the Monroe Doctrine would be invoked; and then at the Tenth Inter-American Conference in Caracas in March 1954 a resolution was passed under the guidance of US Secretary of State Dulles, Resolution XCIII, that the domination or control of any American state by the international movement would constitute a threat to the sovereignty and political independence of the American states.[47]

But change was in the air, here as much as elsewhere.

In 1950 a leftist, Arbenz Guzman, was elected President of Guatemala; and he started by expropriating half a million acres of land owned by the United Fruit Company,[48] the largest producers of bananas in Guatemala, which in turn produced a fifth of all the bananas of Central America. So when the US lodged a strong protest with the Guatemalan Ambassador in Washington, the latter affirmed on 3 September 1953 that his country would never tolerate being treated as a banana republic.

Arbenz didn't stop there. He took over the Anglo-American-owned International Railway of Central America; then he announced he was withdrawing from the Organisation of Central American States. But the kind of solution to the problem that would have been automatic in the first two decades of the century was now impossible. The US had to resort to Guatemalan exiles moving in from Honduras in June 1954, with help from US aircraft which bombed railway stations, barracks, fuel dumps. By the end of that month Arbenz had resigned and a five-man military junta took over to restore the *status quo ante*. But US forces had not actually gone in.

Cuba was even worse. In 1906, as the historian of the Marine Corps[49] writes, 'a revolution of considerable proportions was well under way' there. The US put together the Army of Cuban Pacification, 97 officers and 2,795 men, who went in during September and October of that year. Having pacified the situation they were back in the US by 1909. Three years later there was more trouble. This time a smaller force sufficed; it landed during the course of May and was gone, mission accomplished, by July the same year. But in 1959, when Fidel Castro came to power, so far had the balance of military power changed, nothing more was possible than the use of Cuban exiles in an armed military intervention of April 1961 which, in terms of the traditional story, did (and was intended to) strengthen Castro's hold on power and try to push him more firmly into the Soviet area of influence. Modernity saw this as a debacle which "burdened hegemonic America with the very epithet that the operation was supposed to demolish, 'paper tiger'."[50]

Or take Nicaragua, which was, if such can be imagined, even worse.

In 1909, when President Zelaya, who was liberal but a little too inclined to cultivate the European powers, executed some 500 revolutionaries along with two American advisers, who were trying to overthrow him, the US simply had to tell the Nicaraguan Charge d'Affaires in Washington, 'enough is enough' and hand him his passport; Zelaya resigned. Some US ships did sail into Nicaraguan waters, but no landings were necessary at that time. And when the trouble still didn't subside a battalion of 200 Marines landed at the end of May 1910 and were back on board a week later. This wasn't the end of the story, for revolution was in the Nicaraguans' blood and every now and then, in 1912, then again in 1922, small numbers of Marines had to be landed; each time a few hundred proved enough.

Contrast July 1979, when the Sandinistas, openly Marxist, pro-Soviet, pro-Cuban, came to power. And two months later Castro was hosting a non-aligned movement meeting in Havana, flanked by the leaders of Nicaragua and Grenada, proclaiming the movement was the 'natural ally' of the Socialist nations. In response President Carter did nothing, he couldn't actually do anything and even tried to give this government economic aid; this was only stopped when the Sandinistas helped leftist revolutionaries in El Salvador two years later.

Haiti is another example, though not a typical one, since its inhabitants are more ferociously violent than any other Latin Americans: they were the only ones to fight off successive British, Spanish and French efforts to make Haiti part of their empire, defeating finally a force of 20,000 French and evicting them; declaring independence in 1803, becoming the second country in the hemisphere ever to do so by war, the first having been the US.

In the early twentieth century, of course, they were subject to the same forces as everyone else. Revolutionaries brought down President Vilbrun Guillaume Sam in 1915; they had pushed into the French Legation, where he took shelter, caught hold of him, and thereafter proceeded to cut him up into little pieces, chop off his head and parade it through the streets on a pike. So President Wilson decided to send in the Marines. Three thousand of them comprising a Brigade, the 1st Regiment and an artillery Battalion, apart from several companies went in at the end of July 1915, quickly restored order, supervised elections and the signing by the newly elected President of a Treaty with the US. The Marines then stayed, unopposed, till 1934.

Soon after they left the violence that had characterised Haiti resumed as one elected president after another was overthrown. Then in 1957 came the Duvaliers, 'Papa Doc', who soon declared himself President for life, and his son 'Baby Doc'; and the violence and killing escalated with their private army, the 'Tontons Macoutes' eliminating thousands of his opponents. That went on for thirty years. Finally in early 1986 a revolution overthrew Baby Doc, and he was flown into exile by the US. That was a signal for even more violence and killing as peasants and others who had been at the receiving end during the Duvalier regimes went on the rampage against the Macoutes; then the Macoutes hit back. And so it went. It was, if one was to pay any attention to the traditional story, obviously a situation best left alone.

But here again the opposition between the traditional story and the one of modernity came to the fore, for, according to the latter, the Cold War came to an end around 1990, meaning there was, or should have been, a great surge of democratic sentiment around the world, a surge that was pushed along by a mighty US effort.

In Haiti, elections were held on 16 December 1990 in which Jean Bertrand Aristide, a leftist and Catholic priest, won handsomely. A coup attempt by army officers in January 1991, before Aristide could take over, was foiled; but a second one of September 1991 succeeded. Aristide was exiled and a military Junta headed by General Raoul Cedras took over. The US didn't do much; it had always been inclined to favour military regimes. But on this occasion it was the UN that led the US, overcome by the great democratic surge. The UN passed one resolution after another, imposing sanctions, at the same time, together with the OAS, began negotiations with Cedras to get Aristide back into power. Finally, by July 1993 these efforts led to an agreement between Cedras and Aristide under which fresh elections would be held; so a UN Mission in Haiti, UNMIH, was created, led by the US. It tried to land at Port au Prince in October 1993 and was driven off by demonstrators who had stormed the docks and, seeing the US Ambassador there to welcome the Mission, started kicking his car; he, too, drove off. Months passed; not much changed.

By now the US had got into the democratic surge mood and took the lead in getting the UNSC to pass a resolution of 31 July 1994, describing the situation in Haiti in chapter VII language as a "threat to international peace and security", as also authorising "all necessary means" to remove the military regime and get Aristide back. Unfortunately most of the Latin Americans, Cuba, Mexico, Uruguay, Venezuela, criticised the resolution and even pro-Aristide groups in Haiti attacked it, thinking it an attempt by the US at military intervention, which, of course, it was. The Vatican, which thought Aristide's liberation theology unsound, also opposed any action against the military regime; and gathered their resources in the Catholic world to arouse opposition to any such step. And when the US finally did go in, leading UNMIH II so to speak, former President Jimmy Carter went in first to talk to Emile Jonassaint, the President appointed by the military, and to the military leaders, try to persuade them to see reason; for they were quite ready to oppose any attempt by the US to land forces. He did actually reach an agreement with them on 18 September 1994, a day before the US troops landed. But they landed anyway, and in strength; 20 naval vessels disgorged 22,000 troops in an 'Operation Restore Democracy'. Aristide did return, aboard a US aircraft; and Cedras did go away to Panama, also in a US aircraft, having rented his house and beach villa to the US government.

Then Aristide went from rigged elections to corruption to the use of violence, including the use of armed gangs, Tontons Macoute style, to eliminate his opponents; there were uprisings and a coup attempt; by early 2004 the US was calling on him to leave the country. And that year, on February 29, he did leave, accusing the US of having forced him to do so, calling on his supporters to resist the US. And then a US-led multi-national mission, with yet another acronym, MINUSTAH (United Nations Stabilisation Mission in Haiti), went in, this time a bit smaller, 3,500 strong.

And so it went. Going back to the traditional story, it would be difficult to show that any purpose had been served by all the attempts to bring Haiti onto the democratic path: armed gangs continued to roam unhindered; the economy was in chaos; a sizable cocaine trade had developed.

## Dominica

Two final examples from Latin America further illustrate the changing balance of military power.

The Dominican Republic, in the years 1903-4 (and indeed for years before and after, but we can take these as illustrative) was in a state of continuing revolution. Late in 1903 a new President, Carlos Morales, came into power through an insurrection. No sooner was he installed than another insurrection under a former President, Jiminez, began.

The US had business interests there. US politicians and financiers had in 1892 formed a Santo Domingo Improvement Company to manage Dominica's finances and they were directly concerned that there should not be any untoward development jeopardising those finances. Much of Dominica's revenue came from customs duties and the government there had announced its intention of converting Samara and Manzanillo into free ports which would not only reduce revenues but seemed to benefit Germany most of all.

Furthermore, there was the need for political stability. The continuing revolutions and turmoil led to damage to American property, the destruction of sugarcane owned by Americans, the killing of livestock owned by them as well as indignities upon their persons.

By late 1903, with the continuation of the insurrection, conditions were thought to be serious; one naval vessel, the *Detroit*, under Commander Albert C. Dillingham, proceeded from Port of Spain, where she was berthed, to Puerto Plata on the northern coast of Dominica. On 3 January 1904 a marine detachment of twenty men was sent ashore to enforce a ceasefire zone within a defined area in which American citizens were. Four days later another detachment, this time only ten men, was sent ashore. A few days later their task was accomplished and all of them returned to ship. Later, on 11 February, there were further disturbances, including some shots fired at an American ship; another naval vessel, the *Hartford*, was brought in. This time 330 men were sent in; they came back to their ships the same evening. No further intervention was necessary; the US took over the custom house to collect the revenue needed to pay foreign debtors. There was no further trouble from Dominica till 1916.

Contrast this scene, an easy American action, no consultations with anyone else, everything brought under control within the shortest possible time, with what happened after 1945.

In the early 1960s Dominica faced almost exactly the same problem, but minus the international debt. In September 1963 a three-man military Junta over-threw and sent into exile Juan Bosch, the first freely elected President that the country had had. In April 1965 the Junta was overthrown by a military revolt led by the followers of Bosch. So there were Bosch and his supporters, who were generally leftist, and who had now taken over, and his opponents, generally rightist, in the opposition; and this was now an armed opposition; there was fighting in the streets. Perhaps the Soviet Union was trying to step in; Cuba was already a precedent. The American Ambassador warned that a communist take-over could be the outcome of the fighting.

On 3 May 1965 President Johnson said that a band of communist conspirators were taking control of what had been a popular democratic revolution; the US would not allow another communist state in the hemisphere. He "had decided that the revolt was part of a larger conspiracy" to challenge American interests in the entire region. It was necessary to act unilaterally, despite the fact that the Organisation of American States (OAS) charter expressly forbade such intervention or unilateralism. Johnson remarked in response to such considerations, "The OAS couldn't pour piss out of a boot if the instructions were written on the heel."[51]

US naval vessels had already started assembling in Dominican waters; within days there were forty vessels (contrast the two that had been brought in six decades earlier). And US troops started going in from the armada, in an operation wholly out of proportion to what had been done in 1903-04; first the Marines went in, then the Army's 82nd Airborne Division. By early May there were already 9,500 US troops there; within the next days the count went up to 22,000. The situation was brought under control; though the civil war continued for some months. Elections were held on 1 June 1966; one Joaquin Belagua was elected, defeating Juan Bosch; three months thereafter all US troops had departed. The whole operation cost $ 150 million and attracted considerable criticism within the US, apart from Latin America.

Dominica was, of course, a bigger problem in 1965 than it had been in 1903; for one thing its population was 3.8 million compared to around 600,000; but, altogether, there had been a change of scene which made the new situation unrecognisable. You could no longer imagine that sending in two or three hundred Marines would bring virtually any kind of situation under control.

On the other hand, here is a comment from Juan Bosch which conforms to the modernity story: "I am certain that if a captain in the U.S. mission had said that the government should be overthrown, this would have been done within an hour, because a U.S. captain had greater authority over the Dominican military high command than the people, the Constitutions, and the President."[52]

## Grenada

The case of Grenada is perhaps an even better illustration of how hard it had become for the US to intervene within its own backyard, for this, an island located on the far southern end of the Lesser Antilles, is tiny, about the size of Malta but with a quarter the population, just over 100,000 in 1979.

A bloodless coup of 13 March 1979 by the leader of the left wing

New Jewel Movement replaced the elected Prime Minister Eric Gairy, by then generally regarded as increasingly corrupt and autocratic. This was a pro-Soviet, pro-Cuba regime, an open flouting of the Monroe Doctrine, but for four years the US did nothing. Grenada's military was trained by the Cubans, who were heavily involved in providing instructors and advisers to both military and civil institutions, along with Libyans, East Germans, North Koreans, and Russians. The instructors were more or less permanently stationed there and there seemed no reason for the US to hesitate. The US blocked World Bank loans to Grenada, terminated US aid programmes, issued a travel advisory that Grenada was an unsafe destination, staged large-scale naval exercises in 1981, 1982 and 1983; even a mock invasion of a similar sized island off Puerto Rico.

But for four years it did nothing else.

Then, in March 1983 rumours started of a possible US invasion. By October a US navy task force steamed towards Grenada. Internal dissensions had begun in Grenada, with Prime Minister Maurice Bishop and several of his ministers on one side, his deputy and General Hudson Austin, Commander of the People's Revolutionary Army, on the other. Bishop and his friends were arrested and then executed.

On 22 October the Pentagon announced that a naval task force of two aircraft carriers and ten warships was being sent to Grenada; three days later, in an exercise called 'Operation Urgent Fury' US forces went in. Six thousand troops were sent in altogether, supplemented by another 300 soldiers and policemen from Antigua, Barbados, St. Lucia, Dominica and St. Vincent; none of the latter did any fighting; some of them had only been trained as traffic policemen. On the other side were 1,000 of the People's Revolutionary Army. Even so it took time; there was no question of the troops returning to their ships by evening. There were several hundred deaths, including twenty-four Americans. On 26 October reinforcements had to be called in to deal with the remaining opposition. Thereafter 8612 medals were distributed, including many to those who had never left American shores.

And US Secretary of State George Shultz told a Cabinet meeting thereafter that "this may be a turning point in history. We've let the world know that we are going to protect our interests whatever it costs."[53]

## ENDNOTES

[1] Quoted in David Campbell, *Writing Security, United States Foreign Policy and the Politics of Identity*, University of Minnesota Press, Minneapolis, 1992, p. 27.

[2] Henry Steele Commager, ed., *Documents of American History*, Appleton-Century-Crofts, New York, 1958, Volume II, p. 705.

[3] Stephen E. Ambrose, *Rise to Globalism*, American Foreign Policy since 1938, Penguin Books, Harmondsworth, 1984, pp. 165 and 186.

[4] Dwight D. Eisenhower, *Waging Peace, 1956-61*, Heinemann, London, 1966, p. 625.

[5] Y.M. Primakov, *Anatomy of the Middle East Conflict*, Nauka Publishing House, Moscow, 1979, p. 6.

[6] Karen Brutents, *The Newly Free Countries in the Seventies*, Progress Publishers, Moscow, 1983, pp. 31, 35.

[7] Y.M. Primakov, op. cit., p. 38.

[8] Louis J. Halle, *The Cold War as History*, Chatto and Windus, London, 1967, p. 157.

[9] Quoted in Yu. Ivanov, Marxism-Leninism on Social Progress in the Young States, in S. Pshennikov, ed., *Two Directions of Socio-economic Development in Africa*, USSR Academy of Sciences, Moscow, 1986, p. 37

[10] Karen Brutents, op. cit., p. 18

[11] Col. G.Malinovsky, quoted by Mark N. Katz, *The Third World in Soviet Military Thought*, Croom Helm, London, 1982, p. 107.

[12] See Karen Brutents, op. cit., p. 78.

[13] See David Campbell, op. cit., pp. 158 and 31, respectively.

[14] Stephen E. Ambrose, op. cit., p. 248.

[15] Edward A. Kolodziej, U.S.-Soviet Cooperation: The Role of Third States, in *Annals of the American Academy of Political and Social Science*, Vol. 518, November 1991, p. 119.

[16] Stephen E. Ambrose, op. cit., p. 229.

[17] See Bernard Brodie, *War and Politics*, Macmillan, London, 1973, p. 428

[18] David Laitin, Somalia: Civil War and International Intervention, in Barbara F. Walter and Jack Snyder, eds., *Civil Wars, Insecurity, and Intervention*, Columbia University Press, New York, 1999, p. 156.

[19] Peter Savigear, *Cold War or Détente in the 1980's, The International Politics of American-Soviet Relations*, Wheatsheaf Books, Great Britain, 1987, pp. 141-144.

[20] *Foreign Relations of the United States*, 1961-63, Vol. V, Soviet Union, Department of State, p. 36.

[21] Richard Crockett, *The Fifty Year War, The United States and the Soviet Union in World Politics, 1941-91*, Routledge, London, 1996, p. 226.

[22] John Spanier, *American Foreign Policy since World War II*, Tata McGraw-Hill, New Delhi, 1989, p. 35.

[23] D. Michael Shafer, *Deadly Paradigms, The Failure of US Counter-insurgency Policy*, Leicester University Press, 1988, p. 204.

[24] Stephen E. Ambrose, op. cit., p. 169.

[25] Henry Steele Commager, op. cit. Vol. II, p. 740.

[26] Gabriel Kolko, *Century of War, Politics, Conflict and Society since 1914*, The New Press, New York, 1994, pp. 404, 410.

[27] Quoted by Peter Lyon, *Neutralism*, Leicester University Press, 1963, p. 191.

[28] Jean Baudrillard, *Simulations, Semiotext(e)*, Columbia University, New York, 1983, pp. 45-6.

[29] Henry Kissinger, *The White House Years*, Vikas, New Delhi, 1979, p. 912. This section of the text is based on this volume and on Jack Anderson, The Anderson Papers, Millington, London, 1973.

[30] Jack Anderson, op. cit., p. 265.

[31] Henry Kissinger, op. cit., p. 913.

[32] Stephen E Ambrose, op. cit., p. 193.

[33] Dwight D. Eisenhower, op. cit., p. 267.

[34] James Cable, *Gunboat Diplomacy*, Chatto and Windus, London, 1971, p. 61. Cable's text, now regarded as a classic on the use of limited naval force for political purposes, has no doubt contributed in its own way to enlarging the number of times the so-called great powers' attempt to use force on smaller countries.

[35] Stephen E. Ambrose, op. cit., p. 351.

[36] Ralph A. Hallenbeck, *Military Force as an Instrument of U.S. Foreign Policy*, Praeger, New York, 1991, p. xi.

[37] Karen Brutents, op. cit., p. 83, 84.

[38] Martin Meredith, *The State of Africa, A History of Fifty Years of Independence*, Free Press, London, p. 469.

[39] David Laitin, op. cit., p. 148.

[40] Quoted in Martin Meredith, op. cit., p. 474

[41] Quoted by William G. Hyland, *Clinton's World, Remaking America's Foreign Policy*, Praeger, Westport, 1999, p. 56.

[42] David D. Laitin, op. cit., p. 162.

[43] Martin Merdith, op. cit., p. 482.

[44] Columbia Pictures, 2001; the film, by a 'cult' director, meaning one who should really have been beyond modernity, was nominated for several academy awards and actually won two.

[45] Quotes in this paragraph are from Andreas Behnke, The Re-enchantment of War in Popular Culture, in *Millennium*, Vol. 34, No. 3, 2006, p. 939, 940 and 943.

[46] Henry Steele Commager, op. cit., Vol. I, p. 236, and Vol. II, pp. 213-4, for this and the previous paragraph.

[47] Herbert L. Matthews, Diplomatic Relations, in *The American Assembly, The United States and Latin America*, Prentice Hall, New Jersey, 1963, pp. 144-146.

[48] The Company virtually owned the country; it owned, directly or through subsidiaries, all the railroads, most of the electricity generation plants, as also its distribution, all the port facilities; it was the largest landowner. Secretary of State John Foster Dulles had been a senior partner in the Company's law firm; his brother Allen, and other like Henry Cabot Lodge, US Ambassador to the UN, were major stock-holders.

[49] Captain Harry Allanson Ellsworth, *One Hundred Eighty Landings of United States Marines, 1800-1934*, History and Museums Division, Headquarters, U.S. Marine Corps, Washington D.C. This is the source I have used for material for the actions of the Marine Corps during the early twentieth century.

[50] Thomas J. McCormick, *America's Half-Century, United States Foreign Policy in the Cold War*, East-West Press, New Delhi, 1992, p. 144.

[51] Stephen Ambrose, op. cit. pp. 295-6.

[52] Juan Bosch, *The Unfinished Experiment, Democracy in the Dominican Republic*, Pall Mall Press, London, 1966, p. 217. This was written when he was in exile after the 1963 coup, so it can be rated premature.

[53] Jeff McMahan, *Reagan and the World, Imperial Policy in the New Cold War*, Monthly Review Press, New York, 1985, p. 216.

# 9

# The Other Story: the Cold War

The discursive framework of the Cold War, which is that of modernity, is well known. There is an extensive and authoritative literature on it. Hence what follows is confined to those elements which highlight the contrast with the traditional discourse of what happened in the years 1945-90. It is, in other words, based on the supposition that the Cold War was real, in contrast to the last two chapters, which assumed there was no such thing.

During the Cold War period, war was separated completely from power. As one eminent academic authority put it, "military power has appreciably lost its political utility, compared with previous ages. For a considerable range of foreign policy purposes, military superiority is now at a discount."[1] Indeed, the generally acknowledged specialist, who has been called the 'Dean of Cold War historians', wrote that the "Cold War may well be remembered, then, as the point at which military strength, a defining characteristic of 'power' itself for the past five centuries, ceased to be that."[2]

So the two concepts, war and power were, so to speak, each in free float. Of course, it didn't stay that way; with time each concept attached itself to things, as we shall see.

## Looking at War

As for war, in parallel with the modernity story of imperial efforts, the attempt was to delete it from the political vocabulary, or at least reduce it to irrelevance. Let us look at three aspects of this.

First, any real war in which a great power was involved was excluded from the IR model of the Cold War. For in such real wars after 1945, despite having enormous power, the great powers didn't seem able to win. In fact, they couldn't bring it to bear with advantageous effect in terms of their interests in even weak or small states. Random examples will suffice to make the point.

In the Korean War (1950-53) China, a poor agricultural nation with virtually no industry, and indices near the bottom of world rankings in most categories, held the most powerful nation in the world to a draw. The examples multiplied: the Vietnam and Afghanistan wars; revolutionary Cuba's defiance of the USA; the experience of US military intervention in the third world; and, most dramatically, the collapse of the Soviet control over East Europe and of the Soviet Union itself at the end of the Cold War. So many things were happening in which indices and rankings did not matter at all that even the least tortuous explanations were unconvincing. One comment on the US assisted Bay of Pigs invasion in 1961 to remove the regime of Fidel Castro in Cuba, which failed, was that the debacle "burdened hegemonic America with the very epithet that the operation was supposed to demolish, 'paper tiger', a global policeman without real clout on its own neighbourhood beat."[3]

Klaus Knorr, an academic strategic affairs analyst and former Director of International Studies at Princeton University, noted in 1966 that "the utility of military power – particularly nuclear military power – as an instrument of policy has declined, if not slumped, dramatically", partly because of the diminished value of territorial conquest. But, more important, it has never been more difficult for the strong to impose their will on the weak. Then he goes on to give six reasons for this: the intense competition between the two super powers which prompts them to allow small states to defy or even blackmail them; the change in the moral temper; the diminished legitimacy of displaying military power except in self-defence; the fear and distrust of the Western powers among the nations of Asia and Africa; the new militant nationalism spreading through the non-Western world; and the fact that the military forces of the two super powers are structured in relation to each other and are not appropriate for chastening the small and weak.[4]

US Secretary of State Henry Kissinger made the same complaint. "The most ominous change that marked our period was the transformation in the nature of power … By an irony of history a gargantuan increase in power had eroded the relationship of power to policy. The major nuclear powers would be able to devastate one another. But they would also have great difficulty in bringing their power to bear on the issues most likely to arise ... the capacity to destroy proved difficult to translate into a plausible threat even against countries with no capacity for retaliation."[5] Many others came to the same conclusion; one writes that "American power was vaster than anyone else's, but in many cases it was not usable power and thus could not be translated into diplomatic victory."[6]

Quite a substantial literature has been written about this ability of the weak to withstand or even win wars against the strong.[7] But the short answer given is that they can't really win; it is the strong that faced internal or international opposition and had to abandon the war effort. One author asks why weak actors have regularly been winning these wars and "have won with increasing frequency over time." He answers that the strong were politically vulnerable. The French in Algeria had won the war, but their war brutalities catalysed opposition to the war, so they had to quit. On this count the British didn't lose the 1956 war against Egypt, nor that in South Yemen. Similarly, the Americans won in Vietnam and then "the United States withdrew from Vietnam when and how it did because U.S. public opinion had shifted against the war."[8]

Probably an appropriate summing up of the reasons for this was, "how the strong have often dealt with the weak in ways far more oblique, or less successful than the simple notion of a high correlation between might and achievement might suggest; how and under what conditions the weak have been able to offset their inferiority ... these are issues ... for which, again, far more historical work ought to be undertaken."[9]

In other words it might not be necessary to explain how the weak did so well, because they didn't. There was no sign of the shifting balance that we have read about in the traditional story; in fact, there wasn't ever really much of a war. This is at the core of the Cold War model.

The second aspect was the discourse on war from the viewpoint of great power rivalry, a blossoming literature on nuclear war covering the range and accuracy of missiles, including things like circular error probability; the destructive power in megatons of TNT of the warheads; counter force and counter value targeting; the spectrum of conflict including strategic nuclear war, theatre nuclear war, theatre conventional war and sub-theatre or localised war as brought out, of instance, in the US Defence Posture Statement of

March 1971 which US Secretary of Defence Melvin Laird put out. So the first thing that war as concept attached itself to was nuclear war.

This gave strength to the Cold War discourse.

Where the traditional story took it for granted that there was no real possibility of war between the nuclear powers, one of the most popular and acceptable ways of thinking about international relations, in the modernity story, was to re-categorise war as conflict. A huge literature grew around this. In one of the best-known texts of the Cold War period, *The Strategy of Conflict*, Thomas C. Schelling of Harvard University wrote that 'winning' in a conflict does not mean some kind of competitive winning; "it means gaining relative to one's own value system; and this may be done by bargaining, by mutual accommodation, and by the avoidance of mutually damaging behavior." So if it is possible to conduct war in such a way as to minimize damage or even coercing an adversary by threatening war instead of waging it, that mutual accommodation should be sought; and a "theory of deterrence would be, in effect, a theory of the skilful *nonuse* of force,"[10] which looks like a war without war, something akin to the battle of Valmy in 1792.[11] Clearly Clausewitz, who characterised war as "an act of violence intended to compel our opponent to fulfil our will", would not have approved such an idea of conflict.

The third aspect concerned wars in which smaller powers were involved, generally without the direct participation of one or other of the two great powers, but often with some assistance from one or both of them through the supply of arms, training and aid. This was another thing to which war attached itself, and it was called 'armed conflict'.

Here, too, great power rivalry predominated, since the Cold War meant, among other things, a world dominated by the two great powers, and such a world "implied and even required the indivisibility of international politics. Nothing happened in isolation. War and peace in any region had global consequences."[12] No local war could have any significance other than in the context of great power rivalry; and this gave further strength to the Cold War discourse.

**From Nuclear Confrontation to Local Wars**

The last two aspects are well brought out by a look at the *World Armaments and Disarmament Yearbook*, an annual publication of the prestigious Stockholm Institute of International Peace Research, SIPRI. This is certainly one of the most if not the most widely read regular publications on the subject.

In the year 1981, well into the Cold War, SIPRI was worried, and this was their principal worry for years, a worry shared by countless other think-tanks, strategists and academics, about the nuclear arms race. "In the current international climate (probably referring to the 1979 Soviet invasion of Afghanistan and the destabilising effects of the revolution in Iran the same year, which are seen only within the Cold War context, but this is not clearly stated) we can expect the East-West nuclear and conventional arms races to accelerate ... which will increase the probability of a nuclear world war", because new weapons would provoke moves away from nuclear deterrence strategies to nuclear war fighting strategies.

As far as SIPRI was concerned you would never know, looking at the 1981 or 1982 Yearbooks, which covered events in 1980 and 1981, respectively, that there was a major war going on between Iran and Iraq or that Soviet troops had massively invaded Afghanistan. On the first, the Yearbook did mention that there was a "basic conflict between Israel and the Arab states", the main worry here being the possibility of the involvement of the great powers; and the latent conflict, which became actual at the end of the period, between Iran and Iraq over the control over their joint outlet to the sea. On the second, "the Soviet involvement in Afghanistan indicates that Soviet leaders may not have learnt the lessons of Vietnam any better than have US leaders." That's all there was.

In 1983, there was US military action in Grenada and Lebanon (see chapter 8). The *SIPRI Yearbook* for 1984 writes, "In 1983 the United States used military force in Grenada and Lebanon. It was a new attitude. Secretary Weinberger said in February 1983 that 'our plans and programs must, therefore, focus on strengthening our ability to respond effectively, with military force, if necessary, in several strategically important areas, and in circumstances ranging from small-scale incidents to major military operations'". During all those years SIPRI had clearly decided that the various small wars around the world were insignificant, as had been decided by modernity during the colonial era.

But in those years the focus was clearly on being pessimistic about East-West relations in the context of the possibility of a nuclear war, which in turn was raised or lowered by an escalation or deceleration in the arms race. The traditional story, it will be recalled, was all about the cooperation among the super powers, condominiums, the ground rules that they might have been establishing, already by the early 1970s. But in the story of modernity, super power tensions were spiralling and the *1983 SIPRI Yearbook*, for instance, says there was no progress in arms control or disarmament, military expenditure had been rising faster in the past four years than it did in the previous four, and the world stockpile of nuclear weapons was 50,000 and could rise to 60,000 early in the 1990s.

This gloom on nuclear war continued until and including the 1986 Yearbook. In 1984 and 1985 it said, as far as the risk of a major war was concerned, "things were getting worse". And, it forecast that, if there is no progress towards arms control, if the arms race continued unchecked "then the risk of a major war will continue to increase."

Then, quite suddenly, the *1987 Yearbook* made a turn around. There was no apparent reason for this; no new arms control or reduction agreements had been concluded. Gorbachev and his policies seemed to promise change, but he had been at the helm in the Soviet Union only for two years and had done nothing new yet. Gorbachev and Reagan had met in Reykjavik, October, 1986, but no progress had been made at that meeting on any of the subjects which SIPRI was so worried about over the years. There seemed no apparent reason not to continue focusing on the worldwide global nuclear confrontation, and SIPRI gave none.

But SIPRI didn't continue that focus and the turn around was in the attention paid to problems outside the East-West conflict, those problems that had so far been treated as peripheral: now the Iran-Iraq war; South Africa; the debt crisis or the ticking debt bomb, these were the three singled out for special attention. And there was a whole new chapter, which had never before made an appearance, but was now to be an increasingly prominent and lengthy entry, on armed conflicts, meaning all the small wars, insurgencies and guerilla wars, civil hostilities, ethnic and religious tensions and so on that were happening around the world. There were thirty-six happenings in 1986, all in the third world (except Northern Ireland). And these were summarised: opposition to the

Syrian government from Islamic fundamentalists; ethnic and religious violence in India; a low level separatist guerilla campaign in Baluchistan – thousands dead in the 1970s; terrorist bombings in the North West Frontier Province of Pakistan; Sind as the main trouble spot; ethnic and religious based conflict in Sri Lanka; civil war, invasion, famine in Kampuchea; communists and separatists in Malaysia, the Philippines and Thailand. And so it continued: eight conflicts in the Far East; six in the Middle East; eleven in Africa; six in Latin America. And there were three conclusions: that there have never been as many wars as there are today (which didn't seem logical, since every one of the thirty-six conflicts listed started well before 1986 and, in fact, all but four of them were dated 1980 or earlier!); that the nature of these wars was such that civilians were at greater risk and dying in greater numbers than ever before; and that 'numerous' of them had the potential for escalating into regional wars or super power confrontation. Super power relations were still of concern.

Over the years this chapter expanded to include ways in which the major powers were supplying arms or giving military support to one side or the other in a conflict, the possibilities of linkage between local conflicts due to super power involvement, and the threat of escalation that thereby arose. Soon (1989 Yearbook) another chapter on the role of the UN in the resolution of such conflict was added and, sure enough, by the Moscow summit, May-June 1988, Gorbachev and Reagan were discussing issues that included problems of conflict in South Asia, the Middle East, Central America and Southern Africa.

In any case, by the time of the 1995 *SIPRI Yearbook*, well into the post-Cold War era, major armed conflicts, the entry that has started modestly in 1987, had been promoted to Part I, Chapter I, with a listing of major armed conflicts around the world and an introductory note averring that "special anxiety and concern surround the wars in Afghanistan, Bosnia and Herzegovina, Chechnya, Kurdistan and Tajikistan, the genocide in Rwanda, and a host of long-drawn out and new ethnic and religious conflicts elsewhere."

Others, too, brought this matter of war more firmly into the story of modernity through an effort to formulate it in wholly deterministic terms, governed by universal and timeless laws. For this purpose, a large academic effort was launched, practically an industry to mathematise war, conflict and security issues. One of the best known is by J. David Singer, *The Correlates of War* database project started at the University of Michigan in 1963. This collected and continues to collect and disseminate what are generally taken as accurate quantitative data on war and wider questions of international relations going back over the centuries; and it is available over the internet, so that anyone who wishes to write about war and wants a simple way to get the most detailed data only has to access the website. And, understandably, large numbers did, thus making the episteme ever more popular.

Singer himself has done so, and, to give just one example of a voluminous literature, his "multivariate logistic regression model" evaluates a series of propositions about the chance of civil wars happening around the world: semi-democracy increases the chances; economic development lowers them; more military spending increases them, and so does cultural polarisation.[13] Then there is the University of Uppsala Department of Peace and Conflict Research with an equally accessible database giving details about dozens of conflicts: conflict intensity, dates, the warring parties, battle deaths and so on. One smaller example may be given. The Addington survey on *Patterns of War* (see chapter 4), as far as the post-1945 period is concerned, has no mention of the fact that India and Pakistan were at war in 1947-48 and again in 1965 and 1971; nor does it refer to the clashes between China and the Soviet Union in 1979 along the Ussuri river or the Chinese attack on Vietnam the same year. Only wars involving or risking super power confrontation or East-West tension in some form are included: Korea, 1950-53; the 1956 war on Egypt; the Arab Israel wars of 1967 and 1973; the Vietnam war, 1961-73.

All this also linked up with the World Order Models Project, which argued that "world peace and security are inseparable from problems such as human rights, ecological balance, income inequality, food distribution and malnutrition, over population, energy scarcity, resource exploitation ... global, social, cultural, economic and technological issues." The problem to be solved is much wider than just peace between states; it is about making models that would show the optimum road towards the amelioration of the human condition.[14]

There are many other links.

And so the literature goes on, trying to put war into a framework of timeless and universal principles which will take human agency out of the picture, the idea being to remove war from the uncertainties that had so far plagued it; to make it into conflict and a part of modernity by discovering generally applicable laws that would govern its beginning, its course, intensity and duration, based perhaps on the incompatibilities involved, the goals of the warring parties, their relative strength and so on.

## Power: Europe as the Centre

The concept of power attached itself firstly and in the initial stages to Europe as the centre of the Cold War; secondly, somewhat later, to a world order which was dominated by two great powers, the US and the Soviet Union; and thirdly and all along, to precise measurement.

The Cold War is shown in much of the most relevant literature as the continuation of a history in which Europe is at the centre.[15] Where could the centre of the Cold War be found? "The most obvious answer was in Europe, where the heaviest concentrations of armed strength confronted one another and the two ways of life were in close juxtaposition."[16] The religion, the ideologies, the very culture of Europe still dominate the world, so that the Soviet Union and the USA "have been forced increasingly to recognise that they are Europeans in a sense, after all; that not only their race but that their culture is originally European ... thus that small continent is still the centre of the world – and not only because of the cold war, not only politically so."[17]

According to this story, during the nineteenth century European power was projected around the world so that "the European balance of power had become essentially a world balance of power" and the stage on which the Europeans did their balancing "had become nothing less than the whole world."[18]

As for the others, "robbed of their past freedom to go their own ways politically and culturally, non-Western peoples were subjected to a world order that perpetuated or even deepened their helplessness. Henceforth equality could be attained only on the terms imposed by the West. Western ascendancy was so complete that it left only one rational response: abject imitation as a condition of survival and self-affirmation"; while decolonisation "merely escalated the imitation and hardened the grip of Western institutions and values over the entire world."[19]

The fact that by the beginning of the twentieth century non-European powers, Japan and the USA, had established a position in the hierarchy of the leading powers, did not change the Euro-centric situation. This simply meant that the European balance was no longer self-contained; what had happened was that the European balance had come to involve powers around the world. "Still, however, as in the past, the fulcrum of the balance, the centre of gravity, remains in Europe." With this background it is easy to understand the Cold War as a face-off between the USA and the Soviet Union, for it is "across the heart of Europe that they confront each other face to face". So, like all the previous European contestations for power, in other words, "like its predecessors, the Cold War has been a worldwide power contest in which one expanding power had threatened to make itself predominant, and in which other powers have banded together in a defensive coalition to frustrate it".[20] So now the Cold War had a history that went back several centuries; that gave the discourse even more strength.

Secondly, despite all the problems of actually using the power for any purpose, there was no doubt, in the literature, in the statements of political leaders and commentators, in the attention given by the media, that whatever power existed in the world was in the hands of the two great powers; or at least so much of it that it didn't make any difference.

All those nations which did not have the statistical qualifications to make the grade were excluded. It was clear, says one historian of those years, that "the United States and the Soviet Union loom over all aspects of international relations, still reducing other factors to a miserable impotence ... the overriding characteristic of the superpowers was their common responsibility for power and principle in international relations". In other words, "the history of international relations since 1945 contained a simple message: The world had to accept the primacy of two states, the nuclear giants ...their influence was felt everywhere". In Afghanistan, once the Soviet Union had invaded that country in 1979, the superpowers were "trapped in a competition from which there seems to be no escape."[21] In this scheme, and note here the continuation of the argument of chapter 4, the countries of Asia, Africa and Latin America were reduced to ciphers, non-players in the game of IR.

Anyway everyone else, being far down the international power hierarchy, just had to accept the dominance of the two great powers.

The smaller states can also be regarded as objects, or in the enduring terminology of President Eisenhower, dominoes. "You have a row of dominoes set up, you knock over the first one, and ... the last one ... will go over very quickly."[22]

The existence of an international order is linked to this; this order reigns over world politics; and in it the two great powers predominate. The idea is that "the nations of the world are organised into systems or international orders which persist", for the economic, military and other relations of the weaker states become linked to the order set up by one or other of the two. Here again is the contrast to the traditional story, for "nations are *not* free to shift from one international order to another ... great or small, their whole way of life is geared to the order to which they belong. Its rules are their rules..."[23] Differently put it was asserted that "the dominant states and empires in every international system organise and maintain the network of political, economic and other relationships within the system."[24]

This is partly because these two great powers are in a state of unrelenting rivalry. One Cambridge historian described the relations between the Western powers led by the US and the Eastern powers led by the Soviet Union as a state of incessant hostility, with "aims and strategies like military campaigns, and they involved tactical skirmishes, careful deployment of forces, surprise attacks and improvised counter-attacks in which each side incurred serious losses or made considerable gains."[25] Everything that happened anywhere was about that US-Soviet rivalry. We find in the standard Penguin History of the World that "in those decades world history was dominated by a prolonged and bitter Soviet-American antagonism."[26] For the third world, their development was "taking place against the background of an active confrontation between the two world social systems, the confrontation which cannot help making a profound impact on the dynamics of developments in those countries..."[27] This became an indispensable part of discourse and of history; it was hardly possible to envisage what happened anywhere in the world in the years 1945-90 without some reference to it; and a 'universe' of the Cold War was constructed by historians and commentators, with its own language, structural framework, and analytical tools.

Of course the two great powers are not actually equal; one or the other or both of them claimed to dominate the other, which is thus subordinate, while still dominating over all the rest. Zbigniew Brzezinski, who would become National Security Adviser to the US President in the years 1977-81, was already in the early 1970s writing of US paramountcy, that "the US today is the only effective global military power in the world ... our way of life is the most appealing way of life to most of the people on earth ... we are the only power with far flung global economic investments ... involvement ... trade."[28]

A variant on the same theme is that the twentieth century "is the age of the general transition from capitalism to socialism".[29] In other words it is the Soviet Union that really dominates more than the US. History is on the side of the scientific socialism formulated by Marx and Lenin; and "in the future the development of nations and nationalities will result, in the course of social development, in a changeover of capitalist nations to socialist nations."[30]

So although theoretically the developing countries could choose between the capitalist and socialist systems, and Soviet scholars asserted firmly that "there is no third alternative", but in doing so the options proposed by them are: either the establishment of capitalism, which could be from below or from above; or a "leap directed and controlled from above to a socialist orientation."[31] But then they add that capitalism is going through a general crisis which is "nothing but the 'irreversible decline of capitalism' and there is no way out of the general crisis" except on the basis of Marxism-Leninism, meaning "the revolutionary transformation of capitalism into socialism was and will be governed by certain common laws"; in other words, it is inevitable.[32] History itself will, therefore, push the weaker nations in a specific direction.

Again, they do not have a choice.

**Measuring Power**

Thirdly, and partly because each of the two claimed to be bigger and better, the first problem was to assess, in the absence of war, who has got how much power. There had to be some other way of measuring power, for without any measure there can be no hierarchy, hence no order in the matter; and order, in the world of modernity, just had to be there.

Another criterion or set of criteria was needed. The new criteria would have to fulfil two requirements: that the hierarchy should be appropriate, which means the USA and the USSR should be seen at the top of the hierarchy, that the Europeans, specially those who had traditionally enjoyed great power status, as also Japan, should be next on the listings, and that the third world, a nomenclature that had not yet emerged but can be taken to refer to the colonised and other states of Asia and Africa, be at the bottom.

The appearance in 1948 of Hans Morgenthau's *Politics among Nations* laid the foundations of theory that established the new criteria. The book brought together in a definitive study the most significant work that had been done till then in the field and framed the way succeeding generations of international relations scholars, those who were guided by contemporary realism, thought about it. And "there can be no doubt that Morgenthau's work was the single most important vehicle for establishing the dominance of the realist paradigm within the field."[33] Realism provided the kinds of measurement needed to establish the hierarchical system by which nations could be judged in terms of power. And it decisively separated the possession of power from the making of war; this, and not some advanced level of understanding about how IR works, was its main achievement.

Morgenthau devotes part of his book to listing the elements of national power, things like geography, natural resources and population; industrial capacity, military preparedness and the Armed Forces; leadership, morale and the qualities of government and diplomacy. Some of these can be measured, others cannot; some change over short periods of time, others not, or not at all. All these elements go into the making of the measure of a nation's power which, in turn, is conceptually concentrated at the centre and at the disposal of the nation for use in the international system; the system of nations can then be envisaged as a sort of planetary grouping, planets with varying mass orbiting a complex pattern determined largely by their respective power or weight, a system which is as scientific and objective as Newton's laws. Politics, in the key sentence of the book which was already quoted in chapter 4, "is governed by objective laws that have their roots in human nature. ... The operation of these laws being impervious to our preferences, men will challenge them only at the risk of failure."[34] In essence, the system depicts national power as the attributes of the nation, its weight as determined by the described elements, and makes the assertion that it exists at the level determined by those attributes even if there is no test of it beyond the nation's borders.

It is true that Morgenthau himself referred to the uncertainties involved in actually measuring the power of a nation, but equally so that his work more than any other laid a strong foundation for the belief that somehow this could be done. So instead of linking the concept of power to what a nation could do, or had done in the international arena, it was tied to indices which were entirely internal and autonomous; it became a stand alone concept divorced from applicability.

Thus realist theory took to elaborating the laws governing the discipline of IR and gave rise, *inter alia*, to a considerable body of literature aimed to quantify more exactly the measure of a nation's power.

In the early years after World War II the indices were uncomplicated and firmly attached to military power, actual and potential; and in those years this was thought to be determined largely by the coal and iron/steel industries. But this gradually got more and more complicated. We illustrate the argument here with some samples from the writings over the years.

When the West Europeans wanted to remove the prime cause of war from their mutual relations they first thought of establishing joint control of the coal and steel industries of the potential belligerents, chiefly France and Germany. In the basic texts of the period these industries are identified as the main ingredients of a nation's power; as in this from 1960: "although atomic energy, oil and hydro-electric power get most of the headlines today, the bases of industrial power that determine a country's wealth and often its political power are still coal and iron and steel."[35]

W.W. Rostow, writing in 1971, was still committed to industrialisation as the key to power status, saying that at the end of the 19th century "four great areas – Germany, Japan, Russia and the United States – moved forward rapidly in industrialisation ... the interplay among them was to determine the world's balance of power in the first half of the twentieth century."[36]

Writing in 1974, the Australian geographer J.P. Cole who spent a lifetime developing the application of quantitative methods and computers in geography, tried to give points for world power status based on six indices: area, population, steel and energy consumption, GDP and military strength. This was still relatively uncomplicated. Like H. Kahn[37] and others before him, Cole put the USA and USSR at the top of the list; the first gets 222 points out of 1,000; the second gets 177; the others are way behind, China coming in third with 80, India fourth with 44. Neither Vietnam nor Afghanistan was in the top twenty.[38]

Kenneth Waltz, who wrote the second classic on the subject (1979), this one on neo-realism, a variant of realism, put forward one of the more sophisticated elaborations. He postulated the structure of the international system as the central and, in fact, only concern, of the study of international politics. There are only two such structures and so, in modern history, there was only one occasion when one structure changed into another, "in all of modern history the structure of international politics has changed but once."[39] Each structure is characterised by three elements: the ordering principles of the system; the functions which are performed by the different participants in the system; and the distribution of capabilities among these participants. In simplifying the system so far Waltz is attempting really to make this fully determinate, one governed by universal and timeless laws. As for capabilities, meaning the measure of power, Waltz put in a somewhat more comprehensive list than earlier authors, saying that states "are not placed in the top rank because they excel in one way or another. Their rank depends on how they score on all of the following items: size of population and territory, resource endowment, economic capability, military strength, political stability and competence."[40]

Hans Morgenthau would have approved, but there were critics who said Waltz had "repeated the errors of those economists, and political scientists, who have introduced unduly mechanistic assumptions in the attempt to render human activity fully determinate."[41]

Robert Gilpin, in another realist classic published two years later, 1981, referred only to economic and military power, so that after 1945 "the United States stood at the apex of the international hierarchy of power and prestige. American economic and military power was supreme, and it provided the basis for an American centered world economic and political order."[42]

Then we come to Paul Kennedy, whose books on *The Rise and Fall of British Naval Mastery* and on *The Rise and Fall of the Great Powers* contain a wealth of economic and military detail. His first book came out in 1976 and the second in 1989.

So he had for many years collected valuable data on economics worldwide and on how "European societies entered into a constantly upward spiral of economic growth and military effectiveness" which made them the world leaders from the seventeenth century onwards. He refers to the long-term shifts affecting the power balances, to understand which one has to look at the economic data. His data, as did all the other data generated in this exercise, presumed peace, though he repeatedly applied it to war. For instance, his second book showed that in 1938 Germany was, in every respect, far more powerful than Russia: in levels of per capita industrialisation, four times as powerful; in iron/steel production, 30 per cent higher; or total industrial potential, over 40 per cent greater. Yet in the war that followed it was Russia, almost alone, that defeated Germany; in December 1941, as Russian counter-offensives started to throw the German forces out of the suburbs of Moscow, and the long German retreat began, the latter had no other enemies to face.[43] But Kennedy didn't get into explanations of how this could have happened.

Another writing on international relations, this one from 1990 by Joseph Nye, listed territory and population, then nuclear military power, followed by space military power, then economic power.[44]

There were some problems with this approach, as the criteria for measurement got more complicated. Many analysts continued to favour one or at most a combination of more easily quantifiable domains and among those that favoured a single one, GNP ranked high. Even this, despite the wealth of statistics available, was not problem free: many items in the large and burgeoning service sector of the developed countries could not be logically related to the impact a state might have on the international scene despite the claim that the global spread of blue jeans or coca cola, called America's soft power resource, made a difference; some states consistently overestimated their figures, while others, like China, underestimated them, to compound which a number of scholars in the field maintained that the former were doing what the latter were actually doing and vice versa; exchange rate fluctuations could not always be neutralised by purchasing power parity calculations which again, specially in the case of China, were suspect: under-reported, according to the evidence; over-reported, according to outside observers.

Then there were some authors who thought that accuracy in the measurement of national power would be impossible. One such author wrote that " 'national power', whatever that may be, is today a resultant of many incommensurable factors, of which mobilisable military power is only one, and even that one not easily measured in practice." Then he goes on to include human and raw material resources, strategic position, productivity, technology, domestic unity and morale, the effectiveness of statecraft and propaganda.[45]

But the central thrust of work on IR was based on the assumption that objective measurements of national power, the starting point for an objective model of the international system, would become possible if one did enough research in the matter. And that objective model would put the US at the head of the international power hierarchy and the Soviet Union in second place. No other power could be placed anywhere near these two; the main competition, therefore, was between the statistics and indices of those two powers.

And so, in the final stages of the period, as more and more research was done, more and more publications and websites provided more and more details to help scholars such as have been quoted above with the measurement of national power.

Starting with the 1980s the volume and sophistication of the work done in this direction was unprecedented. Precise indices were proposed using single-variable or multi-variant indicators, rank orderings of nations were developed assigning weightages to the different elements or attributes, so many measures were on offer that one of the problems was to choose among them. The list of rank orderings steadily gained in popularity; whether one nation or another figured in the top ten or the top twenty, in gross national product, industrial development, agricultural production or any other (or a combination) of several dozen criteria or indices. If you were in the top ten you boasted about it; if you were dropped you felt humiliated. Annual publications like the *UN Statistical Yearbooks* or the *World Handbook of Political and Social Indicators*, were devoted to just this comparative exercise. Measurement became one of the central issues for the study of international relations, although there has never been agreement on what are the most relevant indices.

Attributes, which Kenneth Waltz would have called capabilities, are an important aspect of the research done. Two works in particular standardised the study of attributes: *A Cross-Polity Survey*; and the *World Handbook of Political and Social Indicators.*[46] Over the years not only were these data collections expanded, they became the "data library for the entire field of political science."[47] And this was not just for US researchers. Since the data was far more comprehensive than could possibly be collected anywhere else, these two publications and their successors became the standard for work, world wide, in the field of IR. The data covered every country in the world; it went back over the years, back to 1815, then to pre-colonial times, then to the Roman Empire.

As for military attributes, there was, freely available, voluminous data about the relative numbers of strategic bombers and intercontinental ballistic missiles, of nuclear submarines and submarine launched ballistic missiles; apart from SIPRI, which was mentioned earlier and which also went into the statistical details of such things, the prestigious London based International Institute for Strategic Studies published, each year, the *Military Balance*, a quantitative assessment, which was taken as authoritative by scholars everywhere, of the military power and defence expenditure of countries throughout the world. This became more voluminous with each passing year.

## The Importance of Realist Theory

All this helped to locate realism as the central and the most widely accepted paradigm in international relations, in Thomas Kuhn's sense of the word.

Research done by John Vasquez in 1972 showed when international relations' scholars in the US were asked, as many as half responded that Hans J. Morgenthau was the most influential scholar in the field and over a third saw his book as the most important theoretical work in the field. As for establishing the paradigm, Vasquez finds overall that 75 per cent of all the data available in the field of IR would tend to provide information on nation-states and on topics of enquiry that were labeled realist. Therefore, and understandably, the bulk of the research in the field was also centred on the articulation of the realist paradigm theory. Of the major articles on the subject that appeared in the 1960s over 90 per cent of the independent variables, according to Vasquez, 94 per cent of the dependent variables and some 93 per cent of the hypotheses tested were founded on the realist paradigm. "Normal science", in the phrase used by Kuhn, was based on realism. Furthermore this was a British-American intellectual condominium. American authors cited other American authors most of the time, 69 per cent in the years 1948-68, and over 74 per cent in the years after 1970. British authors cited other British authors and Americans with almost equal frequency in the years to 1970, but then, after that American more and more, above 60 per cent. Indian authors, too, cited mostly American and British authors, nearly 60 per cent for the period 1948-70, but thereafter less, around 52 per cent, while their citations of Indian authors rose somewhat.[48]

So realist theory shaped and continues to shape the analysis of scholars, the writings of commentators and the decisions of practitioners. It lies behind the way the USA treated itself on the international stage, and the way others treat it as a hyper-power or sole super-power, destined for leadership in any major international endeavour. Other theories were proposed and found acceptance for a time. But the dominance of American power in the post-1945 world, and the dominance of American writings about power and international relations, ensured that realism always made a come-back.

Note that there is not only no incentive to change or alter this way of thinking, but any attempt to do so would be up against a strong set of disincentives. As Morgenthau himself, ironically enough (having been the first to set up the episteme) was able to note in later years, society itself is at work to conceal the truths of social science from its members in order to erect barriers to those activities which may force change. Political science must work on models that demonstrate the essential truth of, and thereby help to perpetuate, the existing set of relations. It must "cover political relations with a veil of ideologies which mollify the conscience of society; by justifying the existing power relations, it reassures the powers-that-be in their possession of power... ."[49]

In other words those who comment on such matters are primarily concerned to ensure that the existing model is proved to be valid, thus, of course, prolonging its life, for that is the only way to ensure that their discipline becomes respectable and influential.

## ENDNOTES

[1] Klaus Knorr, *On the Uses of Military Power in the Nuclear Age*, Princeton University Press, 1966, p. 79.

[2] John Lewis Gaddis, *The Cold War*, Penguin Books, London, 2007, p. 263.

[3] Thomas McCormick, *America's Half-Century, United States Foreign Policy in the Cold War*, East-West Press, New Delhi, 1992, p. 144.

[4] Klaus Knorr, op. cit., pp. 17 and 75-8; Guy Poitras, in *The Ordeal of Hegemony, The United States and Latin America*, Westview, Boulder, 1990, pp. 111-4 also gives six

reasons for the deflating of US advantage in military power over that of the Latin American countries and they are similar. Joseph Nye, op. cit., p. 182, gives five trends for this: economic interdependence; transnational actors, nationalism in weak states; the spread of technology; and changing political issues.

[5] Henry Kissinger, *The White House Years*, Vikas, New Delhi, 1979, pp. 66-67.

[6]Stephen E. Ambrose, *Rise to Globalism, American Foreign Policy since 1938*, Harmondsworth, Penguin Books, 1984, p. 105.

[7] Two examples may be given here. T.V.Paul, *Asymmetric Conflicts: War Initiation by Weaker Powers,* Cambridge University Press, New York, 1994; and Andrew J.R.Mack, Why Big Nations lose Small Wars: The Politics of Asymmetric conflict, in *World Politics*, Vol. 7, No. 4. Summer 1998, pp. 1-43.

[8] Ivan Arreguin-Toft, How the Weak Win Wars, A Theory of Asymmetric Conflict, in *International Security,* Vol. 26, No. 1, Summer 2001, pp. 96, 121, 123 and 118, respectively. He starts by defining a strong actor as one whose material base is at least ten times as large as that of the adversary.

[9] Stanley Hoffman, An American Social Science: International Relations, reproduced in James Der Derian, ed., *International Theory, Critical Investigations*, Macmillan, Hampshire, 1995, p. 240.

[10] Thomas C. Schelling, *The Strategy of Conflict*, Harvard University Press, 1960, pp. 3, 9.

[11] See chapter 1.

[12] Peter Savigear, *Cold War or Détente in the 1980's, The International Politics of American-Soviet Relations*, Wheatsheaf books, Great Britain, 1987, p. 161.

[13] Errol A. Henderson and J. David Singer, Civil War in the Post-Colonial World, 1946-92, *Journal of Peace Research*, Vol. 37, No. 3, May 2000, pp. 275-299.

[14] K.J.Holsti, *The Dividing Discipline, Hegemony and Diversity in International Theory*, Allen and Unwin, Boston, 1985, p. 48.

[15] Contrast the traditional story, chapter 8, in which Europe had ceased to matter.

[16] P. M.H. Bell, *The World Since 1945, An International History,* Arnold, London, 2001, p. 151.

[17] John Lukacs, *A History of the Cold War*, Doubleday and Company, New York, 1961, p. 274.

[18] Louis J. Halle, *The Cold War as History*, Chatto and Windus, London, 1967, p. 3.

[19] Theodore H. Von Laue, *The World Revolution of Westernization, The Twentieth Century in Global Perspective*, OUP New York, 1987, p. 4.

[20] Louis J. Halle, op. cit. pp. 4, 5, and 9.

[21] Peter Savigear, op. cit., pp. 1, 2, 3 and 25, respectively.

[22] Cited by John Lewis Gaddis, The Cold War, op. cit. p. 123.

[23] A.F.K.Organski, *World Politics*, Scientific Book Agency, Calcutta, 1964, p. 316.

[24] Robert Gilpin, *War and Change in World Politics*, Cambridge University Press, 1981, pp. 29-30.

[25] David Thomson, *Europe since Napoleon*, Penguin Books, Harmondsworth, 1966, p. 836.

[26] J.M.Roberts, *The Penguin History of the World,* Penguin Books, London, 1997, p. 997.

[27] Karen Brutents,., *Cooperation between the USSR and developing countries*, USSR Academy of Sciences, Institute of Oriental Studies, Social Sciences Today editorial board, Moscow, 1986, p. 279.

[28] Cited by Alastair Buchan, *Power and Equilibrium in the 1970s*, Chatto and Windus, London, 1973, p. 68.

[29] Karen Brutents, op. cit., p. 280

[30] M.Kulichenko, *Nations and Social Progress*, Progress Publishers, Moscow, 1984, p. 230.

[31] N.A. Simonya, *Destiny of Capitalism in the Orient*, Progress Publishers, Moscow, 1985, p. 252.

[32] S.P. Novosyolov, The Increasingly Acute Crisis in the 1970s, in, M.K.Bunkina, ed., *Current Problems of Contemporary Capitalism*, Progress Publishers, Moscow, 1982. pp. 6, 20.

[33] John A. Vasquez, *The Power of Power Politics, From Classical Realism to Neotraditionalism,* Cambridge University Press, 1998, p. 36.

[34] Hans J. Morgenthau, *Politics Among Nations* , Scientific Book Agency, Calcutta 1966, p. 4.

[35] Andrew Boyd, *An Atlas of World Affairs,* Frederick A. Praeger, New York, 1960, p. 12.

[36] W.W. Rostow, *Politics and the Stages of Growth*, Cambridge University Press, 1971, p. 217.

[37] H.Kahn and A.J.Wiener, *The Year 2000*, Macmillan, New York, 1967, lists the top ten, with the USA and USSR as the only superpowers, followed by large powers like China and Japan, then intermediate powers like India and Italy. See p. 17.

[38] J.P. Cole, *Geography of World Affairs*, Penguin Books, Harmondsworth, 1974, p. 72.

[39] Kenneth N. Waltz, *Theory of International Politics*, Addison-Wesley, Reading Mass., 1979, p. 163.

[40] Kenneth Waltz, op. cit., p. 131.

[41] R.J. Barry Jones, Concepts and Models of Change in International Relations, in Barry Buzan and R.J.Barry Jones, eds., *Change and the Study of International Relations: The Evaded Dimension*., Frances Pinter, London, 1981, p. 15.

[42] Robert Gilpin, op. cit., p. 231.

[43] Paul Kennedy, *The Rise and Fall of the Great Powers, Economic Change and Military Conflict from 1500 to 2000*, Fontana Press, London, 1989, pp. xvii and 254-59.

[44] Joseph S. Nye, Bound to Lead, *The Changing Nature of American Power*, Basic Books, New York, 1990, pp. 195-6.

[45] Walter Millis, writing in the *New York Times* magazine in August, 1959, cited by Harold and Margaret Sprout, *Foundations of International Politics,* D. Van Nostrand, Princeton, New Jersey, 1962, pp. 138-9. The authors of the book provide their own criteria of judging national power by the accounting of capabilities on pp. 167-77.

[46] Arthur S. Banks and Robert B. Textor, *A Cross-Polity Survey*, MIT Press, Cambridge, Mass., , 1963; and Bruce M. Russett, Hayward R. Alker, Jr, Karl W. Deutsch, Harold D. Lasswell, *World Handbook of Political and Social Indicators,* Yale University Press, New Haven, 1964.

[47] John A. Vasquez, op. cit., p. 83.

[48] See on this also K.J. Holsti, *The Dividing Discipline*, op. cit., pp. 103-7.

[49] Richard Little, Ideology and Change, in Barry Buzan and R.J. Barry Jones, eds., op. cit. p. 33.

# 10

# Vietnam

In what follows Vietnam's struggle against China, France and then the US is recounted from the viewpoint of the traditional story, with some references to that of modernity, in a similar way to the chapters on Indonesia and Algeria.

The earliest French attempt at a foothold in Vietnam was in 1680. A trading office was opened in Pho Hien, which was close to today's Hung Yen. The English and Dutch had started factories there in 1672, then moving on to Hanoi, close by. The three of them could have expanded the toehold to a foothold and more, but the Vietnamese were suspicious; they sold their products at high prices; and refused to allow the foreign traders control over the sources of supply. There was very little profit for any of them and as the years passed the Board of Directors of all three companies were making increasingly anxious enquiries about whether the trade with Vietnam would ever really yield high dividends. Actually, "when the French arrived, trade with Vietnam was in fact about to become unprofitable."

By 1700 all three had shut down their operations in Vietnam.

## Power, War and Empire

The next French attempt came in April 1847. In the intervening century and a half they had eyed Vietnam but recognised that the prospects of again establishing a foothold were bleak. It was only French missionaries who did manage to get in to preach the Catholic faith. The Vietnamese had laws against this but the laws were sparingly implemented, though this did depend to some extent on who was ruling the country. Occasionally, therefore, the missionaries were caught and executed. One of the rulers, Minh Mang, executed several in the years 1835-38. By the latter year, the French or at least the French Society of Foreign Missions, "the spokesmen of French political Catholicism had decided that military intervention alone could save the missionary cause in Vietnam." French warships arrived in Tourane (now Danang), the main harbour near Hue, in 1837 and again in 1838. But the show of force didn't help; the Vietnamese were not impressed; they didn't release any captured missionaries; the French found negotiations and submissions were needed if they were to achieve this objective. When in 1842 Captain Fabin-Leveque of the French warship *Heroine* heard of five French missionaries detained by the Vietnamese he sailed into Tourane, but then had to plead and 'negotiate' his way to their release.

Five years later another French missionary, a Monsignor Lefebvre, was detained and sentenced to death for preaching. This time two warships were sent into Tourane harbour where, on 15 April 1847, they attacked five Vietnamese ships: one blew up; one sank; one fled; and two surrendered. It was the first French attempt to assert their military power in Vietnam. It was not much of an attempt. The French did not try to land; they didn't even make an effort to get Lefebvre released. Actually he wasn't there; he'd been released four weeks earlier and sent off to Singapore. The French were so overcome by this assertion of military power that both warships just sailed off; both ran aground shortly thereafter.

But in the 1850s and 1860s all this changed. France acquired a sense of destiny, reinforced by the surrender of Abdel Kader in Algeria in 1847 and the likelihood that they would at last be able to establish an empire there. A 'Commission on Indochina', established with the encouragement of Count Walewski, Minister of Foreign Affairs, argued in a report of 1857 about how French power was equated with her Asian possessions, that, in short, "France had to enter the race for Asian possessions or become a European power of second rank." Force of circumstances, the Commission wrote, pushes the nations of the West to expand towards the East; the English had done it, as had the Dutch, the Spanish and even the Russians, so "are we going to be the only ones without possessions in the East ...?"[1]

By 1860 another equally powerful argument was added. France

had a mission, said the imperialists, more than that of any other nation, "to civilise the backward people of the world ... Let France demonstrate her generosity by fulfilling the greatest of all her duties toward mankind, which was to educate and to guide the destinies of the black and yellow races."[2]

The effectiveness of Vietnamese resistance meant that all these ideas could only be implemented at rather slow speed. In 1858 one Admiral Rigault de Genouilly was selected to lead the first expedition; its aim was to try and occupy Tourane. To the accompaniment of enthusiastic officially sponsored articles in the French press about the rosy trade prospects and the abundant resources of Vietnam, he reached the harbour at Tourane with fourteen vessels and two thousand five hundred men under his command on 31 August. By 2 September the town had been attacked and taken. It wasn't much of an 'attack'. There was no resistance; there was no one to resist; all the Vietnamese had disappeared; there was no one left even to do the manual work required to make the Tourane landfall into a properly fortified base; so the French had to do this themselves and they didn't do a very good job. Within weeks guerilla attacks on the weakly defended French forces began. Then the rains came down; heat and disease took their toll; in June 1859 came a cholera epidemic; a month later typhus erupted. Reinforcements arrived but the Vietnamese attacks grew more aggressive. There was just no hope of getting further inland. When Admiral Genouilly's successor arrived in Tourane on 19 October 1859 he saw that "the only territory firmly occupied by the French after a year of fighting was the cemetery of the many soldiers who had died of disease." All hope of increasing their territorial control was now abandoned by Paris. Indeed Tourane itself had to be abandoned. The French accordingly decided to pull out and by 22 March 1860 they had all gone.

It was not an auspicious beginning for the French empire in Asia.

However, there was a silver lining. In early 1859 Admiral Genouilly had sailed southward from Tourane and conquered Saigon; and the French managed to hold onto it, rather precariously, in the face of Vietnamese assaults. In February 1861 Admiral Charnier was ordered to take a larger expedition, seventy vessels and three thousand five hundred men, to reinforce the Saigon garrison and to attempt expanding the territory held there. As they advanced from Saigon into the interior of what was called Cochin

China there was considerable resistance and a French historian, Pallu de la Barriere, wrote about the nature of this resistance in words the Americans would have recognised a century later, "the centre of the resistance was everywhere, endlessly sub-dividing into as many units as there were Annamites. It would have been more accurate to consider each peasant tying a sack of rice stack as a centre of resistance".[3] Even so, French reinforcements continued to come in; by June 1862 both sides were ready for a break. A treaty was signed giving France possession of a substantial area around Saigon; the treaty also opened three Vietnamese ports for Western traders and gave freedom of action to missionaries in that part of Vietnam. It was a beginning. By December 1863 a protectorate had been established over Cambodia and in a series of subsequent attacks around the Mekong delta the French were able to establish control over the whole of Cochin China by the end of 1867.

There was another break; and then the French resumed their advance in 1873. After many ups and downs, against continuing Vietnamese resistance, the North was brought under a French protectorate by a treaty of 25 August 1883.

The French methods of quelling the resistance were, in Vietnam, as brutal as in Algeria, so that one Governor-General, de Lanessan, more humane than others, could write in the 1890s "that the burning of villages, the mass shootings, the bayonet slaughters, the execution of notables should be replaced by other less violent procedures."[4]

Nevertheless, the slaughter continued, with perhaps its full extent and brutality dependent partly on the character of the Governor-General. Rene Robin, for instance, who occupied that chair in the mid-1930s, famously shouted "*tres bien. Continuez*". The French legionnaires who he was addressing had just told him that, in response to a peasant uprising north of Hue, every one taken prisoner had been slain. His predecessor, Pierre Pasquier, had set the example. When the Vietnamese garrison at Yen Bay rose and briefly occupied the town on 10 February 1930, Pasquier ordered the aerial bombing of a nearby village, on suspicion that some of the mutineers had taken shelter there; the village, Co An, was reduced to ashes. On one occasion in September 1930, some 6,000 unarmed peasants protesting against the high taxes forcing them into starvation, arrived in the provincial capital of North Annam, Vinh. Again, aircraft were called in, which proceeded to bomb and strafe the gathering. Several hundred were killed, while the rest fled. In the evening the families came to collect the dead; the aircraft were called in again, more bombing and strafing, more killed. You could always say, and the French authorities did say, that they thought this was another demonstration.

Strikes, peasant demonstrations, and even unarmed uprisings in those years were met by brutal suppression. So "known rebels, and hundreds of innocent people were also killed in cold blood, by soldiers as well as by the authorities ... some soldiers bragged that they had sawn off the heads of prisoners ... 'out of ten, we had to kill nine and keep only one for interrogation. These were our unwritten orders' ... a group of Legionnaires on trial went free although testimony showed that they had emptied a truckload of prisoners by stopping and killing a few every few miles... ."

It became common, during Pasquier's stewardship, to give troops the order to fire indiscriminately into crowds celebrating, for instance, May Day.

And it was under one of his predecessors, Albert Sarraut, that in response to a protest by some of the inmates of the Poulo Condore, an infamous concentration camp, an order was given to the guards to shoot at the assembled prisoners and to keep on shooting until no one was left standing. That was in February 1918, just fourteen months before General Dyer ordered indiscriminate firing on a crowd of unarmed villagers who had been gathered in the enclosed confines of Jallianwala Bagh, Amritsar.[5]

Martial Henri Merlin, Governor-General from August 1923 to April 1925, said it aptly when asked about the education of the natives. They should be given, he said, "only horizontal education."[6]

## Vietnamese Nationalism: Endless Struggle

Perhaps the best known example of the way nationalism is nourished and grows would be Vietnam. Here is a nation that has been deeply imprinted with Chinese traditions and culture. It was ruled by China for over a thousand years, from 111 BC to 939 AD. Both Confucianism and Mahayana Buddhism were introduced during those years. The Chinese imposed their administrative systems; the study of Chinese classics was made mandatory for those Vietnamese who wished to rise to higher positions; a programme of intermarriage led in the first century AD to the emergence of a new elite, a pro-Chinese aristocracy that qualified for administrative positions by passing the examinations in Chinese literature and philosophy that the Chinese also had to pass.

But when the Vietnamese look back over their history one theme dominates over every other: struggle, struggle against the Chinese, the super power of the time, which continued throughout the thousand years that the Chinese ruled them; struggle for decades against the French; struggle for years against the US; struggle always against foreign countries that were far more powerful than Vietnam. Struggle, the "steadfast popular resistance marked by armed insurrection against foreign domination" is what shaped the steel frame of Vietnamese nationalism, playing about the same role as the operation of the war machine played in Afghanistan; it "led to the preservation of the Vietnamese people's identity, the emergence of a national consciousness and the establishment of the independent state of Viet Nam."[7] As Vietnamese Prime Minister Pham Van Dong told journalist Wilfred Burchett, "there is nothing in our history except struggle. Struggle against foreign invaders, always more powerful than ourselves ... and the result of this, after two thousand-odd years, is that it has created a very stable nervous system in our people. We never panic."[8]

Struggle has forged a smoothly integrated social system so well integrated that the whole nation is actually treated as a family. This is a family adaptable to the ever changing situation that war creates, with great determination, and a great will to independence and freedom. This is a family where there is genuine amusement that the Chinese can teach them a lesson, or that the outsiders like the French or the US can conquer and subdue them, or even defeat them in war.

And this absence of panic is evident to anyone who travels in Vietnam, specially the North and interacts with the people. This is the people who have lived with death and danger too long to be perturbed by them; who have acquired the stillness, the repose, the mental and physical calm that can only come from years of strenuous effort, effort that consumes every mental and physical reserve. They work at a steady but uniform and unremitting pace, for there is no rush, no need for spasmodic action, they firmly believe that time is with them; that heaven itself is with them.

One of the major traditions of the origins of Vietnam as a unified nation places that origin in 208 BC when a dissident Chinese warlord, Trieu Da, proclaimed himself Emperor of Nam Viet to rival the Han Empire which ruled over China. Though he was Chinese in origin, the accepted tradition is that he assimilated fully with the people; he and his successors managed to rule independently till 111 BC, when the Han invaded and incorporated Vietnam into China as a province. But the Vietnamese struggle for independence from China never ceased. There were highlights in this struggle. In 40 AD the Trung sisters, Trung Trac and Trung Nhi, the former of whose husband had been killed by the Chinese, called on the people to resist them; they led an uprising against Han rule which even led to a very brief period of independence for several months, then two years of war as the Hans tried to re-establish control, which they finally succeeded in doing. The Trung sisters committed suicide and they "entered the Vietnamese legends as gods. To this day they are worshipped."[9] In Hanoi, in the Museum of the Revolution, they have been given pride of place and in the twentieth century there were still attempts to rally the people against the foreign invader in the name of the Trung sisters.

In 544 AD the leader of one struggle, Le Bon, proclaimed himself King of Nam Viet; but in 547 he was defeated by the Chinese forces and his movement collapsed. Another revolt, led by Li Phat Tu, of the same family, began in the year 600 and was only crushed two years later.[10]

Finally, in the year 939, at the battle of Bach Dang River, Ngo Nguyen won independence from the Chinese. The latter tried to regain control, repeatedly and unsuccessfully; internal power struggles among ambitious Vietnamese encouraged them. In 968 invaders from the Song dynasty were defeated. During the Li dynasty which is often regarded as the Golden Era of Vietnam, there were more attempts by the Song Empire to subjugate Vietnam, all of which were unsuccessful. But the signal success of Vietnam was when its Tran dynasty took on the wars against the Yuan dynasty of China, the Mongol empire. In 1257 a Mongol army got as far as Hanoi, but was forced to withdraw. Kubla Khan himself sent Marshall Sogato to subjugate Vietnam; then he sent his son Togan who was also defeated by the guerilla tactics of the Vietnamese. When Marshall Sogato tried to help him the former was killed. In 1287 and then the following year another Mongol army entered Hanoi, and this was a horde of 300,000. It made three attempts to conquer Vietnam. But the Tran king left his capital which was also abandoned by all the citizens who had lived there. The Mongol army was unable to get food or other supplies; they were harassed by guerilla attacks, by repeated counter-offensives by the Vietnamese forces. So each time it was defeated and forced to retreat by the great Vietnamese general of the Tran dynasty, Than Hung Dao.

Six centuries later, when the French were trying to make an empire in Vietnam they had the same experience; the emperor left the capital, and all the people left with him. There is a consistency in the Vietnamese ability to struggle as well as in the methods they have used over the centuries.

So when, in 1941, Ho Chi Minh appealed to the students and other youth to join the liberation movement in his Letter from Abroad, he wrote about the resistance of the Vietnamese against Mongols, that "some hundreds of years ago, when our country was endangered by the Mongolian invasion, our elders under the Tran dynasty rose up indignantly and called on their sons and daughters throughout the country to rise as one in order to kill the enemy."

In 1407 the Ming ruler of China was able to occupy Hanoi and stay there. Le Loi was the leader who waged guerilla war against the Ming Empire. He besieged Hanoi, defeated the Ming general in 1428 and proclaimed himself King. And then, in a gesture of grace, he offered the defeated Chinese generals horses so that they could return in comfort; Vietnamese guides of the mid-1960s, showing visitors around museums where these Vietnamese victories are celebrated, usually said that they would be happy, later on, to provide similar facilities to the defeated Americans.

Dynasties came and went; scholars add up a total of fifteen from 208 BC to 1945 AD when Bao Dai, the last of the Emperors, abdicated. There were internal dissension, civil war and even rebellion; appeals to the Chinese Emperors who did interfere on behalf of one or other claimant to the Vietnamese throne, but did not again try to bring the entire country under subjugation. On one such occasion the Manchu Emperor sent an army south and, in 1787, captured Hanoi to reinstall their client. But then the Vietnamese won a victory after a surprise attack during the Vietnamese New Year, Tet; in the context of Vietnamese historiography this is often cited as the precedent for the 1968 Tet offensive, which changed the shape of the war between the US and Vietnam. Again it was the centuries of war against China that provided the backdrop for the years of war against the US.

So it was not unusual that when the Europeans arrived civil war raged in Vietnam. The Trinh in the North fought the Nguyen in the South from 1620 to 1674 and the struggle stormed back and forth for, as tradition approves, war was the sole occupation of the mandarins who ruled the country. For centuries the Vietnamese had fought pirates from the sea and armies of occupation sent from the North; they had always been ready to mobilise for war and to fight. So they had acquired a firmly held conviction. They may have to struggle long; indeed they would inevitably have to struggle long, for their enemies had always been far larger and more powerful than they; but they would fight and they would continue fighting, and eventually they would win.

### Vietnamese Nationalism: Resources

In 1802 Nguyen Anh established the Nguyen dynasty. He called himself Gia Long: Gia for the short form of the old name of Saigon; Long for the short form of the old name of Hanoi. When the French arrived in August, 1858 it was the Nguyen dynasty which ruled Vietnam. The initial French demands were three: a guarantee of religious freedom for Christians who had been persecuted with particular severity by the Emperor Tu Duc, who ruled from 1848 to 1883; permission to establish a French commercial presence; and to have a French Consul at Hue. The demands were rejected and thus began three decades of war against the Vietnamese nationalists as also against the Chinese who claimed suzerain status and, therefore, the right to sign any agreement with any foreign power on behalf of the Vietnamese.

Against French colonialism, too, the theme is always struggle. The names of the movements of struggle are the ones familiar to every Vietnamese student: the Hich Can Vuong or Monarchist movement from 1885 to 1913; the Dong Kinh Nghia Thuc or Private Schools movement (1907-08); the Dong Du (Trip to the East) or Pan-Asian Movement (1905-1939); the Vietnam Quoc-Dan Dang or Nationalist Movement (1925-33 and 1945-46). One author, citing these movements, writes that "throughout the whole of the French colonial period, armed revolts against the conquerors rarely ceased, and even intermittent intervals in the fighting were marked by non-violent agitation."[11]

When the French under General Genouilly went up the Saigon river in 1859 they were greeted with printed proclamations, "your country belongs to the western seas, ours to the eastern ... As the horse and the buffalo differ, so do we – in language, literature, customs. If you persist in putting the torch to us, disorder will be long. But we shall act according to the laws of heaven, and our cause will triumph in the end."[12]

And as they advanced their colonial enterprise further, it was independent and local national leaders who offered them the most resistance, thus making it more difficult to counter, for these local guerilla leaders seemed to be autonomous; they had no single head. Meanwhile, the Emperor signed agreements with the French which gave the latter an increasing number of concessions, but with considerable reluctance and often at the point of a gun. At the court there had been a consistent emphasis on compromise with the French, and this was the policy called 'Hoa Ngi' (peace with negotiation). Outside the court there was determined opposition, often armed, sometimes non-violent. And the military setbacks piled up. In 1862, as the French were busy putting Residents into place in the provinces, there were rebellions all over Vietnam, which even aroused opposition in France and necessitated the dispatch of more troops to ensure the rebellious provinces were brought more firmly under control. In March, 1885, as they were about to complete their conquest, they suffered a disastrous defeat at the hands of Chinese forces at Lang Son near the Chinese border; the cabinet of Jules Ferry fell as soon as news of this disaster reached France.

And so it was that "everywhere indeed in the new French empire unrest and rebellion were constant factors for many years ... in each case it was a long protracted struggle, and when at last forced to give in the Vietnamese never lost the hope that one day the hated foreigner would have to withdraw."[13]

But finally, by 1884-85 the French had acquired control at least over all the important centres of Vietnam. When, in the final act of conquest, General de Courcy, the Commander-in-Chief of French troops in Indochina, arrived in Hue in 1885 and shelled the Imperial Palace, then occupied it, the Emperor fled to the mountains and launched an appeal, Hich Can Vuong, roughly meaning come to the aid of the Emperor. For in 1883, along with the signing of the treaty making Tongking and Annam into French protectorates, the court officials were also planning the continuation of the resistance. Ham Nghi became Emperor in July 1884 at the age of twelve; a year later he was to symbolise the resistance, having been taken to Tan So, a fortified city which had been built in Quang

Tri province as a centre for the resistance. On July 5, 1885 the attack on French positions began. The resistance had managed to accumulate quantities of arms and other supplies in Tan So; villagers throughout the province, hearing about the resistance and that it was led by the Emperor, came together in groups to attack French positions; it was a war of national freedom and even a somewhat unsympathetic historian of the times had to admit that "the royal uprising at times reached the proportions of a truly national war of liberation."

This, the Hich Can Vuong movement, became over the years the major movement for independence. Phan Dinh Phung was one of the most important and one of the last of the fighters of that militant movement. This Confucian court scholar and rebel fought for years in the 1880s and 1890s to free his country from the French. He was a former 'Ngu Su' or grand imperial censor, and one of the great leaders of the resistance. He had come first in the metropolitan examinations of 1877; but by 1885 he was organising the militants. He used local scholars as his troop commanders. There were in fact hundreds of scholars who took an active part in one militant movement or the other against the French.

As French positions crumbled under the attacks of this movement the countryside went out of control, and for almost a year control was restricted to strongly fortified positions. Then the Emperor Ham Nghi was captured by the French. After the French had attacked and taken Tan So the resistance split into smaller groups and continued to spread throughout Vietnam. Able local leaders assumed control, like Nghe One in the province of Nghe An, Le Truc in the provinces of Quang Binh and Ha Tinh, or Hieu of Quang Tri province. Of the last, for example, one French author of the time wrote "this man, still young and of rare energy, gradually acquired the reputation of a truly fabulous hero. He gave to the insurrection in his province the breadth and prestige of a national movement."[14]

South of the Red river delta the resistance constructed another fortress city called Ba Dinh, inside which they dug a complicated network of tunnels and earthworks. It took three assaults, two months, December 1886 and January 1887, and several thousand troops for the French to take it, and when they did, the defenders were not there.

As for Phan Dinh Phung, once he realised that the movement

led by the Emperor faced defeat, he started travelling through the North Annam countryside, using his prestige as a former Ngu Su to build up support for the revival of the resistance. Four years later, in December 1893, he was ready with a well equipped army of 3000 and with the hope that, once he struck, others would join. And so they did. Phung had his headquarters in the mountainous region of Vu Quang and he was soon able to extend the territory under his control north to Thanh Hoa and south to Quang Binh. He divided this zone into twelve districts and established the beginnings of an administrative system in each of them. For two years the French were again reduced to a few heavily fortified centres. They tried everything; close friends and members of his family were made to write to him urging him to surrender; his family tombs were opened, the corpses removed and exhibited in the town of Ha Tinh, which as far as the Christian church is concerned, would be equal to the burning of churches.

In the year 1895 an appeal was sent to him by a friend who had been with him in the resistance to the French; the appeal, encouraged by French authorities, was to surrender as there was no hope of his forcing out the French. He replied that Vietnam had resisted the Han, the Tang, the Song, Yuan and Ming dynasties of China, a country a thousand times more powerful than Vietnam but none of those dynasties could annex it because "the destiny of our country has been willed by Heaven itself."[15] Then his friend appealed to him in the name of tradition, for the sake of his village, for preserving his ancestor's tombs which the French would otherwise destroy, for his brothers who were threatened by them, and he replied, "From the time I joined you in the Can Vuong movement I determined to forget questions of family and village. Now I have but one tomb, a very large one, that must be defended, the land of Vietnam. I have only one brother, very important, that is in danger, more than twenty million countrymen."[16]

Reinforcements were brought in but it was not till Phung himself died in 1895, that his followers offered to surrender; so, to encourage them, they were offered a pardon, so they did surrender. All were beheaded. His wife and son were spared.

Another great resistance leader was Phan Boi Chau, though, since he spent most of his active years outside Vietnam, he was more inspiration than executor. He passed the examinations in 1900. He used the resulting prestige to travel, write against French rule and even try to set up an underground organisation for armed resistance. This last didn't work too well; he had sought out the survivors of the Can Vuong movement and located in the person of Cuong De a direct descendant of the first Nguyen Emperor, and a person who could serve as a rallying point for those who wished to fight for it. Chau took Cuong De to Japan in 1906, along with several Vietnamese students; from there they inspired militancy within Vietnam. But then in July 1907 Japan and France came to an agreement under which the former recognised the latter's Asian possessions; Vietnamese students and others in Japan, who had been working on plans for the resistance, were squeezed; Chau himself was expelled and went to Siam.

But the Chinese revolution of 1911 gave Chau and his colleagues another opportunity to regroup and organise militancy inside the country, including a number of bombings and assassinations. In March, 1913, for instance, the city of Saigon was targeted for bombs and though they were discovered before exploding, other acts followed, including a bomb thrown on the terrace of a Hanoi hotel in which two French officers were killed. In 1916 the organisation founded by Chau launched an impressive effort: simultaneous uprisings in thirteen of the provinces. This showed that despite French repression and surveillance local level leaders could organise networks of coordinated attack and also that militant leaders in exile had sufficient communication skills and could supervise this organisation. The uprisings included a mutiny by Vietnamese troops in the northern province of Thai Nguyen; 300 soldiers, helped by the townspeople, held the town of Thai Nguyen for several days before the French re-established control.

In June 1925 he was in Canton, from where he was kidnapped by French agents, (it was Ho Chi Minh, see below, who actually gave him away to the French agents), taken to Hanoi, tried and given a life sentence, and then almost immediately pardoned. But his time as inspiration was over.

And then other leaders of the resistance kept rising up against the French, Hoang Hoa Tham, for example, a pirate who had become a nationalist. The French called him the Tiger of Yen Tre; from 1893 he built a volunteer army with which he defended his stronghold in the province of Yen Tre, regularly raiding French garrisons in the North. The French were forced to sign a truce giving him control over twenty-two villages; he continued to attack

French positions from there, and it was not until 1907 that his rebellion was broken.

## The Creation of Nationalism: Ho Chi Minh

There was now a change in the nature of the national movement. Until 1918 the leadership of that movement had comprised Confucian scholars, with a strong allegiance to the Court and its restoration to power. After that new leaders emerged. This was largely due to the socio-economic changes that were brought about by the 1914-18 war and economic growth. During that war almost 45,000 Vietnamese soldiers were sent to the fronts in Europe; another 50,000 were sent as workers, again as part of France's war effort. They returned with different ideas about freedom and the form that it should take. The war also necessitated industrialisation and faster growth. New lands, especially in the Mekong valley, were opened up for cultivation; there were also in the result more tenants and landless labour in the agricultural sector; and there were now more speculators and entrepreneurs in that sector. France needed larger quantities of raw materials for the war effort and more manufactures since its own industry was turned to munitions production. So in Vietnam manufacturing, mining and industry grew, and with this the labour force: from 1913 to 1939 it grew four-fold. Inequalities in the distribution of income sharpened, especially in the South. These changes created the ground for a national movement based on attachment to communist goals rather than to the Court. And it was symbolic of the nature of the change that "when Ho Chi Minh arrived in Canton in June 1925 as an agent for the Comintern ... his first task was to cause the arrest of Phan Boi Chau, the living symbol of the traditionalist protest against French rule."

In June 1925 also Ho Chi Minh founded an Association of Revolutionary Youth, called the Revolutionary League of the Youth of Vietnam while he was in Canton. This was an openly communist organisation and it was the first time a communist force had come on the scene; its membership quickly rose to several thousand; many of its members were given training in the USSR. Ho himself went there in April, 1927 when the Kuomintang cracked down on the communists in China. But the Association founded by him expanded and with it his stature as a freedom fighter and nationalist. His immediate aim was without doubt the nationalist one of achieving independence, while that of communism was for a later stage. At a Congress held in Hong Kong in 1929 he appealed (in absentia) for all classes, workers, peasants, soldiers, merchants, students, to unite against the French. And he wanted it to be a Vietnamese revolution. Moscow disagreed on both counts, saying it had to be a class-based movement. It should be led by the workers and peasants; the bourgeoisie, which Ho wanted to include, should be kept out. And it should not be national; the whole of Indochina should be included. And Moscow chose delegates to that conference who went back to Vietnam and set up a class-based Indochinese Communist Party. In January 1930 Ho went back to Vietnam and actually established a Vietnamese Communist Party, for which the Comintern pulled him up.

At this time his authority within the party does not seem to have been undisputed. When the party decided to launch a combined peasants' and workers' agitation on the pattern of the typical class-based struggles which communists had internalised as a result of Soviet teaching, which was to be in the first half of the year 1930, Ho was against it, arguing that the peasants and workers were not yet ready for this kind of agitation. He was over-ruled. So it was that in October 1930 another unified Indochinese Communist Party was set up. Moscow didn't want independence for Vietnam; it wanted control.

But as the years passed his authority and his control over the Party became complete. By May, 1941 he was fully in control. At the eighth session of the Central Committee of the Party held that month he steered it towards the founding of a Vietnam Independence League, called the Viet Minh, with the goal of mobilising the masses' national spirit. So the communists had now shifted away from an emphasis on the class struggle and towards the national spirit. However, the earliest attempts at revolutionary activity of the 1930s, like the Bac Son uprising of late 1940 in the mountains of North Vietnam, were abortive. They did not sufficiently rely on nationalist, as opposed to class or communist, spirit.

## First Stage: The War Against France

For the next four years after the formation of the Viet Minh, the party prepared its politico-military base in the mountains of North Vietnam. Japanese troops had moved into Vietnam in

September, 1940, as a result of an agreement with the Vichy government in France; and throughout their occupation of the country they "confirmed French colonialism", while, conversely, France was throughout the war "giving support and advantage to the enemy of the Allied powers in Asia." So then it was the Viet Minh that organised the most effective resistance to the Japanese occupation, again by tapping the spirit of nationalism. Military political cells were set up with a view to taking control once the Japanese left. The task of organising these was given to Vo Nguyen Giap. In May, 1945, seeing the impending end of Japanese occupation, Viet Minh attacks on their positions increased; and the Vietminh base inside Vietnam grew stronger and with increased popular backing.

So when Japan surrendered in August, 1945 it was the Viet Minh who were able to move smoothly into place. On the morning of 19 August their first units moved into Hanoi; there was no resistance from the administration of the time which had been set up by the Japanese with the Emperor Bao Dai at the head; Bao Dai himself abdicated on 25 August. And on 2 September Ho addressed a crowd of half a million that had gathered in Hanoi for the purpose, saying the French had fled, the Japanese had capitulated, now the people had established the present Republican government. "We have wrested our independence from the Japanese and not from the French."[17]

He made there a declaration of Vietnamese independence, quoting liberally from the American declaration of independence and from the French declaration of the rights of man; and proclaimed the establishment of the Democratic Republic of Vietnam, with a provisional government which had taken over the administration of Hanoi and the countryside. No one, of course, recognised the government established by Ho Chi Minh, not the US, not (till 1950) the USSR. The US was getting more and more concerned that Ho and his colleagues were communists, as the French never tired of reiterating. But in the North his position was strong.[18]

In the North it was the Chinese forces of Chiang Kai Shek to whom the Allies had given the task of moving in for the concluding business of the war. They entered northern Vietnam in September, 1945 to supervise the surrender of Japanese troops, free the French prisoners of war and generally maintain peace. By the end of the year there were almost 200,000 Chinese troops in North Vietnam, far too many for the 48,000 Japanese troops whose surrender they were supposed to supervise. The Chinese interest seems to have been to loosen French control over North Vietnam so that they could regain some of the suzerainty that they had claimed over the centuries. So they neglected the Japanese surrender business and started to arm the Vietminh. The latter, content to receive as much military equipment as they could get, definitely wanted the Chinese out, remembering the thousand-year rule of China over Vietnam. But, given the generally tattered reputation of the French as far as the battlefield is concerned the Vietminh did feel that the French would be much easier to evict than the Chinese, so French troops should replace the latter. The French also wanted the Chinese out; they calculated that if a few French troops were sent north for this purpose, their numbers could be built up soon enough to take on and eliminate the Vietminh. And what they wanted was in accord with Allied policy throughout Southeast Asia: the early restoration of colonial control.

So on 28 February 1946 the Chinese signed an agreement with the French that they would withdraw their troops and on 6 March 1946 the Vietminh signed an agreement with the French in which they effectively agreed that 15,000 French troops would replace them; the agreement included French recognition of Vietnam as a "free state" within the French Union; that the Vietminh would retain its army, that other institutions would function like a Parliament and a Treasury; that there would be a referendum on Vietnamese unification; and that France would withdraw its troops by 1952.

The French now occupied the Governor-General's palace in Hanoi, also known, appropriately enough, as the *cage doree* or golden cage. But their general position in the North was not strong.

Within weeks the agreement had effectively been torn up by the French, who were frantically embarking troops every week from Marseilles for service in North Vietnam, in an ill-concealed policy of destroying the Vietminh. But there were different voices out of France and perhaps the Vietminh leadership retained some hope that the March, 1946 agreement would be honoured. Leon Blum won the election of December, 1946 and just before being elected he had written an article asserting that "there is one way and only one way of preserving in Indochina the prestige of our civilisation, our political and spiritual influence ... sincere agreement with

Vietnam on the basis of independence."[19] On the other hand, there was De Gaulle, not to be lightly regarded, who said, echoing Count Walewski's report of 1857, that "united with the overseas territories which she opened to civilisation, France is a great power. Without these territories she would be in danger of no longer being one."[20]

Events showed that the latter view prevailed. Clashes between the two sides, which were minor at first, built up in size and ferocity. In the South the resistance had already begun in late 1945 in which, as Vo Nguyen Giap asserted with a mixture of optimism and idealistic commitment, "the pointed bamboo spears of our people under a democratic republican regime had proved to be much more effective than the cannons of the former kings and mandarins."[21]

## Dien Bien Phu: The War Ends

Meanwhile in the North, by November, 1946 the French had more or less completed their build-up; the clashes grew fiercer and there was a rapid rise in the number of casualties. Finally, in the clearest possible statement of their real intentions, on 23 November the French fleet in Haiphong harbour launched a bombardment, backed by air strikes, which left 6,000 dead, mostly civilians. Just four weeks later, on 20 December, 1946, Ho Chi Minh called for a national resistance war on Voice of Vietnam radio and went to his country base at Tan Trao, where he and his companions began a guerilla war. It took time for Ho Chi Minh and Vo Nguyen Giap to build up their strength, but by 1950 they were definitely on the offensive; they had forced a French withdrawal from the northern mountains, had overwhelmed a French garrison at Cao Bang and in a series of other sorties pushed the French into defensive warfare. At Lang Son the French pulled back so rapidly that a large quantity of stores was left behind. There seemed to be little hope of victory and the French considered withdrawing from Hanoi. Then, in the years 1952 and 1953, the tide of war changed and the French made some advances; a series of successful offensives brought back much of the lost ground.

At this point, in July, 1953, the Navarre Plan was adopted by the French cabinet. France had 200,000 troops in Vietnam and had suffered a total of 74,000 casualties already; opinion at home was rapidly turning against the war. It was essential to do something to show that this war was going somewhere. The Plan called for the establishment of defensive strong points which could hold back

Vietminh forces until US aid enabled the French to build up enough offensive strength to launch more aggressive operations. The main strong point was a cross roads in the Northwest that was a major route for military supplies from China and for access to Laos. It was a valley surrounded by hills and mountains; it was called Dien Bien Phu. It could be supplied by air; there was plenty of open space around the French positions so that defence would be easy; anything that moved into the open space could be mown down from a good distance; any attack on the position would have to be based in the mountains, and the Vietnamese had no military hardware that could reach them from the mountains. So the French established their strong point. But all their calculations happened to be wrong. The French had 105 mm artillery and thought Giap had none, but he had 48 of them compared to their 28; all could reach the French positions. And all were so well concealed in the forested hills and mountains around that, despite control of the air they could not be located by French bombers.

Giap's offensive on the entrenched French occupying garrison of 15,000 began on the 12 March, 1954. As his heavy guns started firing the French found that they were so well hidden that they still could not be found. Then Giap's troops started tunneling operations, in which the Vietnamese had centuries of experience; hundreds of kilometres of tunnels were dug which brought Vietminh troops within rifle range of the French and suddenly the open spaces around their positions were of no more use; the French troops were being picked off where they were. Through April and May the world press kept Dien Bien Phu on the front page; the Geneva conference on Vietnam was meeting just then and there was no doubt in anyone's mind that what happened on the battlefield would have a decisive outcome on the negotiations.

After 55 days of siege, on 7 May, 1954, the French at Dien Bien Phu surrendered. Five months later Ho Chi Minh's troops entered Hanoi. The French had lost their empire in Asia. In the meanwhile, the Geneva accords were signed on 21 July, 1954, which provided for French withdrawal from the North and a joint election of North and South within two years on the question of unification. France dissolved Indochina's status within the French Union and now the US stepped in, dealing directly with a South Vietnamese government under Ngo Dinh Diem.

The classic study of the war that the Vietnamese fought against the French is Bernard B. Fall's *Street Without Joy* which in the first three years after publication in 1961 went into several reprints and four editions. When it was published President Kennedy had moved into the White House; he had already assembled the team that was to produce innovative theories about the best way to conduct limited war in the jungles of Asia; and the Americans were just about getting more and more interested in Vietnam. Any American concerned with policy in Vietnam, what to do there, had to read it. The book contains no description of what happened in Dien Bien Phu. Fall describes in some detail the maltreatment by the Vietnamese of French prisoners, comparing the survivors to those of Dachau and Buchenwald; he asks why Dien Bien Phu was chosen at all, and answers that Navarre, the French Commander-in-Chief, Indochina, was probably responsible, meaning implicitly that someone else could have avoided the disaster. But he does not tell us what happened there, far less the consequences on French politics, the economy and society.

And he has some advice to give to the Americans. "Why is it that we must use top-notch elite forces, the cream of the crop of American, British, French or Australian commando and special warfare schools, armed with the very best that advanced technology can provide, to defeat the Vietminh, Algerian or Malay 'CT's', almost none of whom can lay claim to similar expert training and only in the rarest of cases to equality of fire-power?" And he gives the answer: it is because "it takes all the technical proficiency our system can provide to make up for the woeful lack of popular support and political savvy of most of the regimes that the West has thus far sought to prop up."[22]

## Another War Begins: The US in Vietnam

The American conviction that it could and should build a world order in accord with its own design was the start of its involvement in Vietnam (as elsewhere). Furthermore, with Kennedy in the White House from early 1961, and his putting together a group of surpassing talent, the best and the brightest of young people from government, business, the academic world, this would be done with success; the world would be saved from Communism. With this team President Kennedy formulated a composite body of thought and action on how to tackle guerilla warfare in the jungles of Asia.

US interest in preventing the unification of Vietnam or, which was the same thing, ensuring that the joint election of North and South provided for by the Geneva accords was not held or, closer to the US world view, blocking a highly motivated and disciplined North Vietnamese regime taking over South Vietnam from a very pro-West regime, grew slowly. At first this interest was expressed through delaying the joint election. Until 1960 there were, on the ground, only 342 US advisers in South Vietnam; in that year the number was doubled to 685, and other things happened. The National Liberation Front had been formed in the South; infiltration from the North, along what came to be known as the Ho Chi Minh trail, began for the movement of men, finance, and equipment to the NLF. By 1960 it was apparent that the South Vietnamese government led by Ngo Dinh Diem was steadily losing control over the countryside to the NLF.

This was also a time of intense jousting for advantage in the so-called Cold War. In Southeast Asia two factors were relevant in this context, for US policy. One was a general sense of losing. The 'loss of China' provided the backdrop, and as Robert Trumbull wrote in the *New York Times Book Review* about a new book on what went wrong in Southeast Asia, "the free world is steadily losing ground in that part of the world to the Communists." That book, *The Ugly American,* had appeared in 1958, and its authors put it starkly. "Without pitting one Soviet soldier against one American soldier, the Soviet has won a staggering series of victories. In the few years since the end of World War II, Russia has added 700,000,000 people to the multitude already under its direct rule. Its land empire has swollen by about 5,000,000 square miles." Then they go on to cite the way the Communists have won wars, gained prestige, become strong contenders for power; while American prestige diminished and the "Vice-President has been spat upon". Secondly, the Americans could do something about this. "We have the material, and above all the human resources, to change our methods and to win."[23]

The book was a sellout. Within four months it became a 'Book of the Month Club' selection, and had gone into the twentieth printing.

The Kennedy administration decided that they would, indeed, change their methods and win. They brought the academics into Washington, where they evolved even more sophisticated theories about a spectrum of warfare ranging from full nuclear retaliation in the case of all-out war to limited nuclear war to war with only the use of large-scale conventional weapons all the way down to insurgencies and brush fire war, fought in the jungles and deserts of the third world. Counter insurgency methods evolved along with technological fixes for all the military and economic problems of the developing world. And with this came the hardware: area denial techniques; ground sensors; airborne people sniffers; defoliants. And, in concord with the simulacra of IR theory, it was the statistics which would tell you whether you were winning or losing. So it was the statistics that dominated the US war on Vietnam, and Defense Secretary Robert McNamara, who was directing it from Washington, was fully at home only in the world of statistics. That was "the portrait of McNamara in those years at his desk, on planes, in Saigon, poring over page after page of data, each platoon, each squad, studying all those statistics ... looking for what he wanted to see; and he never saw nor smelled nor felt what was really there, right in front of him."[24]

What actually happened was that "the advent of sophisticated theories of limited conflict in the Kennedy defence program complicated the conceptual problem of differentiating war from peace,"[25] because no one actually knew or could work out, in the case of each category of conflict, what the limits were.

Kennedy decided he would increase the number of political and military advisers sent to Saigon. The number of US advisers deputed to South Vietnam was steadily increased as the task seemed bigger than at first thought; and their role changed from pure advice to active combat. And this continued under President Johnson. By late 1964 there were 23,000 and by January 1965 US tactical aircraft had started operating out of South Vietnam, bombing suspected NLF concentrations, interdicting their communications, though there was no activity over North Vietnam, yet.

Then on 7 February 1965 an NLF team broke into the American air base in Pleiku, fired several mortar rounds, killed eight US soldiers, and destroyed six helicopters and an air transport plane.

## Escalation

This had two consequences. First, it enforced an escalation in the number of US ground forces in South Vietnam. The South Vietnamese obviously could not adequately protect the US air bases and other installations; the US would itself have to do the protecting, which, of course, meant getting directly into offensive operations in a way that had not been done before. This built up over the years as US ground forces were used for an increasing range of tasks. Two marine battalions arrived in early March 1965; they were allowed to undertake operations up to eighty-five kilometres from whatever installation they were protecting; then an army brigade arrived, again for base defence; and so it grew, always for defence of US military installations, but that always also meant offensive ground operations.

By mid-1966 there were 300,000 advisers; a year later US force levels had reached 431,000; and finally there were 525,000 US troops in South Vietnam. The advice given by the authors of *The Ugly American*: send out your best diplomats; get them to learn the local language; to know more about the problems of the country than even the local leaders; to mix with the local people, all that was forgotten. Secretary of Defence Robert McNamara wanted the results of the US effort in Vietnam in terms of numbers: the body count of enemy killed; numbers of defectors from the NLF; numbers of weapons captured. The numbers also, of course, covered the debit side, the rising cost of the war: by the mid-1960s a million dollars a day on artillery alone; a hundred tons of bombs costing US$ 140,000 for each infiltrator killed along the Ho Chi Minh trail.

Actually, in the jungles and mountains of South Vietnam the Americans had always had little chance of winning the war. The Vietnamese had fought that kind of war for too many centuries and against too many enemies, all far more powerful than them, to lose. But the NLF could not, on its own, win South Vietnam either. For by 1966 the US was using the technology they had on a large scale. Ninety per cent of the territory of the south had been declared a free fire zone where anything that moved could be bombed or otherwise destroyed. To ensure detection defoliants like Agent Orange were used extensively to destroy anything that grew. C-123 transport aircraft with multiple wing nozzles were used to spray the countryside with this and other defoliants. Ten per cent of cropland and a third of total forest acreage were covered as the Americans blanketed the countryside, destroying trees, bushes, anything which you could hide in and, of course, crops.

That included food crops and so the villages emptied out into the cities; over eight million people moved, and US counter-revolutionary theorists put a name to this strategy, 'forced urbanisation'. And, of course, the NLF moved in with them. This meant that over the months and years the NLF mastered the art of urban guerilla tactics; for the US this was particularly unfortunate.

But in the towns and cities American bases and garrisons were, by and large, secured. To win the war the NLF needed help in men and material from the North, a constant replenishment that would enable them to keep engaging and killing Americans; and as the war progressed tens of thousands of trained troops from the North did move South; they were essential for the war. Conversely, therefore, the Americans, in order to win the war in the South, had to stop the North from sending men and material into the South. As the experts in General Westmoreland's headquarters said to correspondents in private briefings, "Granted, we cannot win the war in the South in the *South*. But we will win the war in the South in the North – by breaking the North."[26]

Second, therefore, and far more important, the attack on Pleiku marked the beginning of the air war against the North, which became known as Operation Rolling Thunder. That began on 13 February 1965; in order to defend against these attacks on the bases the source had to be neutralised, and that meant air attacks against the North. Of course, other explanations were also given: that this would revive the morale of the South Vietnamese government; that 'something' had to be done since otherwise the Communists would win.[27]

So the Americans desperately wanted to, had to, win the air war; when they lost the air war, they lost the Vietnam War.

For the air war it was the Defence Department that put out the figures. By 1966, a little over a year after the air war began, the American had dropped more bombs on Vietnam than in the entire Pacific theatre during World War II; by 1967 one and a half million tons of bombs had been dropped over Vietnam, more than in the entire European theatre in the same war; by 1968 it was more than all the bombs dropped anywhere during that war; and by 1970 it was more than all the bombs ever dropped anywhere in the whole of human history. And that was before the 1972 Christmas bombings, which were heavier than all the bombings of the previous three years put together. All this was surely enough to win the air war, as the American planners thought.

But it didn't help. Take the so-called Ho Chi Minh trail, the route along which most of the supplies of men, weapons and other material moved from the North to the South. It was one of the prime aims of the bombing to stop the truck traffic along this and the US Air Force claimed victory more than once, that all the trucks had been destroyed, that there were no more trucks, the North had none to send across to the South. As one CIA official said, "North Vietnam theoretically ran out of trucks at least seven or eight times while I worked on the North Vietnam desk. Each time when this happened, the Joint Chiefs of Staff demanded to know why they were still seeing trucks in North Vietnam."[28] At one point *The New York Times* of 9 May 1966 quoted a military spokesman saying that all railroads and highways leading into Hanoi had been cut; the Vietnamese capital was isolated; but American correspondents there were travelling freely into and out of Hanoi at the time, reporting that all roads into the capital were functioning normally.[29]

## The Air War and the Blockade

From the broadest viewpoint, the Americans had three objectives in the air war.[30] First, to stop the NLF from getting aid from North Vietnam in the shape of troops and supplies or at least substantially which in turn would reduce the flow to raise the morale of the South Vietnamese forces. Second, destroy the military and economic potential of North Vietnam and thus eliminate its war-making capacity; and, third, to shake the morale of the people in the North.

On the other hand, the North Vietnamese aims were national; they had little to do with Marxist-Leninist ideology or with what the Soviet Union or China might advise them. As Wilfred Burchett reports them saying, "Whether Peking or Moscow existed or not, whether the socialist camp existed or not, we would have no choice but to take up arms and fight, as our ancestors have always done for national salvation ... we accept no advice that runs contrary to our ideas of how we should fulfil that task."

North Vietnam had three aims. First, to continue building socialism in the country; second, to intensify the supply of men and material to the South; and, third, to win the air war.

As for the American strategy of breaking the North to win in the South, when Burchett asked Ho Chi Minh about it he laughed (the Vietnamese always seemed genuinely amused by the idea that the Americans could win the war, any war against Vietnam), and said, "The Americans are deceiving themselves in thinking that by bombing the North they can win in the South. Never, never will we submit ... we are determined to fight on if it takes five, ten, 20 or even more years. We will win this war..."[31]

There were actually three air wars. The first started on 13 February 1965 after the attack on the Pleiku air base and continued till 31 March 1968 at which point, and this was reinforced by the Tet offensive, the US was forced to call it off. The second was from 9 May 1972 to 22 October 1972 which included a blockade of North Vietnam by naval action and mine laying. In contrast to the first, which concentrated largely on military targets with some civilian casualties resulting from collateral damage, the second was aimed specifically at both military and civilian targets. The third was from 23 October 1972 to 15 January 1973, the so-called Christmas bombings. As part of this one, during "twelve days of December the Air Force pounded North Vietnam with a greater tonnage of bombs that the total of the past three years, reducing areas of Hanoi and Haiphong to rubble, destroying Hanoi's airport, factories and power plants."[32]

In general the air war saw the US using whatever strength they had: 1260 tactical aircraft including tactical bombers were used, 32% of total US tactical air strength; and 93 B-52 bombers or 40% of total US strength.[33] There was, in other words, not much more that they *could* put in; if this was not going to be enough nothing was enough and it wasn't.

The Vietnamese defences were effective against the US air attacks. These were in several layers, backed by a dense radar network; as the US aircraft approached for their bombing runs the first to take them on in coordinated feints to divert them from their targets were aircraft of the Vietnamese air force comprising MIG-17's, MIG-19's and MIG-21's. Then there were the strategic weapons, the surface-to-air missile batteries, of which the most effective proved to be the SAM-2. These were reinforced by modern anti-aircraft artillery as well as somewhat old-fashioned ones. Then there were the militia with small arms, mainly machine guns, but also rifles. Three thousand three hundred units of the militia were organised, spread all over the country; so if the pilots came down for precision runs they would run into a hail of fire from the small arms held by militia units, each of which was as enthusiastic as the next to get a kill. This proved demoralising for the pilots; casualties were so high that they flew high and fast and confined themselves to a single run. Not many targets were hit. One of the most publicised air attacks was early in the air war, on the road at the critically important Mu Gia pass leading into Laos, on which 109 bombs were dropped; four of them hit the road, which was cleared within hours; the rest had fallen harmlessly in the jungle. Several weeks later the Americans flew over and discovered this, so they bombed it again, with roughly the same results.

It was important for successful air defence to know what American technology could do; so every aircraft downed had its radar jamming and other electronic equipment taken away. Research was done on this by the Vietnamese scientists to ensure that it was rendered ineffective if the same technology was used during future air raids. "North Vietnamese electronics experts had made certain small but crucial modifications to their Soviet-supplied equipment, and ... the modifications involved adding one or more bands to their radar sets which US ECM gear was not prepared to jam".[34] They also had to enhance the range of the SAMs by adding boosters since they found that the missiles given to them were falling 2,000 feet short of the 30,000 feet cruising altitude of the B-52's.

In the result the US went on losing aircraft at a rate which they could not afford. They lost 4,181 aircraft from 1964 to 1973; and this Vietnamese figure ties roughly with that of the Pentagon, which, in an excessively conservative estimate admitted to 3,689 fixed wing aircraft lost by the end of 1972, plus 4,857 helicopters, a cost of US $ 10 billion. Indeed the loss of helicopter gun ships over Laos was so high due to the deadly anti-aircraft defences there that from mid-1966 their use was suspended in that sector. During the most intense twelve days of the 1972 Christmas bombing, mentioned above, 34 B-52 and 47 tactical fighters were lost; dozens of pilots captured by the Vietnamese, and those who were still flying were quite demoralised. So while it was officially claimed that "Hanoi was on its knees" the fact was that the Air Force was unable to function much longer.[35] As signs of low morale there were occasions when tactical aircraft failed to appear to protect the B-52 bombers and there was at least one case of a Commander of the latter refusing to fly and being tried for it.

The economy of North Vietnam actually continued to grow during the years of the air war, though not rapidly. Industry grew. Plant was dispersed; one machine tool plant was dispersed to sixteen different locations; petroleum stocks were put into 55 gallon steel drums and "the random dispersal of these drums by the thousands in city, town and rural rice paddy fields insured that they could not effectively be attacked by American air power."[36] Rail track, signaling equipment, all manner of other industrial products were scattered around the countryside and in the fields, much as had been done in the Soviet Union during World war II.

And the flow of supplies to the South not only increased; it increased substantially: 9.8 times from the years 1961-64 to the year 1968; and it continued rising thereafter. The Americans repeatedly claimed that the railroads and the highways had been hit and hit again and they were out of use. But they were always back in use in a day or two and American pilots who had seen bridges put completely out of action came back 48 hours later and there, sure enough, the bridge was fully functional. It was very demoralising.

The Vietnamese dealt in substantially the same way with the blockade, code named Sea Dragon, accompanying the second air war. The US planted 21,973 mines at 43 points altogether along the Vietnamese coast, concentrated outside the main harbours like Hong Kai, Haiphong and some river mouths. Some 55 warships were deployed to reinforce the blockade, starting with a heavy bombardment of the coastal defences. This was apart from the 15 aircraft carriers (that's all that the US had) which were deployed by rotation off the coast. The US assessment was that since 85% of supplies for the war were coming in by sea, an effective blockade could win the war. For the Vietnamese it was essential to strike at the enemy ships as often as possible, for some waterways had to be kept clear so that supplies could continue to come in from abroad. However, since the Americans were clearly much superior, this could only be done by feinting actions and diversions by the use of coastal artillery, naval ships and aircraft. Militia, regional and regular artillery forces were deployed to attack the US ships; the navy was also used, though in a very carefully planned manner, on a small scale and only at the most favourable moments, given their inferiority. Some US ships were sunk by the navy, about six by the air force, and at the end of the war it was true and a matter of pride for the Vietnamese that the US navy could not destroy their minute navy. As for the mines, some were of the improved variety, and some twice improved, which proved to be particularly dangerous, taking a long time to deactivate. Overall 12,664 were deactivated; some of the remainder were self-deactivating; while some were marked and left till the end of the war. In sum a sufficient number of water ways were kept open to keep up the supply line.

So the Americans were losing the air war and they were losing the blockade, though this was not generally known, and not even recognised by the American political and military leadership; it was only the North Vietnamese that really knew it.

## The Impact of Tet

Meanwhile, even as the air war and blockade continued to go badly, another unfortunate development had taken place within American society. In the late 1940s and 1950s many Americans sincerely believed that the social values associated with the aims of World War II would prevail; that liberal economic reforms would gradually bring equity; that poverty would either diminish or disappear; that the distinctions of race, class and gender would be eliminated. But none of this happened. Levels of poverty remained as high as ever; equity was not even attempted; civil rights movements were brutally crushed; those who might have benefited from change came to believe that nothing would change and they turned to radicalism. University campuses erupted, starting with Berkeley University in 1964-65, and spread rapidly to other campuses. The civil rights movement turned towards the black power advocates. And by late 1967 the broad spectrum of social protest issues seemed to narrow its focus to the one all the movements agreed on: the Vietnam War. Thousands came out into the streets all through 1966 and 1967 to protest against the war; and the "anger, bitterness and ugliness of anti-war confrontation with the government mounted ... Robert McNamara's car was pounded on at Harvard ... the President himself became a virtual prisoner in the White House."[37]

Johnson decided that the radicalisation of American society and the focus on the Vietnam War could both be handled by convincing the public that America was winning the war. Since not much was known about how the air war was going, and since on the ground in South Vietnam there was not much that the NLF seemed able to do, this should be easy. If only he could get Americans convinced that victory was around the corner in Vietnam, the protests would end, the students would go back to the classrooms and the whole protest movement would fizzle out. So he called General William Westmoreland, the US Commander there, back to the US in late 1967 to deliver a series of lectures and to brief the media: the

Americans were winning the war; the military could now see the light at the end of the tunnel; the Communists were definitely on the run; and the year 1968 would bring the turning point.

Then came Tet, and it exposed the truth about both the air war and the fact that by losing the air war, the Americans were also losing the war on the ground.

The Communist Party of Vietnam had been planning for a major offensive in January 1968 for a year. The basic idea of such an offensive was to make an impact on American public opinion, which would then render it difficult for the US administration to continue to propagate that the war was being won. There was also some hope that the war could be shortened, particularly if the offensive led to general uprisings in the urban areas. Militarily there would be major losses, but the Party also believed "that it could compensate for its military losses quite quickly."[38]

On 21 January, 1968 North Vietnamese and NLF forces began the siege of Khe Sanh, a US base in the northwest corner of South Vietnam, near the 17th parallel. It began with an artillery barrage, just like at Dien Bien Phu. Reinforcements were rushed there, in anticipation of another large-scale attack, but this was a feint. It was a feint designed to metamorphose into a major conventional battle and to keep American forces occupied there for the three months. Those forces would then not be available to counter the Tet offensive, designed to continue for the same period.

The latter was the real attack and it came ten days later, on Vietnamese New Year day, Tet, the 31 January. The North Vietnamese and NLF forces, some 80,000 strong, launched a nation-wide offensive concentrated in the urban areas. Thirty-six of the total of 44 provincial capitals were attacked, as well as dozens of district towns. Scores of towns and cities came under their control. In Saigon just one thousand NLF and regular Vietnamese forces were involved; there were 11,000 US and South Vietnamese troops trying to hold them off; but they entered the American Embassy compound and were there almost the whole day before they were picked off. In Hue, one of the largest cities in the South, 12,000 of them held out for a month; the aerial and artillery barrages needed for the Americans to flush them out and re-establish control were so heavy that there was hardly anything left standing. The city, one of the most ancient in Vietnam and with a priceless heritage of historical treasures became (wrongly) the site for one of the most quoted remarks of the entire war, that 'it was necessary to destroy the city in order to save it.'[39] Most of the towns and cities were retaken in a week or ten days; but it all meant street fighting, often block by block. And the American casualties mounted daily. The marines were not used to this; they had been trained for jungle warfare. But the NLF were, thanks in part to defoliation, highly skilled in urban warfare.

Then came another phase of the offensive, starting May 1968, in which nearly 120 cities, towns, and military bases were hit by the NLF and North Vietnamese forces; and then a third, from 17 August, largely concentrated on US installations, attacked this time with small units. So it was not just the TV pictures of the American Embassy in Saigon under occupation by the NLF that did the damage, but claims that the Tet offensive was a last gasp, that now the enemy had been decisively defeated, were given the lie by these successive offensives.

For Americans the month following Tet brought only bad news: 543 US combat deaths in a week, the highest since the war began; the 800th aircraft shot down over North Vietnam; and then the Senate Foreign Relations Committee began hearings challenging the very need of the war. And on CBS, one of the best known figures in American broadcasting, Walter Cronkite, said, "What the hell is going on? I thought we were winning the war."

Until Tet it was assumed that the war would go on and on unless the Americans substantially increased the number of troops they had on the ground, but if that could be done, it was winnable; after Tet it was known that the war was lost, that no amount of additional troops would change this fact, and would only prolong the war with more and more American casualties. Until Tet it was assumed that if the US wanted to, it could escalate the ground and air war and this would bring victory closer; after Tet it was known, certainly by those concerned in the administration, that no escalation was possible, not because it would not help, for it would not, but also because it was not possible. It was not politically possible because of student protests, the burning of draft cards, black violence directed at the administration; it was not economically possible because there was simply not enough money available, and the run on the dollar had made that quite clear. Before Tet it was assumed that America would stop the expansion of communism in Asia, and perhaps even around the world; after Tet it was known that America would have to live with the expansion of communism. Till Tet Americans believed the enemy was a fugitive: weak, dispersed, hunted, running for his life. Tet made it clear that the Americans were losing the war. So until Tet, and despite the demonstrations and protest, a majority of Americans supported the Vietnam War. After Tet, "overnight, a majority opposed the war."[40]

And then there was the post-Tet run on the dollar. Looking at the expenditure on the Vietnam war Senator Jacob Javits called for an end to the gold pool under which the dollar was, at least theoretically, pegged to gold. This started a flight from the dollar as members of the pool from Europe, having lost the certainty that the American commitment to gold convertibility would be honoured, started withdrawing from it; within four days of March, 1968 a billion dollars in gold were withdrawn and the pool suspended operations at that point. As the European members of the pool, bankers, arrived in Washington for consultations the US tried to persuade them to forgo their right to claim gold against dollars. They refused since there was no indication that the Americans were ready to manage their economy more responsibly. This meant that the US managed its economy more responsibly, meaning stopped spending more and more on the Vietnam war or its position as leader of the world economy would be in danger.

## Cracks in the US Politico-military Structure

With that realisation the US politico-military structure began to crack. General Westmoreland said he would need 206,000 troops more for the war; and Chairman of the Joint Chiefs of Staff Wheeler went to Vietnam and brought back this figure and presented it to Washington. It was greeted with shock; there were 525,000 troops there already and through 1967 the raising of the force level even to this figure had been controversial. And, anyway the administration knew it couldn't afford it, with the economy already in such a parlous condition. Then, on 10 March, 1968 *New York Times* revealed this figure, so it was not only the administration but the entire nation that was shocked. Johnson's new Defence Secretary Clark Clifford said the US should not send more troops there; on the contrary, it should get out of Vietnam. Then Johnson announced that Westmoreland would be replaced by June. And on 31 March, just two months after Tet, he went on TV to say he was implementing a freeze on troop levels in Vietnam; limiting the air war on North Vietnam; that he would seek a negotiated peace; and that he would not run for another term for President.

Polls showed that while before Tet Johnson had led his rival, McCarthy, 63 to 18, after Tet it was even and weeks thereafter he was behind 1 to 2. And, of course, the anti-war demonstrations, now often led by people like Jerry Rubin who wanted a social revolution, became larger and more aggressive; hundreds of thousands marched repeatedly in Washington; the number of sit-ins in college campuses increased and, when it is seen that 1968 witnessed also the assassinations of Martin Luther King and of Robert Kennedy, "the nation seemed to come apart as, one blow after another, it reeled from psychic and emotional wounds unprecedented in the modern era."[41]

Then there were the long-term blows to the economy. Having spent so much on the war the US was no longer internationally as solvent. The dollar had so far been convertible to gold, at least theoretically and by internationally accepted convention, as a demonstration of this solvency, and despite the problems that immediately followed Tet,

But over the years confidence in the dollar eroded, while the European currencies were getting stronger; by early 1971 it was known that the German mark, in particular, was under-valued. In expectation of a revaluation dollars started flowing into Germany, one billion in May alone, as European banks again redeemed dollars for gold. On August, 15, 1971, the US unilaterally suspended this convertibility; and in December it officially devalued the dollar; and imposed a ten per cent special tariff on all imports. Academics started bemoaning the decline of the US as reflected in the statistics. "In 1945", wrote one, "the US economy accounted for almost 45 per cent of world GNP, while Soviet GNP was one-seventh that of the United States, less than seven per cent of the world GNP. By the mid-1970s the US share of world GNP was down to about 24 per cent, and the Soviet Union's had grown to approximately 15 per cent."[42]

Some of this, like the assassinations, was unconnected to the Vietnam War, but it is true to say the "Tet offensive of 1968 had a devastating political and psychological impact on the US approach to the war in Vietnam."[43] There were also long-term effects on the global position of the US, for losing the war meant there was no more Cold War consensus, no more conviction that America would be able to win the Cold War, that the Soviet Union had to be taken on and defeated or at least held so that it made no more gains. Tet spelt the end of the strategy that had been initiated by George Kennan and NSC 68. It "left the country deeply divided and for years opposed to almost any use of military force."[44]

One result was the decision to withdraw US troops and on 8 June 1969 Nixon announced the first batch of withdrawals; if the war was lost they might as well, without admitting that the war was lost, start minimizing casualties. In Vietnam, meanwhile, talks between the Americans and the North Vietnamese had continued off and on. The Americans had to put the best face on a lost war, since great powers do not easily admit to losing any war. This best face was achieved by a great deal of publicity for the issues involved, US prisoners of war, that the North relinquish the use of force to unite the country, wider matters like 'linkage' between the war and Soviet behaviour, a favourite expression of Henry Kissinger.

By early 1972 troop levels were down to 70,000, and the withdrawals continued; by January 1973 they had all gone and with the signing of an agreement with the North all American participation in the war came to an end. The war had taken a toll of 45,000 Americans killed; another 300,000 wounded. Expenditure on it was something like US $ 20 billion annually for nearly a decade, a total of $ 150 billion over and above what would have been the normal military budget.[45] All this was quite apart from the breakdown in national and military morale which would take years to rebuild. In the military particularly heroin use increased until it was thought one-third of the troops in Vietnam were addicts; racial tensions rose since the blacks felt they were being used as cannon fodder while the whites occupied a disproportionate number of officers positions. Troop attacks on officers, fragging or the attempted murder of officers by soldiers, mounted as troops were assigned to especially dangerous missions and refused to go.

## Other Effects of Defeat

Another early result was the Nixon Doctrine, announced at a press conference in Guam, July, 1969, "the premise that countries threatened by Communist aggression must take the primary responsibility for their own defence."[46] He was equally specific in Manila the same month, saying "Peace in Asia cannot come from the US. It must come from Asia. The people of Asia, the governments of Asia, they are the ones who must lead the way to peace in Asia."

This was elaborated in Nixon's Foreign Policy Report to Congress, February, 1971: "The post-war order in international relations – the configuration of power that emerged from the Second World War, is gone. With it are gone the conditions which have determined the assumptions and practice of United States foreign policy since 1945." This was part of a broader picture of US retreat. "The U.S. retreat that is now in progress is a mixture of drawing back from overextended forward commitments to less exposed and, therefore, more secure ones, and of recognition that even the richest country in the world needs to husband its resources at home and abroad more economically and more effectively."[47]

In other words, the US would now have to compromise with the Soviet Union. One of the earliest compromises was the agreement on Berlin, 1971. The same year Nixon decided to accept the basic conditions imposed by the People's Republic of China for diplomatic relations, the starting point of any effort to take advantage of the Sino-Soviet rift to gain the additional leverage which the US now needed, it being no longer possible for the US to take on the Soviet Union single-handed.

More followed. At the May, 1972 US-Soviet summit Nixon agreed to sign a formal document, which would also be signed by all the European countries as well as by the Soviet Union. This document would recognise existing borders in Europe and thereby tacitly confirm the dominant role of the Soviet Union in Eastern Europe."[48] And, at the same summit, the two sides signed an agreement on Basic Principles of Relations[49] that they would avoid military confrontation, accept the principle of equality and the renunciation of the use or threat of force, prevent the outbreak of nuclear war and not try to obtain unilateral advantage at the expense of the other. It read almost like a declaration of the non-aligned movement. At the same time the first strategic arms limitation agreement was signed, limiting the numbers of strategic weapons as well as anti-ballistic missile defence systems on each side; strategic parity had been accepted; the arms race was over. The ripples of Tet went on and on. Even when Carter became President in February, 1977 he felt obliged to announce no more Vietnams, the aim of his administration would be the elimination of nuclear weapons, the defence of human rights everywhere.

The media had, of course, lost faith in the administration as soon as Tet happened. More important, in the long term, Congress lost faith. In 1973 the War Powers Resolution was passed by Congress, then vetoed by President Nixon, then passed by a two-thirds majority of both House and Senate to over-ride the veto. It provided that: the President would have to consult with Congress before, or at least soon after, committing US troops in any situation other than a genuine national emergency; there would be a 60-day clock by which US troops would have to be withdrawn unless Congress specifically gave an extension.

A year later, using its new-found powers, Congress cut military aid to South Vietnam; within months the South collapsed; in March, 1975 its military position started breaking apart; by the end of April it had surrendered to the North; Vietnam was unified.

One author summed up all that had happened. US power and military capabilities had eroded along with US resolve; "strategic superiority had given way to nuclear parity … SEATO and CENTO had come apart; the US military presence in Southeast Asia had ended (except for bases in the Philippines) and ended in failure; economic and military assistance programs were diminished; the number of overseas bases had declined; and access to some regions was no longer secure. The United States had even abrogated its defence treaty with Taiwan … the optimism of US purpose and capability had declined markedly … there was a lack of confidence in the efficacy and to some extent legitimacy of US power being exercised abroad."[50]

Later, much later, the explanations and the justifications came. Robert S. McNamara gave six reasons for losing the Vietnam war: that the US misjudged the geo-political intentions of the adversary and exaggerated the dangers from him; thought that South Vietnam had a thirst for freedom and democracy; underestimated the power of nationalism to motivate people to fight and to die; ignored the history, politics and culture of the area; failed to recognise the limitations of modern high technology military equipment, forces and doctrine; didn't draw the American Congress and people in or recognise that the US was not omniscient.[51]

But Nixon was more assertive. The US had won the war, according to him. "We had won the war militarily and politically in Vietnam. But defeat was snatched from the jaws of victory because we lost the war politically in the United States." He also blamed the media; it was the first war in which they were more friendly to our enemies than to our allies. And the Soviets provided arms to Hanoi in violation of the peace agreement. Vietnam was lost because, finally, of "a failure of skill and determination at using power", not lack of power.[52]

## ENDNOTES

[1] Joseph Buttinger, *The Smaller Dragon, A Political History of Vietnam*, Frederick A. Praeger, New York, 1958, pp. 209, 304 and 343 for this and the previous four paragraphs.

[2] One Francis Garnier, a naval lieutenant, was particularly forceful in putting forward this argument; see Joseph Buttinger, op. cit. above, p. 349 and footnote 69 on p. 408.

[3] Nguyen Khac Vien, *Vietnam, A Long History*, The Gioi Publishers, Hanoi, 2007, p. 135. This is the officially approved history, and in my view the best available in the English language.

[4] Joseph Buttinger, op. cit. above, pp. 347 and 384 for this and the previous three paragraphs.

[5] Martial law regulations prohibiting meetings were in force in Amritsar; on 13 April 1919 a crowd of villagers had come into the city to attend a fair; they were unaware of the regulations. General Dyer, who was responsible for enforcing martial law, took a body of troops, herded the villagers into an enclosed space with no exit (Jallianwala Bagh) and gave the orders to fire to kill. Over six hundred villagers died, though the exact count will never be known; many more were injured and it was reported that they were left there unattended. The government said only 379 died, and Dyer was given a rousing welcome when he returned to England.

[6] Joseph Buttinger, *Vietnam: A Dragon Embattled, Volume I, From Colonialism to the Vietminh*, Pall Mall Press, London, 1967, pp. 219-220 and 103 for this and the previous three paragraphs.

[7] Nguyen Khac Vien, op. cit. p. 35.

[8] Cited in Michael Maclear, *Vietnam: The Ten Thousand Day War*, Thames Methuen, London, 1981, p. 244.

[9] Harrison E. Salisbury, *Behind the Lines – Hanoi, December 23, 1966 – January 7, 1967*, Secker and Warburg, London, 1967, p. 51.

[10] See D.G.E. Hall, *A History of South-East Asia,* Macmillan, London, 1964, p. 184.

[11] Hoang van Chi, *From Colonialism to Communism, A Case History of North Vietnam*, Pall Mall Press, London, 1964, p. 14.

[12] Quoted in Joseph Buttinger, *Vietnam: A Dragon Embattled*, p. 495.

[13] D.G.E.Hall, op. cit. pp. 628 & 718.

[14] Joseph Buttinger *Vietnam: A Dragon Embattled*, p. 127, for this and the last two paragraphs.

[15] Quoted by David G. Marr, *Vietnamese Anti-colonialism, 1885-1925,* University of California, Berkeley, 1970, p. 67.

[16] David G. Marr, op. cit., p. 63.

[17] John T. McAlister, Jr., *Vietnam, The Origins of Revolution*, The Penguin Press, London, 1969 op. cit. pp. 83, 110 and 194 respectively for this and previous four paragraphs.

[18] Meanwhile, post-war developments in the South were quite different. British troops had moved into and occupied Vietnam south of the 16th parallel. Their task was to accept the surrender of the Japanese and to intern them, free the French and to rearm them so that they could, if required with British military help, restore their imperial position. So as the French in the South started to try and take back their pre-war positions and the clashes with the Viet Minh began, it was British military help that they could rely on.

[19] Quoted by John T. McAlister, Jr., op. cit., pp. 312-3.

[20] Cited in Michael Maclear, op. cit., p. 21.

[21] General Vo Nguyen Giap, *Unforgettable Days,* Foreign Languages Publishing House, Hanoi, 1978, p. 117.

[22] Bernard B. Fall, *Street Without Joy*, Pall Mall Press, London, 1964, p. 373.

[23] William J. Lederer and Eugene Burdick, *The Ugly American*, Crest Books, New York, 1960, pp. 239-40.

[24] David Halberstam, *The Best and the Brightest*, Pan Books, London, 1973, p. 304.

[25] Richard K. Betts, *Soldiers, Statesmen, and Cold War Crises*, Harvard University Press, Cambridge, Mass., 1977, p. 13.

[26] Wilfred G. Burchett, *Vietnam North*, International Publishers, New York, 1966, p. 161.

[27] See for more details, Harrison E. Salisbury, op. cit., p. 216.

[28] David Marr, The Technological Imperative in US War Strategy in Vietnam, in Mary Kaldor and Asbjorn Eide, eds, *The World Military Order, The Impact of Military Technology on the Third World*, Macmillan, London, 1979, p. 38.

[29] Wilfred G. Burchett, p. 26.

[30] What follows on the air war is largely based on briefings given to me by Vietnamese civil and military officials during a visit to North Vietnam in 1981; where other sources are used these have been indicated.

[31] Wilfred G. Burchett, pp. 179-180 and 165 for this and the previous two paragraphs.

[32] Barbara W. Tuchman, *The March of Folly, From Troy to Vietnam*, Michael Joseph, London, 1984, p. 372.

[33] These figures, given by Vietnamese officials, do not tally with those of the Military Balance, 1971-1972 (Institute of Strategic Studies, London), which gives US tactical strength at the time at 2,700 aircraft and B-52's at 540, included in the strategic forces, but there is no mention there of B-52's being used in Vietnam.

[34] David Marr, op. cit., p. 40.

[35] Gabriel Kolko, *Vietnam, Anatomy of a War, 1940-1975*, Allen and Unwin, London, 1986, p. 441.

[36] Harrison Salisbury op. cit., p. 91.

[37] William H. Chafe, *The Unfinished Journey, America since World War II*, OUP, New York, 1991, p. 325

[38] Gabriel Kolko, op. cit., p. 304.

[39] Actually an American colonel had made this remark about Ben Tre, a provincial capital of 140,000 which had been levelled to the ground even more completely than Hue.

[40] William H. Chafe, op. cit., p. 348.

[41] William H.Chafe, op. cit., p. 380.

[42] Lawrence Grinter, The United States: Military and Political Perspectives, in Sam C. Sarkesian, ed., *Non-nuclear Conflicts in the Nuclear Age*, Praeger, New York, 1980, p. 62.

[43] Richard Shultz, Strategy Lessons from an Unconventional War: The US experience in Vietnam, in Sam C. Sarkesian, ed., op. cit., p. 154.

[44] Bruce W. Jentleson, *American Foreign Policy, The Dynamics of Choice in the 21st Century*, W.W.Norton and Company, New York, 2004, p. 155.

[45] Barbara Tuchman, op. cit., p. 374.

[46] See Richard Nixon, *The Real War,* Warner Books, New York, 1980, pp. 106-07.

[47] Henry Brandon, *The Retreat of American Power*, The Bodley Head, London, 1973, pp. 80 and xii for this and the last paragraph.

[48] Alexander L. George, *Managing US-Soviet Rivalry: Problems of Crisis Prevention*, Westview Press, Boulder, Colorado, 1983, Chapter 2.

[49] See the reference in chapter 8 on this agreement.

[50] David W. Tarr, The Strategic Environment, US National Security and the nature of low intensity conflict, in Sam C. Sarkesian, ed., op. cit., p. 49-50.

[51] Robert S. McNamara, *In Retrospect: The Tragedy and Lessons of Vietnam,* Times Books, New York, 1995.

[52] Richard Nixon, op. cit., pp. 114-123.

# 11

# Afghanistan

This chapter tells the story of Afghanistan's struggle, first against the British, then the Soviet Union.

This is told along the lines of the traditional story, that this was a nationalist struggle, not tribal or religious. Chapter 12 continues this story after the US invasion of Afghanistan.

Geography and topography explain a great deal of what to expect from Afghanistan in the future. It is at a cross roads through which have passed, for thousands of years, invaders, pilgrims, priests and traders on their way to or from India, Iran and Central Asia. Its people are used to war and fighting, the transmutations of religion and culture, how to make money from trade and the tax on trade.

As for topography, it is part of an arid and semi-desert belt that stretches from the Iranian plateau eastwards, for the most part rock and gravel and limestone, with a barren central mountain range, the Hindu Kush, which starts from the quadri-junction in the Northwest Karakorum (Black Rubble in Turkish) range where Afghanistan meets Tajikistan, China, and India (Jammu and Kashmir state); then extends south and west across central Afghanistan. It is also a big country, 652,000 square kilometres; often compared to Switzerland, it is actually sixteen times the size; bigger than France or Germany. About equal to Germany and Poland put together.

Only 12 per cent of the land area is arable as compared to 54 per cent in India and 62 per cent in Bangladesh, the highest in the world. Of this only two and a half per cent is dry land farmed.

Most of the agriculture is on irrigated land. Afghanistan is not densely populated but because of the above factors it has twice as many people per hectare of arable land as India (which has a population density of 358 persons per square kilometre, almost twelve times that of Afghanistan). And it is not fertile: one hectare feeds two people compared to eight in India. This is not due only to technology but also to topography.

Extremes of temperature are another disincentive to settled arable farming: very hot summers and very cold winters; sharp variations between day and night.

Altogether this is not a country for settled farming on a large scale; but the grass lands in the mountains encourage animal husbandry, large migrations of people in search of summer and winter pastures, and nomadism.

## The Nature of the Nomad

The starting point for the understanding of the Afghan is the nature of the nomad, which has often been commented on in the course of history. For the Europeans, yesterday and today, it is the Scythian and the Tatar who represents the essence of the nomad. Herodotus, often called the Father of History, describes how the Persian king Darius tried to expand his empire into the territory of the Scythians beyond the river Danube. The Scythians, "having neither cities nor forts, and carrying their dwellings with them wherever they go; accustomed moreover, one and all of them, to shoot from horseback; and living not by husbandry but on their cattle, their wagons the only houses that they possess, how can they fail of being unconquerable."[1] The Afghans are unconquerable.

Edward Gibbon ascribes to the attacks by these nomads or barbarians one of the four principle reasons for the fall of the Roman Empire. "The thrones of Asia have been repeatedly overturned by the shepherds of the North, and their arms have spread terror and devastation over the most fertile and warlike countries of Europe." War and the hunt are the two activities of the nomad: war for itself, for glory and for prestige within the tribal social framework; the hunt "as the image and as the school of war."[2] At a later date, writing in the early part of the twentieth century, the historian Arnold Toynbee agrees that one of the principal causes of the decline of civilisations like that of Rome is the attacks by the trans-frontier barbarians, for whom this warfare "is not a burden but an opportunity, not an anxiety but an exhilaration."[3] That, as anyone who has lived in Afghanistan for any length of time will tell you, is the attitude of the people there towards war.

So at individual level the Afghan has endurance and strength, the ability to bear hardships which others could not sustain, as can be expected from the meagre livelihood that comes out of hard labour in almost uninhabitable terrain; but the people of the mountain, as Fernand Braudel[4] calls them, are also pragmatic individualists, self-assured, even proud to the point of arrogance, and never back away from a fight; and honour is prized above all other virtues. Violence and cruelty and vendetta run through their histories.

As for the social level, despite the ethnic and tribal mix in Afghan society, the attitudes of the people, particularly those of the Pashtuns, are of the mountain. They live under laws and rules made by the community or the tribe, by social custom and tradition; they reject central control in their ethics, their institutions and their codes of reward and punishment. Personal honour (nang), the tribal code of honour (pashtunwali), hospitality (melmastia), asylum (nanawaty), revenge (badla) and custom in general (rawaj), are more important than the constitution or the laws and decrees passed under it; and, of course, far more important than anything written into international law and codes, such as accountability for terrorist acts. Equally, the Afghans reject centrally imposed religion or dogma. Islam in Afghanistan since the Ghazni Empire (late years of the tenth and early years of the eleventh centuries) has been accompanied by belief in shamans and mystics, by the strength of the Sufi tradition with its saints and songs, by pilgrimage to the graves of holy men, the pirs and khwajas. Religious belief has had to adjust, to conform to local custom and tradition. Tribal custom has always been more important than Sharia law.

It was melmastia and not religious fundamentalism or any agreement with Al Qaeda's objectives that prevented the Taliban, in late 2001, from handing over Osama bin Laden to the US.

Socially the organisation goes from family to tribe to sub-clan to clan to tribal confederation in a pyramid with an eponymous or mythic ancestor. It is vertical. The Pashtun social identity, which is central to Afghanistan, is defined by his place within the pyramid, and no horizontal relationship can claim priority over the vertical. Other ethnic groups like the Uzbeks have the same social organisation. This again is of nomadic origin. The extended family and tribe are the most important economic and social units, the units that command loyalty, not horizontal affiliations like caste or language or religion as in India or most of Europe. All men are equal and only personal achievement, personal qualities can bring you to a higher social level, not rank or inheritance. Hence the chief of the tribe is there not because of his seniority within the family group, but because of his prestige, his ability to sense the desires of the group; and he is always in danger of being abandoned and replaced if he loses these qualities. He has no institutional or delegated power upon which he can presume to take decisions on behalf of the family or tribe.

The society has thus an in-built mechanism of resistance not just against a state which may already be in existence but against the emergence of a state-like structure with their society. So they are best understood in terms of the war machine proposed by Gilles Deleuze and Felix Guattari in *A Thousand Plateaus*, in which the nomad plays the most important role, and whose organisation is coexistent with the state, directed against the state and exterior to the state. War is part of the essence of such a society; not just war against a neighboring civilisation, but war within the society. For war in primitive societies "is the surest mechanism directed against the formation of the State: war maintains the dispersal and segmentarity of groups."

## The War Machine and the State

Deleuze and Guattari take up for consideration the proposal of Pierre Clastres that the war machine is directed against the apparatus of the state. He put it in evolutionary format: that the state form arises by the destruction of the nomadic war machine, that is, the one form replaces the other. They propose, on the other hand, that it is in terms of "coexistence and competition in a perpetual field of interaction" that we should conceive of the relations between the war machine and the state apparatus: within all social fields; within religious formations, commercial organisations, and others. Within all these fields there are the areas which have been appropriated by the state apparatus, where people have opted for servitude to wider norms. And there are the areas which are external to the state, where the free flight of an unbounded self-expression reigns and "which continue to affirm the rights of segmentary societies in opposition to the organs of state power."[5]

What needs to be added to the account given by them is, first, that while within any particular society both tendencies always exist together, yet the balance between them differs from society to society as also within that same society, from one era to another; secondly, that both tendencies exist within the same individual, and, again, the balance between the two varies from person to person, of course, but also between one period and another of the life of the same individual. Most of us have those moments, when we give full reign to the free flight of an unbounded self-expression.

Given that the balance between the two tendencies could be very different, depending on the particular society, it is true that, in the case of Afghanistan, the balance has always been, is, and is always likely to be, heavily tilted towards the kind of operations that are found in the war machine. This is the steel which frames Afghan nationalism and that results in an unrelenting resistance to any kind of foreign rule.

Over the years Afghanistan has been called 'Land of the Unruly' or 'Land of the Free' or 'Land of the Rebels' or even 'Land of the Insolent'. It is unusually difficult to subjugate them; since they are not easily tempted by the lures of civilisation, and are willing to fight for their freedom, centralised political systems generally attempt, fail and then abandon the effort to bring them within the fold; there is among them a persistent refusal to accept centrally administered law, or, for instance, to pay taxes.

This is so not only in Afghanistan but in the Apennines, Kabylie and Switzerland, to give a few examples. Buzkashi, the game without rules, symbolises the Afghan resistance to the well regulated orderliness of a system put in place by the state. Here there are no rules, no limit to the number of teams that may take the field at one time; no limit to the number of players in each team (as many as 1000 players have been known to take to the field at one time); no limit to the tactics used such as pushing, whipping, hitting, so that you get twenty or more horsemen around an oiled stitched up calf carcass in a melee, trying to pick it up before taking it by the hand, carrying it around a distant pole and depositing it back in the circle from which it was picked up.

## Afghan Nationalism

There is duality in the Afghan's attitude towards the external world: defending his country fiercely in the name of Jihad when invaded, but refusing to go outside it for the same purpose, unless lured by the prospect of wealth. For the Afghan, Jihad has meant the national struggle against the foreigner occupier, not the struggle of the believer against the unbeliever. As a consequence, over the years mobilisation in the name of religion has been as difficult as it has been easy to mobilise the disparate ethnic and tribal groups in the name of defending Afghanistan's freedom as a nation. Despite the predominance of ethnic and tribal affinity in the Afghan self-identity, nationalism rather than religion has occupied second place; but it usually surfaces in opposition to the foreigner as aggressor or hostile neighbour: the British in India from the first Afghan war (1839-42) till 1919; Pakistan from 1947 till 1979; the Soviet Union from then to 1989; and the US presence today.

This turns the most widely-held theories of nationalism and the nation-state on their head. According to these theories, "in modern Afghanistan, the national or patriotic idea remained very weak and undeveloped, altogether lacking appeal of influence", and this is because it is "a congeries of different ethnic communities, linguistic groups, and tribes" with no ethnic or linguistic homogeneity and where state borders were essentially fluid.[6] The reality, and this corresponds to the traditional story, is the opposite: that while the different ethnic and tribal groups attach great importance to their own particular customs and traditions, the lands inherited from their ancestors, their own versions of Islam, this very strength of the local has reinforced nationalism. "Both history and recent memory show us that it is the presence of these strong, well-armed and organised local community structures in Afghanistan that have assured national independence – not the presence of any kind of strong but dependent, centralised state apparatus."[7]

This means that if a nation is to be constructed it must be done on the basis of confederacy, an agreement among equals.

Nevertheless, in 1747, Ahmad Shah of the Abdali (later Durrani or its Mohammadzai branch, from which all Afghan rulers came) tribe brought together the heads of the different Pashtun tribes as well as of the other ethnic groups, including the Tajiks, the Uzbeks, the Hazaras and Baluchis, to form a united and even expansionist Afghanistan; Ahmad Shah's dominions stretched in time to include the northern part of India. In 1762 he defeated the Sikhs near Lahore and annexed Kashmir and was within 100 kilometres of Delhi.

During the next two centuries Afghanistan continued to be constructed as a nation; and the divisions in Afghan society continued. At the broadest level this was between the Pashtuns and the non-Pashtuns. There were also divisions within the Pashtuns; and within the non-Pashtuns.

Among the Pashtuns there was the struggle between the two main branches, the Durrani, now ruling, and the Ghilzai, which had been dominant before 1747; the struggle has continued over the centuries; it continues unabated today. The two sides came together when there was an external threat, as during the wars against the British and later against the Soviet Union and then the US, then separated and fought each other when the threat was gone. The Durrani continued to rule the country, though even within this tribe different branches or sub-tribes came together, parted and fought each other in a bewildering kaleidoscope of combinations.

Here we can only give some examples. The Popalzai is one branch of the Durrani; and the Taliban in their origin were of Durrani origin. It was not till late in 1996, as they were getting ready for the final assault on Kabul, that some Ghilzai joined them. In any case they remained more or less exclusively a Pashtun gathering. The Barakzai is an offshoot of the Popalzai, an offshoot which, early in the twentieth century, grew so exceptionally powerful in eastern Afghanistan, that the Durrani rulers split them by dividing their land and settling one segment, the Achakzai, south of Kandahar; it was the Achakzai whom the Taliban had to fight to gain control of the Kandahar-Chaman road in October 1994.

The same holds for the Ghilzai. Noor Mohammed Taraki, who overthrew the government of Mohammed Daud (a Durrani) in April 1978, was a Ghilzai. But then Hafizullah Amin, who killed and replaced Taraki in September 1979, was also a Ghilzai. So was one of the major resistance leaders who fought the Soviet Union, Gulbuddin Hekmatyar, who used his tribal origin to garner support against the Soviet forces and, when they were gone, to induce senior Ghilzai members of the armed forces to attempt a coup against President Najibullah. That failed, but the Ghilzais who had tried it joined Hekmatyar's Hizbe Islami. So the tribes and the sub-tribes join hands, fight each other, join up again, and it is that bewildering kaleidoscope again.

The non-Pashtun ethnic groups are also divided. The largest of them is the Tajik, some four and a half million people inhabiting an area north of Kabul upto Badakhshan and Kunduz on the Tajikistan border. Between the Tajiks of Badakhshan and of Panjsher, for instance, there have been differences for centuries. This was one factor in the problems that emerged between the political leadership of the Jamiat-e-Islami under Burhanuddin Rabbani, a Badakhshani who became President of Afghanistan in June 1992, and the military leadership of the same party under Ahmad Shah Masoud, a Tajik from Panjsher. The Panjsheris still dominate the Tajiks and this has been a cause of some unhappiness among other, non-Panjsheri, Tajiks.

The Hazaras, about one and a half million inhabiting central and western Afghanistan, are the third largest ethnic group, and have also been divided. Unified by their deep-rooted suspicion and dislike of the Pashtuns (though one of their commanders sided for a short time with the Pashtun-dominated Taliban) the Hazara divided along religious lines between Shia (the majority), Sunni and Ismaili; between ultra-conservatives, modern radicalists and Maoists; and, through the 1980s and early 1990s, between allegiance to different commanders like Ismail Khan in Herat, Abdul Ali Mazari south of Kabul, Karim Khalili along the northern highway and Jaffar Naderi in the north.

The Uzbeks are the fourth largest ethnic group, some one million located in Balkh and Jawzjan provinces along the borders with Uzbekistan and Turkmenistan. The divisions among them were shown most dramatically when the Taliban attacked Mazar-i-Sharif in May 1997. An Uzbek general, Abdul Malik, separated from his leader Abdul Rashid Dostum, to help the Taliban; and then, four days later, turned on the Taliban to drive them out of the city. In general the Uzbeks, however, are less divided than the other major ethnic groups.

There are others, in smaller numbers like the Turkmens, the Baluchis, the Aimaq, the Kirghiz and the Nuristani which have not played such an important role in recent developments.

It is not just tribe and ethnicity that divide the Afghans. At the religious level there is the divide between Sunni and Shia, which, since it broadly corresponds to the ethnic divide between non-Hazara and Hazara, reinforces the latter. There are also divisions among the Sunni, between the Deobandis of the Hanafi sect for instance, which included the Taliban leadership, and those influenced by the Wahabism of Saudi Arabia.

The above examples are not to essentialise the ethnic or tribal or religious divisions in Afghanistan, but to amplify that, recognising such divisions, and assuming (wrongly, as is obvious from earlier chapters of this book), along with the theorists of nationalism, that they signify weakness, every neighbour from the British and Tsarist Russia to the Soviet Union and then Pakistan, has consistently followed a policy of sharpening them, of trying to weaken the Afghan nation through socio-political fragmentation.

## The First British Effort at Empire

First came the British.

As the territory under the control of the East India Company expanded towards the Northwest of India, it was decided to bring Afghanistan, too, under control. By the first decade of the nineteenth century British territory or that under British protection extended to the river Sutlej. Beyond that lay the domains of Ranjit Singh of the Punjab, who was still, in the 1830s, too strong for the Company to take on; a Treaty of Alliance had been signed with him in 1809.

The plan for Afghanistan was to oust the ruler, the Amir, Dost Mohammad Khan, with the help of Ranjit Singh. A puppet would be installed who would agree, as had been the pattern with protectorates in India, to British control over his foreign policy and to accept a British Resident with a military unit stationed for his security. From there on, not many steps would be needed to bring Afghanistan fully into the empire.

The Court of Directors in London was hesitant about such a forward policy in general and this plan in particular. But they were worried about, and wanted to do everything that was possible to counter, Persian and Russian influence in Kabul. A dispatch of 1836 from the secret committee of the Court instructed the Governor-General to "adopt any interference in the affairs of Afghanistan 'either to prevent the extension of Persian dominion in that quarter or to raise a timely barrier against the impending encroachments of Russian influence.'" And, in fact, the Persian army did besiege Herat from November, 1837; while a Russian envoy, a certain Captain Vitkavich, who had been with the Persian army in its march to Herat, arrived in Kabul in December, 1837, and then rumours floated that he was offering money to the Afghan ruler to fight against Ranjit Singh and the British.

All this continued only for a few months. The Persian siege was lifted in September, 1838, since it had achieved nothing, though the British were to claim that it was lifted due to their pressure; the Russian envoy returned to St. Petersburg, was disavowed by the Tsar, and committed suicide.

Meanwhile, a Tripartite Treaty had been signed: the East India Company; Ranjit Singh; and Shah Shuja, who was to be the British puppet in Kabul. It was agreed that Shah Shuja, with a British force, would march on Kabul via Kandahar in the South, while Ranjit Singh would provide a force to march on Kabul from the East through Peshawar, accompanied by Shah Shuja's son. Governor-General Lord Auckland issued a manifesto, the Simla Manifesto, on 1 October, 1838, some three weeks after the Persian siege of Herat had been lifted, which referred to the fact that "intrigues were actively prosecuted throughout Afghanistan, for the purpose of extending Persian influence and authority to the banks of, and even beyond, the Indus... that the siege of Herat had now been carried on by the Persian army for many months;" and that now it had been decided that Shah Shuja would be installed on, or restored to, the throne in Kabul, with due support from a British army, so that these intrigues are rapidly arrested, aggression is resisted and tranquillity established along the western frontiers of the British possessions in the East."

And so the 'Army of the Indus' was assembled at Ferozepur: 20,000 of the army; nearly 38,000 transport and camp attendants; large quantities of money to pay off the Afghan tribal chiefs en route; a huge moving city of shops where every requirement of the men could be bought, shoes mended, equipment repaired; with Sir William Macnaghten in command. And began its march to Kabul. There was no fighting. In April, 1839, having rewarded the local chiefs with money, Kandahar was taken. On April 25, "with pomp and circumstance, Shah Shuja re-entered Kandahar." By the end of June the Army had reached Ghazni, where there was a skirmish. As reported by Henry Durand, who took part in it, the attack on Ghazni fort, the "crowning achievement of the campaign" was completed without a blow from a sword or the loss of a man. With the further advance of the expedition towards Kabul the Amir, Dost

Mohammad Khan left for Bukhara; so on 7 August, 1839 Shah Shuja entered Kabul without being opposed or welcomed by any of his subjects.

The problems began rather slowly. British units, moving back and forth between India and their locations in Afghanistan, as also those moving between Kabul, Kandahar, Ghazni and so on, came under sporadic attack from large and small Afghan groups which seemed to appear out of nowhere. In early 1840 Dost Mohammad Khan reappeared; he had collected an army of 6,000, with which he attacked British forces; when a large force was sent out from Kabul to meet him, he engaged them, and on 2 November, 1840, at Parwan inflicted a decisive defeat on them. Then, a few days later, unpredictably, he surrendered to the British. But the attacks continued. The British had some of the strategic positions, but their communications between those positions and with India were under constant attack; and the attacks seemed to get progressively more aggressive. The Court of Directors in London was by now getting uneasy. As the occupation of Kabul lengthened over time, as the attacks on British patrols mounted in intensity, as the sequestering of food and forage for the troops and their animals from the local population led to famine and unrest, that occupation was also and above all, getting to be increasingly expensive.

In November, 1841 came the great Kabul uprising. In a concerted effort the Afghans attacked the British positions there, killed the senior officers and sacked the treasury. One of the officers, Alexander Burnes, tried to escape disguised as a woman, was discovered and promptly killed. The British food stores were seized; their artillery captured. The strategic heights around Kabul were captured and, in the course of the action, several hundred British troops and their officers killed. Appeals were sent out for reinforcements; they went unanswered. There was nothing for it but to pull out. Finally, on 11 December, Macnaghten rightly fearful that the situation would get worse and worse, signed a treaty under which British troops would entirely withdraw from Afghanistan, "shall speedily quit the territories of Afghanistan and march to India, and shall not return"; all their military stores, all their weapons, excepting only six guns, would be left behind; Dost Mohammad Khan would be released by them and allowed to return to Afghanistan; and six of the British (in fact there were more by the time the retreat began) would he held back, as "our guests" –

the word hostages was not used.

It looked like the ultimate humiliation for British arms; but it was not, since far worse was to follow. On 6 January, 1842, in bitter cold, a dispirited and demoralised army, all that was left of the Army of the Indus, 4,500 officers and men with 12,000 camp attendants which included women and children, started to make its way down from Kabul to Jalalabad. As they made their way down through the snow and frost, seriously short of rations, transport and forage for the animals, a long, defeated, dispirited line, the stragglers came under attack and were picked off in twos and threes. From the hills around the route the Afghans fired on them by day and by night. In panic thousands sought shelter and safety by charging ahead, leaving baggage behind. So the shortage of supplies, already acute, became worse; hundreds died of hunger, cold and exposure. The retreating force became smaller and smaller. At Gandamak, just thirty miles southwest of Jalalabad, it was down to twenty officers and forty-five soldiers. At Fatehabad, sixteen miles from Jalalabad, only six were left. Finally only one man, a Dr. Brydon, who seemed to have been left alive so that he could tell the tale of the rout, got back to Jalalabad. Meanwhile, all the other British positions in Afghanistan outside Kabul also felt the onslaught of Afghan attacks, though not all of them were abandoned.

The epitaph on this attempt at expanding the empire was written by a British military officer and historian, Sir Henry Rawlinson, that "there was never an occasion on which the Afghans could stand for an hour against British soldiers or Indian Sepoys."[8]

Retribution did follow. The British sent in a punitive expedition in August, 1842 whose main purpose was to burn as much of Kabul and kill as many of the occupants of that city as possible. But by 1843 Dost Mohammad Khan was back in power in Kabul.

## The Second British Effort at Empire

The second British invasion of Afghanistan (1878) was, if allowance be made for variations in detail, a replica of the first. So much so that William Ewart Gladstone, then leader of the opposition, said in Parliament as he saw events unfold, "we made war in error upon Afghanistan in 1838. To err is human and pardonable. But we have erred a second time on the same ground and with no better justification ...in the face of every warning conceivable and imaginable ..."[9]

A large part of the answer to the question, why then was such a policy followed, lies in the renewed European urge to expand the limits of their empires. This was felt by all the imperial European powers by the late 1870's. The greatly accelerated rate by which the area of the empire increased after 1878 has been mentioned in an earlier chapter. But the major part of the answer, as it applies to Afghanistan, lies in the inability of the British to leave behind the framework provided by the modernity story; and this will emerge in greater detail as we look at the so-called Cold War era.

This second invasion was, like the first, intended to control and colonise Afghanistan. Like the first, the British representative in India, here the Viceroy Lord Lytton, was more eager to move into Afghanistan than his government in London, so he had to provide justification to them in terms of the pro-Russian leanings of the Afghan ruler. There had, in fact, been a clear understanding of 1873 between Britain and Russia. This specified that the northern border of Afghanistan would extend up to the river Oxus, while Russia avowed, and then repeated, that Afghanistan "lay wholly outside her sphere of influence."[10] But Lord Lytton referred to a Russian mission to Afghanistan, this one led by a certain General Stoletoff, and then the Russian Foreign Office denied that there had been any such mission. Lytton went ahead anyway with a demand that a British mission be allowed into Kabul; the Afghans refused. The mission went anyway in September, 1878, and was turned back at the border. An ultimatum was sent to the Afghan ruler: apologise and agree to a permanent British mission in Kabul. It was a barely disguised declaration of war, given the circumstances.

So on 21 November, 1878, three columns of British forces, some 50,000 in all, invaded Afghanistan. There was little opposition, exactly on the pattern of the previous occasion. Just small-scale skirmishes. The ruler, Sher Ali, left Kabul and went to Balkh, leaving Yakub Khan as regent. Yakub Khan ordered that all resistance to the British advance be ended; then he went to the British camp at Gandamak and signed the Treaty of Gandamak on 26 May, 1879. Under its terms Britain agreed to protect Afghanistan from external attack, to station a British Resident at Kabul, and would give to the ruler an annual subsidy of Rupees 600,000 (six lakhs). Afghanistan's foreign relations would be conducted 'in accordance with the advice and wishes of the British Government'. That meant that no engagements, no quarrels would be entered into with any foreign powers except with the concurrence of the British Government.

Louis Cavagnari, the British envoy, reached Kabul on 24 July 1879. Exactly as had happened thirty-eight years earlier, though this time it only took six weeks for the Afghans to react, they attacked the mission. That was on 3 September; Cavagnari was killed and everyone else in the mission along with him; the mission itself was burned to the ground. The Afghans took control of Kabul, while Yakub Khan abdicated. And Lord Lytton wrote mournfully to his Prime Minister, "The web of policy so carefully woven has been rudely shattered."

British forces were again assembled and marched on Kabul. Again there was little fighting, just a few skirmishes. The forces entered Kabul on 12 October. Then in late November the Afghans attacked again, cutting the British lines of communication to India and forcing them out of Kabul. By 15 December the Afghans controlled the whole of Kabul. The British called for reinforcements; when these arrived there followed another attack on Kabul, which was taken a month later. But in the meanwhile British forces elsewhere were also under attack.

Lytton thought one solution might be to break up Afghanistan into pieces. He had, of course, no idea of how the nomadic war machine operates. So Kandahar province was detached from Kabul and Sher Ali Khan placed there as ruler, with assurances of British military support in case he was attacked. In fact, a British military force was stationed there for purposes of reassurance and to ensure that Kandahar was not reintegrated into Afghanistan. Then a certain General Ghulam Haidar Khan Wardak, who was ruling the northern provinces, beyond the Hindu Kush, tried to get the help of the Emir of Bokhara to consolidate his rule. And a certain Ayub Khan ruled in Herat and was, to all intents and purposes, not only independent of Kabul, but had the ambition of extending his rule starting with Kandahar. In Herat he had foundries, adequate military supplies and a large army. When he marched on Kandahar in July, 1880, the British decided to give battle, since the ruler they had installed there was obviously not going to be able to do so; indeed Sher Ali Khan's troops were probably not even loyal to him and would cross over to Ayub (which actually happened when the time came to give battle). At the ensuing battle of Maiwand, late July, 1880, the British found that Ayub outgunned them, outclassed them in tactics and strategy, out-generalled them. The result was, as one British historian wrote somewhat condescendingly, "one of the most notable victories ever gained by oriental troops in conflict with a European army." After 2001, when the British joined the US in sending troops into Afghanistan, whenever the Afghans engaged those troops someone or other would recall Maiwand, urging that a similar defeat now be inflicted on the British troops.

Ayub, who was by then regarded as a national hero and continues to be so today, was eventually prevented from taking Kandahar, but the problem of whom to place in Kabul remained. Here, by chance or design, Abdur Rehman Khan, a member of the ruling Mohammadzai family, the grandson of Dost Mohammad Khan who had been Amir in the 1840s and 1850s, who had been in exile in Russia for over decade, decided to return and stake a claim to the rulership. The British welcomed him. On 22 July, 1880 he was installed formally as Amir in Kabul; a letter had been written to him two days earlier by the British Foreign Secretary, a memorandum of obligation in which the British agreed not to appoint a Resident, not to interfere in the internal affairs of Afghanistan, and that the Amir should have no political relations with any other power than Britain.

Then they hastened to leave and were gone by September, 1880. None of their aims had been achieved. "The policy which had been the main motive for the war was definitely and explicitly given up."[11] They wanted a Resident mission in Kabul; this was renounced. They wanted the break-up of the country, but by the end of the year Abdur Rehman Khan had not only Kandahar within the bounds of his rule, but had also taken Herat and the provinces north of the Hindu Kush. They wanted to control Afghan external relations and this was specified in the letter of 20 July, although the Afghans chafed under the restriction, and in due course of time launched a war to dispense with it.

But they were able to console themselves. "My Lords", said Prime Minister Disraeli to the House of Lords, "the Key of India is not Merv or Herat or Kandahar. The key of India is London. The majesty and sovereignty, the spirit and vigour of your Parliaments, the inexhaustible resources of a free, an ingenious and a determined people, these are the keys of India."[12]

## The Afghans Make War

In May 1919, the ruler of Afghanistan, then Amanullah Khan, launched a war, a jihad, to secure abrogation of British control over his external relations. That seemed like a good time to do this. Amanullah felt the unity and cohesion of Afghanistan built by stages over four decades had reached a level at which he, as a ruler, could challenge the British. Secondly, the spread of Pan-Islamic sentiment across West Asia after Turkey entered the 1914-18 European war meant that such a challenge would be popular and seen as a jihad by the religious leaders. Furthermore, the British and Indian forces in India had not yet recovered from the 1914-18 war in Europe. British troops had been demobilised in large numbers; many of those remaining were on extended leave. The Indian officers and men, too, were on furlough in substantial numbers. Stores of arms and ammunition were down; they had been used up in the war and not yet replaced. And, above all, conditions in India gave the British a lot to be preoccupied about. The Rowlatt bills had been introduced in February, 1919; they provided for extraordinary powers to the executive to detain without trial, restrict the right to appeal and abridge court procedures. A movement against them was launched by Mahatma Gandhi; there were strikes; and the British replied with intensified repression. At one place, Jallianwala Bagh in Amritsar, an unarmed crowd was fired on and several hundred killed (see chapter 10, endnotes). Massive discontent was building.

Having collected some 50,000 troops against the 140,000 that the British were able to muster, Amanullah launched his Jihad on 4 May, 1919. Afghan forces launched attacks at several points along the Durand line: across from Kandahar towards Quetta in the South; from Khost and Ghazni in the Southeast; across the Khyber pass towards Peshawar in the East. Some of their offensives gained territory across the border; others were repulsed. The British bombed Kabul and Jalalabad from the air. But most of all they feared the warring tribes along the border belt, the Afridis and the Masuds, the Waziris along the Tochi river who had been bribed to stay loyal, but who could change sides quickly, as also others, whose society was organised on the principles of the nomadic war machine, who always therefore waited for such a chance to attack. Many did; British garrisons along the border regions had to be pulled back.

So it was a short war. By 31 May both sides were ready to call a truce; an armistice of 3 June brought it to a formal end. As on earlier occasions the British claimed that they had won. But what the Afghans called the War of Independence ended with Afghanistan gaining complete control of its foreign affairs. Its acceptance of the Durand line was confirmed.

So Amanullah got what he wanted, leading to the justifiable question of how, if the British had actually won the war, the terms on which it was ended were such as if the Afghans had won it; and some criticism from senior army officers, who actually did believe that they, the British, had won. So when the Treaty of Peace was signed on 8 August, 1919, there was no mention of a British Resident; as for their control over Afghan external relations, this was expressly repudiated. In a letter of the same date from the British representative it was clarified that all previous treaties between the parties stood cancelled and that the Treaty and letter left Afghanistan "officially free and independent in its internal and external affairs."

In later years, under Amanullah, with the prestige of victory in the war, a new phase of secular modernisation began the next step in further consolidating central rule, this time by reducing the position of the Ulema. This nationalism used the concept of the Fatherland, or Watan, in which the King played the central guiding role and was the focus of the citizens' loyalty. Though Amanullah took Afghanistan too fast along the road to secular nationalism, and had to abdicate in 1929, his successor Zahir Shah was able successfully though very gradually to modernise Afghanistan along the same lines. From 1933 to 1973, helped by a small but growing group of modernisers, he gave a nationalist focus to the Afghans. History was rewritten to show that Afghanistan existed as a national entity even before 1747, traditional culture was developed including the printing of old Pashtun and Farsi literature, and above all Islam was more firmly co-opted into the state apparatus.

In any case 1919 ended the three rounds of the first bout that the Afghans fought with a great power. The next bout which led to the defeat and destruction of the Soviet Union began sixty years later in 1979. There was also a third bout, against the US, which began twenty-two years after that.

## The Soviet Union Goes in

In the late 1970s the Soviet Union was well on the way to becoming the most powerful country on the planet.

It was already the world's leading economic power, ahead of the US and, of course, everyone else. In that era it was the production figures of a few key sectors of the economy that showed who was ahead. When W.W. Rostow, Professor of Economic History and author of the classic *The Stages of Economic Growth*, tried to assess who would achieve world economic primacy, he listed six sectors: coal, oil, pig-iron, steel, electric power, and cement. These were the keys to meaningful economic primacy, the list of sectors for becoming the global economic, and, of course, thereby automatically political, super-power. He suggested that though the Soviet Union had achieved much higher rates of growth than the US in all these sectors in the 1950s, this was because the Soviet economy was actually some sixty years behind that of the US, going through a stage of high growth which the US had long passed. So Soviet economic growth would now slow down.

But he wrote all this in 1960 and, as the years passed, it didn't. In fact, it went ahead of the US in all the sectors identified by him: in cement by 1963, and by the 1980s the Soviet Union produced twice as much as the US; in pig-iron by 1970 and in steel by 1971; in primary energy, which included coal, oil and electric power, by 1985. Commentators had to accept the relative decline of the US; despite the continuous growth of the US economy and its gross national product, as one commented, "by the late 1960s the U.S.A. was feeling the effects of its relative decline as a world power."[13] A better-known commentator and historian, Paul Kennedy, assessing the changing economic balance during the years 1950 to 1980, had to admit, gloomily, the erosion of America's economic position, and the imposing gains of the Soviet Union in the output of steel, electricity, and even automobile production[14] (in which the Soviet Union never caught up, by the way, and was never even close).

So if we take the list of specific sectors which in 1960 were considered not just by Rostow, but by many other economists and political scientists, most relevant for economic power, then the power of the Soviet Union was, in 1980, much bigger than that of the US. (Although, by the latter date, the list had changed and, according to the new list, it wasn't.)

In terms of international politics also, the Soviet Union was ahead of the US. Within the socialist bloc this was shown most dramatically in the August 1968 invasion of Czechoslovakia, which under Alexander Dubcek had granted freedom of the press, civil liberties and even took steps towards a multi-party political system, all anathema to the Soviet system. The Brezhnev doctrine, enunciated as a consequence, clarified that "the Soviet Union would use force to eliminate any threats to 'the course of socialism'". No secession from the Soviet bloc would be allowed; and no fundamental change within it, no departure from the basic principles governing the socialist world on the acceptable political and economic system, foreign policy and security matters, as per the standards of acceptability laid down by Moscow.[15]

Outside the bloc there was also advance, especially in Africa. In Angola the approach of independence in November 1975 saw three groups in contest for the power to run the government thereafter: the Popular Movement for the Liberation of Angola (MPLA); the National Union for Total Independence (UNITA); and the National Front (FLNA). The Soviet Union backed all three at one point or another, but one of them, MPLA, was a favourite. It was eventually backed with arms, economic aid, and the provision of air and sea transport for the lifting of some 30,000 Cuban troops which turned the tide of the war so that it emerged victorious. It was a notable triumph, all the sweeter because the other two had been backed by the US and even by South Africa, which had intervened militarily, but to no good effect. If, as even an American historian wrote, "nothing more nor less than great-power rivalry was involved", then indeed it must be true that history is on the side of the scientific socialism formulated by Marx and Lenin, and, as one Soviet author triumphantly declared in 1979, that imperialism is less and less able to impose its will on the developing countries.[16]

And the triumph in Angola was followed, within months, by another, this one in Ethiopia (see chapter 8). In the autumn of 1977 the Ethiopians under Mengistu Haile Mariam were losing the war with Somalia, the result, almost entirely, of Soviet arms and money given to the latter in the earlier 1970s. So the Ethiopians were boxed into a small enclave around Addis Ababa with no access to the outside world; the Somalians had cut off rail link to Djibouti, while the only other access, through Assab in Eritrea, was subject to sabotage when not actually in rebel hands. Now the Soviets went boldly to the aid of Mengistu; signed an arms supply agreement in September 1977; sent in a small command team led by a General V.I. Petrov, airlifted 15,000 Cuban troops into Addis Ababa and the tide turned. By March 1978 the Somalis had been thrown out of

Ethiopia altogether, the rebellion crushed and Eritrea was back under government control.

With these achievements it was reasonable to talk about "an utterly novel boldness on the part of Soviet military leaders" and a new confidence in the professional competence of the military which would lead to "far less prudence in external policy".

The 1970s was also a decade in which US military morale was at its lowest following defeat in Vietnam, its armed strength reduced further each year as a result of budget cuts, and its nerve for external intervention now seriously frayed. So the contrast was especially sharp, and "the Soviet Union could indeed look forward to the day when it would become the world's greatest military power, and its only true global power". Indeed, "the total stock of Soviet military equipment has grown to the point where it exceeds in quantity the combined inventories of the United States, the rest of NATO and the People's Republic of China..."[17]

Or, as a Soviet text of the period put it, the "invincibility of the socialist military organisation and its supremacy over the imperialist military organisation are a direct result of the supremacy of the socialist social system over the bourgeois in material and spiritual respects."[18]

There were some branches of the military in which it had established an incontrovertible supremacy. Insofar as the space and missile race was concerned it had, as the launch of Sputnik, the very first ever man-made satellite in late 1957 showed, always been ahead. That launch had generated a cascading panic, a "wave of near hysteria", as President Eisenhower put it, in the US.[19] And it was followed by more: the testing of an intercontinental ballistic missile; then the serial production of those missiles; and finally a claim by Khrushchev in early 1960 that the Soviet Union had achieved superiority over the USA in the production of all types of intercontinental ballistic rockets, and in March 1960 that "the Soviet Union is now the world's strongest military power."[20]

In other areas, to give just one example, Soviet airlift and sealift capacity had been expanding throughout the 1950s and 1960s, and was then demonstrated dramatically in the cases of Angola and Ethiopia cited above. One American expert, who was also the editor of *Jane's Fighting Ships*, the bible of the world's navies, recorded in 1974 that while two decades earlier Soviet sea power was essentially unimportant, "today, the Soviet Union can boast of the world's largest and most modern surface navy; the largest and most modern ocean research and fishing fleets; one of the largest and fastest growing merchant fleets ..."[21]

To summarise the argument it appeared to many, and more particularly the Soviet leadership, by the late 1970s, that the Soviet Union was not just on the way, it had already become the most powerful country on the planet.

## The Soviet Military Effort

In 1979 they decided to use all this to extend their power into Afghanistan.

In autumn of that year the headquarters of the 40th Army, normally located in Samarkand, was moved to Termez on the Afghan border. On 23 and 24 December Soviet commandos flew into Kabul, took control of the airport and held it while reinforcements were brought in; by 26 December other commando units had set up a perimeter control line around Darul Aman, the palace in Kabul in which Hafizullah Amin (who had proclaimed himself President on 16 September 1979) had set up his headquarters in expectation of just such an attack. On 27 December the palace was stormed while, simultaneously, the telecommunications centre was blown up and the Radio and Television broadcasting station occupied. There was some fighting in and around Darul Aman but by early morning of 28 December it was over; Amin had been captured and then executed. And, meanwhile, Soviet land forces had completed the circuit of the main highway that circles Afghanistan. Two mechanised divisions from the 40th Army moved from Kushka on the border to Herat in the West and then on to Kandahar in the South; another two moved from Termez through Kunduz in the Northeast and thence south to Kabul, with detachments continuing on to Kandahar.

The whole operation had been carried out too swiftly and cleanly for any opposition to develop; it demonstrated not only the high level of training of the Soviet troops, especially the commandos who had been responsible for taking over the airport and the operation in the Darul Aman palace, but also a high level of intelligence and of control.

In the initial weeks some 80,000 Soviet troops were deployed to Afghanistan, but as the months went by and the resistance grew in strength, this figure rose to 120,000. Over the next three years, these were supplemented by around 120,000 Afghan forces, comprising 60,000 army, 30,000 in the police and 30,000 in the state security organisation, KHAD, the infamous Khidmat-e-Ittalat-e-Daulati. The Afghan forces were of uncertain reliability; desertion rates from the Army and the Police were high, usually above 30 per cent of those recruited; but KHAD was known to be far more reliable, and when the Soviet Union decided to retreat, they put the head of KHAD, Najibullah, to oversee the transition, since he and his forces would fight better.

The Soviet troops, of course, had their problems. Within the armed forces the elite units had always been deployed to the European theatre. The units assigned to Afghanistan comprised largely reservists from Central Asia who were badly trained and who, while inside Afghanistan, often developed sympathies with resistance forces such as the Tajiks or Uzbeks who came from the same ethnic group. They and their eventual replacements had no training in mountain warfare or counter insurgency operations; Soviet military thinking was focused on a traditional land war across the flat plains of Europe, and many of their soldiers assigned to Afghanistan had never even seen a mountain until then. So they favoured road bound and mechanised operations, and when they had to get off the roads, as they had to all the time, they got stuck.

Overall, Soviet strategy was "to hold the cities, secure the lines of communication, limit infiltration, and destroy resistance strongholds and their lines of communication at minimum cost ...a combination of 'scorched earth' and 'migratory genocide."[22] But with this level of forces there was no hope of controlling a country with an area twenty per cent larger than France. It was necessary to reduce the strength of the resistance to the point where Soviet casualties from year to year were not unacceptably high; hope that the resistance would eventually tire of a war which (they must surely presume) they could never win; and depend on the further supposition that diplomacy, persuading Pakistan and the US to reduce or stop supporting the resistance, could also play a role at some stage.

In order to reduce the strength of the resistance Soviet forces carried out a scorched earth policy, burning crops over extensive areas, mining cultivable fields, destroying whole villages so that large parts of the country-side would be depopulated and the resistance lose their sources of recruitment, support, sustenance and concealment among the people. The aim of depopulating Afghanistan was fairly successfully achieved: whole villages left; whole tribes who were not trusted emigrated from their homes; Afghan refugees streamed into Pakistan and Iran; there were eventually nearly five million, three million in Pakistan, two million in Iran, altogether twenty-five per cent of the total population of the country was displaced. But it had no perceptible effect in diminishing the strength of the resistance. And apart from creating a man-power pool of nearly three million Afghans in Pakistan and nearly two million in Iran from which the resistance could be recruited, this Soviet policy enabled the Pakistan authorities, in particular, to tutor a substantial proportion of the Afghan population with its own version of Islam. Equally important, the polarisation of society, which had so far been confined to the urbanised middle class, was now extended to the people in every region and village of the country.

With Pakistan diplomacy was used, of course; air and artillery attacks were launched across the border as an additional inducement to Pakistan to curb support for the resistance.

### Dividing the Afghans ...

Within Afghanistan Soviet policy was to intensify the tribal and ethnic divisions that had always been part of Afghan society.

This was, in effect, a continuation of British policies, specifically those of Lord Lytton, to try to disintegrate Afghanistan. To mention briefly the background, by 1973 the gradual modernisation of Afghanistan through expansion of the government apparatus, infrastructure and the economy including the private sector had led to demands for political liberalisation. A growing, but still tiny, urban middle class demanded rapid westernisation, the abandonment of traditional socio-religious practices, and the reduction of religious influence. At the opposite pole, there was an Islamic revival led by scholars educated at Al Azhar University, or influenced by Maulana Maududi. Traditional Afghan society has been moderate: one of the reasons for the gradual consolidation of internal cohesion was the ability, under the guidance of the successive rulers or Kings, of Sunnis and Shias, Pashtun and non-Pashtun, to tackle the problems of socio-political development with an accommodating flexibility. There was very little domestic support for leftist or Islamist extremes; the representatives of both were from the newly educated urbanised middle class. But the pressure of external forces pushed Afghanistan's polity into a mounting confrontation between these extremes in which the voices of the moderates were silenced.

In July 1973 Mohammad Daoud, a cousin and brother-in-law of King Zahir Shah, with the help of a group of army officers, had staged a bloodless coup in which he abolished the monarchy, declared Afghanistan a Republic and proclaimed himself President. The Soviet Union was the first to recognise the new government; the size of the Soviet aid programme was substantially increased, and followed up with a regular exchange of high-level visits between Kabul and Moscow, while relations with Washington cooled.

The coup brought not only the leftists in the army to power, but also the People's Democratic Party of Afghanistan (PDPA), some of whose members became ministers. This party, described by the Soviet official media as a vanguard party, which had split soon after it was founded in January 1965 into a largely Pashtun-dominated Khalq group and a more generally non-Pashtun Parcham group, remained divided, and the Soviet officials assigned to look after its interests ensured that roughly equal favours were bestowed on both groups so that it stayed so.

As the weight of one branch of politics shifted to the left and to inspiration from the Soviet Union, the Islamists at the other end of the spectrum looked increasingly to Pakistan. By 1975, after a series of uprisings to overthrow the government of President Daoud had failed, several of the more radical of them had taken shelter there, and in stages thereafter even the moderates went into exile. The stage was set for the next step in fragmenting Afghan society.

The Saur revolution of April 1978 and its second stage of December 1979 took the polarisation of Afghan internal and external politics all the way into open warfare. On April 27, 1978, the PDPA took over power, killed Daoud and proclaimed the birth of the Democratic Republic of Afghanistan. The Khalq group in the party played the dominant role. In the second stage of the revolution the Khalq leadership was replaced by the Parcham, Soviet troops entered the country, and for the next decade domestic and external policy was directly controlled from Moscow. At the other extreme the Islamists, fighting a jihad against the Soviet occupation of their country, came increasingly under Pakistan's control.

The pre-1978 policies of promoting cohesion were being reversed in other ways also as the Soviet occupation of Afghanistan continued.

A 1985 constitution provided for the creation of administrative units based on national characteristics. By 1988 the PDPA, under Soviet guidance, was actively encouraging the different nationalities such as the Pashtuns and Tajiks, the Hazaras and Uzbeks, to develop distinctive identities by promoting their particular culture. Where previously national Jirgas or Assemblies brought the different nationalities together, now separate Jirgas were organised for each; and each was offered autonomy within its area, so that the local tribal or national leader would exercise effective power with minimal administrative interference from Kabul.

Devolution of power to the different regions was also encouraged through external contacts. Direct discussions between Afghan provinces and neighbouring Soviet Republics on expanding economic, cultural and educational co-operation began. Three Soviet Republics, the Turkmen, Uzbek and Tajik, bordered northern Afghanistan's provinces, and the latter were encouraged to, and did, enter into direct co-operation with them. That the provinces had substantial populations of Turkmen, Uzbek or Tajik ethnic origin, and that they were the most highly developed industrially with gas, fertilizer, power and irrigation projects set up over the years with Soviet assistance, facilitated such co-operation. And as the 1980s progressed reports came in that the ethnic divisions were being firmed up, with Hazaras moving out of non-Hazara areas, Uzbeks out of non-Uzbek areas and so on. Abdur Rahman's policy of ensuring an ethnic population mix within each province was being reversed.

### ... with Help from the US and from Pakistan

The US and Pakistan, as we have seen external powers invariably do in similar situations, helped the Soviet Union in as many ways as they could.

The US had decided to confine its disapproval (which had to be shown for public consumption) to rhetoric and some symbolic gestures like the boycotting of the 1980 Olympic Games, halting high technology sales, and stopping US feed grain shipments. Diverse reasons were trotted out for not doing more. It was argued, for instance, that helping the resistance, particularly with the supply of weapons, would make it the first time US lethal weapons were used to kill Soviet citizens.

In order to illustrate this we can cite the debate about the pros and cons of supplying the Stinger anti-aircraft missiles to them, given particularly that Soviet aircraft and helicopters became over time the biggest danger for the resistance. Deputy Director John McMahon of the Central Intelligence Agency, which was directing all operations in regard to the resistance, thought US involvement could be directly traced to it, and "raised the danger of public exposure and political scandal that could damage the agency". The CIA clung to the tenet of 'plausible deniability'.[23] Some thought more US aid through lethal weapons would upset super-power relations in areas like arms control, which should get higher priority than getting the Soviets out of Afghanistan; or might risk Soviet counter-escalation, especially against Pakistan; others that the resistance was too unsophisticated to handle a high technology like this.

Pakistan too was against the supply of the Stinger to the resistance. President Zia-ul Haq told CIA Director Bill Casey in late 1982, and a visiting congressional official in early 1984, that the key in Afghanistan was to keep the pot boiling; too much escalation would make the pot boil over, leading to Soviet retaliation against Pakistan. Besides he was also afraid that one of the missiles could be used on his presidential plane.[24]

Finally the Stinger was not given to the resistance till 1986, and by then it was clear to the Soviet leaders as well as to the Americans that the Soviet Union had lost the war; so giving the missile at that late stage was designed, as the traditional story would have it, to obliterate or at least dilute the credit that the resistance might get for that outcome, to assert, in other words, that it was the super power that did it.

After the war was over and the Soviets had left Afghanistan, there was, expectedly, another heated debate: the Stinger did it, said some; it was truly man-portable, a true fire and forget weapon, flew faster, over a longer range, undeceived by flares. Compared to it the British Blowpipe, a weapon with the same objective, was a disaster; an ISI official describes one engagement in which the Blowpipe was used against aircraft that were just sitting there; thirteen missiles were fired, and there was not a single hit; as he says, a "duck shoot in which the ducks won."[25] In short the Stinger had a decisive impact on the war, forced an early Soviet withdrawal, which in turn led to the collapse of communism and of the Soviet Union and the end of the Cold War. In other words, it was the Stinger that won the Cold War.

There were others who said the Stinger kept the Soviets in Afghanistan longer than they would have stayed otherwise; it made the armed forces determined to stay, not give in under duress, as former Foreign Minister Shevardnadze said.

But the most important aspect of Pakistan's policy towards the resistance was its decision to use the freedom given to manage the war and whatever money and weapons were required, for its own purposes: the weakening of Afghan national strength.

Pakistan, even more than the Soviet Union, was opposed to a future Afghanistan being united and strong, hence its policy vis-à-vis the Mujahidin was precisely complementary to that of the Soviet Union towards the PDPA government. For a dozen years, since the early 1980s, the Pakistani leadership planned an Afghanistan that, after the Soviet troops pulled out, would be both friendly and subservient; this meant also weak and unstable, for obvious reasons. Pakistan's leadership has always felt the need for strategic depth vis-à-vis India; secondly, it has to try to settle its own Pashtun problem; and, thirdly, if Afghanistan remains in such an unsettled state that there is little prospect of the former Mujahidin returning to peacetime occupations, then a large pool of battle-tested fighters would become available for use in Jammu and Kashmir as also elsewhere in India. So these three factors became the drivers for Pakistan's policy during the years of the Soviet occupation.

In the implementation of this policy Pakistan had two main levers: the supply of arms, money and material to them; and Islam.

In regard to the first, resistance activity in the early months was disparate, without co-ordination. Even before the Soviet occupation there had been several parties active in Peshawar; immediately after that occupation began the numbers multiplied and by 1981 some forty parties or groups were jockeying for position in Peshawar; there were others in Quetta, not to mention those operating out of Iran. Each of them claimed leadership of the struggle against the Soviet Union. Few had any links with the commanders in the field, who were doing the actual fighting.

By agreement with the USA and Saudi Arabia, who were the main foreign suppliers of arms, material and money for the purpose, all such supplies were channeled through the Pakistan authorities.

Pakistan's Inter-Services Intelligence (ISI), which had been in touch with the leaders for several years, was given the task of coordinating of the different resistance groups. Resistance unity was obviously going to be the best thing to fight the Soviets, but unity was the one thing Pakistan didn't want. So they decided to support not one, or two, or three, but seven of the resistance groups[26] in the shape of political parties. These parties received the arms, money and other supplies from the ISI and passed it on to the commanders, hence the strength of the commanders in the field was dependent on what the parties received from the ISI.

All the groups except these seven found their resources of arms and money drying up, and disappeared. The ISI thereafter ensured by the judicious distribution of arms and other supplies, that none of the seven could become too powerful. Gulbuddin Hekmatyar's Hizb-e-Islami, which specifically rejected a nationalist ideology for Afghanistan, attached the greatest importance to the Islamic ideological content of its programmes (which were modelled on the ideas of the Jamaat-e-Islami of Pakistan) and at one stage proposed a confederation between Afghanistan and Pakistan, was the only one often (for even he was not always trusted) given more generous treatment. In general while a nominal balance was maintained between such Ghilzai groups and those of the Durrani who supported the return of Zahir Shah, Pakistan consistently favoured the former, and above all the Hizb-e-Islami.

Pakistan also in general kept the Pashtuns divided for it had been the Pashtuns that had been most vociferous in demanding Pashtunistan; as a consequence the Tajik, Uzbek and Hazara groups, particularly those led by commanders located within Afghanistan, gained in strength, upsetting the traditional balance between Pashtun and non-Pashtun.

By 1982, already the differences between the different resistance groups, Shia and Sunni, Pashtun and non-Pashtun, Pashtun and Pashtun, were so deep that at the OIC Foreign Ministers' Conference of August that year they could not agree on a spokesman. At that conference and at later international gatherings where the same problem arose repeatedly, each side would appeal to the Pakistan leadership, the latter would appeal to them to settle their differences, play off one against the other; and the matter would be left at that. There followed clashes in the field between Pashtun and Tajik, between Pashtun and Uzbek, or between different Pashtun groups such as Durrani and Ghilzai, and even within the same group. But the ISI were able to ensure that none of the seven groups was eliminated.

As for the second, Pakistan's policy was that the war had to be kept going, and converted by stages into an Islamic Jihad, a war of the believer against the infidel. Such an Islam would destroy and replace that other, liberal, Islam which Amir Habibullah had promoted, and which brought together Shia and Sunni, Tajik and Uzbek, Hazara and Pashtun to form a unified nation state, the Islam accepted and supported by an urbanised middle class and which brought cohesion to the country. This would hopefully help to create a large body of fighters, prepared to go to war for the promotion of Islam outside Afghanistan, something the Afghans had always been reluctant to do.

## The Resistance: Commanders and Parties

Meanwhile, on the ground in Afghanistan, where the issue of whether the Soviet Union had won or lost would be decided, the resistance commanders were largely autonomous. Occasionally they fought one another but, now that they had a common enemy, more rarely than ever before. Occasionally they coordinated an operation, but that, too, was not frequent; each had a clear-cut operational territory and took his own decisions on how to pursue the war.

There was Ahmed Shah Masud in the Panjsher valley, one of the best organised of them, who even organised comprehensive training courses within his area for his own fighters and for foreigners; carried out military exercises to keep his forces fighting fit; and had a well thought out defence plan for the valley. The Soviet military showing against his defences of the Panjsher valley was particularly dismal. Over the years Masud repeatedly attacked their Bagram air base, as well as the Salang highway that led from Kabul to the Soviet border, both strategically important targets since these were the lifelines for Soviet re-supply.

There was Ismail Khan in Herat, a former army officer who was able to recruit a large number of soldiers from the Afghan army, divided the functioning of his organisation on the model of a state, and "was unique in recruiting his senior aides with no regard for communal or political affiliation."

On the other hand, the Helmand commander, Abdul Wahid, set up a clerical system, for that is what he knew; his fighters were tightly controlled, had to wear uniforms and worked within a clearly established hierarchy. Then there was Qari Baba in Baghran, also a cleric, but whose system was more liberal, with decisions taken by consensus.

These are random examples of some of the better-known commanders who fought the war and defeated the Soviet Union. There were many more. But two points cannot be overstressed: that the commanders built their strength along the tribal and ethnic lines that had divided Afghan society for centuries; and that the resistance against the Soviet occupation overrode all these divisions. That resistance was called a Jihad, which in this case (for the word has many interpretations) must be taken to mean the Afghan national struggle for freedom from the Soviet Union, for "as long as the Soviets were there, belief in the jihad stood out in opposition to all ethnic and national demands."

Then there were the parties based in Pakistan and Iran.

The parties operated in exile. Partly for reasons of security it was rare for any of them to send a senior representative into the interior of Afghanistan, though forays into the border areas were fairly common, and reports did occasionally appear about such and such leader travelling into the interior. The task of the party leaders was to be the link between the commanders and the outside world.

One group of parties, the Sunni parties, were based in Pakistan. As pointed out above the most prominent among them, the favourite of the ISI, was the Pashtun based Hizbe Islam led by Gulbuddin Hekmatyar, who was something of a loose cannon on the Peshawar deck, but made up for it by his unquestioning loyalty to Pakistan. Then there was the Jamaat-e-Islami led by Maulana Burhanuddin Rabbani, whose great advantage was to have Ahmed Shah Masud as well as Ismail Khan affiliated, but its strength was largely in the non-Pashtun areas, which was a disadvantage. Another, the Harakat Inqilab Islami led by Maulavi Mohammed Nabi Mohammedi, had strong religious affiliations but was even more strongly nationalist. Two religious families dominated the Ulema of Afghanistan, and each of them had one resistance group under them: the Mujaddedi, who came to Afghanistan from India in the early nineteenth century, set up religious schools and acquired a following; and the Gailani from the Qadiri brotherhood in Iraq. The Jabhe Nijat was the party of Maulana Sebgatullah Mujaddedi, while the Mahaz-e-Milli was that of Sayyed Gailani.

Iran, too, provided support for the parties based there, but this was limited; in particular, while maintaining its relations with the Shia-led parties, which naturally gravitated to Iran, and even extending moral support, it was "at the same time not providing them with any significant military assistance in order not to damage its own relations with the Soviet Union."[27]

The Shia parties, therefore, though largely affiliated to Iran, also had links with Pakistan, which also supplied them with arms and aid. One of the prominent among them was the Shura Inqilabi led by Seyyed Beheshti, who had organised a gathering of Shia representatives in Bamiyan province in September 1979, before the Soviet invasion, and as a demonstration of unity among the Hazara people. Then there was Sazman Nasr, founded in 1979 by a group of Ulema who had trained in Iran and were led by Sheikh Abdul Ali Mazari. Another, perhaps better known, was the Sepahi Pasdaran, led by Sheikh Akbari, who had trained as an Alem in the Iraqi city of Najaf, and whose links to the Iranian religious leadership were strong enough for him to get official Iranian recognition of his party in 1983.

## Phases of the War

Nothing that the Soviet Union did, nothing that the Americans and Pakistanis did to help them, brought them any closer to victory in the war.

True, the air-borne operations were effective; the helicopter gunship, the Soviet Hind, was feared by the resistance, but, as the Americans found in Vietnam, this was true only up to a point. As soon as the resistance decided to stand up and fight, then, "many eyewitnesses have noted that the use of primitive air-defense weapons by the resistance will cause Soviet and Afghan pilots to take evasive actions, severely degrading the effectiveness of their bombing or strafing run."

But in a war of this kind you could not depend only on control of the air; you had to go onto the ground, and here it was not so much the problems faced by the Soviet troops as the strength of the resistance that affected their morale. Over the years it was not the resistance that tired. As the casualties mounted, year after year, it was the Soviet troops, then their commanders and then the leaders in Moscow that tired of a war they came to realise they could only lose now, or many thousands of casualties down the road, later.

And it was the resistance that took heart from Soviet demoralisation, asserting that the latter's forces were addicted to 'cook-book warfare', readymade recipes for battle, applied unthinkingly to every situation.[28]

Added to this was the collapse of support at home for the continuation of the war, as the dead were taken back year after year, the hundreds going up to thousands, never ceasing, no matter what the authorities said about how well the war was going. The war counted an eventual total of at least twenty thousand, perhaps many more. Twice that many were wounded.[29] Then there were half a million Afghan war veterans, *Afghantsy* who were angry at having been made to fight a war with no meaning, who in their own society were resented by the people around them for all their atrocities while at war, and who were themselves resentful at the less than adequate recognition and facilities given to them by officialdom. The murmurs of criticism came out in the open, in the form of open acts of defiance from Moscow to the remotest village whenever and wherever the dead body of a soldier was brought back from Afghanistan. These problems were compounded by the nature of the Soviet system; as Gorbachev recalled, Soviet society was not aware of the scale of the war in Afghanistan; there was no anti-war movement as there had been in the US during the Vietnam War.[30]

So three things happened. Soviet civil society, what there was of it, developed hitherto unknown resentments against the regime as well as against the armed forces; official attitudes towards those who had served in Afghanistan became callous, for they didn't want any part of such an unpopular war; and the veterans became resentful of a system that had treated them so badly, refused to recognise the contribution they made to the war. All three, at the end of the war, hastened the collapse of the Soviet Union.

A considerable effort was put in to counter all this: making people believe that the soldiers were only "helping villagers plant trees, clean out irrigation ditches, and build schools;"[31] lauding, in case the mention of combat operations was unavoidable, the 'limited contingent' of Soviet troops who were really defending the homeland, fighting a small war in a foreign country in order to defend against a larger war that could threaten the country or its resources, given the inter-connectedness of military operations; describing the heroes of the war such as Sergeant Nikolai Chepik, an icon venerated through displays in schools;[32] and generally glorifying the veterans of the war. None of all this helped, since the war was going so badly.

The war can be conveniently divided into three phases. In the first, 1980-1983, the Soviets tried to wear down, tire out and thereby gradually eliminate the fighting abilities of the resistance. During this first phase perimeter protection was installed around the main towns by security patrols and extensive mine laying; efforts, by and large, successful except in the South and East, were made to keep the roads open, and here the highway going north from Kabul through the Salang pass to the Soviet border was especially important. Air attacks were mounted on resistance bases and supply lines from Pakistan; there were even air attacks into Pakistan's border areas for this purpose; efforts were made to get some of the resistance leaders living in Pakistan assassinated. But Soviet forces tried their best not to launch land attacks on resistance positions away from the main highways, not wanting high casualties while their counter-insurgency skills were still rudimentary. So it was the Afghan army that was given the task of flushing out resistance hideaways far from the main highways. But even so the Soviet casualties mounted: 1,500 dead in 1980; 2,000 in 1981; 2,300 in 1982; and there were many more wounded. As for the Afghan army, which had a strength of 100,000 in 1978, desertions had reduced it to 30,000 by 1982 and it never really recovered; that was still the figure despite forced conscription and a lowering of the age of conscription, at the end of the first phase of the war.

In the second phase, 1985 and 1986, the Soviet Union's leaders realised that they were never going to win this war; the resistance would never lose it; so, in effect, they were going to lose it. Two military actions in particular demonstrated the truth of this.

One of these, part of a series of attempts to dislodge Ahmed Shah Masud from the Panjsher valley, was a massive attack on the valley in April 1985; one whole Soviet division (108 Motor Rifle Division) accompanied by air assault units and thousands of Afghan troops moved into the valley in an effort to remove Masud from there. TU-16 bombers flew in from their bases in the Soviet Union in repeated sorties, a rolling barrage, a wall of fire intended to flatten anything that moved and behind which the ground forces moved forward. All this "forced Masud to withdraw his men from the valley and take up positions higher up in the mountains." It didn't help. The very next month Masud's forces attacked a convoy on the Salang highway destroying three hundred trucks; another month, June, 1985, and he attacked a fort held by the Afghan army; "complete surprise was achieved ... the result was a complete victory for the Mujahideen" who captured over a hundred officers and NCOs and several hundred enlisted men.

In like manner six major offensives were launched in 1985, but despite extensive attacks on the villages in the valley and the burning of crops neither the first nor the others were successful. The refugees continued to pour into Pakistan; but Masud still controlled the valley and Soviet casualties were mounting.

The second major military action was the war for Khost and this further signified the end of the Soviet imperial venture; this was a static war, with set piece battles as against the mobile engagements with Masud. Khost is the capital of Paktia province on the Pakistan border and had a major garrison of Afghan troops, under constant attack from the resistance led by Jalaluddin Haqqani, based in Zhawar, not far away. Early in 1986 the Soviet military command decided to make an example of it; the resistance was to be decisively defeated and a major Soviet force would do this job. So they moved in, thousands of specially trained commandos, *spetznatz,* behind a heavy aerial bombardment, riding on hundreds of tanks, accompanied by armoured personnel carriers and MI-8 helicopters. They immediately came under attack; several of the helicopters were shot down, half of the first wave of commandos killed, while "the other half surrendered to the freedom fighters."[33] Eventually, of course, Zhawar was captured and the resistance driven out, but the price paid had been too high.

So by 1986 the Soviet leaders knew they were never going to win this war. Actually Gorbachev tells us that "as early as 1985, during discussions in the Politburo, the question of ending the war in Afghanistan was raised. In February 1986, at the Twenty-seventh Party Congress, the political report from the party Central Committee publicly declared that the war must be ended." That was the occasion he used to describe the war as a 'bleeding wound', adding that he would like Soviet troops to withdraw from Afghanistan 'in the nearest future'.

By the end of 1986, in any case, and now we are on the verge of entering the third phase of the war, all this provided further confirmation that the war was being lost.

Mikhail Gorbachev put it neatly that "if at the first phase of the invasion into Afghanistan, Soviet leaders could nourish hopes for a favourable outcome, it became clear after two or three years that we would be stuck for a long time without any chance or resolving the matter in our favour ... Afghanistan turned into a whirlpool ...." sucking in and crushing manpower and a huge and unbearable expenditure. So "in general this war was one of the causes for the economic and political crisis that necessitated *perestroika*."[34] Soviet Foreign Minister Edward Shevardnadze also linked *perestroika*, or even the whole of the 'new thinking' in Soviet foreign policy, to the war in Afghanistan.

The third phase was the tacit admission of defeat and the decision finally to withdraw from Afghanistan. By 1987 with the war going so badly, anti-militarism grew, especially in the non-Russian republics of the Soviet Union. Reports started surfacing of corruption at the higher levels of the armed forces, of incidents of looting and plundering and even worse, drug abuse, the sale of military equipment to the resistance to obtain drugs, food, electronic gadgets.

Nevertheless, withdrawal and the admission of defeat were not going to be easy. This had never happened to the Soviet Union; Tsarist Russia had been defeated in war; the Soviet Union, never. So there was the deep military humiliation that the Soviet Union "failed to demonstrate either its vast military power or its ability to use that power as a political instrument."[35] And there was the international humiliation; the Soviet leadership remembered the vivid scenes of the last American leaving Saigon from the rooftop of the Embassy building, clinging to the struts of departing helicopters as the North Vietnamese forces moved in. Then there was the Soviet geo-strategic position, from Africa to Latin America, even the Gulf, its blue water navies operated across the world's oceans, all of which would be gone. In Cuba and Vietnam, in South Yemen, Ethiopia and Angola there would be no respect left for the power and ability of the Soviet Union. So Gorbachev was not going to rush into a withdrawal. Much later he gave his own version. "I am often asked" he wrote, "why I failed to end the war promptly in 1985", as soon, presumably, as it was clear that it was lost. And he gave the reasons: the need for a unified position within the Soviet leadership; and within the Afghan leadership; and with the others, Pakistan, Iran, the US;[36] and it all sounded quite lame.

Finally, early in 1988, he announced that, in accordance with the Geneva accords, all Soviet troops would leave Afghanistan by February 15, 1989; and they did, actually completing the withdrawal a day ahead of schedule; and the last of them crossed the bridge over the Amu Darya with the sound bite: "Our nine-year stay ends with this."[37]

## The Impact of Defeat

"In January 1990, Shevardnadze most clearly linked the withdrawal from Afghanistan (and unveiling the fallacy of using military force) to the goals of *perestroika.* He noted: 'the deliverance of our country from the oppressive moral and material burden of involvement in the Afghan war is one of the biggest international achievements of *perestroika*." Indeed, the whole policy of *perestroika* flowed from the decision to leave Afghanistan.[38]

So from now on defeat in Afghanistan was first paired to *perestroika* or more generally the new thinking, or *novoe myshlenie* which, while it "could be applied to all of Gorbachev's reforms, it referred most specifically to foreign policy and in particular to the Soviet Union's relationship with the West;"[39] then later the new thinking took over and, so to speak, stifled the fact of that defeat.

A major consequence of defeat was that the Russians seemed to have lost the desire for an empire. "The protracted, bloody war in Afghanistan appears to have gradually drained ethnic Russians of a willingness to support the use of Russian lives to preserve the so-called 'outer' Soviet empire. By the beginning of the 1990s, this sentiment had spread to the issue of the forcible preservation of the 'inner' Soviet empire."[40]

But even more important, if it was true that "the Soviet army was the glue that held the diverse Soviet Republics together, its defeat had profound implications for the survivability of the Soviet Union."[41]

And perhaps it was true for, after the defeat, and probably as consequence, Soviet power dropped with cascading effect. Already in December 1988 Gorbachev had announced to the United Nations that he would cut Soviet forces by ten per cent and this would be done by thinning down their presence in East Europe; now its Warsaw Treaty allies announced similar cuts in their force levels. The muscle to enforce political decisions was no longer going to be available. This meant three things: no insistence on a Soviet style domestic political or economic system; no insistence on a particular foreign policy or even defence policy line; and, above all, no enforcement at all.

Hungary was the first to go. In November 1988 a second party was legalised; the Communist party, called the Hungarian Socialist Workers' Party since 1956, no longer held a monopoly; soon Hungary had a multi-party system. Then came Poland which held free elections in June 1989 in which Solidarity candidates won every seat they contested against the Communist Party. Then Bulgaria and Czechoslovakia where Vaclav Havel took power in December 1989. Romania came last, soon after.

Through all this Soviet troops in East Europe continued to withdraw; and the East Europeans continued to cut down the size of their forces. The Brezhnev doctrine was no more and this was made clear as early as March 1988, when, during a visit to Yugoslavia, "Gorbachev publicly repudiated the notion of limited sovereignty for socialist states." He repeated this in a speech to the Council of Europe, Strasbourg, France, in July 1989 elaborating that "any interference in domestic affairs and any attempts to restrict the sovereignty of states, both friends or allies or any others, are inadmissible."[42]

The inability and unwillingness to insist on a foreign policy line in conformity with that of the Soviet Union was most dramatically shown by the breaching of the Berlin wall in November 1989. German unification was then only a matter of time; it came on 3 October 1990 "and with it the liquidation of the Soviet role in eastern and central Europe which they won in the carnage and devastation of World War II." The Warsaw Treaty came to an end in July 1991. All the allies of the outer empire were gone.

That left the Soviet Union itself, and that too dissolved. First Lithuanian independence came, March 1990, then that of Estonia and Latvia, and then the Ukraine in the autumn of 1991. That last was a particularly hard blow since the Ukraine produced half the agricultural produce and over one-fifth of the industrial goods of the Soviet Union; it had a "unique combination of demographic and economic weight."[43] One by one the component parts of the Soviet Union, its allies and even its friends, were asserting their full independence of action. "If national awakenings in the Baltic republics set the process of Soviet disintegration in motion, the Ukrainian awakening sealed the country's fate."[44]

In the last act on 21 December 1991, the heads of all the now independent states that had once been part of the Soviet Union agreed at Alma Ata to form the Commonwealth of Independent States and the Soviet Union ceased to exist.

At this point it is as well to recollect that modernity, which turns the traditional story upside down, is sure that the end of the Soviet empire and of the Soviet Union itself was the result of the US winning the Cold War. It was American pressure applied in a sustained manner through the policy of containment, as well as the American example of how to run an economy, that turned the Soviet Union, its empire, its ideology, in the words of the most read Cold War historian, into "a sandpile ready to slide."[45]

The Gorbachev view is a variation on this, and reinforces the modernity story that is widely accepted today. It was that the Soviet intervention in Afghanistan "buried the possibility of improving international relations for a long time."[46] So if the new thinking were to come into play, and in his interactions with western leaders Gorbachev ceaselessly underlined the imperative of this new thinking, a Soviet withdrawal had to be a pre-condition. He records discussions with world leaders who came to Moscow for the funeral of Konstantin Chernenko (his predecessor), discussions with the French President, with US Vice President George Bush and Secretary of State Schultz and the content was the same: the relations between the Soviet Union and the West must come out of the ice age in which they seemed to be stuck; there was no fatal conflict of interests between the two sides; peaceful coexistence was the only alternative. In brief, the main force behind the Soviet withdrawal was not defeat, nor even the cost of the war in economic or human terms; it was that in order to achieve *perestroika* or economic restructuring the Soviet Union needed, as essential inputs, the economic and technological cooperation of the West and a détente which would allow the shifting of resources from military to economic use. This would not be available unless Soviet troops were withdrawn from Afghanistan.[47]

## ENDNOTES

[1] Herodotus, *Histories*, Wordsworth, Hertfordshire, 1996, p. 321.

[2] Edward Gibbon, *The Decline and Fall of the Roman Empire,* The Modern Library, Random House, New York, undated, Vol. I, pp. 901 and 905.

[3] Arnold Toynbee, *A Study of History*, abridgement of Volumes VII-X by D.C.Somervell, OUP, London, 1957, p. 129.

[4] See chapter 6 on Algeria for more on this subject.

[5] Gilles Deleuze and Felix Guattari, *A Thousand Plateaus*, Continuum, London, 2007, pp. 394 and 396-8.

[6] Anthony Hyman, Nationalism in Afghanistan, *International Journal of Middle East Studies*, Vol.34, 2002, pp. 299, 301.

[7] M. Nazif Asrani, The Future of the state and the structure of community governance in Afghanistan, in William Haley (ed.) *Fundamentalism Reborn? Afghanistan and the Taliban*, Hurst, London, 1998, p. 238.

[8] For this and the last seven paragraphs see Percy Sykes, *A History of Afghanistan*, Vol. I, Munshiram Manoharlal Publishers, New Delhi. The dispatch of 1836 quoted on p. 406; the Simla Manifesto in Vol. II, p. 340; the Army of the Indus in Vol. II, pp. 7 and 10; the Treaty of December 1841, Article 1, on p. 350 of Vol. II; and the last quote on p. 37, Vo. II.

[9] P. E.Roberts, *History of British India under the Company and the Crown*, OUP, Oxford, 1923, p. 441

[10] Percy Sykes, op. cit., p. 88.

[11] P. E. Roberts, op. cit., p. 449 for this and last two paragraphs.

[12] Quoted by P.E.Roberts, op. cit. p.451.

[13] J.P. Cole, *Geography of World Affairs*, Penguin Books, Harmondworth, 1974, p. 393.

[14] Paul Kennedy, *The Rise and Fall of the Great Powers*, Fontana Press, London, 1989, p. 555.

[15] Michael Kort, *The Soviet Colossus, The Rise and Fall of the USSR*, M.E. Sharpe, New York, 1993, p. 270.

[16] Karen Brutents, *Cooperation between the USSR and developing countries*, USSR Academy of Sciences, Institute of Oriental Studies, Social Sciences Today editorial board, Moscow, 1986, pp. 10-11.

[17] Edward N. Luttwak, *The Grand Strategy of the Soviet Union*, Weidenfeld and Nicolson, London, 1983, pp. 60, 30 and 43. Note the sameness, bordering on seriality, of statements made in the 1990s about American power, that its defence expenditure was equal to the combined expenditures of the next fifteen countries.

[18] *Marxism-Leninism on War and Army*, by authors from Soviet military educational establishments, Progress Publishers, Moscow, 1972, p. 270.

[19] Dwight D. Eisenhower, *Waging Peace, 1956-1961*, Heinemann, London, 1966, p. 211.

[20] Quoted in Hannes Adomeit, Soviet Risk Taking and Crisis Behaviour, in John Bayliss and Gerald Segal, eds., *Soviet Strategy*, Croom Helm, London, 1981. p. 189.

[21] Norman Polmar, *Soviet Naval Power, Challenge for the 1970s*, Crane, Russak and Co., New York, 1974, p. 1.

[22] Joseph Collins, Soviet Policy Towards Afghanistan, *Proceedings of the Academy of Political Science*, Vol. 36, No. 4, 1987, Soviet Foreign Policy, p. 204.

[23] Alan J. Kuperman, The Stinger Missile and U.S. Intervention in Afghanistan, *Political Science Quarterly*, Vol. 114, No. 2, Summer 1999, p. 222.

[24] Alan J. Kuperman, op. cit., pp. 250 and 225 for this and the last paragraph.

[25] Mohammed Yousaf and Mark Adkin, *The Bear Trap*, Leo Cooper, London, 1982, pp. 87-88.

[26] These were, in alphabetical order: 1. Ettehad-e-Islami led by Abdul Rasul Sayyaf; 2. Harakat-e-Inqilab led by Mohammad Nabi Mohammadi; 3. Hizb-e-Islami

(Khalis) led by Yunus Khalis; 4. another, a Hizb-e-Islami (Gulbuddin) led by Gulbuddin Hekmatyar, which was Pakistan's favourite; 5. Jabhe Nijat-e-Milli led by Sibgatullah Mujaddedi; 6. Jamaat-e-Islami led by Burhanuddin Rabbani; and 7. the Mahaz-e-Milli led by Sayyed Ajmed Gailani.

[27] Gilles Dorronsoro, *Revolution Unending, Afghanistan: 1979 to the Present*, Hurst, London, 2005, pp. 127, 126, 181 and 146 for this and the previous six paragraphs.

[28] Joseph Collins, op. cit., p. 206.

[29] The precise number of casualties has never been established. Krasnaya Zvezda, the Soviet Defence Ministry newspaper, wrote in 1990 that there were 14,454 killed in action and 50,000 wounded. Russian Defence Minister Pavel Grachev said in 1994 that 23,258 were wounded and 26,798 injured, maimed or shocked. See Henry S. Bradsher, Afghan Communism and Soviet Intervention, OUP, 1999, p. 251.

[30] See Bruce W. Jentleson, *American Foreign Policy, The Dynamics of Choice in the 21st Century*, W.W. Norton, New York, 2004, p. 283.

[31] Henry S. Bradsher, op. cit., p. 242. Note the remarkable resemblance between these tasks and those of the Provincial Reconstruction Teams of a later, post-9/11, age.

[32] Reported in the *New York Times,* 16 January 1985.

[33] Matinuddin Lt. Gen. (Retd) Kamal Matinuddin, *Power Struggle in the Hindu Kush, Afghanistan (1978-1991)*, Wajidalis, Lahore, 1991, pp. 140, 141 and 145 for this and the last paragraph.

[34] Quoted by Bruce W. Jentleson, op. cit., p. 283.

[35] Ted Daley, Afghanistan and Gorbachev's Global Foreign Policy, *Asian Survey*, Vol. 29, No. 5, May 1989, p. 499.

[36] Gorbachev (the book cover does not mention his first name, Mikhail), *On my country and the world,* Columbia University Press, New York, 2000, p. 198.

[37] Michael Kort, p. 307.

[38] Rafael Reuveny and Aseem Prakash, The Afghanistan war and the breakdown of the Soviet Union, *Review of International Studies*, 1999, Vol. 25, p. 699.

[39] Michael Kort, op. cit., p. 297.

[40] John B.Dunlop, Russia: Confronting a Loss of Empire, 1987-1991, *Political Science Quarterly*, Vol. 108, No. 4, Winter 1993-94, p. 628.

[41] Rafael Reuveny and Aseem Prakash, op. cit., p. 698.

[42] David Cox, *Retreating from the Cold War, Germany, Russia and the Withdrawal of the Western Group of Forces*, Macmillan, Hampshire, 1996, pp. 59, 65.

[43] Raymond Pearson, *The Rise and Fall of the Soviet Empire*, Macmillan, Hampshire, 1998, p. 153.

[44] Robert Strayer, *Why did the Soviet Union Collapse, Understanding Historical Change*, M.E. Sharpe, Armonk, New York, 1998, p. 156.

[45] John Lewis Gaddis, *The Cold War*, Penguin Books, London, 2007, p. 238.

[46] Gorbachev op. cit., pp. 198 and 177, for this and the last paragraph..

[47] For a succinct statement of this argument see Alan J. Kuperman, op. cit. p. 236.

# 12

# The US Goes into Afghanistan

This chapter tells the story of how the US went into Afghanistan; the outcome is not yet known, but at the end of the chapter an attempt has been made to project how it will come out, based on the assumptions of the traditional story.

The American military incursion into Afghanistan, from this viewpoint, was an attempt to extend American military power, made because of the conviction of the US leadership that they now had the most powerful country on the planet, probably the most powerful country ever in the history of the planet. In this sense it echoed the Soviet invasion of Afghanistan of December 1979, and the US' own invasion of Vietnam in the 1960s, while the US incursion into Iraq in 2003, also arising from the same basic motivation, echoed it.

After 1990 the US was, as has been pointed out with examples and in more detail in chapter 14, quite generally acclaimed as the sole super power, comparable or even exceeding Rome at the peak of its imperial power. In accordance with the traditional story it had, therefore, to extend its power abroad, even if an empire of the kind the British or French had had was not possible.

There were three themes attached to this: that there was now a new structure of international relations called unipolarity; that the US occupied the top position in it; and that it was, therefore, for the US to take the lead in all IR matters, indeed to make an empire of some kind.

Just two short quotations will suffice; there are several more in chapter 14. The new structure of international relations, with the USA occupying a solitary position at the apex, was compared by Henry Kissinger to the great empires of history: "At the dawn of the new millennium, the United States is enjoying a pre-eminence unrivalled by even the greatest empires of the past ... during the last decade of the twentieth century, America's preponderant position rendered it the indispensable component of international stability."[1] This line of thought led to the transfiguration of the unipolar moment into the imperial moment: "Empires are not always planned", according to an article in *Foreign Affairs*, the American establishment quarterly, and here we glimpse the old argument about the British being reluctant imperialists, followed by "the United States will be an even more reluctant imperialist. But a new imperial moment has arrived."[2]

It was clearly time to acquire an empire.

Two caveats, pointed out in chapter 7, can be reiterated here. First, the war equals power equals war equation was no longer normatively acceptable in public declarations. So while in its dealings with smaller states the US believed in the three-way link between war and power, this could no longer be said in public, where other justifications had to be found for waging war. Second, and more important, the effectiveness of the use of military force by the great powers was declining and that of the smaller countries was increasing. For the US specifically there was the experience of the Vietnam War, which had been added to its somewhat pungent taste of even small-scale military action thereafter. That had been encapsulated in the so-called Tarnoff doctrine. Peter Tarnoff, Undersecretary of State for Political Affairs in the Clinton administration had suggested in May 1993 that the US no longer had the resources to run the world. This was, of course, immediately repudiated by more authoritative commentators, but, as noted at that time by Charles William Maynes, editor of *Foreign Policy*, the US had three serious problems with running the world: the news media had a growing ability to set the country's international agenda; the Cold War geopolitical compass was no longer available to guide the administration; and the American public refused to make available the resources for a vigorous foreign policy.[3]

And so the US became less and less willing to use the military on a large scale, hoping that just a little bit of war, supplemented by simulacra and a general reputation as a great power would somehow achieve the aim. And the decisions to go to war, in Afghanistan and in Iraq eighteen months later, were preceded by much prevarication and foot dragging.

## The US Goes in

In sum, the urge for empire was circumscribed by the reluctance to get one by military means. In any case the US went into Afghanistan not just to extend its power into that country but to extend it into the entire region, since that's the kind of thing great powers, and especially super powers, do; eliminating Al Qaeda was secondary; eliminating the Taliban probably even more remote, tertiary.

It is true that the Al Qaeda attack of 9/11 gave the US an immediate and overwhelming justification to go in. It is equally true that eliminating Al Qaeda and the Taliban could have been done quite simply by an air attack against their defensive positions, which were known. The Northern Alliance (NA),[4] the main group opposing the Taliban government at the time, had, and that too was known, enough strength to complete the job; and, given their history of enmity with both Al Qaeda and the Taliban, and that their leader Ahmed Shah Masud had, two days before 9/11, been assassinated by an Al Qaeda suicide squad, this completion would have been thorough and irreversible. But such an action would have seriously jeopardised American power and influence in Pakistan, the sponsor, actually the creator, of the Taliban; and the US wanted to bring Afghanistan within the fold of their power, while also bringing Pakistan more firmly in.

Recall that this had been US policy since the Taliban emerged, that is, to support the Taliban against the NA. Robin Raphel, for instance, then US Assistant Secretary for South Asia, told a Congressional hearing in 1995 that the Taliban leaders supported a peaceful political process, which was in contrast to the 'factional leaders' (meaning the NA) who did not want to give up their power for the overall good of the country. US officials expressed the hope that, being largely Durrani in origin, the Taliban would allow the return to Afghanistan of Zahir Shah, then in exile in Italy, under whose rule there had been forty years of peace; this would then create the conditions for the construction of gas and oil pipelines from Central Asia through Afghanistan and Pakistan. This was being pushed by Union Oil Company of California, UNOCAL, its partner

Delta Oil of Saudi Arabia and Bridas of Argentina, each of which reportedly put considerable quantities of money into Taliban hands.

In June 1996, a three-day conference on Afghanistan was held in Washington, sponsored by the chairman of the Foreign Relations Sub-committee on the Near East and Southeast Asia of the US Congress, which questioned the legitimacy of the Rabbani government, then battling to keep the Taliban at bay, and called that government the major obstacle to the restoration of peace and stability. Benazir Bhutto, then Prime Minister of Pakistan, told the BBC on 14 October 1996 that the US and Britain had supplied weapons to the Taliban with money provided by Saudi Arabia. Even after the Taliban attracted general opprobrium for their human rights record and the way they treated women, a spokesman of the US State Department said that there was nothing objectionable about the kind of Islamic laws they were enforcing. Robert Oakley, formerly US Ambassador to Pakistan and by then a consultant to UNOCAL, declared at a seminar late in 1996 that the Taliban ideology represented the restoration of traditional and village values to the cities. He suggested to the UNOCAL board that they should get into Kandahar somehow, so the company gave a million dollars to the Taliban for 'training', ostensibly in the technical skills needed for oil exploration, constructing a pipeline; then another twenty million dollars was spent, which seemingly went into Taliban pockets. And Bridas actually opened an office in Kandahar to which they sent three high-powered executives for weeks of negotiations with the Taliban, who, of course, knew no English and certainly no Spanish; actually they knew only Koranic studies.

The time soon came when the Taliban went too far. They arrested and tried to intimidate the European Union Commissioner for Humanitarian Affairs Emma Bonino (along with two prominent journalists, William Shawcross and Christiane Amanpour) on 29 September 1997 because she had a camera which their edicts banned. Press reports against the Taliban also became more strident, since they refused to make any kind of concession, taking a special pleasure, when western reporters were around to watch, in beating up women who violated their dress code and beating up men who didn't have long enough beards. Even so, the statements that US officials made about the Taliban were only mildly critical, and there was still no mention of Osama bin Laden, who was known to have been in Afghanistan under Taliban protection since 1994. And there were not many such statements; in fact, reporting on Afghanistan came down to a trickle; the world tended to lose interest; the Americans didn't want their strategy for Pakistan to run aground on a bank of adverse opinion there.

So that strategy continued after 9/11. President Bush had announced, three days after that attack, in a speech at the National Cathedral, "our responsibility to history is already clear; to answer these attacks and rid the world of evil." He had, if such were required, the authority of the UN Security Council which in Resolution 1368, passed the day after the attack, condemned it as a threat to international peace and security, thus bringing it under chapter VII, which is about military action; as also the authority of NATO; and of the US Congress, which had given him a blank cheque to use "all necessary and appropriate force against those nations, organisations, or persons he determines planned, authorised, committed or aided the terrorist attacks ... or harboured such organisations or persons." But with all those authorizations in his hands he waited; so the Americans did nothing; it began to look like they were stalling. The first choice was to take Pakistan along; to do nothing which would jeopardise the relationship with Pakistan. So an effort was made to persuade the Taliban to hand over Osama or at least get him to leave Afghanistan so the Taliban could continue to rule. A delegation of Pakistani religious figures, accompanied by Mahmood Ahmed, a director in the ISI, went to Kandahar on 17 September, then again on 28 September, in an effort to achieve this; there was no result. Parallel efforts went on to find 'moderate' Taliban who might replace people like Mullah Omar. President Musharraf and Colin Powell held a press conference in late September and proposed this; and the CIA was particularly keen for this to happen, that moderate Taliban "would rise to denounce Mullah Omar, hand over bin Laden to the Americans, and join a new coalition government in Kabul."[5]

Weeks passed; the US conducted some light bombing raids against symbolic targets, raids which were designed not to trouble the Taliban too much. The US still thought, so it seemed, that just a little bit of war would somehow do the trick. October came. On 7 October the US announced that Operation Enduring Freedom, the military action in response to the 9/11 attacks, had begun. Still nothing happened. Musharraf continued to say the moderate Taliban would appear; some people would change sides. A spectacular action was planned and carried out: a Special Operations Force attack on Kandahar on 29 October to get both Mullah Omar and Osama bin Laden; it was badly planned; the US forces were surrounded and suffered heavy casualties; the attack collapsed. It was, finally, not till the first week of November that the US, which now really looked as if it were shilly shallying, decided that the Pakistan option was less important than its own interest in taking decisive action. That meant two things: sustained and heavy bombing of Taliban defenses so that the NA could get in to attack and defeat them in the northern and central towns; and sending US forces into Kandahar and the South and East, since the NA was weak in Pashtun territory and would not be able to deliver the two men that the US wanted. Even at that stage the Pakistan option had not been altogether given up; the US tried to put pressure on the NA not to occupy Kabul once the Taliban government fell.

Heavy bombing raids were accordingly conducted on the Taliban's defensive positions in and around the major towns. Mazar-e-Sharif fell to the NA on 9 November, Maimana two days later, Herat a day later, and Kabul (despite the US pressure) fell to them within a day of that; in less than a week after the heavy bombing started the entire north of Afghanistan had fallen to the NA. The South took longer since the NA was not strong there, Kandahar did not fall till 9 December.

Again, rhetoric, the 'destruction of evil', for instance, demanded that Kandahar be quickly surrounded by US troops so that the leadership of Al Qaeda and the Taliban did not escape. But it was not till late November that significant numbers of US troops arrived there; and there was considerable hesitation in the way they were deployed, reportedly due to the consideration that casualties were to be minimized. So Mullah Omar, who was in Kandahar till early December, escaped to Pakistan; a large number of senior Taliban officials and commanders had already arrived there, airlifted from Kunduz and other centres in the North by the Pakistan Air Force. Note that even after the fall of Kabul the discrepancy between US rhetoric and their actions on the ground continued; for during that airlift it was reported that US forces stood guard while the hundreds of Pakistani regular troops which had been fighting on the side of the Taliban, along with Taliban and possibly Al Qaeda leaders, were whisked away. So the US commitment to Pakistan had not been diluted despite the criticism about its shilly shallying.[6] The Al Qaeda leadership, including Osama bin Laden, went to the Tora Bora caves, on the route to the Pakistan border; the Americans tried to use local commanders to flush them out, the latter were on doubtful commitment, and none of the Al Qaeda leaders was captured or killed.

The war continued its wavering course, as a reading of presidential statements, especially the annual State of the Union message to the US Congress, reveals.

The crusading zeal along with the description of all the dangers presented by terrorists and extremists continued though with decreasing intensity. In his January 2002 message George Bush had described how "thousands of dangerous killers, schooled in the methods of murder, often supported by outlaw regimes, are now spread throughout the world", so first "we will shut down terrorist camps, disrupt terrorist plans, and bring the terrorists to justice"; and second, "we must prevent the terrorists and regimes who seek chemical, biological, or nuclear weapons from threatening the United States and the world." A year later it was a different picture for in January 2003, in his message to Congress, Bush said Al Qaeda and the terrorists "are no longer a problem to the United States and our friends and allies" because key heads of the organisation had been arrested "or otherwise dealt with". In all three thousand had been arrested and "many others have met a different fate." Another year and the picture changed again; in the January 2004 message he stressed "America is on the offensive against the terrorists who started this war" suggesting that there was, after all, a problem, though "our coalition is leading aggressive raids against the surviving members of the Taliban and Al Qaeda." Two years passed and, January 2006, "we remain on the offensive in Afghanistan." It was not a very reassuring message.

And, as the years passed, the message did not get any more cheerful. By 2007, far from the terrorists being no longer a problem, their ambitions seemed to have grown. Now they were on the offensive for in Afghanistan "NATO has taken the lead turning back the Taliban and Al Qaeda offensive"; and now there was mention of the "shoreless ambitions of this enemy ... our enemies want to overthrow moderate governments and establish safe havens from which to carry out new attacks on our country ... they want to force our country to retreat from the world and abandon the cause of liberty ... be free to impose their will and spread their totalitarian ideology."

From the perspective of the traditional story the US, wishing to extend their power into Afghanistan and further consolidate it in Pakistan, had adopted the strategy of a 'light footprint', or, as it was generally said to be, "the desire for a quick cheap war followed by a quick cheap peace"[7] that would achieve all their objectives in Afghanistan without committing too many troops. Until late 2007 the total number of US troops deployed was only 15,000. The UK had some 7,000, Canada and Germany 3,000 each, and total foreign forces were around 41,000. It was not till 2009 that the US decided to increase the numbers of its troops; the numbers would then go up to 68,000, over half of those the Soviet Union had at peak strength level. But then the Soviet Union had to cope with US as well as Pakistani, Iranian and other help to the Mujahidin, including substantial financial aid from Saudi Arabia. For the US there is no such problem; the Taliban are supposed to be on their own, perhaps with some help from Al Qaeda and other like sympathisers, none of whom has comparable resources in money and weapons.

## The Opposition

That brings in the nature of the opposition. There are three groups in opposition. A clear separation needs to be made between Al Qaeda; other terrorist groups, in this case particularly the Pakistani group known as Tehreek-e-Taliban Pakistan or the Pakistani Taliban; and the Taliban of Afghanistan and their supporters.

The first threat is from Al Qaeda. Reports suggest that this continues to be a going concern. Periodic statements from Osama bin Laden and Ayman Zawahiri suggest that it is still being led by the two of them. From time to time Arabs and Uzbeks and others are still found among the dead or injured in the battles for control over the North-west of Pakistan. There is some debate about how active Al Qaeda still is; there have been attacks after 9/11, bombings in Algiers, April 2007, another bombing of the Danish embassy in Pakistan, June 2008, an attack on the US embassy in Sana'a, Yemen, in September 2008; and there have been others, perhaps not as well reported in all cases.

Al Qaeda is a millenarian terrorist group on the lines of the Japanese Aum Shinrikyo, the Ugandan Lord's Resistance Army and the extreme right militias supporting the return of Nazism under a new Hitler. Al Qaeda is bigger, better funded and stronger internationally, but the genre is the same: all the groups set targets which seem, in the face of any reasonable assessment, impossible to achieve: Aum Shinrikyo to save its members from the coming Armageddon or Apocalypse; the Lord's Resistance Army to set up a state based on the biblical ten commandments; the right militias to create or recreate the world of *Mein Kampf*.

And Al Qaeda carries forward the ideas of Sayyid Qutb (1906-1966), often regarded as the leading theoretician of Islamic radicalism. Qutb himself took forward the ideas of Maulana Maududi (1903-1979), Hassan al Banna and others like Muhammed Abd al Salam Faraj. Briefly these focus on establishing by violent means a planet ruled by the tenets of orthodox Islam. As Maududi who categorically placed nationalism and Islam in diametric opposition wrote, "Islam wishes to destroy all States and Governments anywhere on the face of the earth which are opposed to the ideology and programme of Islam". And this is not just to remove those which oppose Islam, but to establish Islam everywhere, meaning that "the objective of Islamic 'Jihad' is to eliminate the rule of an un-Islamic system and establish in its stead an Islamic system of State rule. Islam does not intend to confine this revolution to a single State or a few countries", the aim is a universal revolution.[8]

Qutb took this argument forward by emphasising the violent part of the Jihadi revolution to establish Islamic rule over the world; he insisted that every true Muslim had an obligation to take up arms in order to spread the faith throughout the world and to the whole of mankind. Abdullah Azzam, the mentor of Osama bin Laden, was a disciple of Qutb. It is reported that he was the one who conceptualised Al Qaeda in 1987. "Azzam's greatest contribution was undoubtedly the creation of a mystique of Muslim invincibility."[9]

Azzam inculcated his ideas into Osama, who had actually studied in King Abdul Aziz University, Jeddah, Saudi Arabia, under Mohammed Qutb, Sayyid Qutb's brother. As the two of them worked together in the North-west of Pakistan in the early 1980s to support the Mujahidin in their war against the Soviet forces in Afghanistan, they started seeing the war in Afghanistan as the first step in the coming worldwide Jihad. There, in 1988, Al Qaeda was founded, and within three years Osama had established himself as the chief coordinator of radical Islamic forces worldwide.

Even before 9/11 the classic argument of a division of the world into two, the House of Faith, Dar al Islam and the House of War, Dar al Harb, comprising everyone who was not a believer, was used by Osama and his followers, as in the much publicised World Islamic Front statement or fatwa of 23 February 1998, that to "kill the Americans and their allies – civilians and military – is an individual duty for every Muslim who can do it in any country in which it is possible to do it." Between the two houses there is an obligatory state of war which will continue until the final and inevitable triumph of Islam. This justifies every act of violence, the killing of Germans in Tunisia, of the French in Karachi, the British and Australians in the Bali explosions. After 9/11 this division between the two worlds sharpened, and Osama emphasised that the war waged by the Americans in Iraq is not between the US and Iraq, or between Saddam and Bush; it is "between you, all our Muslim brothers, and us on the one side and the crusaders and the Jews on the other."[10] After 9/11, of course, the same division of the world into two, those who are with us and those who are against us, with a perpetual state of war between the two, was sanctified by the US President.

Osama's statements repeatedly stress the importance of the defence of Muslim brothers and sisters in Palestine and the liberation of the holy places, meaning Mecca and Medina, but more broadly the whole of Saudi Arabia, from the presence of foreign troops, or from US occupation; and even justifies the 9/11 attacks for these two reasons.[11] However, far from the larger global aims such as converting the planet into Islam, even these more modest goals cannot be achieved by terrorism. These millenarian goals are intended to give heightened motivation and inspiration to individual acts of terrorism, specially suicide terrorism, and to bring legitimation to a sacred leadership. This does not make Al Qaeda and its sister organisations like the Pakistani Taliban less dangerous; in some ways it makes them more so, since Muslims everywhere get increasingly conscious of the persecutions and deprivations suffered by Muslims in different parts of the world, and with the kind of sophisticated material produced by organisations like the Global Islamic Media Front, and the use they make of the internet, there is a much higher chance of some of them taking action into their own hands.

Secondly, there is the Pakistani Taliban or Tehreek-e-Taliban Pakistan (TTP), formed in December 2007 largely by the efforts of Baitullah Mahsud. He did say that he was a follower of the Taliban Emir, Mullah Mohammed Omar, but then he goes on to apocalyptic aims, which are far beyond any capabilities he could ever acquire, saying he will wage jihad in Pakistan and Afghanistan, in Palestine, Bosnia and Iraq as well; and eradicate Britain and America, destroy the White House, New York and London; and ends with 'soon, we will see the miracles of jihad."[12] Over time the TTP seems to have become "more and more integrated with Al Qaeda both from an ideological and a strategic-military standpoint." One of the organisation's deputies said that the TTP and Al Qaeda are two sides of the same coin, the former fighting the infidel on the international front and the latter within the Pakistan-Afghanistan region.[13]

## The Main Opposition

But the Afghan Taliban is a very different opposition, different from the other two in leadership, in aims, and in what they have achieved so far; and now increasingly different from that Taliban which was created by Pakistan; and it has a quite limited aim: freeing Afghanistan from foreign military occupation. The Taliban has not, except in passing, made mention of a global Jihad or struggle between Muslims everywhere and non-Muslims, or of an Islamic universe; they wish only to expel foreign troops and establish an Islamic Emirate in Afghanistan, roughly on the lines that existed from 1996 to 2001. It is a limited territorial aim.

So this third is the main threat to the US in Afghanistan.

True, the Afghan Taliban did give shelter to Al Qaeda leaders and cadres during the period they were in government in Afghanistan, 1996 to 2001. This was in recognition of their contribution to the struggle to expel Soviet troops. And they undoubtedly knew about Al Qaeda's plans to attack various targets during that time, including the 9/11 attacks. But they seem not to have played any role in the planning of any of these attacks; nor were there any Afghans who took part in any of them. They did, after 9/11, refuse to hand over Osama bin Laden to the Americans, at thus risking the destruction of their leadership and government. However, even had the Americans produced reasonably conclusive evidence of the involvement of Al Qaeda, that would have been irrelevant, since Melmastia is one of the strongest Afghan traditions, that you must never hand over a guest to those he is wanted by, even if that guest be your sworn enemy, and even if those who want him do so for the right reasons.

Admittedly also the Afghan Taliban originated as a Pakistani creation, unlike Al Qaeda and the TTP. The aim was to bring Afghanistan firmly into the Pakistani sphere of influence. But it was also the aim of Pakistan that the Pashtuns should remain divided among themselves, the Durrani from the Ghilzai, as well as other divisions, so that from both sides of the border they would have to look to Pakistan for leadership, rather than to the prospects of an autonomous or independent state. The Pashtuns should also remain divided from the other ethnic groups, so that nationalism weakened and the unsettled status continued. However, after the fall of the Soviet-backed Najibullah government in April 1992, Ahmad Shah Masud and the Hazaras were quick to move into Kabul seizing all the strategic points and taking control of government; the Pashtun groups supported by Pakistan especially the Hizbe Islami of Gulbuddin Hekmatyar was excluded from control over the capital but Pakistan continued to instigate and to back its efforts to get in by force. The August 1992 rocket attack on Kabul, and the more intense barrage of rockets fired from January 1994, which destroyed half of what remained standing and killed some 25,000 civilians, were parts of this effort; and this, of course, was what led to criticism of the Mujahidin and the allegations about their creating a civil war. At the end of all this Gulbuddin Hekmatyar was no closer to controlling Kabul. Indeed, those of the local commanders of the jihad against the Soviet forces who had retained some independence from Pakistan, appeared to be getting stronger, and this included many Tajik, Uzbek and Hazara leaders and groups, the exact opposite of what had been intended.

So the Taliban was launched by Pakistan as a Pashtun group to get the drivers of Pakistani policy going again. A considerable change of direction was involved. Financed largely with foreign money seven major Mujahidin groups or parties had been trained and equipped for over a decade. All of them would have to be abandoned. The success of the Taliban is traceable to the resolute manner in which Pakistan accepted the need for and then implemented this radical change of direction. Liberal assistance to the Taliban was paralleled by the stoppage of all aid to the other groups from early 1994. Pakistani manpower was used not only to boost the strength of the Taliban militarily, but, once Kabul had been captured, to man the government departments as advisers.

This did not entirely change after 9/11. When Mullah Mohammed Omar sought shelter in Quetta thereafter he was allowed to do so, and even to reorganise the leadership of the Taliban. By then the Jamaat-ul-Ulema Islam (JUI), which had been crucial for the initiation of the Taliban, was in power in both of Pakistan's provinces bordering Afghanistan. So, as the Taliban fighters flowed into Pakistan, fleeing from the American attack, "the full state machinery and facilities of the provisional (sic) governments were now available to the Taliban, with the help of ministers such as Maulana Faizullah, the JUI minister of agriculture in Baluchistan who had fought in Kandahar alongside Mullah Omar until the city was abandoned." At a later stage, in June 2006, US, NATO and Afghan intelligence compiled their information in a report which "described Pakistan's role in the most unflattering light of any intelligence report so far", including references to ISI operatives paying the Taliban, the fact that many of the fighters were continuing to fight because of pressure by the ISI, and the essential role of the sanctuary in Pakistan for the survival of the Taliban.[14]

Despite all this the traditional story is clear that today the Afghan Taliban have to be treated as a separate entity whose sole aim is to create a movement to expel US forces, one which accommodates as many as possible of those who have battle experience. But it is increasingly a national movement. Spokesmen for the Afghan Taliban have been repeatedly emphasising that their links with the Pakistani Taliban are based solely on the brotherly sympathy of one Muslim for another who is struggling. But the struggles are quite different. As the *New York Times* reported on 26 March 2009, the spokesman for the Afghan Taliban, Zabiullah Majid emphasised that no emissaries had been sent by the Afghan Taliban to the Pakistani Taliban, nor was there any meeting between them, for "we don't like to be involved with them, as we have rejected all affiliation with the Pakistani Taliban fighters. We have sympathy for them as Muslims, but beside that, there is nothing else between us." In another interview conducted by Nic Robertson and reported by *CNN* on 5 May 2009, Majid stressed that "Taliban is one thing and Al Qaeda is another. They are global but we are just in the region. We are not under the command of Al Qaeda".

So it is generally true that since those years things have evolved; the Taliban has not remained entirely subservient to Pakistan. There were, of course, Pashtun personnel from the Pakistani paramilitary and armed forces in it from the outset; but there were also breakaway officers and personnel from the Khalq wing of the PDPA, the Soviet-sponsored party in Afghanistan; and a mixed groups of Pashtun fighters from some of the seven original Mujahidin groups, particularly from the Harakat-e-Inqilab Islami of Maulvi Mohammed Nabi Mohammedi, a former parliamentarian and supporter of the former King Zahir Shah, and a breakaway faction of the Hizbe Islami, led by Maulvi Yunus Khalis, a Pashtun from the Khugiani tribe which is strong in Kandahar. Another one is Jalaluddin Haqqani of the Jadran tribe, one of the leading commanders of the war against the Soviet troops and a Minister in the 1996 to 2001 Taliban government; he has built up considerable strength along the Pakistan-Afghan border, in Khost and Paktika, and now his son Sirajjudin Haqqani is reported to have launched a number of attacks against the American forces. There is also Gulbuddin Hekmatyar, often but not always subservient to Pakistan, who at one stage was opposed to the Taliban and is now reportedly with them. His party, the Hizbe Islami, has been successful in recreating its base of support in some of the northern provinces, including Badakhshan and Kunduz. Another component is the Talib or religious students from the madrasas along the Afghan-Pakistan border, from which the name Taliban came, but these were the least important, there only to give Islamic respectability. The Taliban have also successfully sought support among the Tatars, the Turkmens and the Uzbek populations of the North. So now, the Taliban have successfully co-opted many of those who were against them, had fought the Soviet troops and, therefore, had considerable battle experience.

As the war goes forward it can be anticipated that the Afghan Taliban will attempt to build alliances with other groups also, including non-Pashtun groups, though Pashtun dominance of the movement is likely to continue. However, it is fundamental to understand the traditional story's version of Afghanistan's future that this now looks more and more like a nationalist movement attempting to evict foreign forces from their country and that this will be successful. It has always been, as Mullah Omar rightly says, a matter of Afghan pride expressed now through the Taliban that the foreigner whose armies enter the country should be seen off by violent means.

Over the years since 2002 frequent visitors to Afghanistan report that the Taliban has become a unified, highly centralised, well coordinated and insistently motivated organisation. It is flexible enough to give local commanders the autonomy they need to carry out operations, and has shown a continuing ability to improve their fighting abilities. So it is not divided into disparate groups, it is not primitive or loosely organised but the local autonomy given to commanders is a strength not a weakness.[15]

It is, in other words, a growing force and one which is decreasingly under Pakistan's full control.

There is still a great deal left of the original Taliban aims, when Mullah Mohammed Omar declared himself Amir-ul-Momineen at a council of Ulema held in the early 1990s with the aim to end the mischief, meaning the fighting between the different Mujahidin groups, to establish peace and security, to protect life, wealth and honour and to enforce the Shariah. The last aim is still as prominent as before in Taliban pronouncements. And there is still no idea of social or economic reconstruction in their aims. But there are no millenarian aims such as those of Al Qaeda or the Pakistani Taliban. The Afghan Taliban has focused on Afghanistan, on driving out the foreign forces and on implementing an Islamic social order. On 29 December 2006, for instance, Mullah Mohammed Omar released a statement through his spokesman Mohammed Hanif, that "Afghans have a history of expelling their enemies as no enemy and invader has quit Afghanistan willingly", so that is their aim, to totally defeat them and force them out of the country.

## The Course of the War

By early 2003, the Taliban had recovered sufficiently from the initial American attack to start launching attacks. These started in Helmand and Zabul and Kandahar provinces in the South bordering Baluchistan, where Mullah Mohammed Omar had his operational headquarters. The attacks, small scale at first, increased in numbers with time: an ICRC convoy held up in Uruzgan in March; two US soldiers shot dead the same month in Helmand; an Italian tourist killed in April in Zabul; as well as others of the same magnitude.

In June 2003 Mullah Omar had reorganised, set up a ten-man

leadership council, launched vigorous training schedules for his fighters and ordered increased attacks. So "in the summer of 2003 one or two attacks by the Taliban occurred every other day ... on a single day, August 13, 50 people were killed in multiple attacks in three provinces."[16] These were also in larger formations, up to 300 men in one operation rather than the twenty and thirty-man teams that had launched the attacks so far. And by mid-2005 there were new tactics: sophisticated and continuously improved IEDs, of which the number deployed increased exponentially from year to year; motivated suicide bombings, both learned from the Iraqi resistance; and the Taliban were increasingly learning that to reduce your own casualties while increasing those of the enemy, you had to stand up and fight, no matter how inferior your weapons; that way the casualties would at first be heavy, but as you learnt to deal with the heavier equipment of the enemy in the long run, they would come down. They also learnt, with time, how to launch frontal attacks on US and other international coalition positions, which were unknown till 2006.

So the attacks went on increasing. During the years 2005 and 2006, as the US military reported, the number of suicide attacks increased from 27 to 139; remotely detonated bomb attacks from 783 to 1677; and armed assaults rose three times, from 1588 to 4542. From 2006 to 2007 attacks overall rose 27 per cent; 60 per cent in Helmand province. As a United States Congressional Research Service (CRS) report, see following page, observed somewhat coyly, "an upsurge of violence in mid-2006 took some observers by surprise because the insurgency had been at low level for several years, and there has been a widely held view among observers that the Taliban are politically unpopular, even in the conservative Pashtun areas where the movement is operating."

Above all, and most important, they have consistently been ahead in the propaganda battle; through videos, the internet, cell phones, night letters and word of mouth they have managed to convince the people that the foreigner is targeting civilians, is there to stay and must be evicted, that all must join in this effort. And this is not a message directed to Pashtuns alone; it is to all Afghans.

As for the US effort to counter all this, an early indication of the way the war could go was 'Operation Anaconda' launched on 1 March 2002 by US forces into the mountains near Gardez in order to smoke out Taliban fighters who had taken shelter there.

Everything went wrong. Two Chinook helicopters were shot down by the Taliban almost immediately. And they were present in much larger strength than US intelligence had estimated. Eight Americans were killed and eighty wounded, many of whom would also have been killed but for body armour. The Taliban fighters retreated into Pakistan with no significant losses, though the Americans claimed eight hundred killed.

The US launched a further series of offensives: 'Operation Mountain Viper' in August 2003; 'Operation Avalanche' in December that year; 'Operation Mountain Storm' in March to July 2004; the appropriately named 'Operation Lightning Freedom' from December 2004 to February 2005, to mention just a few. By then the US commanders did believe, as indicated in the CRS report by Kenneth Katzman, titled *Afghanistan: Post-War Governance, Security, and U.S. Policy* and updated on 1 November 2007,[17] that they had been able to weaken the insurgency to the point of virtual irrelevance. But all these operations were just a prelude, skirmishes in which the Taliban were sizing up the enemy.

This was apparent from the way the territory under their control expanded. By the end of the year 2003 the Taliban reportedly controlled eighty per cent of Zabul province and extensive border areas in the three provinces of Paktika, Khost and Kunar.

By 2006 there was a Taliban presence (as opposed to control) in 75 per cent of the country, meaning it had spread to the North, the non-Pashtun areas, as contrasted with the previous year, when it had been confined to the South and East of Afghanistan. The International Council on Security and Development, an independent think-tank, reported that in 2007 the Taliban controlled 54 per cent of the country. So in any case by 2007 the Taliban were almost fully in control of some provinces, like Wardak, where they had set-up a government, installed mayors in the towns, police chiefs and an entire administration; or in Logar, where they had completed the establishment of a parallel judiciary, administrative set up and policing system, a province in which, excepting the main highway and the NATO forces camp, everything was under Taliban control.

Seeing this former British Foreign Secretary Malcom Rifkind asserted that the Taliban was stronger than at any time since 9/11, and suggested in June 2007 that since the war was not being won the West must turn to Pakistan. For winning in Afghanistan "the key will be winning full Pakistanis' support ... it needs a more sophisticated approach, one that recognises legitimate Pakistani concerns and interests."[18]

By 2008 the area under control had increased to 72 per cent, and the Council put maps on their website[19] showing in dark pink precisely the areas controlled, and where it was dangerous for international travellers or Afghan government employees to go. In Kabul itself three out of the four roads leading out of the city were "compromised by Taliban activity", as the Council reported; the roads leading west through Wardak to Kandahar, south to Logar, east to Jalalabad as well as one of the roads leading north, the one to the Bagram airbase, were unsafe. As for the city, most of it was dark pink, meaning either there was a significant Taliban presence or criminal activity of other kinds made the areas unsafe.

Other reports suggested that by 2008 Badghis and Kunduz in the North, Farah and Ghor in the West, areas where the Taliban had never really had any strength, were insecure as far as the travel of foreigners and of Afghan officials was concerned; other NGOs published maps showing areas where it was unsafe to go and these got filled up, as the year passed, with shades of pink and yellow, the pinker the more extreme the risk.

There was thus reason for Admiral Michael Mullen, Chairman of the US Joint Chiefs of Staff, telling the House Armed Services Committee on 8 September 2008: "I'm not convinced we're winning the war."[20] A British officer summed it up more succinctly, saying in October 2008, "we're not going to win this war. It's about reducing it to a manageable level of insurgency that's not a strategic threat..." And he suggested talking to the Taliban, which is "precisely the sort of progress that concludes insurgencies like this."[21] Some months later David Miliband, the British Foreign Secretary, echoed this. July 2009 had been the deadliest month for British casualties and he suggested a viable political solution was essential alongside the military offensive; the insurgents should be reintegrated into society, given a role in local and central government. "Talk to them" he summed up. We are back to the Pakistan option, with which it all started.

Here we also glimpse elements of modernity, as if the war was not really important. Michael Mullen, for instance, added in his statement that what is needed is better Afghan governance, more foreign investment, a viable alternative to poppy farming, greater cooperation with Pakistan and more US non-military assistance. Over the years there has been no shortage of reports recommending similar action. Just one can be cited: a report of 2 November 2006 by a think-tank, the International Crisis Group, suggests: that the Government of Afghanistan should launch an anti-corruption drive, revive and push ahead with action for 'Peace, Reconciliation and Justice', identify why the Afghan National Army is doing so poorly in retaining personnel; while the US and Allied Governments should emphasise the rule of law; the NATO/ISAF Governments should pressure Pakistan to hand over Taliban leaders; and the UN should ensure all parties are called to account.

After Barrack Obama became the President, in particular, modernity emerged stronger. Now it was suggested that the Taliban were disunited, divided into an ideological or hardcore group; a larger number of mercenaries who could be brought over the side of the government by political and financial means; and the largest number, the foot soldiers, who had joined only for the sake of earning some money and who could be brought or bought over by job offers. Fareed Zakaria, formerly editor of the influential *Foreign Affairs*, wrote in *Newsweek* (9 February 2009) that US policy should separate, "as often as possible, the global jihadist from the accidental guerilla", and this was a policy approach fully approved by the Afghan government. Obama himself said at one time that there "may be some opportunities in Afghanistan" and Karzai seized on this with approval, saying Obama "accepted and approved the path of peace and talks with those Afghan Taliban who he calls moderates".[22]

The traditional story suggests that all these are signs that the war is being lost. So the Americans and their NATO allies are not going to win the war in Afghanistan. An inevitable consequence of this, and it is a consequence that will be seen quite soon, is that American, and probably even before that all the other NATO forces, will leave Afghanistan without having defeated the Taliban.

The US retreat may not mean the immediate establishment of a Taliban government in Kabul; in Vietnam after the US forces completed their withdrawal, in Afghanistan after the Soviet forces finally left, governments friendly to each of them remained in power for two years or more. But the retreat will point to a future in which the Taliban has a much greater say in Kabul, even if the possibility of prolonged factionalist strife, as happened after the fall of the

Najibullah government in 1992, cannot be avoided.

But while the situation in Afghanistan may remain fluid after the US retreat, that retreat will have major consequences for US power worldwide. Some of these consequences have been sketched out at the end of the next chapter.

## ENDNOTES

[1] Henry Kissinger, *Does America Need a Foreign Policy? Towards a Diplomacy for the 21st Century*, Simon and Schuster, New York, 2001, p. 17.

[2] Sebastian Mallaby, The Reluctant Imperialist, Terrorism, Failed States, and the case for American Empire, in *Foreign Affairs*, Mar/April, 2002, Vol 81, No. 2, p. 6.

[3] *Foreign Policy*, No. 93, Winter, 1993-94, p. 3.

[4] The government left behind when Soviet troops withdrew from Afghanistan was led by President Najibullah and fell in April, 1992, to be replaced by one led by a combination of Mujahidin groups; when the Taliban came to power they replaced this. President Rabbani and his Mujahidin group, who had been evicted by the Taliban, became the core of the Northern Alliance, now led more notably by Ahmed Shah Masud, who we have come across in chapter 11. The Tajiks were dominant in it, but there was also representation from the Uzbeks, the Hazaras and some Pashtuns.

[5] Ahmed Rashid, *Descent into Chaos*, Allen Lane, London, 2008, p. 72.

[6] Gilles Dorronsoro puts it rather delicately: some of these were evacuated to Pakistan by air, with US approval, in a nocturnal operation lasting two weeks. See p. 325 of his book *Revolution Unending, Afghanistan: 1979 to the Present,* Hurst, London, 2005. See also pp. 317-324 for an account of how the US tried the 'Pakistan solution' for weeks after 'Operation Enduring Freedom' got under way, and failed.

[7] The phrase used by the International Crisis Group, see their *Asia Report* No. 123 of 2 November 2006, available on their website.

[8] For Maududi's views on nationalism see Wilfred Cantwell Smith, Islam in Modern History, Princeton University Press, 1957, p. 75, n. 61. The quote is from Abul ala Maududi, *Jihad in Islam*, Islamic Publications, Lahore, Pakistan, pp. 8 and 9.

[9] Walter Laquer, *No End to War, Terrorism in the Twenty-First Century*, Continuum, New York, 2003, p. 51.

[10] See the *FBIS*, Foreign Broadcast Information Service report of January 2004, on the internet, giving a translated compilation of statements by Osama bin Laden from 1994 to January 2004: p. 56 for the World Islamic Front fatwa; p. 230 for the statement on the war being between all the Muslims on one side and the crusaders and Jews on the other. There are several statements in this selection of quotations highlighting the nature of this war being between all Muslims and all crusaders and Jews.

[11] See, for instance, *FBIS*, n. 3 above, p. 234, for a statement made in an interview given on 21 October 2001.

[12] From an interview with Baitullah Mahsud, describing himself as the Emir of the Pakistani Taliban, given to *Al-Jazeera*, aired on 25 January 2008, and reported in The Middle East Media Research Institute, Special Despatch series No. 1830, 30 January 2008.

[13] From Claudio Franco, The Evolution of the Taliban in Pakistan during the February-May 2008 Period: The Peace Accord Era, on the website: nefafoundation.org

[14] Ahmed Rashid, op. cit., pp. 243 and 368.

[15] See Gilles Dorronsoro, *The Taliban's Winning Strategy in Afghanistan*, Carnegie Endowment for International Peace, Washington D.C., 2009.

[16] Ahmed Rashid, op. cit., p. 247.

[17] This is available on the CRS website; accessed on 30 November 2007.

[18] Malcolm Rifkind, If we ignore Pakistan, we won't solve Afghanistan, in *The Independent*, 11 June 2007.

[19] The website is icosgroup.net and the information given here is from the different pages of that site, including one titled 'Advance of the Taliban: Maps'.

[20] As reported by *CBS New.com*, Washington, on 10 September 2008.

[21] Brigadier Mark Carleton-Smith quoted by Caroline Gammel in *The Telegraph*, 5 October 2008.

[22] See Syed Salahuddin, Afghan Leader Karzai Backs Obama's Call on Taliban, *Reuters*, 8 March 2009.

# 13

# Iraq: the 2003 Invasion and After

On grounds very similar to those that dictated the invasion of Afghanistan, the US decided to extend its power into Iraq in March 2003. This chapter tells that story, again with an attempt to project it into the future on the basis of the traditional story.

At the end of the chapter I have inserted a section on the consequences of the traditional story for the global distribution of power.

## The US Goes in

Despite the ripples of the Tarnoff doctrine (see chapter 12) when George Bush became President in 2001, there was less foot dragging in the approach to the war in Iraq than there had been in the case of Afghanistan. In contrast to the latter, where the *cause finale* was evident here, there was none, or at least it was difficult to demonstrate. So domestic opinion was against it; so was international opinion.

But Iraq, looked like an easy target to the political (though not the military) leadership, in contrast to that graveyard of invaders, Afghanistan.[1] Furthermore, though opinion might have been against the war, nobody liked Saddam Hussain, nobody would really mind if he was removed; while in Afghanistan, though the Taliban government was unpopular, there were complications about how Pakistan would react, about access to a landlocked country, about the terrain on which fighting would happen.

Anyway a small group led by the neocons was determined to launch this war. Already by 1994 Paul Wolfowitz, later to become

Under Secretary for Policy in the Defense Department under the Bush presidency and Dick Cheney, later to be Vice-President, had explicitly proposed a military invasion of Iraq. Over the years other neo-conservatives joined him and in January 1998 he, along with Donald Rumsfeld, later to be Secretary of Defense, and William Kristol wrote a letter along with others urging President Clinton "to take all necessary diplomatic and military measures to depose Saddam Hussein."[2] Later that year the US Congress passed an Iraq Liberation Act authorising financial support for approved Iraqi opposition groups.

After George Bush became President a new 'Office of Plans' was set up under the Secretary of Defense Donald Rumsfeld mainly to prepare plans for the invasion of Iraq. And then came the attack on the US on 9/11; both Dick Cheney and Donald Rumsfeld hoped they could take advantage of this to promote their agenda on Iraq, meaning launch the invasion by blaming Saddam Hussain for the attack; Deputy Secretary of Defense Paul Wolfowitz actually argued for a simultaneous attack on Iraq and Afghanistan.[3] Attempts were made to overcome possible domestic opposition to such a course, to convince the American public that the invasion of Iraq was necessary. The resources of a think-tank, *The Project for the New American Century,* were brought in; articles appeared in the newspapers and in important journals about Iraq's continued efforts to acquire weapons of mass destruction, Saddam Hussain's brutal repression of his people and his alleged 1993 sponsoring of an attempt to assassinate former President George H.W. Bush.

As for opinion in the international community, the doubts were to some extent overtaken by the enormous wave of international sympathy for the US after 9/11. As one writer noted, before 9/11 many countries had reservations about assertive US behaviour. But thereafter, "all those already hesitant moves came to an abrupt stop. Instead, governments cheered and much of the world stood by as the US asserted the rights of empire …there was a rush to join the US crusade even before it was clear just what it was that other nations were joining. Seventy-six governments granted landing rights in their countries for US military operations. Twenty-three governments offered bases for US forces involved in offensive operations."[4]

And after the Taliban had been removed from Afghanistan the efforts by this group to get the Iraq war going redoubled. Henry

Kissinger wrote in the *Washington Post* on 13 January 2002 that the US could build on Phase I of the anti-terror campaign and move on to Phase II, Iraq. Bush also took full advantage of all this to work up international enthusiasm. His State of the Union address, 29 January 2002, was a ringing call to arms, "once again, this nation and all our friends are all that stand between a world at peace, and a world of chaos and constant alarm..." adding that the US is called to defend the hopes of mankind. In September that year he was at the United Nations telling the assembled delegates that they have to make a stand to prevent the great horrors that would result if Iraq's regime is left intact, that "by heritage and by choice, the United States of America will make that stand." Other things followed: Secretary of State Powell's plea to the United Nations Security Council about Iraq's nexus with the Al Qaeda terrorist network, Saddam's determination to keep and to make more weapons of mass destruction, his violations of human rights, imprisoning, torturing and killing hundreds of thousands of Iraqis. The idea was to build up international enthusiasm for military action in Iraq; trends had been such that the Americans didn't want to go it alone. The US did need allies and would have preferred the whole operation to go forward under cover of a UNSC resolution.

But it didn't, eventually, work out that way; they were not able to get any UN approval and by the first week of March it had become clear that only the UK, Spain and Bulgaria would support the US; even permanent members of the Security Council, on whom so far they could rely, backed out; as Bush stated somewhat delicately on the eve of the invasion, 17 March 2003, they shared the US assessment of the danger, "but not our resolve to meet it." France and Germany openly opposed the war and even declared they were not convinced Iraq had links with Al Qaeda. Turkey, another NATO ally, refused to give the US the rights of military passage, so there was not going to be a northern front; in the event the Kurds had to be persuaded to make diversionary maneouvres.

In any case, as far as the US Congress was concerned, Iraq's links with Al Qaeda, its 'continuing to aid and harbour other international terrorist organisations' and the past efforts of the US Congress and the President to fight terrorists, could be, and were, added to the text of the resolution that was finally presented to the Congress in October 2002, and passed that month, authorising the President to use the Armed Forces of the United States, as he determines to be necessary and appropriate, to defend US security against the continuing Iraqi threat and 'to enforce all relevant United Nations Security Council Resolutions regarding Iraq.' So on that side the path was clear.

The US military was still reluctant, though plans for the invasion of Iraq had been initiated at the beginning of the year 2002. Iraq had a large army; its elite units in the Republican Guard were still intact. William Arkin, for instance, had reported in the *Los Angeles Times*, 7 May 2002 that a February 2002 Defense Agency plan showed what a military attack on Iraq would look like, that the plan "clearly presents toppling Hussain's regime as a challenge so formidable that only tremendous military resources could accomplish it. Then a more detailed invasion plan was leaked in June 2002 which reflected military unease and acknowledged that up to 250,000 American troops would have to be deployed.

But Iraq had to be weaker than ever before; it certainly was, compared to the early years of Saddam Hussain's rule. In 1990, when it invaded, occupied and annexed Kuwait, it had some 450,000 under arms, although its armed forces had not yet fully recovered from the eight-year war with Iran, 1980-88. At that time, in order just to get Kuwait free of Iraqi troops with no intention of pushing on into Iraq itself, the US needed almost a million troops: nearly 700,000 of its own, helped by another 200,000 of its allies, mainly Saudi Arabia (75,000), the UK (45,000), Egypt (35,000) and France (18,000). Withal a bombing campaign of over five weeks, some two thousand sorties a day, conducted round the clock, hitting Iraq's air defences, military command centres, airports, oil refineries, was needed to soften it up before the ground forces felt confident enough to advance into Kuwait. And at that time there were no international political obstacles; the UN Security Council had given the go-ahead; the coalition which the US had put together included all the Arab gulf states, Syria, Morocco, even Pakistan and Bangladesh.

Iraq's infrastructure had already been destroyed in the initial bombing: communications, electricity, water purification plants; a UN official had reported after a March 1991 visit about the devastation that "has wrought near-apocalyptic results upon the economic infrastructure" relegating Iraq, for some time to come, to a pre-industrial age.[5]

For twelve years thereafter Iraq was systematically and progressively weakened further. First by the sanctions that prevented food and medicine getting in; Iraq had always been heavily dependent on imports of these. Malnutrition and disease caused infant mortality to triple from 1984-89 to 1994-99.[6] UNICEF concluded that they killed half a million children, with concomitant effects on adults; other reliable estimates were that altogether almost a million people had died of malnutrition and disease traceable to the sanctions. Inevitably this degraded Iraq's fighting abilities. And secondly there were the air strikes. Through those twelve years Iraqi targets, anything that looked like an anti-aircraft battery or other defensive installation, buildings which looked suspicious or not, other random targets, were periodically hit by American aircraft; sometimes British aircraft joined in. In December 1998 came four days of far more intense bombing with a code name, 'Operation Desert Fox'; the targets were suspicious buildings, suspicious because they might hold Iraqi weapons of mass destruction, but this also served to further weaken Iraq. In February and April of that year the main oil export pipeline was hit and destroyed. In 2000 there were friendly visits to Iraq by the Presidents of Venezuela and Indonesia; the US didn't like that; more air strikes. "The United States justified these strikes in ideological and moral terms, demonising Saddam as a personification of the world evil ... used the strikes as an instrument of political pressure almost every time the UN Security Council met to discuss the Iraqi problem."[7]

So Iraq was much weaker than it might have been.

The military operation began on 20 March 2003. The US had deployed 250,000 troops, followed by the UK with 45,000. Others, Spain, of course, but also Australia and Denmark, contributed; even Poland put in a two hundred-man contingent. Opposing them were 540,000 Iraqi defenders plus, reportedly, 80,000 elite Republican Guards, and 650,000 reserves.

There was no extensive preliminary bombardment from the air, as had been done in 1991. That kind of bombardment was not necessary; there had already been twelve years of bombardment. But as proof of just how far ahead US military technology was, compared to anyone else, the munitions used got a great deal of publicity: laser-guided hell fire missiles; thermobaric weapons, the MOAB or massive ordnance air blast bomb, at 21,500 pounds the 'mother of all bombs'. And there was not a lot of fighting; many

Iraqi units surrendered without any fight at all.

Here and there the Iraqi defence forces fought. Umm Qasr, the only Iraqi port, took several days for the Americans to clear; Nasiriyah, several hundred kilometres up the Euphrates, was the site of the first major battle from 23 to 29 March and there were significant US losses, nearly 30 killed and 50 wounded, but you would not call that major casualties. At the Debecka pass, an important junction between Mosul and Kirkuk in the North there was a five-hour tank battle on the 6 April. Baghdad saw some heavy fighting and was finally occupied by 9 April and the last major centre, Tikrit, Saddam Hussain's home town, was taken on 15 April. Saddam himself was not there, nor was he caught in Baghdad; some months later he did get caught and was hanged in public.

Meanwhile, on 1 May 2003, on board the USS Abraham Lincoln, President Bush stated that major combat operations had ended; 139 Americans had been killed, many by their own colleagues, accidentally.

## History, Geography and the Iraqi Nation

Now we can look at the other side of the picture.

History and geography make Iraq a nation in the most elemental sense. The earliest known civilisation appeared along the valleys of the Tigris and the Euphrates, and the lands around. This meant a number of things: the replacement of herding by the domestication of animals and of a hunter gatherer economy by settled farming; a dramatic increase in the density of population since settled farming could support many more people than nomadism; hence urbanisation, cities where the production of goods became specialised, generating surpluses over and above those of settled farming; a political organisation to maintain an ordered hierarchy and a religious organisation including the evolution of a priestly class; and, of course, culture, above all, a written language but also the development of the visual and performing arts.

There were three places where civilisation flowered earlier than anywhere else, and in each case this was due to the existence of a fertile plain irrigated by dependable water from a perennial river system: Mesopotamia; the Nile valley; and the Indus valley. In each case, apart from the consciousness of the ancient roots of their civilisation, people through the generations have retained a culture founded on the geography of water, the ceaseless effort to acquire and build upon the engineering skills necessary to control and to make use of the perennial water supply, to construct and maintain irrigation systems, to expand the area under crops and to intensify cropping and cultivation patterns, in short, the effort to control the forces of nature.

Iraq and the river systems at its heart are inextricably bound together. Indeed al-Iraq is the expression that has been used for twelve hundred years to describe the shores all along the Tigris and the Euphrates, the irrigated farming land beyond and the grazing areas further beyond.

Long before that, around 3,500 BC, the civilisation of Sumer had appeared in the region. There were a number of city states, frequently at war with each other, but with a shared culture. The great cities like Eridu, Ur and Uruk yielded thousands of cuneiform tablets to later archaeologists, with prayers, hymns, legends and the more mundane records of business transactions written on them. Each city had a political hierarchy, a priestly class charged with acquiring the skills of the soothsayers, propitiating the pantheon of gods, which included the goddess Ishtar, the Sumerian Aphrodite, through elaborate ritual, and organising education. One of the best-known products of the Sumerian language, the epic of Gilgamesh, is about a ruler who restlessly attempts to control the forces of nature. He was not only the first hero of literature; he was probably the first man ever to have been known to succeeding generations of mankind by a name.

Meanwhile, Sumer had been under attack by nomad populations to the West and North-west; sometime around 2,400 BC it succumbed to a nomadic ruler, Sargon I, who conquered the cities and began the Akkadian supremacy. He combined the city states under one empire, and then went further afield, into Egypt in the West and up to Ethiopia in the South, probably the first imperial venture in history. In effect, the nomadism of Akkad and the culture of Sumer combined to produce a new great empire from 1,800 BC: Babylon under the rule of the great Hammurabi who ruled for about forty years from 1792 BC, and famously gave his people a Code of Law, again the first ever, 285 articles covering property, business and commercial law, the land, family law, injuries, labour. Even more famously he prescribed *lex talionis*, an eye for an eye, as a principle of law, as well as the practice of trial by ordeal.

Babylon under Hammurabi and his successors was a great state not just for its imperial and legal system; not just for the opulence and grandeur of its palaces and public buildings where consumption for pleasure reached levels unknown till then, but also for its attainments in science and astronomy: the sexagenary system on which the circle of 360 degrees and the hour of 60 minutes are based; the detailed mathematical tables for practical application, calculating the movements of the stars.

Then the Assyrians came who starting around 800 BC began establishing an empire further northwest up the Tigris based on the cities of Assur and Nineveh. They had been at war with Babylon since the eleventh century BC and now, under a great ruler, Tiglath-Peleser III, conquered Babylon in 729 BC and retained it till 606 BC, when the Scythians destroyed Assyrian power and empire. One more Babylonian ruler was to retain a prominent place in the history books. Nebuchadnezzar was a great conqueror who expanded the Babylonian empire once more in the sixth century BC, from Suez and the Red Sea all the way across Mesopotamia. Once again the economy prospered, trade flourished, Babylon renewed its place as the centre of the ancient West Asian world. Great temples were built, a ziggurat was raised to a height of 650 feet in the city centre and there, nearby, were the Hanging Gardens, one of the seven wonders of the world, built tier upon tier to a height of seventy-five feet, with water carried up by hydraulic engines, to remind one of his wives of the hills for which she pined.

Then, in 539 BC, Babylon was conquered by the Persian ruler Cyrus, who had his capital in Susa, across the hills to the northwest of the South Mesopotamian plain. In power political terms Iraq was no longer the centre of the West Asian world, although Cyrus did assume as one of his titles, 'King of Babylon, King of the land', such was the almost mythic power and prestige still attached to the idea of ruling Babylon. But it was dissipated, gradually and over the centuries. In 331 BC Alexander of Macedon defeated the Persian ruler Darius, the last of Cyrus' successors to the greatness of the Persian Empire and incorporated Mesopotamia into the Greek Empire. But after Alexander died in Babylon, 323 BC, his empire quickly broke up.

Other rulers came to wield power over Iraq in succeeding centuries: the Seleucids; the Parthians; the Sassanians, who restored Persian rule for a while and even established, in Ctesiphon on the Tigris, a capital city of wealth and splendour that some historians could compare to Babylon; for none of them was Iraq the heart of empire, and Persian rule was not something that could be incorporated into the nationalist upsurge.

## The Resources of Nationalism

Then came Islam; Arab armies defeated the Persians in 637 AD; Iraq was the first region outside Arabia into which the conquering armies from there went. But it was still not the centre. It was not till 762 AD that the Caliph Abu Jafar, called Al Mansur, the victorious, decided that his capital should be in Baghdad. He had spent a night there, on the west bank of the Tigris, and not far from Ctesiphon, "the sweetest and gentlest night on earth", so that is where he decided his capital would be built.[8] But, more practically, it was also a strategically important site. For, as Al Mansur remarked, "it is excellent as a military camp. Besides, here is the Tigris to put us in touch with lands as far as China and bring us all that the seas yield as well as the food products of Mesopotamia, Armenia and their environs." So he had it built; a hundred thousand labourers, craftsmen and architects were brought from all parts of the empire, took four years and used up, apart from everything else, most of what was left of Ctesiphon for building material; at the end of which appeared a city of a magnificence that had never yet been seen, in concentric circles with the Caliph's palace as the centre, with four broad highways leading to the four city gates which in turn led to the four corners of the vast empire. The opulence of the city's architecture was matched by the opulence of its lifestyle. When the Caliph al-Mamun got married in 825, to give one example, a thousand pearls of a size not yet seen were poured from a gold tray onto the bridal couple, who sat on gold mats studded with pearls and sapphires. That wedding "lived in Arabic literature as one of the unforgettable extravaganzas of the age." When in 917 AD Constantine VII sent envoys to the then Caliph, Al Muqtadir, they were shown into a hall which had a tree reaching to the ceiling made of silver and gold in which were sitting elegantly carved birds, also made of silver and gold, and which chirped with the help of automatic devices as they sat. All this was Arabic with a strong Persian influence, inevitably, given the location of Iraq as the eastern outpost of the Arab empire. Persian titles were introduced into the court, "Persian wines and wives, Persian mistresses, Persian songs, as well as Persian ideas and thoughts, won the day."[9] It is not surprising, then, and not at all incongruent, that within a framework of nationalism founded on the Arab and Islamic inheritance, the Persian influence continues strong in Iraq today.

But there was also the cultural renaissance: musicians, singers, and dancers came to Baghdad not just from the Arab world but from Europe, India and China. One Caliph found time to personally direct the performance of an all-night ballet. More important, it became the intellectual centre of the world. Texts from Sanskrit, Persian and Greek were translated into Arabic. Scholars were sent out to procure Greek manuscripts, the philosophy of Aristotle, the mathematics of Euclid, the astronomy of Ptolemy, the medical treatises of Galen and of Hippocrates, which were translated first into Syriac or Aramaic, since the Arabs knew no Greek, and then into Arabic. It was, by the way, the retranslation of these texts into European languages, Latin in particular, that laid the foundations of the renaissance in Europe; none of the original Greek texts was available. In any case, all this influence from around the world made Arabic into the most superb medium for intellectual communication at the highest level, from the precise expression of scientific and mathematical ideas or the comprehensive conveying of philosophical or ethical speculations, to systems of jurisprudence or treatises on geography and history. The translations were, of course, far less important than the original work done by the Arabs under the Abbasids in all these subjects. And the real foundations for the progress made in these subjects in later centuries were in this original work.

With the growth of the political and economic power of the empire there was a growth in trade. As the heart of a great globalised network, Baghdad was equipped with miles of wharves along the river front; shipping from China, India, from Russia and Scandinavia, brought in goods from all over the world.

All this peaked in the three quarters of a century after Baghdad was built, say till the reign of the Caliph Al Mamun (813-833). After that there was a slow decline.

The Abbasid rulers, over the years, had got into the habit of hiring mercenaries, Turks or Circassians, for their personal security, for delicate missions and, as time passed, for the regular army. These Mamlukes were more reliable, having no tribal or family connections which could tempt them into disloyalty or ambition. But over time they too became more powerful, and, as the rulers and their ministers lost their grip on the levers of power, so the Mamlukes became ambitious in their own right; in 945 the leader of the Baghdad Mamlukes, Ahmad ibn Buwaih, forced the Caliph to hand over all power to him and assumed the title Amir Al Umara or Commander of Commanders. He and his successors ruled in Baghdad till 1055. Then the Seljuk Turks came who ruled till 1194; but the decline of the Caliphate continued. Finally, in January 1258 a large Mongol army under Hulagu, grandson of Genghis Khan, demolished the defences of Baghdad, leaving them in ruins, broke the irrigation dykes holding back the river waters so that the city and its surroundings were flooded, and occupied Baghdad. The entire Abbasid army was ordered into a plain outside the city and slaughtered; then the entire population hacked or shot down; almost a million men, women and children died; the Mongol soldiery plundered the city. Nothing was left of it but a devastated and unpeopled ruin, a collection of piles of rubble.

In the late fourteenth century, the Mongol emperor Tamer Lane (1336-1405) came, added Iraq to his empire for a few years and went. The Safavids, again Persian, came to rule over Baghdad and Mosul in the early fifteenth century. And then the Ottomans under Suleiman conquered it in 1534; Iraq was reduced to a province or *vilayat* of the Ottoman Empire for three and a half centuries, and then, at the end of the nineteenth century Baghdad, Basra and Mosul were separated, so it became three provinces of that empire and stayed that way till 1917.

Britain and Turkey were at war then; in March of that year a British force under Major-General Sir Stanley Maude marched into Baghdad. The three provinces were brought together again and, in effect, Iraq became a part of the British Empire.

## Whether Iraq is a Nation

And this is the point at which we can look at how all this history and geography, all these resources, figures in Iraqi nationalism.

As a preliminary let us dispose of the modernity argument. It has become commonplace to assert, especially after the March 2003 US invasion, that Iraq is not a nation at all, that it exists at all only because the Europeans wanted it to; that "the Iraqi state owes its existence almost entirely to the constellation of forces among the European imperialist powers at the end of World War I".[10] In other words, "Iraqis lack a sense of national identity. They are deeply divided along ethnic and sectarian lines."[11] This is because Iraq has three distinct communities, Sunni, Shia and Kurd, which are mutually hostile. "Iraqi politics has always been, and will continue to be, animated by deeply held communal antipathies ... there can be only one policy option: the situation will be stabilised by dividing the country into three smaller, ethnically purer and more manageable units."[12] According to this thinking it was held together only by the oppression of Saddam Hussain. In fact, since the autocratic state like Iraq under Saddam is "held together entirely by repression and not by performance, an end to, or an easing of, repression could create destabilising battles for succession ... anarchy and the rapid rise of non-state actors."[13]

So democracy could mean break-up. In other words "if the Iraqi people are genuinely given the right to shape their own future, it is possible that what emerges out of contemporary Iraq could be three distinct entities ... many argue that the removal of Saddam's regime from power will ultimately result in the disintegration of Iraq in any case."[14] The Treaty of Sevres between the Allies and Turkey, August 1920, had actually recognised the possibility that an independent state of Kurdistan might come into existence, though it was to be largely carved out of Turkey, yet this would certainly make it more feasible for Kurdish areas in Iraq also to join it, had it ever been realised.

The latest appearance of such a scheme for dividing Iraq was the so-called Biden-Gelb plan, put forward in the *New York Times*, 1 May 2007 by Joe Biden, then a senator and now US Vice-President, and Leslie Gelb, President of the Council on Foreign Relations, New York, who had already, in November 2003, urged a three-state solution, for "such a course is manageable, even necessary, because it would allow us to find Iraq's future in its denied but natural past."

In June 2007 a Brookings paper enlarged on this plan to divide Iraq into three autonomous regions, one each for the Sunnis, the Shias and the Kurds, under which US troops could start withdrawing since the security of each of the three zones would be, by a natural division of labour, the responsibility of each of the three homogeneous people.

Recall that all these arguments of modernity assume that the nation, meaning all those people that wish to live and work within the same political, economic and social space, is a pre-existing fixed entity.

## The Creation of Nationalism: The State

In this chapter, however, we focus on the traditional synthesis or story by treating the nation flexibly, constantly in the process of evolution, needing to be made and remade, dependent on a leader or group of leaders to chart out the lines along which it may move from one stage to the next. People's ideas about history, culture, religion, and so on, which change and can be made to change, are the resources to develop the strength of nationhood, not essentials that can make or break the nation.

In the case of Iraq there are three fairly representative aspects of this exercise.

First that the state is the best mechanism to make use of those resources. For "economic and fiscal administration, education, employment, military conscription, the media and social and cultural organisation – all make the nation a fact, compelling on the cognition and imagination of its members ... in Iraq (as in many other countries) it is the state that made the nation." This is quite understandable, for the "most 'national' of all strata in an incipient nation-state are the functionaries and politicians of that state. Their world outlook and life chances revolve around the national idea."[15]

Put differently, there is "the power of the state to act as the centre of gravity, gradually drawing people into a field of Iraqi politics"; and for this to happen those in positions of command have continuously to construct narratives, "accounts people give of themselves and others in relation to the state, as well as to their efforts to make the history of the state conform to their self-image."[16]

Secondly, for Iraq this exercise is made easier because of the fact that Sunni and Shia Arabs, the Kurds, the Turkomans, Persians, indigenous and immigrant Assyrians, Chaldean Christians, Armenians from west of the Caspian sea as well as other ethnicities and faiths, "all express their own separate identity while subscribing in differing degrees to an identity acknowledged a distinctly Iraqi."[17] Individuals and even parts of the different communities have constantly, over the centuries, moved across the dividing lines. They inter-marry Kurds, Persians, Arabs, Shia and Sunni. The Christians have through the ages played a far greater role in the bureaucracy that their proportion of the total numbers, giving them a stake in the viability of the unified state. The Kurds have similarly had a larger proportion of representation in the government. Furthermore, the fragmentation in the Kurdish socio-political system is a reflection of their primary loyalties to tribe, even village and kin group and clan as well as horizontal divisions into classes. In one tribe there could be both Shia and Sunni, and, in any case, "the Kurds are far from having articulated a unified pattern of loyalty to a Kurdish nation ..."[18] On the wider canvas of Iraq as a whole, one leading historian Hanna Batatu took the horizontal divisions along social and economic interests as the main determinants in political dynamics. According to him, "vertical categories of ethnic and religious affiliation were subordinated to the horizontal, class-structured ones. These vertical lines were supposed to fade as society evolved."[19]

The third aspect is that, above all, and this is a key area of nation-building, Iraqis see their history as a struggle against the foreigner; so "for most Iraqis with consciously held ideas about the nation's history – and this includes the illiterate villager with access to the coffeehouse radio as well as the educated townsman – Iraq's recent past is seen as a struggle for national independence."[20]

And so, when polls were conducted in Iraq in February and November 2005 they showed seventy per cent of the population wanting a unified Iraq with a central government in Baghdad; only twelve per cent of the Kurds wanted Iraq to be broken up into separate states; the polling data "indicate a popular sense of national identity and a widespread wish for a strong unitary state centred in Baghdad."[21]

It is of interest to see how, during the last half a century, and within the context of the three aspects outlined above, Iraqi leaders brought the resources of historical and cultural experience into play in the effort to strengthen the idea of an Iraqi nation, starting with pre-Islamic history.

In the early years after the three Ottoman provinces were brought together into a single state in 1920, the pre-Islamic past was ignored. At that time the glories of Iraq's Arab past formed, almost exclusively, the input to the people's construction of nationalism. The example of education is the one most often given here. Under Sati al-Husri, who was Director General of Education of Iraq in the 1920s, and later a Professor and then Dean of the Law College in the 1930s, as well as others, the emphasis in the school and college curriculum was shifted to pan-Arabism. Indeed it has been pointed out that "the leaders and designers of Iraq's educational system in the 1920s and 1930s were a number of pan-Arab nationalist activists who had made a vital contribution to the development and expansion of pan-Arab nationalist ideology throughout the Arab world."[22]

Al-Husri "enjoined teachers not to present any history but that of the Arabs in a positive light and admonished them against teaching anything critical of the Arabs." Teachers of history were instructed that their goal in teaching it "was to present the history of the fatherland, and the past of the nation, in order to strengthen the national patriotic consciousness"; history made exciting through the stories of Arab heroes, their bravery, courage, determination and noble deeds.[23] These included, more specifically, the Abbasid Caliphs, Al Mamun, Al Rashid and Al Mansur. "Special attention was ... given to the ideological, conceptual and intellectual links existing among the Arab peoples."

But when General Abdel Karim Kassim overthrew the monarchy on 14 July 1958, putting in place a three-man Council – a Sunni, a Shia and a Kurd – he added to this Arab resource by resurrecting ancient or pre-Islamic Iraq as a foundation for the building of the nation. So "postage stamps suddenly bloomed with Sumerian and Assyrian art. The Akkadian sun, an eight-pointed star with light waves connecting its points, and the hexagonal star of Ishtar took their place as the new emblems of Iraqi nationalism."[24] The first was made into the national emblem; the second put into the national flag. Inscriptions of Hammurabi's laws, models of Ziggurats and symbols of Tamuz-Dumuzi, the ancient spring god, made their appearance.

After the Baath party seized power in 1968 this was taken much further. An Iraqi Fashion House, whose declared purpose was strengthening of the links between modern Iraqi garments and the dress used in Mesopotamia, was established. With attractive models to take the ramp, 130 extravagant costumes, designers and musicians, the Fashion House presented its shows, inspired by the civilisations of Sumer, Akkad, Babylon, Assyria, from the cities of Basra, Kufa, Baghdad, Samarra, and Mosul, from past millennia to the present day, in Iraq as well as all over the world. Plays were produced which were set in ancient Sumer or Babylon; one of them, Gilgamesh, was staged spectacularly in an amphitheatre in Babylon with two thousand spectators watching. And Babylon itself was reconstructed, with the famous Ishtar gate, a statue of the Lion of Babylon and wide processional avenues.[25] On national days floats depicted these as well as, among others, the hanging gardens of Babylon, the towers of Nineveh, the Ziggurats of the Assyrians.

This did not mean that after the 1958 revolution the Arab and Islamic past was neglected. The Baath party at its foundation in 1947 by Michel Aflaq and Salah al-Din al-Bitar, a Christian and a Muslim who met for the first time in Paris, 1929, was the heart of the idea of Arab unity, that a unified Arab state based on language, culture and history would overcome the narrow religious, tribal or sectarian thought processes of the Arabs, lead to a unified Arab identity and liberate the Arabs from western domination. By the late 1940s Baathist cells and student circles had come up all over the Arab world, including Iraq. But when the Baath party actually came to power in 1968 the assertion of Arab nationalism was layered with that of Iraqi nationalism. Then came the 1980s, differences with Syria, the springboard of the Baath party, the war with Iran which needed more Iraqi nationalism and, above all, Saddam Hussain, who saw the party as an instrument for his personal rule rather than one for building nationalism.

Note that nearly four centuries of Ottoman rule did not figure in any of these narratives of nationalism. Those years were described, if at all, as a period of stagnation and decay and not fit for consideration by serious Iraqi historians, nor any other historians, for that matter.

The Shia-Sunni divide, in particular, which has received a great deal of attention in recent years, was not an obstacle in the building of nationalism. Actually the role of sectarian conflict as an obstacle to nation-building has been constrained by the generally secular outlook of the Iraqi villager, the urban man in the street, and the nomad. True, the rulers, the Abbasids and then the Ottomans, were all Sunni except for the periods of Persian dominance, so the Shias today understandably feel suspicious of any move which could put the Sunnis again on the road to dominance. True, also, that the Sunnis have reason for suspicion, for it was the Shias who, during Ottoman rule, helped the Persians enter Iraq. Two further aspects are relevant. First, the Shia is not a united political community. Some, led by the clerics of Najaf and Karbala, mobilised their people to resist the increasing Sunni domination of political and economic life. But some also identified with Arab nationalism, which, of course, clashed with the commitment to the clerics who were usually of Persian origin, and actually were often Persian. So it becomes true that the Shia intelligentsia, for instance, identified with Iraq as an Arab nation, and often "the Sunni-Shi'i contest in Iraq centred on Arab Shi'is, speaking Arabic and taking pride in their contribution to the Arab culture and heritage."[26]

## Resistance to the British

So these provided the resources based on which the Iraqis opposed British occupation. But leadership was missing; there was no one who came forward to build the kind of nationalism that forcibly evicts the foreigner; nor did Iraq have the societal pattern in which every man, every household, every village is a centre of resistance. So the British were able to dominate Iraq for nearly thirty years, stay on in their air bases for twenty-five.

The most active resistance came during the Iraq revolt, or *thawrat al-ishrin*, the great revolution of 1920, often cited as a prime example of Arab national forces against the imperialist ambitions of Britain. Having seized control of Iraq, or the three Ottoman provinces of Baghdad, Basra and Mosul, the British were inclined to incorporate it into their empire, though there were some dissenting voices within Britain; in any case, only the revolt stopped them.

The British were given Iraq as a mandated territory by the League of Nations in April 1920 as part of the arrangements for the future of the Ottoman Empire, though a meeting of Arab leaders had proclaimed Iraqi independence the previous month. The British, quite sure that the Iraqis were not fit to govern themselves, abolished Ottoman institutions of indirect rule and substituted contact with, and direct rule over, the tribal leaders in the first place. In response, by May 1920 mass meetings were being held in both Sunni and Shia mosques demanding independence. Poets emerged who sang the praises of the Iraqi land, encouraging an Iraqi identity that would be acceptable to Sunni. Shia, Kurd and nomad, and obliterate sectarian and ethnic differences.

In June 1920, 100,000 fighters, Sunnis and Shias, tribal leaders and their followers, Kurds and other minorities, rose in armed revolt against the British occupation forces. It was a struggle for independence. Shia leaders played an important role: Ayatollah al-Shirazi, the Imam of Karbala, issued a fatwah declaring that service in the British administration was unlawful.[27] He and his son

Mohammed Riza made Arab flags, printed pamphlets demanding total independence and urging the tribal leaders to revolt against the British. By July Mosul and the Kurdish areas were in open rebellion which spread south as the days passed. Military outposts and garrisons were attacked and taken, lines of communication were cut, and by August most of northern Iraq was in the hands of the Iraqis; the rebels had taken Baquba near Baghdad and much of the Euphrates valley; they even set up a provisional government of independent Iraq; only the lower Tigris valley remained firmly under British control.

The British suppressed the rebellion ruthlessly; and this was done largely by air, using poison gas, bombing and strafing villages; there was also extensive use of artillery. Winston Churchill was Colonial Secretary at the time and the supervision of the suppression largely fell to his charge. He was strongly supportive of the use of poison gas, saying "I do not understand this squeamishness about the use of gas. I am strongly in favour of using poison gas against uncivilised tribes." By spring 1921 this phase of the independence struggle had largely been crushed.

So it was, as in every other colony, the enforcement power of a British military presence that really ensured domination. To meet the threat presented by the 1920 struggle for independence some 5,000 British and 25,000 Indian troops had been deployed to Iraq. But it was air power, the British believed, that had played the crucial role in quelling that revolt. And so, while most of the ground troops were withdrawn, the air power remained and was used repeatedly to deal with the resistance which kept showing its face over the years. "The continued presence of the Royal Air Force in the region, even after Iraq had secured its nominal independence, was assumed to be a powerful deterrent" to any anti-British sections of the Iraqis.[28]

Now the British tried indirect rule. An Iraqi Council of Ministers was appointed in November 1920, under British supervision. A few months later it was decided to put Amir Feisal on the throne of Iraq; he was the son of Husein ibn Ali, Sherif of Mecca, and, therefore, carried considerable weight with the Iraqis. Feisal was enthroned on 23 August 1921. So, now British domination was to be implemented through the King and a small group of Iraqis who had been in the service of the Ottomans known as The Covenant. These were conservatives who came from *sayyid* families, notables who came to occupy most of the cabinet and senior government offices over the years. They didn't really represent anybody, not even the Sunnis, so below the surface anti-British and nationalist feelings continued to grow. And as the resistance in which this expressed itself came from several directions, air power was repeatedly used.

One was the Kurds of Mosul and the North. Though the August 1920 Treaty of Sevres, under which they were promised autonomy if not independence, was never implemented, the Kurds did take courage from there; tribal leaders under a Sheikh Mahmud took control over Sulaimaniyya in the North by early 1923 and he had Turkish help. The RAF started bombing raids over the area which continued for a year. Finally British and Iraqi forces were able to occupy Sulaimaniyya in July 1924, while Sheikh Mahmud left for Iran, where he maintained guerilla fighting units which attacked Iraq again in 1931. Again ground forces were called in; again they couldn't handle the problem and air power had to be invoked, which turned the tide of battle and by the spring of 1932 the British were once more in control.

Another source of resistance was a combined labour unrest, public demonstrations and tribal insurgency which broke out also in 1931. As a result of the economic problems associated with the depression of those years, different groups combined to form the al-Ikha party, Hizb al-Ikha. There were Sunni notables in it, there was some popular Shia support, and a large number of trade union leaders and small traders, all concerned about the impact on their earnings of the depression, came together into the party and launched a campaign to stop tax payment, and asked the King to dismiss the cabinet. In July of that year a general strike was declared which spread to most of southern Iraq; and then there were huge demonstrations in the streets with slogans against the government and the monarchy; and then tribal insurgency broke out in the mid-Euphrates region, Najaf, Karbala and their surroundings. Once again, the RAF was called in, though this time mostly for purposes of *demonstratio ad oculo,* and the situation was brought under control.

There was another tribal insurgency in March 1935, when various grievances of the Shia tribal Sheikhs in the Najaf and Karbala areas, encouraged by a certain Ayatollah Muhammad Kashif al-Ghita and by some of the leaders of al-Ikha, resulted in violent revolt, but this one was controlled by negotiation and concession.

October 1936 brought a coup d'etat by General Bakr Sidqi, acting Chief of Staff, at the head of an army group (the Chief was in Ankara at the time and General Bakr sent him a telegram to stay on there). Some bombs were dropped; two battalions advanced on Baghdad; Bakr wanted the King to appoint a government headed by Hikmat Sulaiman, a radical leftist who had also been with the al-Ikha party. By August 1937, Bakr was assassinated by an Air Force Commander; another army group was formed, Hikmat Sulaiman was asked to and did resign. More coups d'etat followed; there were a total of seven from October 1936 to April 1941 when the then acting Chief of General Staff Amin Zaki, and Rashid Ali, also from the al-Ikha party, came to power with a government of National Defence. This one was overtly pro-German.

The turn to Nazi Germany in 1941 was another way of continuing the earlier anti-British movements. In September 1933 King Feisal had died; he was succeeded by his son Ghazi who seemed unable to establish the kind of control Feisal had over the multiple groups, interests and factions that made up the Iraqi military-political scene, but who became known for promoting pan-Arab causes. Ghazi was something of a playboy, fond of fast cars; in 1939 he drove one of them straight into a telegraph pole and died, to be succeeded by his three-year-old son, Feisal II, and a regent. But his death did bring new evidence of anti-British feelings as mourning crowds, convinced the British had contrived to do him in, streamed into the streets shouting at the British embassy, "Thou shall answer for the blood of Ghazi."[29] And anti-British feelings continued to grow.

Rashid Ali cut the oil pipeline to the Mediterranean; Hitler ordered arms and military advisers to Baghdad to help him; and a large contingent of British ground forces set sail for Basra; air power wasn't going to be enough to deal with this one. Rashid Ali didn't last long, only till the end of May 1941. Amidst warnings to him to offer no opposition British forces began the landings on 18 April. Meanwhile Iraqi forces surrounded the land around the British air base at Habbaniya, and aircraft from the base started to bomb and strafe their positions. More aircraft arrived from Egypt and the Iraqi military position began to disintegrate. So on the night of 29 May Rashid Ali, his German and Italian friends and a few close supporters left for Iran.

Through these years, apart from the Rashid Ali interregnum of the early 1940s, British domination continued.

Nominal independence came in 1930 with membership of the

League of Nations, while a new 25-year treaty of June 1930 gave Britain the right to maintain two air bases in Iraq, supply all of Iraq's military equipment, training and advisers, and the right to move British troops into Iraq if necessary in time of war. In 1955, shortly before it expired, it was replaced by the Baghdad Pact. Designed ostensibly against Soviet aggression (though Iraq has no borders with what used to be the Soviet Union) it was initially signed by Turkey and Iraq and then joined by the UK, which, at that point, handed over the two air bases to Iraqi control.

Independence really came only when General Abdel Karim Kassim overthrew the monarchy on 14 July 1958 and thereafter withdrew from the Baghdad Pact. Serious efforts were then made to put Iraqi nationalism on stronger foundations, as indicated above, but, in what seemed a repeat of the late 1930s, internal problems hindered these: Kassim was overthrown after some considerable fighting by the armed forces under a Revolutionary Command Council in February 1963; his successor died in a plane crash three years later; a year more, July 1968, and there was a coup, this one peaceful; yet one more year and Saddam Hussain became Vice-President of the Revolutionary Command Council, soon to be virtually the sole ruler of Iraq till the Americans came in 2003.

## And Now It Is the Insurgency

In response to the US invasion, Iraqi nationalism led to an anti-US insurgency which soon became an effective military opposition.

It started even as US ground troops moved in, and by 1 May had built up a considerable momentum. The attacks were by trained fighters who had served in one or other of the armed forces units built up by Saddam Hussain; so they were adept at handling rocket launchers, setting up improvised explosive devices and coordinated attacks on convoys. Here it may be recalled that the traditional story provides for a continuously increased cohesion of Iraqi nationalism. Although its evolution began recently, in 1920, it has the considerable resources of a history and civilisation going back to ancient times, to draw on; and through the years of the monarchy, republic and one-man rule this cohesion was gradually strengthened. So the Iraqis wanted the US out and, over the years, their power and ability to do so, as was the case of the power of many smaller countries vis-à-vis the great powers, had been increasing; and here it was expressed through the insurgency. Note that religion had very little to do with it. Most of the insurgent groups assumed a name with an Islamic connotation: Badr; Islamic Front; Ansar al-Sunnah, among others. This was the call to war as distinct from the war itself, which is only and always about overpowering the opponent. National cohesion meant that, had there been an Islamic army of foreign occupation, the opposition to it would have been just as strong.

In what follows the Iraqi insurgency will be covered with a broad brush; it is a continually changing picture and precludes too much detail.

There have been a number of big battles; one of the biggest was for Falujah. It started on 31 March 2004 when four Americans, private security contractors hired for deployment in Iraq by a company called Blackwater, were killed and their bodies hung over a bridge across the river Euphrates. In response the US commenced 'Operation Valiant Resolve'; marines supported by the army and air force went into Falujah on 5 April. The insurgents were, according to American accounts, well armed and organised as also highly motivated. US casualties rose while they were still on the outskirts of the city; they fell back to regroup, and then withdrew. The Iraqis celebrated their victory in the streets. It was not till November 2004 that the US felt strong enough to go on the offensive again, and this time it was a repeat of the offensive by which Hue was retaken from the Vietnamese after the Tet offensive, 1968. Falujah was virtually reduced to rubble from the air, including the use of white phosphorous; and then the ground troops went in. Even so the US military called it the most intense urban combat since Hue as the insurgents concealed in the rubble engaged US troops for a total of forty-six days before the latter were able to establish control over the city.

Insurgent attacks fluctuated over the years; after the battle for Falujah there was a drop; then in May 2005 there was a sharp increase; that was later called Iraq's bloodiest month in two years. Then they dropped again, only to surge during the latter half of 2006; December that year saw almost a thousand attacks a week, the highest since the invasion began. In January 2007 President Bush decided to send in another 21,500 troops as well as a new Commander of the Multi-National Force – Iraq, General David Petraeus. By March 2008 there had been reportedly a significant decline in insurgent attacks on US forces.

Geographically the insurgency has been spread out from Mosul and Tal Afar in the North through the main towns of the Tigris valley, Tikrit and Samarra, to Baghdad and the South; as also from the Syrian border where the Euphrates enters Iraq, through Ramadi, Falujah, Karbala, and to Najaf and beyond. The Kurdish areas to the North have seen insurgent activity as well as the Shia areas to the South. However, the focus has been in and around Baghdad, where twenty-five per cent of the attacks have taken place. The insurgency "is taking place mainly in the center of the country around Baghdad and western Al Anbar, Iraq's largest province, which borders on Syria, Jordan and Saudi Arabia"[30] including the cities of Al Qaim, Haditha, Hit, and Abu Ghraib.

As for the total number of insurgents, there are widely varying estimates. The more recent estimates suggest a hard core of about 25,000, though there could be up to 100,000 if one includes all those who sympathise enough to be potentially available for action. An example of the problem is that during a three-year period, from May 2003 to May 2006, official estimates of the total number were between 15,000 and 20,000; but in those three years 64,000 had actually been killed by the US and coalition forces, so maybe there was an inexhaustible source keeping the numbers at that somewhat low level.

The number of groups, different reports suggest, are as many as seventy or as few (if the really active ones only are counted) as a dozen.

There are, to start with, the Shia militias which have fought against US forces, and have thereafter joined the Iraqi government set up by the US.

One of the largest and once reputedly the most powerful is the Mahdi Army comprising the followers of a young (born August 1973) Shia cleric Muqtada al-Sadr. He may have some 10,000 fighters (the US claims he has 40-50,000) who are firmly nationalist, meaning they "remained decidedly opposed to the US-led coalition and its policies. Al Sadr's political discourse resembled that of the Sunni based groups with its emphasis on the unity of Iraq, ant-federalism, and withdrawal of foreign troops from Iraq" who are treated as foreign occupiers.[31] They have worked against any effort to break up Iraq. However, while maintaining his cadre of armed fighters, Muqtada has also taken part in the December 2005 elections as part of the United Iraqi Alliance, UIA winning 32 seats.

At the other end of the spectrum, according to American intelligence officials, he has ties with Hezbollah in Lebanon and with the Revolutionary Guards in Iran; some say the latter have infiltrated numbers of their own people into the Mahdi Army.

Another Shia group, again close to Iran, is the Badr corps, under the Supreme Council for the Islamic Revolution in Iraq, SCIRI, established in 1982 by Iraqi exiles in Iran and, of course, with Iran's blessings, and has been led by Ayatollah Mohammed Baqir al-Hakim; his brother, Abdul Aziz al-Hakim, took over the leadership after he was assassinated in August 2003. The Badr corps strength is like that of the Sadrists, in Baghdad and the South, more especially the Shia concentration areas in the South, cities like Najaf, Karbala, Diwaniyah, Nasiriya and Samarra. They can reportedly field up to 30,000 fighters, though half that is probably a more realistic figure; in any case a large number of their fighters have been inducted into the government security forces. Meanwhile, in May 2007 the SCIRI changed its name to Supreme Islamic Iraqi Council of Iraq, SIIC. It fought the election as a component of the UIA and became one of the largest groups in the Iraqi Parliament in December 2005, with 36 seats out of the total of 275.

Yet another Shia group is al-Dawa, started in the 1960s under the leadership of Mohammed Baqir al-Sadr (not to be confused with Sadeq al-Sadr, who was his cousin, or Muqtada al-Sadr, who married his daughter) and was involved in anti-Baath militancy during Saddam Hussein's rule; it attempted to assassinate Saddam and when he was eventually hanged it was primarily for the reprisals he took against them. It was also involved in the bombing of the US and French embassies in Kuwait in December 1983,[32] one of the perpetrators of which incident was elected to Parliament in December 2005. Al-Dawa has been close to Iran, as have the other Shia groups, and moved there during the Iran-Iraq war since it backed Iran. In 2003 it moved back to Iraq. Then in January 2005 it contested the election as part of the UIA and its leader, Ibrahim al Jaafari became Prime Minister. It also contested the December 2005 election; its Secretary-General, Nouri al-Maliki became Prime Minister in May 2006. And now he is working closely with the US, visiting often, while maintaining his links with Iran.

Among the Sunni groups the Islamic Army in Iraq, IAI, formed in 2003 after the US invasion, is probably the most powerful; though its exact strength is disputed it seems to have some 15-17,000 fighters, with many Baathists having joined. IAI has claimed a number of attacks, including the April 2005 downing of a Blackwater group helicopter north of Baghdad which concluded with the execution of the co-pilot, the only one who survived the downing. It claims to have conducted a thousand attacks on the US and the Iraqi government forces each month. In October 2007 a grouping was announced called the Political Council of the Iraqi Resistance, including the Islamic Army in Iraq; the al-Mujahideen Army; Ansar al Sunna, which has been regularly advertising the frequency of their attacks on US forces and is reportedly close to Al Qaeda; the al-Fatiheen Army; and the Islamic Front for the Iraqi Resistance.

Izzat Ibrahim al-Douri, former Vice-President of Iraq, keeps appearing despite a ten-million-dollar bounty on his head by the US. He is reported to have been spotted in the southern suburbs of Diyala; gave an interview in June 2008 to the editor-in-chief of an Egyptian newspaper, *Al-Mawqif Al-Arabi*; and earlier, in October 2007, announced the setting up, with himself as the Supreme Commander, of the Jihad and Liberation Front comprising twenty-three resistance groups, including the Kurdistan Liberation Army; most of the members of the Front are former Baathists. As with all the other groups it is for the unconditional withdrawal of US troops from Iraq.

There are other Baathists who are in the Army of Mohammed, said to have been formed by Saddam himself in April, 2003; other Sunni Muslims, sometimes called nationalist; and there have been those sponsored by or with linked to Al Qaeda; Kurds as in the Ansar al-Islam; Marxists, some in a group called the Iraqi Armed Revolutionary Resistance. Different groups come together from time to time: in September 2007 the Jehad and Change Front was announced comprising eight of the smaller resistance groups including names like the Army of Rashideen, the 1920 Revolutionary Brigade (commemorating the 1920 revolt against the British), and the Islamic Movement of Mujahideen of Iraq.

One writer who spent time in Iraq asserted that of the Sunni groups, "the largest ones were Al-Jaish al-Islamiya fil-Iraq (the Islamic Army in Iraq), Al Jabha al-Islamiya lil Mujawama al-Iraqiya (the Islamic Front of the Iraqi Resistance) and Jaysh Ansar al-Sunna (Army of the Partisans of the Sunna)". On this reckoning the al-Rashideen, Mohammed's Army and other Sunni groups, were much smaller.[33]

Within this overall picture of variety and change some things are consistent and have been since the resistance began in April 2003, and they are applicable in general to the resistance groups.

The first is that the target for the resistance groups is the US occupation: its armed forces; its private military contractors; its civilian support systems. The Iraqi armed forces have been targeted but not consistently; the Iraqi police forces have also been targeted but even less consistently; and, as far as the resistance groups' claims are concerned, innocent civilians never. The resistance leaders do not tire of explaining that attacks on mosques, on other civilian buildings and on civilians, as also the sectarian killings are the work of the US and their agents. This seems consistent with the stated earlier US aim of breaking up Iraq, which has now been abandoned. But there are also reliable reports that some of the sectarian killings of Shias have been by groups affiliated to Al Qaeda.

Hence, secondly, there is a widespread belief that both Shia and Sunni must make an extra effort to ensure no conflict arises between them. There was, of course, some history of such conflict during Ottoman rule in particular as the Shias supported periodic Iranian efforts to wrest control of Iraq from Turkey, but thereafter the attempt has been to build inter-sectarian harmony. On 9 April, 2007, four years after the US occupation began, a million demonstrators came out into the streets of Iraq's major towns; they were overwhelmingly Shia, but "Sunni clerics marched with their Shia counterparts at the head of the massive and peaceful procession", thus blowing a hole in the assumption that "Iraqi nationalism had been wiped out by religious sectarianism" or that without the occupation forces Iraq would descend into civil war.[34]

Thirdly, the overwhelming majority of resistance groups and fighters consider themselves nationalist; they do not welcome foreign fighters and here again, Al Qaeda is the exception; the US has claimed that several hundred foreign fighters have been killed or captured but these figures are suspected. In general the resistance groups assert that their task is to get the US out of Iraq; after that they will manage. And in this they have the support of the Arab world, the people if not the rulers.

## The Course of the War

Overall, the opposition to the US in Iraq is growing. It is growing in commitment, and one sign of this is said to be the growing strength of Al Qaeda, which, according to a mid-2007 article in the American establishment journal *Foreign Affairs*, "is a more dangerous enemy today than it has ever been before." The conclusion is that its reach has spread throughout the Muslim world, while Osama bin Laden's ideas now attract more followers than ever; Zarqawi's death meant little, since the operation is so thoroughly decentralised; it is global and Zarqawi's successor even thanked the US for sending forces into Iraq so that Al Qaeda now has a historic opportunity to engage US forces on Arab soil.[35] One authority noted that the US invasion of Iraq has "inspired a new generation of young Muslims around the world ... Saddam had crushed the jihadists ... today his country is full of them ... forming a network similar to the one formed in Afghanistan during the anti-Soviet struggle.[36] Even the National Intelligence Estimates of the US (which have inputs from different US intelligence organisations) assessed in July 2007 that terrorist groups continue to adapt and improve their capabilities, with Al Qaeda promoting cooperation among them, and that the continuation of the war gives operatives lethal experience, raises money from the Islamic world and make Al Qaeda into a hero. And the operatives keep on improving their technical skills; for instance, new generations of improvised explosive devices continue to appear, each one overcomes the defensive measures taken by the US for the last. Major-General James E. Simmons was reported in the *Washington Post*, 3 June 2007, to have said that they are following increasingly complex tactics in ambushes, like widely separated units, say, three in all, each in communication with the others.

The US has not been able to keep pace with the growing commitment, strength and war-fighting ability of the armed resistance. Every now and then there is an admission of this: a certain Lt.-Col. Paul Yingling referred in April 2007 to the "intellectual and moral failures common to America's general officer corps in Vietnam and Iraq" which constitute a crisis in American generalship, so that they now faced the prospects of military defeat in Iraq.[37] A month later, the former head of MI6 (British Intelligence) asserted that Al Qaeda was thriving while the position of the US and the UK was "strategically weak" in Iraq and elsewhere.

Others have suggested that the US reliance on high technology warfare is not working. This enables the military to locate, identify, track, target and destroy enemy weapon systems without ever interacting or engaging with enemy soldiers. But it was tried in Vietnam and failed; so neither network centric warfare nor the Revolution in Military Affairs, has succeeded in reduced reliance on manpower, which was the intention. This means the US has to revert to a greater dependence on manpower; but the manpower is not available; the new millennium saw a manpower crisis in the US military.[38]

Given the US military performance in Iraq, the resistance (and the traditional story) sees that it is in retreat. In a war like this it may be possible and necessary to exit the battlefield or largely exit the battlefield, without being seen to have been defeated; but it is not certain that the US will be able to do this successfully.

The continuingly modified goals of the war might help it to do so. It was begun with the intention at least of ridding the 'Middle East' from tyranny and despair and anger by introducing democracy and freedom there. Sometimes this got to be part of a global strategy, as President Bush announced in his fifth State of the Union message, January 2005, "our aim is to build and preserve a community of free and independent nations, with governments that answer to their citizens ... freedom in Iraq will ... inspire democratic reformers from Damascus to Tehran". A year later it was not just the region from Damascus to Tehran, for "we seek the end of tyranny in our world ... every step towards freedom in the world makes our country safer." But these worldwide aims were gradually modified. By the 2007 State of the Union message the aim was not the worldwide end of tyranny, but only to "help men and women in the Middle East to build free societies" and "a democratic Iraq that upholds the rule of law, respects the right of its people." By late 2008 an agreement had been signed between the US and Iraq providing for the withdrawal of US forces from Iraq; the US called it a Status of Forces Agreement, a SOFA which is usually signed by countries at the start of the deployment of US forces there; but in Iraq this was the endgame.

By the end of February 2009, with President Barrack Obama in the White House, and having completed a review of US strategy on *Responsibly ending the War in Iraq,* it was no longer US policy to build freedom in the Middle East, nor even a democratic Iraq; the US would now aim at an Iraqi government that is just, representative and accountable and that provided neither support nor safe haven to terrorists. And since the US cannot police Iraq's streets forever, as the review clearly asserted, the very first part of the strategy would be "the responsible removal of our combat troops from Iraq, so by end-August 2010 the US combat mission in Iraq will end." Thereafter 35-50,000 US troops will remain to support the Iraqi government and its security forces, for training and to conduct targeted anti-terrorist missions, but even they will go by the end of 2011. Even by mid-2009 many of those who had joined the US coalition had left: Ukraine much earlier, January 2005; Italy by end 2006; Denmark by 2007; then a whole lot of them in 2008, including Australia, Poland, Georgia and Kazakhstan, Japan; South Korea in early 2009; the British also by early 2009; signs that it is all about to come to an end.

So, to demonstrate that this was indeed the endgame it was also agreed that US forces would pull out of all cities by end-June 2009; they would then be confined to their barracks outside the cities. And Iraqi Prime Minister Nouri al-Maliki announced on 29 June, the day before the pull out, that this was a 'great victory', the result of Iraq's successful effort to repel the invader (meaning the US, by the way, not Al Qaeda); that 30 June would be a national holiday in celebration of the victory.

As for the battlefield, the resistance has taken the withdrawal of US forces from the cities as a sign that they cannot any more take the kind of casualties that urban war entails. They are not convinced, however, that the US will go on with the rest of the withdrawal plan without encouragement. US officials, for instance, have been saying that for purposes of training and advice US forces in thousands may continue to be present in Iraq for years, maybe ten years. So the resistance has stepped up attacks and US casualties have started mounting again.

The Jihad and Change Front announced that they will continue attacking US forces till the last US soldier is out of Iraq and increased the number of attacks on US air bases. The Islamic Front for the Iraqi Resistance, JAMI, claimed that in the first months of 2009 they were able to launch some fifty to seventy-five attacks each month. Several groups have stepped up the level of their activities or are preparing to do so. Overall violence has increased since the beginning of the year and by some accounts April 2009 was the deadliest month since early 2008.

Given the nature of the war and the kind of retreat that is being planned, that will in any case have a dramatic effect on the US political, military and economic position in the world in the short term. We can see already that apart from the steady drain on US economic resources, the war has damaged US global standing and strengthened Iran's position in the region.

## The Effects of Defeat

The traditional story concludes that while the Americans are not going to win the war in Iraq in any convincing way, they may be able to declare victory and leave. But in Afghanistan this will be more difficult, due to the Afghan conviction that they must live up to the tradition that enemies not only need to be expelled forcibly, but be seen to have been expelled forcibly or else they will be back. So the Americans and their NATO allies are going to be seen to have lost the war there. They will leave Afghanistan without being seen to have defeated the Taliban.

The US defeat may not mean the immediate establishment of a Taliban government in Kabul; in Vietnam after the US forces completed their withdrawal, in Afghanistan after the Soviet forces finally left, governments friendly to each of them remained in power for two years or more. But the retreat will point to a future in which the Taliban has a much greater say in Kabul, even if the possibility of prolonged factionalist strife, as happened after the fall of the Najibullah government in 1992, cannot be avoided.

But it will have major consequences for US power. In Afghanistan and Iraq the US will not any longer exercise any power; and the retreat of US power certainly will not stop there. So there will be no more references thereafter to America as the world's unchallenged military and economic power and comparisons to Rome. The use of nouns that have become familiar, like colossus, hyper-power, unbearable power, will disappear; and the US will no longer design or build the global picture we are all familiar with; nor seek, as one part of that global picture, to promote freedom around the world as an instrument to expand its power, nor campaign against evil; or to put out hierarchical rankings, the countries of the world ranked according to freedom, or corruption, or human rights, or being terrorism prone, among the many other rankings that we are given from time to time. The whole business of putting countries into a hierarchical list, for whatever, may well subside or go into disuse.

Beyond that, and since the US will remain one of a handful of major global powers, the question of how far and in which geographical areas or sectors of interest US commitments will be diluted or even revoked, can only be speculatively answered.

Politico-military commitments like the expansion of alliances like NATO or the trilateral security initiative (the US, Australia and Singapore) or a still vaguely outlined quadrilateral one (India, Australia, Japan, US), new security initiatives with ASEAN, are all likely to be abandoned. And troop deployment abroad will be reduced, for the US military presence abroad is a profound symbol of US pre-eminence worldwide. In the Gulf the US has a larger or smaller military presence in every country on the southern coast. The troops are there in large numbers, almost half a million, nearly half of whom are in Iraq and Kuwait. Then there are small numbers scattered in Bahrain and Qatar, Oman and the United Arab Emirates.

They have also been there in Pakistan since the 1950s, with a strong build-up in the 1960s to an average strength of 15,000. Japan and South Korea have a major presence, and there are small numbers in Australia, Singapore, Thailand, and Diego Garcia of course.[39] All this will change; the troop presence will be drastically thinned down or eliminated.

The global retreat of US power will be accompanied by a further relative shrinkage of the US economy, already struggling to find a way out of a slowdown or even recession. The traditional measures here would be a sharp fall in the international value of the dollar, especially against other major currencies like the Euro and the Yen.

Taking the speculative extrapolation a little further, China will thereafter be in a position to assume the role of colossus or hyper-power. This has already been envisaged by several authors, whether as having happened or about to happen. One example of such writings will suffice, of the world having entered a new era from 2008, "one of those rare historical periods that is characterised by a shift in global hegemony from one great power to another … the rise of China and the decline of the U.S. …a period profoundly unstable, deeply uncertain and fraught with danger."[40]

To argue that China is already there, with an economy larger than that of the US, which is the traditional IR criterion, has firm logic behind it.

Three things may be said here on the subject. First, if we go by somewhat old-fashioned indicators of power, the ones that were commonly used in the 1960s as the staple for IR analysts such as by W.W.Rostow, then China has had a larger economy than the US for some years. In cement its production overtook that of the US in 1980; in fertiliser it was in 1984 that it overtook the US; in coal 1988; and in steel 1995. Even in the production of primary energy, which includes oil, electric power, coal and other sources of energy, and where the US took pride in having an unbeatable lead over everyone else, China was by 2008 just about level.

The second thing is that those old-fashioned indicators were actually given up by the 1970s because the Soviet economy was growing so fast that it overtook that of the US, in 1963 for cement, 1971 for steel, 1983-84 for fertiliser production. At that point total GDP statistics came in to replace those old indicators. Since services occupy a large place in GDP, and since the US has a high output of services, there was an expectation that here at least the US was too far ahead for anyone else to catch up. But even here the picture became a bit complicated. GDP comparisons can be made by adding up each country's GDP in the local currency, then converting it into dollars at the market exchange rate (MER). But exchange rates often fluctuate wildly, as a result, for instance, of the movement of so-called 'hot money'. Furthermore, a fully comparable item, such as a ton of steel or cement, may cost far more in one country than another, thus typically sending up the GDP of the former without reflecting any real production difference. So it was thought better to compare goods produced; then a ton of steel or cement produced anywhere adds the same amount to the GDP, and this is the purchasing power approach. This produced the 'Purchasing Power of Currencies' (PPC) based indices of GDP. As the World Bank's World Development Report put it, "the Purchasing Power of Currencies (PPC) is defined as the number of units of a country's currency required to buy the same amounts of goods and services in the domestic market as one dollar would buy in the United States … so that cross-country comparisons of GDP based on them reflect differences in the quantities of goods and services free of price-level differences."[41]

Even on this basis the US was, if not so far ahead, still comfortably enough ahead not to concern itself about the gap closing too quickly.

In the UN Statistical Yearbook, the standard publication used by IR students and other statistical compilations, the year 1990 saw

US GDP at constant prices (not PPC) to be $ 5793 billion; that of China at $ 338 billion.[42] This emboldened the UN and the 39th Statistical Yearbook, giving data to the end of the year 1993 published GDP figures based on purchasing power. For the year 1991 that of the US dropped a little (it is generally below the MER level) to $5610 billion; but China had been grossly under pricing its economy and its GDP jumped to $3430 billion, or 61 per cent of that of the US. And then, as it had for years, the Chinese economy continued to post high rates of growth, 14.2 per cent in 1992; 13.5 per cent in 1993; 12.6 per cent in 1994; and so it continued. And that of the US showed rather low rates, an average of 3 per cent or lower for the early 1990s. It was easy to see that China's GDP, based on purchasing power, would overtake that of the US by 1996 at the latest.

At this point it is necessary to mention the overall Chinese attitude towards all this. At the 16th National Congress of the Communist Party of China, November 2002, Jiang Zemin, who was still General Secretary of the party,[43] brought out his assessment that the first two decades of the new century comprised an 'important period of strategic opportunity' or in acronym form IPSO. In order to take full advantage of this he had already in July 1991 told the next generation of the party leadership that China would have to stay cool-headed, stand firmly, never try to take the lead, bide their time and above all hide China's capabilities. The Chinese leadership had decided that the changed world situation after the end of the Cold War gave China time for peaceful development and while this was going on everything about IR should be played low key.

So, thirdly, ipso facto, it was now necessary to correct these UN statistics. It wouldn't do to have the published figures showing China's GDP higher than that of the US. Two Chinese scholars worked on the problem and in 1995 concluded that China's GDP was overstated. Supposing they wrote in a paper they put out in that year and on the basis of which all later UN data were based, "it was assumed that the productivity of a Chinese doctor is equal to one half of that of an American doctor because American doctors have better facilities and assistance, and longer training time … the purchasing power parity for GDP changes from 0.8709 to 1.1805 and dollar GDP per capita of China in 1986 decreases from I $ 1044[44] to I $ 770 …it is easy to see that if the same productivity adjustments were made for the education and government sectors, the PPP over GDP would be much higher and real income level would be much lower."[45]

So, as in the rabbit that comes out of the magician's hat, China's GDP on the basis of purchasing power dropped and in 2005 it was still at 70 per cent of the US, leading to predictions that it would take years to overtake the latter.

However, over ten years earlier, as if in preparation of what was to come, the PLAAF, the People's Liberation Army Air Force, had decided to expand the three brigades of its 15th Airborne Army (roughly equivalent to the US Marines), into three divisions, meaning from a total of 3-4,000 men to around 15,000. This seems to have been a follow-up to Jiang Zemin's address to the 14th Party Congress, October 1992, when he said in the post-Cold War world there would be an outbreak of ethnic, territorial and religious conflicts, and that China should be prepared with a Rapid Reaction Force. The expansion of this force continued and by the turn of the century articles had started appearing in the world's defence journals about the Chinese Rapid Reaction Force.

In any case the broad conclusion must be that almost at the turn of a switch, China can, as far as IR analysis is concerned, assume the role of (sole) global super power. We may then expect it to bask in that role for several years before using the capabilities it is already developing to undertake a military expedition to expand its power, again on the basis of the traditional story. Where that expedition will be can only be guessed at; but the story leaves no doubt about the outcome.

## ENDNOTES

[1] Or graveyard of empires, as Rand Corporation analyst Seth Jones put it, see his *In the Graveyard of Empires, America's War in Afghanistan*, W.W.Norton, New York, 2009.

[2] Prem Shankar Jha, *The End of Saddam Hussein, History through the Eyes of the Victims*, Rupa, New Delhi, 2004, p. 75.

[3] See Ahmed Rashid, *Descent into Chaos*, Allen Lane, London, 2008, p. 64.

[4] Phyllis Bennis, *Before and After: US Foreign Policy and the September 11th Crisis*, Olive Branch Press, New York, 2003, pp. 82, 88.

[5] Extract from *Report of the United Nations to Assess Humanitarian Needs in Iraq*, by a mission led by Martti Ahtisaari, UN Under-Secretary General for Administration and Management.

[6] UNICEF report quoted by K.P. Fabian, *The Commonsense on the War on Iraq*, Somaiya Publications, Mumbai, 2003, p. 80.

[7] Ekaterina Stepanova, The Unilateral and Multilateral Use of Force by the United States, in David M. Malone and Yuen Foong Khong, *Unilateralism and U.S. Foreign Policy, International Perspectives*, Lynne Rienner, Boulder, 2003, p. 187.

[8] Geoff Simons, *Iraq: From Sumer to Saddam*, Macmillan, Hampshire, 1996, pp. 154-5.

[9] Philip K. Hitti, *History of the Arabs, From the Earliest Times to the Present*, Macmillan, Hampshire, 1985, pp. 292, 302-303 and 294 for quotes in this paragraph, except the first one.

[10] Mohammad Sohrab, Mono-Ethnic Domination in a Multi-Ethnic Society, in Hari Vasudevan et al. eds., *The Global Politics of the Iraq Crisis and India's Options*, Aakar Books, Delhi, 2004, p. 257.

[11] David L. Phillips, *Losing Iraq: Inside the Post-War Reconstruction Fiasco,* Westview, Boulder, Col., 2005, p. 337.

[12] Toby Dodge, State Collapse and the Rise of Identity Politics, in Markus E. Bouillon et al. eds., *Iraq, Preventing a New Generation of Conflict*, Lynne Rienner, Boulder, 2007, p. 25.

[13] Robert I. Rotberg, Introduction to Robert I. Rotberg, ed., *State Failure and State Weakness in a Time of Terror*, Brookings Institute, Washington, DC, 2003, p. 5.

[14] Liam Anderson and Gareth Stansfield, *The Future of Iraq, Dictatorship, Democracy, or Division?*, Palgrave, Macmillan, New York, 2004, p. 11.

[15] Sami Zubaida, The Fragments Imagine the Nation: The Case of Iraq, in *International Journal of Middle East Studies*, Vol. 34, 2002, p. 214, 211.

[16] Charles Tripp, *A History of Iraq*, Cambridge University Press, 2000, p. 1.

[17] Sandra Mackey, *The Reckoning, Iraq and the Legacy of Saddam Hussain*, W.W.Norton, New York, 2002, p. 59.

[18] George L Harris, *Iraq, Its people, its Society, its Culture*, HRAF Press, New Haven, 1958, p. 41.

[19] Liora Lukitz, *Iraq, The Search for National Identity*, Frank Cass, London, 1995, p. 6.

[20] George L. Harris, op. cit., p. 9.

[21] Toby Dodge, op. cit., p. 29.

[22] Michel Eppel, The Elite, the Effendiya, and the Growth of Nationalism and Pan-Arabism in Hashemite Iraq, 1921-1958, in *International Journal of Middle East Studies*, Vol. 30, No. 2, May 1998, p. 233.

[23] Reeva S. Simon, The Teaching of History in Iraq before the Rashid Ali Coup of 1941, in *Middle Eastern Studies,* Vol. 22, No.1, January 1986, p. 41.

[24] Sandra Mackey, op. cit., p. 182.

[25] See Amatzai Baram, Mesopotamian Identity in Baathist Iraq, *Middle Eastern Studies*, Vol. 19, No. 4, October 1983, pp. 428-9.

[26] Liora Lukitz, op. cit., pp. 113 and 149 for this and the previous three paragraphs.

[27] Charles Tripp, op. cit., p. 41.

[28] Geoff Simons, op. cit., pp. 213 and 217 for this and the previous three paragraphs.

[29] Sandra Mackey, op. cit., p. 143.

[30] Mohammed M. Hafez, *Suicide Bombers in Iraq*, US Institute of Peace Press, Washington, 2007, p. 94.

[31] Abdel Salam Sidahmed, Islamism, Nationalism and Sectarianism, in Markus E. Bouillon et. al., eds, op. cit., p. 78.

[32] Not to be confused with the April 1983 Beirut bombing of the US embassy, which was done by the Islamic Jihad Organisation, also affiliated with Iran, by the way, and reportedly with Hezbollah in Lebanon.

[33] See Oliver Poole, *Red Zone: Five Bloody Years in Iraq*, Reportage Press, London, 2008, p. 176.

[34] See Mike Marqusee, Growing Resistance, in *The Hindu*, 22 April, 2007.

[35] Bruce Riedel, Al Qaeda Strikes Back, in *Foreign Affairs*, May/June 2007.

[36] Daniel Byman, Who Wins in Iraq? Al Qaeda, in *Foreign Policy*, March/April, 2007, p. 43.

[37] Quoted by Atul Aneja, Chinks in the Armour in Iraq, *The Hindu,* 28 April, 2007.

[38] See, for example, Frederick W. Kagan, The U.S.Military's Manpower Crisis, in *Foreign Affairs*, July/August, 2006, Vol. 85, No. 4, pp. 98-102.

[39] See Tim Kane, Global US Troop Deployment, 1950-2003, The Heritage Foundation, Centre for Data Analysis, on the heritage.org website.

[40] Martin Jacques in *The Hindu,* 21 April 2009.

[41] *World Development Report*, 1993, p. 320.

[42] That of Russia was $ 967 billion, also far behind.

[43] He was replaced by Hu Jintao at that Congress.

[44] 'I' is an international dollar, used also for comparisons of GDP based on purchasing power, and explained by the World Bank as "one international dollar has the same purchasing power over domestic GNI (Gross National Income) that the US dollar has over US GNI". See the *World Development Report*, 2002, p. 244.

[45] Ren Ruoen and Chen Kai, An expenditure based bilateral comparison of Gross Domestic Product between China and the United States, The World Bank, International Economics Department, Socio-Economic Data Division, Policy Research Working Paper 1415, January 1995, p. 31.

# 14

# Modernity: the Post-Cold War Era

After the Cold War was over the separation of war from power, which was noted in chapter 4 as typifying the colonial era and in chapter 9 as a characteristic of the Cold War, continued. This chapter looks at these two things from the viewpoint of the story of modernity after 1990 and then it attempts to project some of the consequences of that story beyond the first decade of the third millennium.

## Looking at War

Take war first.

During the Cold War attention had come to be focused on scenarios of nuclear war, which produced a substantial literature; and, as the years passed, on local war, guerilla campaigns, civil conflict and the like, the 'host' of small wars around the world. So war in general as a concept had diffracted and scattered; it yielded a growing mass of statistics and then it became possible for academic efforts to hope to bring its study on to a mathematical basis.

Now, in the post-Cold War period nuclear war fighting scenarios took a back seat. All that was left were the small wars and they became so much more diffuse and diffracted that war as concept could no longer hope to be put into the kind of framework of timeless and universal principles that mathematical precision demanded. There was also another change. During the Cold War such small wars or conflicts had the potential of escalating into super-power confrontation; thereafter they were a threat in their own right to the sole super-power, to the civilised world, to freedom and even to things like the environment. So this was now a diffused threat as well as a diffusion of things under threat.

Let us first of all see how this theme was developed over the years by leaders and others. In the second place we will see the way it came to focus on one thing: terrorism; that meant it was no longer diffuse. Thirdly, how did people propose to meet this threat.

Some examples will illustrate the first aspect. Here is President Clinton speaking to the UN General Assembly in September 1994 on the diffusion of the threat. "The dangers we face are less stark and more diffuse than those of the Cold War, but they are still formidable – the ethnic conflicts that drive millions from their homes; the despots ready to repress their own people or conquer their neighbours; the proliferation of weapons of mass destruction; the terrorists wielding their deadly arms; the criminal syndicates selling those arms or drugs or infiltrating the very institutions of a fragile democracy"; and then he continues on to the diffusion of the things under threat: "a global economy that offers great promise but also deep insecurity and, in many places, declining opportunity; diseases like AIDs that threaten to decimate nations", and then he goes on to the population explosion, environmental threats, families breaking down, and ends, "these are the dangers we face today."

Over the years the threat stayed diffused. Here is Clinton again, in his January 1998 State of the Union address where he spoke of "an unholy axis of new threats from terrorists, international criminals and drug traffickers".

To give another example of the kind of threat that could well develop, by 2001, as the US believed, 29 nations had ballistic missile capability. Many of these like Iraq, Iran, North Korea or Libya were nations of major concern. They were on the road to acquiring nuclear, chemical and biological weapons or had already done so, despite having signed and ratified the relevant disarmament treaties and non-possession pledges. Their leaders emerged from socio-political systems that knew no freedoms and "that have a different appreciation for the value of human life, that have a different appreciation for what happens to their regime ... I don't think you can assume that their calculations are entirely rational ...".[1] This approach was not entirely new; under the Clinton administration Anthony Lake, the national security adviser, had referred to 'backlash states', those who did not want to be part of the family of freedom-loving, pluralistic, democratic, free-market nations; these comprised the future threat which would have to be contained. But it was being more clearly and persistently articulated as the years passed.

Such a regime might well not hesitate to attack the US mainland or US troops even knowing that their own and probably their country's destruction would inevitably follow. The September 11 attacks dramatically highlighted the reality of the threat arising from the conflation of a rogue state and a radical terrorist group with weapons of mass destruction, and that multilateral diplomacy and disarmament treaties, formal and well-structured alliances, could never stop such threats. The conflation would put the nation concerned on a US watch list. President Bush underlined the problem in an address to an audience in Atlanta, Georgia, on February 1, 2002. "If you're one of these nations that developed weapons of mass destruction and you're likely to team up with a terrorist group or you're sponsoring terror and you don't hold the values that we hold dear true to your heart then you too are on our watch list."[2]

Later, Bush took Clinton's axis idea into his State of the Union address, 29 January 2003, speaking of an axis of evil comprising North Korea, Iran and Iraq and their terrorist allies, "arming to threaten the peace of the world".

Successive US Presidents were talking the same language: one cannot negotiate with a source of threat that is so diffracted; for it personifies evil, and the ambitions of evil are unlimited. "No concession will appease their hatred", said President Bush at the White House on March 19, 2004, in a speech on Operation Iraqi Freedom and Operation Enduring Freedom, "no accommodation will satisfy their endless demands. Their ultimate ambitions are to control the peoples of the Middle East, and to blackmail the rest of the world."

Again and again, US spokespersons came back to the theme that every kind of danger was lurking in the background. US Secretary of State Condoleezza Rice addressed the UN General Assembly on the U.N.'s 60th anniversary, 2005 and referred to all the new threats that had emerged in the post-Cold War period, terrorism, the proliferation of weapons of mass destruction, pandemics, shifting "the very terrain of international politics beneath our feet"; threats emerge within states and "melt through their borders"; earlier the threats came from strong, aggressive states, while now they were from "weak and poorly governed states" which were unable to ruling their countries with justice and generated crises "from civil war and genocide, to extreme poverty and humanitarian disaster."

The threat could, of course, have come from a particular country but now it was usually a group of countries, sometimes a group of countries with specified character traits, often such a group mixed up with non-state actors, who were thought to have some sort of independent role in the worldwide threat making.

Still later, during the campaign for the 2008 presidential election, several candidates stepped in with elaborations on the same theme. One was Mitt Romney's campaign ad that America was in a struggle with people who aim "to unite the world under a single jihadist Caliphate. To do this they must collapse freedom-loving nations. Like us." Romney was backed by neo-conservative opinion-makers like Norman Podhoretz who wrote about the Islamofascist ideology against which America had been fighting since 9/11 and which wished to create a world shaped by their wishes, as in this example, "by the end of the 21st century the whole of Europe will be transformed into a place to which they give the name Eurabia."[3] Now, said Podhoretz, having defeated communism in the Third (undeclared) World War, America is engaged in the Fourth World War against Islamofascism. In brief, "for the American right, the September 11 attacks were a new Pearl Harbour, and served as a warning that a new gathering storm of terrorist groups and their state sponsors had arrived to threaten freedom around the world."[4]

Soon academic writers on the subject joined in. One interpretation of the above developments was that the era of Clausewitzian war was coming to an end, and "we are entering a period of anarchy, of uncontrollable generalised disintegrative violence … the new wars do not presuppose the existence of states" which could ensure peace within their territories.[5] Another author refers to the idea that states decompose and, as this happens their elites rely on plunder to annex wealth, corruption spreads, identity politics emerges, and then "violence is decentralised, war is conducted by militias and criminal bands as much as by regular forces."[6]

Perhaps one of the leading exponents of this thinking was Martin van Creveld, who portrayed a future in which war was fought by non-state entities, tribes, guerillas, bandits, terrorists, robbers with organisations motivated by fanatical, ideology-based loyalties, not by the expectation of territorial gain as was traditionally the case and, going further, such a war could become an end in itself, there may be situations in which motivation does not lead to war but war to motivation; they will target individuals; and the war will be low intensity, with skirmishes, bombings, massacres with small cheap gadgets as the weapons, perhaps even poison gas and others which are forbidden today, not the massive expensive ships and aircraft of today.[7]

But to get back to the story of modernity, depictions of this diffused worldwide threat led to the generation of a generalised fear, often without anything to be afraid of.

Years before, in October 1999 the Federal Bureau of Investigation had released a report which suggested that many groups – White Supremacy, Christian Identity, Black Hebrew Israelites, Wotanists, the Asatru-Odinic Alliance, or other apocalyptic cults – would engage in violence with the approach of the year 2000, and in the belief that the end of the world was nigh. This was the Megiddo report, named after a hill in northern Israel, said to be the setting for Armageddon (from Megiddo) the final war between good and evil; this now encapsulated what was almost a new lifestyle.

Zygmunt Bauman compared it to living in Europe in the sixteenth century. It was a life of fear, lived in ubiquitous fear, of the darkness that "started just on the other side of the hut door and wrapped the world beyond the farm fence ..." And "ours is, again, a time of fears" fears from a threat which may come "from dark streets and from brightly lit television screens ... earthquakes, floods, hurricanes, mudslides, droughts", and from that unknown zone, "a sense numbing and mind-chafing grey zone, as yet unnamed, from which ever more dense and sinister fears seep, threatening to destroy our homes, workplaces and bodies ...".[8]

## Terrorism Encapsulates all Threats

That brings us to the second aspect, way the threat came gradually to focus on one thing: terrorism.

After 1970, in stages as the word terrorist came into wider use, the state had already taken the lead in using it to describe more and more of the groups which used force against it. This was broadly in line with the diffusion of the threat from small wars.

For the terrorist threat this meant that terrorist groups were dispersed and the members of each group were dispersed. Each was given only general directions, back-up in terms of finance, a supply of weapons, logistic support, but they decided on and carried out specific actions independently. These networked groups were far more difficult to track down. "Increasingly, counter-terrorism law enforcement officials find themselves operating within a nebulous milieu of fluid terror group profiles, where transient, special purpose coalitions incorporate temporarily, sometimes for only a single action."[9] This also meant that groups involved in drugs, or in international crime, come together with terrorists. Former adversaries "are modifying their structures and strategies to take advantage of networked designs, e.g., transnational terrorist groups, black-market proliferators of weapons of mass destruction, drug and other crime syndicates, fundamentalist and ethno-nationalist movements ..."[10]

The traditional effort, in the matter of studying and finding ways to counter terrorism, was to try linking the causes of terrorism with terrorist actions and their aims. This continued for about three decades after 1970.

The causes were found, of instance, in the increasing numbers of internal and external refugees which made for a large reservoir from which terrorists could be recruited. And there were the socio-economic problems, the poverty, deprivation, inhuman treatment of refugees and others which made recruitment easier. The debate on this issue, which continued and intensified for a while after 11 September 2001, can best be illustrated by two sample quotations. "No amount of police action, however cooperative, can stop terrorism without addressing the conditions of misery and injustice that nourish and aggravate terrorism."[11] And this: that problems like the rich-poor division, lack of social justice, the Palestine issue, "it is these unsolved problems that had in large measure incubated the monster of terrorism in the underbelly of the poor and deprived societies in both the developing and the developed nations."[12] So writings on the subject linked terrorism with the kind of deprivation, poverty, and persecution associated with deprivation, the denial of rights and low human development indices.

As for the actions and aims, these also were dispersed. Media coverage was one common purpose of a terrorist attack; then it was called performative violence. Acts of performative violence were "like religious, ritual and street theatre, or dramas designed to have an impact on the several audiences that they affect."[13] Financial gain may be the purpose, as in cases like the kidnappings of businessmen in Italy, or the hijackings of aircraft in West Asia, which were largely for money. After 1970 terrorist groups got into the drug trade. "Originally, the terrorists and the guerillas were mortal enemies of the drug producers and traders ... But, over time, the production and smuggling of drugs have been practised by guerilla and terrorist groups of the left as well as the right."[14] Yet a different kind of purpose was where the violence was solipsist: the Montoneros of Argentina undertook very risky tasks because they hoped for martyrdom and immortality; better known were the groups who carried out attacks with certain death for the perpetrators at the end like the LTTE often did. There was also Fanonism: a violent attack against an oppressor, even if it serves no other purpose, is worth undertaking because it is liberating and empowering.

The ultimate aims of terrorist groups were also dispersed: there were the socio-economic or political aims, as were those of the Baader Meinhof group who claimed to be the vanguard of the weak and the oppressed; the Tupamaros of Uruguay, the Montoneros of Argentina and the later Shining Path or Sendero Luminoso of Peru all of whom wanted socio-political revolution; and, at the other end of the political spectrum were the extreme right militias. Outside such aims were those of the millenarian and messianic groups like the Lord's Resistance Army of Uganda, the Japanese Aum Shinri Kyo, and, of course, Al Qaeda. Then again groups changed their ultimate aims frequently with a constant inflow of new groups with new aims like the eco-terrorists who sank whaling vessels, attacked hydro-power stations and tried to sabotage nuclear power plants. There were violent animal rights activists; there was agro terrorism.

But there was agreement that the actual attacks seemed to become more destructive and easier to execute with each passing year. There were many reasons for this: a steady increase in the destructive capacity of individuals and small groups due to technological advances in materials engineering, the chemistry of explosives and the miniaturisation of electronics; a frequently expressed fear, both officially and in other writings on the subject, that one or other terrorist group will one day acquire weapons of mass destruction; the evolution of communication and information systems meant new targets in cyber-terrorism as well as more easily available data about targets, about the design of aircraft, the structural specifications of buildings, and the movements of VIP's; and economic and technical systems becoming increasingly vulnerable due to their complexity and interdependence.

In sum, "we're easy prey because of two key trends: First, the growing technological capacity of small groups and individuals to destroy things and people; and, second, the increasing vulnerability of our economic and technological systems to carefully aimed attacks." The consequence is that "the advantage in this war has shifted towards terrorists. Our increased vulnerability – and our newfound recognition of that vulnerability – makes us more risk-averse, while terrorists have become more powerful and more tolerant of risk."[15]

This diffusion of threats and things threatened, so far as terrorism was concerned, was gradually reversed after 9/11. The scope or even the desire to seek the sources of grievances in socio-economic or political causes waned; there was a state-led effort to place all those who sought redress for such grievances through violence, or took to violence for other reasons, under one label and to deal with them through the promulgation of one or a few laws. There was no longer any effort to analyse the dispersal or diffusion of threat; now there was only one source of threat and it was religious based. It was also not necessary, according to the post-9/11 thinking, to seek the causes of terrorism, since there were no causes other than the destruction of western civilization itself and its replacement by an Islamo-fascist system. As for aims these were also linked to fundamentalist religion.

Academic research yielded data such as that collected by the ITERATE project, International Terrorism: Attributes of Terrorist Events, and this seemed to show that "because they believe that they speak for God and view all non-believers as legitimate targets, the fundamentalists are not worried about alienating the public" which the left wing and secular terrorists of the 1980s were. So the act "is a sufficient end, particularly if it kills the non-believers, including women and children." Hence there is greater carnage, especially suicide attacks, which lead to thirteen fatalities per attack compared to only one for other kinds.[16] There was, indeed, much to be afraid of, since it was also found that since 1980 the number of religious-based groups has increased as a proportion of active terrorist groups. And, "today, fundamentalist terrorist groups purposely seek out mass casualties, viewing anyone not with them as a legitimate target."[17]

At first this trend of thinking was largely concentrated in the West; thereafter it became universal.

## The Destruction of Evil

The third aspect was the question of who was to meet this threat, who was to destroy this new evil.

This task fell to the US and the US alone.

For, as Vice President Cheney told the Council on Foreign Relations on 16 February 2002, "only we can lead the war on terrorism; only we can rally the world in a task of this complexity against an enemy so elusive and so resourceful. The United States and only the United States can see this effort through to victory." The claim to a sole right to leadership had been articulated before, and one quote will suffice to illustrate the point. President Reagan in 1983 proclaimed "the undeniable truth that America remains the greatest force for peace anywhere in the world today ... the American dream lives – not only in the hearts and minds of our countrymen but in the hearts and minds of millions of the world's people ... who look to us for leadership."[18] But now, after 9/11 it was reiterated more forcefully.

With this duty to the world's people in mind President Bush told the United Nations in September, 2002, that in the matter of the "permanent rights and hopes of mankind" a stand must be taken and "by heritage and by choice, the United States of America will make that stand." Again, as he told his audience at the State of the Union address, 2003, "history has called America and our allies to action, and it is both our responsibility and our privilege to fight freedom's fight." In this task, such was the structure of the international order; the US did not have to depend on anyone else. They were welcome to join in the task, but were not necessary for it to be completed. This is well expressed by what Bush told Indonesian President Megawati Sukarnoputri on 19 September 2001, just a few days after the attack on the US, that "some nations will be comfortable supporting overt activities, some nations will only be comfortable in providing information, others will be helpful and only feel comfortable on financial matters. I understand that."

Indeed allies were a hindrance in some ways; "in the realm of air and space, the United States so outstrips its allies that technology actually inhibits effective military cooperation with allies and friends, exposing the United States to more strident global criticism"; in Afghanistan to give an example the US supplied "nearly 100 per cent of the lethal force", which had to be technology based, while its allies could only supply ground troops.[19]

One of the most important reasons for which this task fell naturally to the US was its construction of the idea of freedom (not to be confused with democracy, by the way), a sort of ultimate safeguard against the new religion based terrorism and its ideologies.

Post-1945 historiography traces the concept of freedom inaccurately to the American civil war where its negative was slavery; but, in fact, it was spelt out for the first time in detail by President Roosevelt in the Four Freedoms speech of 6 January 1941, and applied in the Truman doctrine of 12 March 1947. Greece for which President Truman asked Congress for aid was not a democracy at the time, nor was Turkey, the other country to receive US aid. But he said that their freedom and their very existence were "threatened by the terrorist activities of several thousand armed men led by the communists....". Here freedom's negative was not slavery, but terrorism and totalitarianism.

Another phase in the development of this concept began in June 1950 with the Korean War, encapsulated in Secretary of State Dean Acheson's Strategy of Freedom speech of 29 November 1950. Six elements were listed comprising the strategy of freedom; democracy or the democratic way of life was not among them.

The concept continued evolving, but it always remained basic. Freedom comes from a Book into which the law was laid down by forces beyond man's control. President Bush said it best in his inaugural address, 20 January 2001. "America remains engaged in the world by history and by choice, shaping a balance of power that favours freedom ... we are not this story's author, who fills time and eternity with his purpose. Yet his purpose is achieved in our duty, and our duty is fulfilled in service to one another."

Nine days after 11 September 2001, in an address to a Joint Session of Congress, he traced the lineage of those who had opposed it over the decades. "They are the heirs of all the murderous ideologies of the 20th century ... they follow in the path of fascism, and Nazism, and totalitarianism. And they will follow that path all the way, to where it ends, in history's unmarked grave of discarded lies." A little over four months later Bush delivered his State of the Union address, 29 January, 2002. The word democracy finds no place in an address which largely dealt with America's response to the attacks. But freedom occupies centreplace. Those killed by the terrorists "gave their lives for freedom"; with terrorists at large "freedom is at risk"; and there would be created a new USA Freedom Corps to supplement the work of the Peace Corps.

In this epic struggle, there can be no bystanders, no middle ground. George Kennan had written in 1931 that "the present system of Soviet Russia is so unalterably opposed to our traditional system, that there can be no middle ground or compromise between them."[20] Sixteen years later, in the enunciation of the Truman doctrine, there was this: "At the present moment is world history, nearly every nation must choose between alternative ways of life, one distinguished by free institutions, the other relying on terror and oppression." The quotations can be multiplied, but one more will suffice. Talking about neutralism, a word which Secretary of State Dulles used for non-alignment, he told an Iowa State University audience in June 1956 that unless there were exceptional circumstances neutralism was "an immoral and shortsighted conception."

Right the outset of the campaign against Al Qaeda, therefore, Bush said on 20 September, "Every nation, in every region, now has a decision to make. Either you are with us, or you are with the terrorists." Announcing Operation Enduring Freedom on 7 October, he reverted to this theme, "Every nation has a choice to make. In this conflict there is no neutral ground." Amplifying this point President Bush told the United Nations in September, 2003 that there is "the clearest of divides between those who seek order, and those who spread chaos; between those who work for peaceful change, and those who adopt the methods of gangsters; between those who honour the rights of man, and those who deliberately take the lives of men and women and children without mercy or shame. Between these alternatives there is no neutral ground."

With the US having taken the lead, there was little scope for doubt about the outcome of the war against terror. More or less in parallel with the terrorist groups the US maintained that this war had no end but total victory. This was Armageddon, the war to end all wars, the final war between Good and Evil.

The negative to freedom had to be destroyed completely,

however long it took; it was not conceivable that even a little bit of evil should be allowed to survive, for freedom is always already under threat. Its negative, as posited by National Security Council directive 68 of 1950 (the policy document that appeared shortly before, and was given the status of the key Cold War document of the US by the Korean War), "cannot tolerate the very existence of freedom as an idea and must systematically attempt its liquidation." President Bush told the United Nations on September 12, 2002, that the outlaw groups and regimes "accept no law of morality and have no limit to their violent ambitions". Hence, unless the evil is completely destroyed some threat, however small, will remain. "As the United States is the repository of freedom, any threat to it is a threat of enslavement and is against the basic principles of humankind."[21]

In order to dramatise the total destruction of evil the US resorted to the concept of justice. Initially the military deployment to the region around Afghanistan was named 'Operation Infinite Justice'. But infinite justice, both in Christianity and in Islam, is the prerogative only of God. So this was changed to 'Operation Enduring Freedom'. But the idea of justice found other expressions. On 20 September Bush said to the US Congress, "Whether we bring our enemies to justice, or bring justice to our enemies, justice will be done". He had already elaborated to the press on 17 September, "I want justice. There's an old poster out West that as I recall said – Wanted, dead or alive." And on 15 September, "we will smoke them out of their holes, we'll get them running and we'll bring them to justice". Over two months later, as the Taliban faced certain defeat, he reverted to the metaphor that suggested that these were vermin rather than people. "We're smoking them out", he said on 26 November, "they're running and now we're going to bring them to justice."

So, to summarise, there are all these threats on one side; on the other there is the remaining sole super-power and its propagation of freedom as the antidote. The world can then be divided into those for freedom and those against. The purpose served by Social Darwinism during colonial times and ideological rivalry during the Cold War is thus served by freedom during the post-Cold War era.

## The Measure of Power

Expectedly, as far as power was concerned, Europe was not now at the centre, as it was in the modernity version of the Cold War; now it was the US alone.

Let us take a look at the ways in which the US was described.

During the post-Cold War era, as noted briefly at the beginning of chapter 12, the US was acclaimed as the sole super-power. First, there was now a new structure of international relations. This was celebrated with an exuberance typified by Charles Krauthammer in an oft-quoted article on the unipolar moment: "The immediate post-Cold War world is not multipolar. It is unipolar." Secondly, continuing with the Krauthammer quotation, "the centre of world power is the unchallenged super-power, the United States ... The true geopolitical structure of the post-Cold War world ... a single pole of world power that consists of the United States at the apex of the industrial West" and with a pre-eminence "based on the fact that it is the only country with the military, diplomatic, political and economic assets to be a decisive player in any conflict in whatever part of the world it chooses to involve itself." Thirdly, the US has to take the lead in all global matters, and here, as mentioned above, the idea of sheriff enters, for mankind's best hope lies in American strength and will, "the strength and will to lead a unipolar world, unashamedly laying down the rules of world order and being prepared to enforce them."[22]

After 9/11 Krauthammer returned to the theme emphasising that now US relative power had increased. "American military spending exceeds that of the next twenty countries combined. Its navy, air force and space power are unrivalled. Its technology is irresistible. It is dominant by every measure, military, economic, technological, diplomatic, cultural, even linguistic." So he averred that while his earlier prediction of unipolarity lasting thirty or forty years seemed bold at the time, now that was modest, for "the unipolar moment has become the unipolar era."[23]

Others, equally exuberant, agreed. "America today is by any measure the world's unchallenged military and economic power ... the world counts on us to be a catalyst of coalitions, a broker of peace, a guarantor of global financial stability ... our success is so apparent to others that one of our biggest challenges now is to manage the resentment it sometimes generates,"[24] wrote one author. Another even averred that words were not enough. After the destruction of the twin towers of New York on 9/11, he wrote "words alone did not seem to be enough to describe just how formidable the last remaining super-power had suddenly become", so the problem is not that the US has too little power, "but that it now has too much."[25]

It was, of course, compared to Rome; here is one quotation: "The strength acquired by the United States in the aftermath of World War II was far greater than any single nation had ever possessed, at least since the Roman Empire."[26] And another: "Probably not since classic Rome or ancient China has a single power so towered over its known rivals in the international system. Today, only the US military retains the ability to reach into any region in the world within mere hours. The US economy has become the envy of the world".[27] And yet another, this one from the acclaimed international relations theorist Kenneth Waltz, "never since Rome has one country so nearly dominated its world." The examples could be multiplied but these three give the general flavour of the gladness with which the world welcomed the protection of the US against all those nameless fears.

Then the French, somewhat unexpectedly, joined in with praise for US leadership flowing out of US power. Foreign Minister Herbert Vedrine said in a speech to the Association France-Amerique in early 1999 that to describe the US as a super-power was not enough, he defined it as a "hyper-power, a country that is dominant or predominant in all categories", economics, technology, military might, the domination of attitudes, concepts, language and modes of life.[28] Even Jean Baudrillard, hardly a traditional admirer of the US, refers to its "unbearable power", its "dominant world power" which monopolises every situation.[29] So it has to be sheriff. "Today, the American hegemon is the only possible sheriff ... it is literally unstoppable by any combination of polities and institutions."[30]

We are reminded that in his *Study of History* Arnold Toynbee had identified the 'universal state', namely, those empires and civilisations whose rulers believe they have achieved a system of values and a culture which are of universal appeal and applicability; and whose citizens believe their state is blessed with immortality. He quotes Aristeides who saw a situation such as "has moved the whole world to cleave to Rome with might and main ...You must have seen bats in a cave clinging tight to one another and to the rocks; and this is an apt image of the whole World's dependence on Rome." Then Aristeides goes on to pity those people who got left outside the Empire of Rome, "if there are any such people left."[31] And, if we shift the scene to China under the Manchus, another universal state, and suggest that people outside it not only existed but were also organised into governments, then, according to the belief system of the Manchus those governments must exist only by their permission, given at some undefined period in the past.

As for measurement there has been no other perceptible advance in the concepts according to which power was measured from the Cold War to the post-Cold War era. In general we can say that, in continuation of the total separation of war from power there was a great deal of list making and reiteration that the US was the greatest ever.

Even Noam Chomsky, a severe critic of the way the US uses its power, is nevertheless among those who are prepared to draw up at least a tentative list of components which puts it right up there at the unapproachable peak. The US had half the world's wealth, was the greatest military power, had no enemies nearby, dominated both the oceans and "the richest and most developed regions across the seas, and controlled the world's major reserves of energy and other critical resources." Hence it was that "its planners could realistically design and execute a global vision."[32]

Others, more admiring, have drawn up longer lists, but two examples will have to suffice here. Joseph Nye lists hard power, meaning that of the military and of economics, and soft power meaning the ability to get other people, through admiration, envy, emulation, to want what you want or even to want what you want them to want. So there is the hard power of population, territory, natural resources, economic strength as measured, for instance, in GDP (the US has a 27% share of the world product), manufacturing value-added and high-tech exports; high defence budgets and military force, especially the possession of a large number of nuclear warheads; literacy, and political stability, all of which means "holding the high cards in the international poker game."[33] And there is the soft power, the inherent attractiveness of US culture as the largest part of the wider attractiveness of western culture, which includes western institutions and ideology.

Then there is Harvard University's Stephen M. Walt, who writes that the US has had "the world's largest economy for over a century", between 25 and 30 per cent of the world total since 1960;

American companies were the top innovators in the automotive, aerospace, biotechnology, pharmaceuticals, chemicals, computers, telecommunications, and semiconductor industries, among a host of others; the US spends nearly 40 per cent of the global total on defence, equal to the next thirteen countries combined; its R & D expenditure alone is more than the entire defence budgets of Germany, Great Britain, France, Russia, Japan or China. It plays a unique role in the most important global organisations like the UN, NATO, the IMF and the World Bank. And it has an "ability to shape the preferences of others – to make them want what America wants through the inherent attractiveness of US culture, ideology, the continued effort to promote US ideals of democracy and human rights and institutions."[34]

## Some Decline

Those who tell this story accept the evidence that recent decades have seen some decline in the relative numbers that put the US on top of the international pecking order. The share in world GDP, for instance, of the West generally and of the US, in particular, has declined since the peak reached immediately after the Second World War; so has, in relative terms, the amount spent on the armed forces. Two years before the Cold War ended Paul Kennedy pointed to the relative decline of the American economy relative to the rest of the world and cites statistics. Its share of world GNP dropped from 25.9 per cent in 1960 to 21.5 per cent by 1980. Even more dramatic was its decline in manufacturing production. It had half the world's share in 1945; by 1953 it had dropped to 44.7 per cent and by 1980 to 31.5 per cent, "and it was still falling."[35] Actually the World Development Indicators show that it had reached 23.5 per cent by 1990, but then stayed around there for over a decade. Meanwhile, during that last decade of the century China increased its share of world manufacturing production by two-and-a-half times.

But this decline will be slow. The US will continue to be the sole super-power for a great many years to come. Kennedy himself, after 9/11, compared the US position to that of Great Britain after 1815, when for decades more it continued to rule the seas and expand its empire. If military expenditures are not forced down, "America should remain unchallenged by a single rising Great Power for a generation or more."[36] Others agree. Joseph Nye quotes a Canadian political scientist, Kim Nossal saying in July, 1999 that "there is only one way that the relative balance of power capabilities between the United States and the other major powers extant at the turn of the millennium will change, very slowly, and over many decades."[37]

And Harvard University political scientist Samuel Huntington locates three major characteristics of the decline of the West, the very first being that "it is a slow process. The rise of Western power took four hundred years. Its recession could take as long". Even so, he adds, the power of a state or a group being estimated by measuring the resources it has at its disposal compared to the others (by the numbers in other words), "the West's share of most, but not all, of the important power resources peaked early in the twentieth century and then began to decline relative to those of other civilisations."[38]

## Afghanistan and Iraq

With these assumptions the projection of the consequences for Afghanistan and Iraq becomes straightforward.

The US will increase its military deployment to Afghanistan, perhaps helped by some increase in that of its allies, especially the British, the Canadian, the German and some other forces, all of whom, seeing as time goes by that the situation becomes more secure, will also agree to conduct combat operations in the south and east of the country. And all these forces will stay as long as needed to degrade the military capability of the radicalised Taliban while coopting or integrating the moderates, and this exercise will be completed successfully. The parallel work of winning hearts and minds will continue apace, based on a renewed action plan for peace and reconciliation, the willing cooperation of Pakistan, and the expanded activity of the Provincial Reconstruction Teams to the areas so far neglected by them.

Overall this means not only economic development projects, but also job creation, alternative sources of income for farmers so that the drug trade subsides, and for middle men so they too turn away from this trade.

This also means a substantial though perhaps gradual improvement in the functioning of the Afghan National Army, the police and judiciary to better handle law and order problems, the reduction of corruption and, at the apex level, not only regular elections which are seen to be free and fair, but legislation for good governance and accountability.

With all these changes and improvements, brought about through the mediation of the US and under the eye of a US military presence, the extension of that presence would be welcomed by future Afghan governments; and Afghanistan will be firmly within the American sphere of influence if not empire, while Pakistan's policy would be as closely attuned to US interests as during the best days of the early Cold War.

As for Iraq, the story of modernity projects that the process that had already begun by the Transition Government of early 2005 and continued with the December 2005 election to a National Assembly with a four-year lifespan will continue on track.

Insurgency and sectarian conflict will continue to decline; having withdrawn from active combat and from the urban centres, the further reduction of US and allied troop deployment will continue as political reconciliation makes further progress, not only between the Shia and Sunni communities, but also between the Arabs and Kurds. There has also been some violence between Shia and Shia; that, too, will be resolved. Possibly there will be some reorganisation of the power structure to give more voice to the Sunnis' reconciliation with Iraq's Arab neighbours, which has begun, will also accelerate.

Then there is the matter of economic reconstruction, which will go forward, largely funded by Iraqi oil money, with a supplement of foreign investment, which has already begun, by China and South Korea, for instance.

The US troop deployment will proceed according to the plan already laid down by a US-Iraq security agreement approved on November 2008: all US troops will leave Iraq by August 2010, while 35-50,000 will stay to train the Iraqis until end-2011, by when they too will leave. The security agreement does not provide for any to stay, but modernity suggests that the Iraqis will welcome and probably need several thousands of them to stay on beyond 2011, and that the US will agree to that.

## ENDNOTES

[1] US Undersecretary of State for Arms Control and Disarmament John Bolton in an interview given on August 15, 2001, before the terrorist attacks on the US, and quoted in *Strategic Digest*, Vol. 31, No.9, September 2001, p. 1243.

[2] As quoted in *The Hindu*, February 2, 2002.

[3] Quoted by Paul Krugman, Fearing fear itself, in *The Hindu,* 30 October, 2007.

[4] Michael J. Boyle, The war on terror in American grand strategy, *International Affairs*, 84:2 (2008), p. 195.

[5] Mary Kaldor and Basker Vashee, *Restructuring the Global Military Sector*, Vol. I, New Wars, Pinter, London, 1997, pp 3, 9.

[6] Paul Hirst, *War and Power in the 21st Century, The State, Military Conflict and the International System,* Polity, Oxford, 2001, p. 83.

[7] Martin van Creveld, *The Transformation of War*, The Free Press, New York, 1991, Chapter VII, Future War.

[8] Zygmunt Bauman, *Liquid Fear*, Polity Press, Cambridge, 2006, pp. 2-5.

[9] Joseph W. Foxell Jr., The Debate on the Potential for Mass Casualty Terrorism: The Challenge to US Security, in *Terrorism and Political Violence*, Vol.11, No.1, Spring 1999, p. 100.

[10] John Arquila and David Ronfeldt, The Advent of Netwar: Analytic Background, in *Studies in Conflict and Terrorism,* Vol.22, No.3, July-September 1999, p. 195.

[11] Rosalind P. Petchesky, Phantom Towers, Reflections on the Battle between Global Capitalism and Fundamentalist Terrorism, in *Economic and Political Weekly*, Vol.XXXVI, No. 43, October 27-November 2, 2001, p. 4120.

[12] Sumanta Banerjee, Afghanistan, Islam and the Left, in *Economic and Political Weekly*, Vol. XXXVI, No.44, November 3-9, 2001, p. 4179.

[13] Mark Juergensmeyer, *Terror in the Mind of God,* Oxford University Press, New Delhi, 2000, p. 124.

[14] Walter Laqueur, *The New Terrorists*, Oxford University Press, New York, 1999, pp. 211-212

[15] Thomas Homer-Dixon, The Rise of Complex Terrorism, in *Foreign Policy*, January/February, 2002, pp. 53 and 62.

[16] Walter Enders and Todd Sandler, *The Political Economy of Terrorism*, Cambridge University Press, 2006, p. 48.

[17] Enders and Sandler, op. cit., p. 31.

[18] Quoted in David Campbell, *Writing Security, United States Foreign Policy and the Politics of Identity*, University of Minnesota Press, Minneapolis, 1992, p. 31.

[19] Phillip S. Meilinger, Force Divider, How military technology makes the US even more unilateral, in *Foreign Policy*, Jan-Feb. 2002, pp. 76-77.

[20] David Campbell, op. cit., p. 251.

[21] Quotes in this paragraph from Anders Stephanson, Liberty or Death: The Cold War as US Ideology, in Odd Arne Westad ed., *Reviewing the Cold War*, Frank Cass, London, 2000, pp. 85 and 87.

[22] Charles Krauthammer, The Unipolar Moment, in *Foreign Affairs,* special issue on America and the World 1990/91, Vol. 70, No. 1, pp. 23, 24, 33.

[23] Charles Krauthammer, The Unipolar Moment Revisited, in *The National Interest*, Vol. 70, Winter 2002/03, pp. 5-17.

[24] Samuel R. Berger, A Foreign Policy for the Global Age, in *Foreign Affairs,* November/December 2000, Vol. 79, No. 6, p. 23.

[25] Michael Cox, Meanings of Victory: American Power after the Towers, in Ken Booth and Tim Dunne, eds., *World's in Collision, Terror and the Future of Global Order*, Palgrave Macmillan, Hampshire, 2002, p. 153, 184.

[26] Robert Kagan, The Benevolent Empire, in *Foreign Policy*, Summer 1998, No.111, p. 26.

[27] Charles William Maynes, The Perils of (and for) an Imperial America, in *Foreign Policy*, Summer 1998, No. 111, p. 37.

[28] As reported in the *International Herald Tribune*, 5th February, 1999.

[29] Jean Baudrillard, *The Spirit of Terrorism and Requiem for the Twin Towers,* Verso, London, 2002, pp. 5-8.

[30] Colin Gray, World Politics as usual after September 11, Realism Vindicated, in., Ken Booth and Tim Dunne, eds., op. cit. p. 233

[31] Quoted in Arnold J. Toynbee, *A Study of History*, Abridgement of Vols. VII-X by D.C. Somervell, OUP London, 1957, p. 7.

[32] Noam Chomsky, *World Orders, Old and New*, OUP, Delhi, 1998, p. 83.

[33] Joseph Nye, Jr. *The Paradox of American Power, Why the World's only Superpower can't Go It Alone,* OUP, New York, 2002, pp. 4-5.

[34] Stephen M. Walt, *Taming America's Power, The Global Response to US Primacy*, W.W. Norton, New York, 2005, pp. 31-37; p. 53 for ideology.

[35] Paul Kennedy, *The Rise and Fall of the Great Powers, Economic Change and Military Conflict from 1500 to 2000,* Fontana Press, London, 1989, p. 558.

[36] Paul Kennedy, Maintaining American Power: from Injury to Recovery, in Strobe Talbott and Nayan Chanda, eds., *The Age of Terror*, Basic Books, New York, 2001, p. 62.

[37] Joseph Nye, Jr., op. cit., p. 38.

[38] Samuel P. Huntington, *The Clash of Civilisations and the Remaking of World Order*, Simon and Schuster, New York, 1996, pp. 83-4.

# Index


Abbas, Ferhat (1899–1985), Algerian nationalist leader, 80, 121, 131–3, 136, 143, 390
1936 declaration 121
Abbe Charles–Irene Castel de Saint Pierre (1658–1743), French writer and radical 23
*Project for Making Peace Perpetual in Europe* 23
Abdali , Ahmed Shah (1723–1773), founder of Afghanistan 280
Abdallah Abdallahi (1846–1899), Sudan, heir to the Mahdi 68
Abdel Kader, Amir (1808–1883), Algerian nationalist, xvii, 119, 126–31, 135, 237
Abdelmalik, Mohammed El Amjed Ibn (mid-19th c.), Algerian nationalist, called Bou Baghla 129
Abed Si Mohamed El, Algeria (mid-19th c.), Touareg leader 130
Abu Jafar al Mansur (712–775), second Abbasid Caliph 344
Aceh, northern Sumatra 98–100, 109
Acheson, Dean (1893–1971), US Secretary of State 166–7, 174, 381
*A Cross–Polity Survey; and the World Handbook of Political and Social Indicators* 231
Addington, Larry H. 66
*The Patterns of War Since the Eighteenth Century* 66
Addington Survey (1990), history of warfare 222
Aden 32–3, 166–69
Afghani, Jamaluddin (1838–1897), Islamic activist 124
Afghanistan 54, 60, 66, 154, 158, 216, 219, 221, 224, 229, 241, 275–315, 317–37, 362, 365, 381, 383, 388–9
Afghans Make War 290
British Effort at Empire 283, 286
Commanders and Parties 303
custom and tradition 277
Impact of Defeat on Soviet Union 310
Kabul uprising 285
Khalq leadership 298
Khyber pass 290
Northern Alliance (NA), 317, 320
Soviet Military Effort 295
Soviet occupation of 299
Soviet policy 297
Treaty of Peace 188, 291
Tripartite Treaty 284
US and Pakistan 299
Aflaq, Michael (1910–1989), founder of Baathism 160, 351
Africa, 31–2, 38–9, 45, 47, 49–50, 52, 54–60, 65, 67, 69, 71–2, 75, 81, 85–6, 116, 119, 123, 125, 130, 137, 145, 157, 159, 166, 172, 180–81, 196, 203, 216, 220–21, 224, 227, 293, 309
partition of 50

Agung, Sultan, 17th c. Mataram ruler 95
Ahidjo Ahmadou (1924–1989), First President of Cameroun 47
Ahmed Bey (1784–1850), Algerian nationalist 129
Ahmed Gen. Mahmood, Director General, ISI (1999–2001), 319
Ahmed , Orabi 49, *see also* Pasha, Arabi
Aideed Mohamed Farah (1934–1996), Somali leader, 198–203
Ait Ahmed Hocine (1926–), Algerian nationalist leader 133
Akbar (1542–1602), Mughal emperor 80
Akbari Sheikh, mujahidin leader 305
Albania 184
Al Banna, Hassan (1906–1949), founder of Muslim Brotherhood 323
Albright, Madeleine, US Secretary of State 201
Albuquerque, Affonso (1453–1515), Governor of Portuguese India 32–5, 60, 82, 92–3, 167
al–Dawa (1957–), Militant Iraqi party 359
Alexander of Macedonia (356–323 BC), 3, 31, 36, 285, 292, 343
Alexandria 34, 49, 164
Algeria 31, 54, 116–49, 158, 168, 217, 236–7, 239
  Algerian Communist Party (PCA), 121, 130, 133, 138
  Algerian National Front (MNA), 137, 140
  Algerian People's Party (PPA), 133
  Association of Algerian Muslim Ulema (AUMA), 132
  Association of Friends of the Manifesto and Liberty (AML), 133
  Casbah operation 142
  Club des Neuf 135
  Dey 117, 118, 125–6
  French 143
  French forces in 118, 137, 143
  French occupation of 127
  integration of 131
  *Manifeste du Peuple Algerien* 132
  Movement for the Triumph of Democratic Liberties (MTLD), 133
  National Liberation Army (ALN), 136–7
  National Liberation Front (FLN), 135–42, 143, 144, 145, 146
  Numidia 123
  post–independence 132
  reign of Muawiyah 123
  Revolutionary Council for Unity and Action (CRUA), 135
  *toute–presence* colony 119
  Treaty of Tafna 127–8
Al–Harthi, Abushiri ibn Salim, 19th c. Tanzanian nationalist 49
Al–Husri Sati (1882–1968), Arab nationalist 349–50
Ali Amar, Ali la Pointe (1930–1957), Algerian war hero 139
Ali, Chaudhary Rahmat, (1897–1951), proponent of Pakistan 46
Alighieri, Dante (1265–1321), Italian poet 19
Al–Jalili, Abdel Kader (1077–1166), Islamic leader 126
Al Mamun, Caliph (783–833), Abbasid Caliph 345
Almohads (1130–1248), Berber rulers of North Africa and Iberia 125
Almoravids (1050–1130), Berber rulers of North Africa and Iberia 125
Al Qaeda 277, 317, 320–29, 338, 360–62, 364, 378, 382
Al Shihab 132
Amanpour Christiane (1958–), British journalist 318, 422
Amer General Abdul Hakim Egyptian Vice President (1958–65), 181
American War of Independence 80
Amin Hafizullah (1929–1979), President of Afghanistan 281, 295, 355
Amir of Mascara, *see* Abdul Kader

Amir ul Muminin, Commander of the Faithful 125–6
Amir ul Muslimin, Commander of Muslims 125
Amma, Sheikh Bou 130
Amouche, village in Algeria 120
Anderson Benedict (1936–), English American IR Professor 40, 75–6, 93–4
Angell Norman (1872–1967), English author 151
Angola 176, 293–4, 309
Angre Kanhoji (early 18th c.), Maratha admiral 37
Animism 96
Antigua 211
Arabia 35, 168, 191, 283, 301, 318, 322–4, 339, 344, 358
Arabian Sea 34, 37, 160
Arabi/Orabi Ahmed (1841–1911), Egyptian nationalist leader 49, 360
Arabisation 125
Arab League 137, 141, 192
Arab Legion (1920–), Jordanian Army 161
Arch of Triumph in Paris 13
Aref, Abdul Rahman, (1916–2007), Iraqi President 165
Argentina 180, 318, 378
Aristide Jean Bertrand (1953–), Haitian leader 207–8
Aristocracy 12, 240
  Chinese 240
  Prussian 12
Aristotle (c. 384–322 BC), Greek philosopher 3, 345
Arnaud, Saint, (1798–1854), French colonialist 120
Arnold, Edwin (1832–1904), English poet 80
  *Light of Asia* 80
Aron Raymond (1905–1983), French political scientist 150
Arthashastra (c. 300–310 BC), Indian treatise on statecraft xii–iii, xvi
Arthur, King , legendary early 6th c. Briton 9
*Art of War* 154
Ashanti or Asante, Ghanaian ethnic group, founded Ashanti Kingdom (c. 1670 to 1900), 55–7, 66
Asantewa, Yaa (1840–1921), Asante queen 56
Asoka (304–232 BC), Maurya Emperor, grandson of Chandragupta 4
Ataturk Kamal (1881–1938), founder of modern Turkey 43–4
Attlee 54
Auckland Lord (1784–1849), Governor-General of India 1, 284
Augustine, St. (354–430), Algerian Christian theologian 9, 123
Austin Hudson (1938–), Grenadian leader 1, 211
Australia 108, 340, 364, 366
Austria 74
Awami League, Bangladesh political party 1, 187
Azzam Abdullah (1941–1989), mentor of Osama bin Laden 323

Baader Meinhof, active 1968–77 German terrorist group 378
Baba, Qari 304
Bacon Francis (1561–1626), English author 36
  *Of True Greatness of Kingdoms and Estates* 36
Badis Sheikh Abdul Ben (1889–1940), Algerian nationalist 132
Badr corps (1983–), Iraqi paramilitary force 359
Baghdad 125–6, 161, 341, 344–6, 349–50, 352–3, 355–6, 358–60
Baghla, Bou, *see* Abdelmalik
Bakhdash Khaled (1912–1995), Syrian communist leader 163
Banda, Dutch conquest of 70
Banda Aceh, Sumatra 99
Banerjee , Surendranath (1848–1925), Indian nationalist 46

Bangladesh 275, 339
Bao Dai (1913–1997), Last Emperor of Vietnam 243, 251
Baratieri General Oreste (1841–1901), Italian army officer 58–9
Barbados 211
Barbarism 48
Barbarossa Khairuddin (1478–1546), Turkish admiral 125
Barre Mohamed Siyad (1919–1995), President of Somalia 196–9
Bartholomew Reginald, US Ambassador, Beirut, 1983–86 196
Basic Principles of Relations 182
Batatu Hanna (1926–2000), Iraqi historian 349
Battle of Adowa 59
Battle of Algiers 139–40, 146
Battle of Bach Dang River 242
Battle of Gettysburg 42
Battle of Maiwand (July 1880), 288, 289
Battle of Marne ( Sept. 1914), 150
Battle of Omdurman (1898) 68
Battle of Oued Sebaou 129
Battle of Somme (1916), 150
Battle of Surabaya (1945), 103, 106–7
Battle of Valmy (1792), Between French and Prussian forces 7, 218
Battle of Verdun (1916), 150
Baudrillard Jean (1929–2007), French philosopher 186, 385
Bauman Zygmunt (1971–), Polish sociologist 376
Bay of Bengal 48, 189
Bay of Pigs 216
Beagle H.M.S. (1831–1836), Charles Darwin's ship 71
Beel C.J.M. (1903–1977), Dutch Premier 107
Beirut 192–6
Belagua Joaquin (1906–2002), Dominican President 210
Belgium 31, 50, 172
Belgrade nonaligned conference, 1961 186
Bellounis Mohamed 140
Ben Bella, Ahmed (1918–), Algerian leader 133
Ben–Gurion (1886–1973), first Israeli Premier 162
Beni Chougrane, Algerian tribe 130
Benin 176
Ben Saada, Algerian tribe 120
Ben Salem, Algerian village 120
Bentham Jeremy (1748–1832), English jurist and philosopher 11, 28
*A Plan for Universal and Perpetual Peace* 28
Berbers, North African ethnic group 122–3, 129
Berenike, Berenice, Ptolemaic Red Sea port 34
Berlin 49–50, 56, 157, 270, 311
Berlin conference 49–50
Bernhardi Friedrich von (1849–1930), Prussian general and military historian 13
*Germany and the Next War* 13
Bertrand, Louis (1866–1941), French colonial novelist 117
Bhambatha, uprising of 1906 57
Bhutto, Benazir (1953–2007), Pakistani Premier 318
Biden, Joe (1942–), US Vice-President 347
Bishop, Maurice (1944–1983), Grenadian politician 211
Biskra 123
Bismarck, Otto von (1815–1898), first German Chancellor 50
Bitar, Salah Al–Din al (1912–1980), co-founder of Baath Party 351
Black Sea 202–3
Blenheim, Battle of (1704), 67
Bloch, Marc (1886–1944), French soldier and historian 42
Bohemia 20
Bonino, Emma (1948–), Italian diplomat 318
Borobodur (9th century), Buddhist complex in Java 94

Bosch, Juan (1909–2001), Dominican politician 209
Bose, Subhas Chandra (1897–1945), Indian freedom fighter 54
Bou Amma, Sheikh, 19th c. Algerian nationalist 130
Bou Baghla, *see* Abdelmalik, 129
Boulaid, Moustafa Ben (1917–1956), FLN Commander 136
Boumezrag, (late 19th c.), Algerian nationalist 130
Bourdonnais, Bertrand Francois Mahe de la (1699–1753), French naval officer 48
Bourges–Maunoury, Maurice French Premier (1950s) 142
Boutros–Ghali, UN Secretary–General 199
Agenda for Peace, 1992, 199–200
Braudel, Fernand (1902–1985), French historian 122, 125
Brazil 180
Brito, Horge de (early 16th. c.), Portuguese commander of Malacca 99
Brown Bess, (early 18th to mid–19th c.), Musket commonly used by British army 67
Brussels Treaty of 1890 50
Brydon, Dr. 286
Brzezinski, Zbigniew (1928–), US National Security Adviser 226
Bu Maza, (19th c.), Algerian nationalist, 129
Buddhism 48, 95, 96, 240
Bugeaud, General Thomas Robert (1784–1849), Governor-General, Algeria 118–20, 134
Bulganin, Nikolai (1895–1975), Soviet Premier 162, 163
Bulgaria 184, 311, 338
Burchett, Wilfred (1911–1983), Australian journalist 241, 260
Burke, Edmund (1729–1797), Irish statesman and political theorist 10
Burma 54, 82
Bush, George (1946–), US President 200, 312, 319, 321, 336–7, 341, 357, 363, 374, 380–83
Buwaih, Ahmed ibn, 10th c. Mamluke ruler in Baghdad 346

Cabral, Pedro Alvares de (1468–1520), Portuguese navigator and explorer 35
Cairo 134, 138, 141, 161–2, 181, 191
Cambodia 95, 239
Camoens, Louis Vaz de (1524–1580), Portuguese poet 31
*Lusiads* 31
Camus, Albert (1913–1960), French author 141
Canada 60, 179, 322
CARE 200
Carter, Jimmy (1924–), US President 206–7, 270
Carthage 122–3
Casey, Bill (1913–1987), Head of CIA 300
Castro, Fidel (1926–), Cuban leader 205, 216
Cavagnari, Louis (1841–1879), British administrator 288
Ceasefire 6, 106–8, 110–11, 114, 145, 162–3, 189, 200, 209
Cedras, Gen. Raoul (1949–), Haiti Army 207–8
CENTO 271
Cetshwayo, Zulu King (1872–79) 57, 66
Challe, General Maurice 143
Chamoun, Camille (1900–1987), Lebanese President 192–3
Charlemagne (742–841), King of France 41
Charles X, French King 117
Charnier 238
Chehab, General Fuad (1902–1973), Lebanese President 193
Cheney, Dick (1941–), US Vice-President 337

Chepik, Sergeant Nikolai 306
Chiang Kai Shek (1887–1975), Chinese leader 251
Child, Josiah (1630–1699), Governor, English East India Company 70
China 77–8, 94, 124, 143, 149, 177, 185, 216, 222, 229–30, 236, 239–40, 242–3, 247, 249, 252, 254, 256, 260, 270, 275, 294, 344–5, 366–9, 385–7, 389
  Manchu, conquest of 149
Chinese revolution 248
Chomsky, Noam (1928–), American linguist 386
Chougrane, Beni, Algerian tribe 130
Christendom 9, 76
Christianity 50, 69, 123, 383
Christison, Gen. Philip (1893–1993), British army officer, 106
Churchill, Winston Spencer (1874–1965), British imperialist 68, 110, 353
Cirta, Berber capital, now Constantine 123
Citizenship 28, 131
  world 28
Civilisation 13, 43, 44, 46, 50, 67, 69, 74, 77, 83, 117, 121, 152–3, 252–3, 276, 278–9, 341–2, 350, 356, 385, 388
  disintegration of 153
  Latin 117
  modern 74
Clastres, Pierre (1934–1977), French anthropologist 278
Clausewitz, Carl von (1780–1831), Prussian military historian and theorist 2, 11–12, 155–6, 218
  *magnum opus* 12
Clauzel, General (1772–1842), French colonialist 129
Clemenceau, Georges (1841–1929), French Premier 130
Clifford, Clark (1906–1998), US Secretary of Defense 73, 267
Clinton, William Jefferson (1946–), US President 202
Clive, Robert (1725–1774), English freebooter 93
CNN 202, 327
Code 118, 263, 277, 318, 340
  civil 118
  political 118
  religious 118
  tribal 277
Code of Conduct against Ballistic Missile Proliferation 179
Coedes, George (1886–1969), French archaeologist 94
Coen, Jan Pieterszoon (1587–1629), Governor-General of Dutch East Indies 92
Coghill 161
Cole, J.P. (1928–), Australian geographer 228
Colonialism 57, 85, 100, 102, 244, 251
Colonisation 85, 91–2, 116, 121
Combes, Col. A.V.A., French imperialist, late 19th c 55
Commission on Indochina 237
Communism 50, 102, 111–2, 143, 155, 164, 174–5, 188, 190–91, 193, 204, 250, 266, 301, 375
  international 102, 188, 191, 193
  Russian 112
CTBT, (1996), Comprehensive Nuclear Test Ban Treaty 179
Conference of Afro-Asian nations 137
Congress of Eastern Peoples 132
Connelly, Matthew (1970–), American historian 146
Continent of Dinia 46
Couperus, Louis (1863–1923), Dutch novelist 100
  *The Hidden Force* 100
Court of Directors, London 283, 285
Cromwell, Oliver (1599–1658), English revolutionary xix
Crusades 124
Ctesiphon, Mesopotamian city 343–4
Cuba 205, 207, 209, 211, 216, 309
Culture 2, 10, 39, 41, 43–4, 46, 67, 72,

75–7, 79, 86, 94, 122, 124, 160, 187, 223, 240, 271, 275, 291, 299, 341–2, 348, 351–2, 385–7
French 79
human 46
Curzon, Lord (1859–1925), Viceroy of India 159
Cyprus 166
Cyrus (600–530 BC), Persian King 343
Czechoslovakia 157, 292, 311

Da Gama, Vasco (1460–1524), Portuguese explorer 31, 33, 87
Cape of Good Hope 87
Dante Alighieri (1265–1321), Italian poet and writer 19, 20
Dao, Than Hung (1228–1300), Vietnamese General 243
Dar al–Harb, House of war in Islam 5
Dar al–Islam, House of peace in Islam 5
Darwin, Charles (1809–1882), British scientist 12–3, 71
*Origin of Species by Means of Natural Selection or the Preservation of the Favoured Races in the Struggle for Life* 71
Darwinism, Social (late 19th century onward), 10, 12–3, 60, 66, 68, 71–2, 383
Daud, Mohammed (1909–1978), Afghan President 281
Dee, Dr. John (1527–1609), English navigator and imperialist 36
Defoe, Daniel (1661–1731), English writer and journalist 7
De Gaulle, General Charles (1890–1970), French general and statesman 55, 142–6, 165, 253
Deimachos (2nd c. BC), Greek Ambassador to the Court of Bindusara xiv
De Lanessan 239
Deleuze, Gilles (1925–1995), French philosopher 278
*A Thousand Plateaus* 278
Delhi 54, 59, 124, 281
Demak, town in central Java 96
Democracy 3, 10, 26, 119, 152, 175–6, 222, 271, 347, 363, 373, 381–2, 387
constitutional 3
promotion of 10
revolutionary 176
De Monarchia 19
De Montagnac, Colonel, 19th c. French colonialist 128
Denmark 31, 340, 364
De Rovigo, 19th c. French colonialist 119
Descartes, Rene (1596–1650), French philosopher and mathematician xx–xxi, 23
De Suffren, Admiral (1729–1788), French admiral 48
De Tocqueville, Alexis (1805–1859), French liberal political philosopher 119
Deutsch, Karl W. 79
Devavarman (2nd c. AD), King of Java 94
Dey of Algiers (1830s), Ottoman Governor, 117
Deykerhoff, Colonel Governor of Indonesia, late 19th c. 99
Dharmawangsa (late 10th c.), Singasari ruler 95
Dieman, Anthony van (1593–1645), Governor-General of Dutch East Indies 34
Dien Bien Phu, Battle of (1954), 142, 253–5, 265
Dilks, Charles 71
Dillingham, Commander Albert C. 209
Disraeli, Benjamin (1804–1881), British imperialist 57, 85, 289
Diversity 42, 104
multi–cultural 42
Divisiveness 79
Dogali 58
Dominica 208–11

Dong, Pham Van (1906–2000), Vietnamese Premier 241
Dostum, Abdul Rashid (1954–), Afghan nationalist 282
Douri, Izzat Ibrahim al (1942–), Iraqi nationalist 360
Doyle, Michael W. (1948–), American IR scholar 27
  *Liberalism and World Politics* 27
Drake, Francis (1540–1596), English privateer 36
Dubois, Pierre (1255–1312), adviser to the French King 20
  *De Recuperation Terre Sante* 20
Dulles, John Foster (1885–1959), US Secretary of State 160, 174, 190–91, 204, 382
Dupleix, Joseph Francois (1697–1763), French would-be imperialist 93
Durand, Henry 284
Durban 57
Duvaliers, Haiti, Francois (1907–1971), and Jean Claude (1952–), 206
Dynasty 242–4
  Li 242
  Nguyen 244
  Tran 242, 243
  Yuan 242

EAM, Greece, National Liberation Front 183
East India Company, English 36, 70, 82, 283–4
East India Company, Dutch (VOC), 92
Economic crisis 83
*Economist*, The 153
Eden, Anthony (1897–1977), British Premier 160–62
EDES, Greece, right wing party 183
*Edinburgh Review* 73
*Egalite* 133
Egypt 20, 34, 49, 123–5, 132, 136–7, 143, 160–5, 173, 180–81, 192, 217, 222, 339, 342, 355
  Cold war adventure 162
Eisenhower, Dwight D. (1890–1969), US President 160, 162–3, 174, 176, 182, 190–91, 193, 225, 294
El Cid (1040–1099), Spain's national hero 41
El Jezairi, Abdel Kader, *see* Abdel Kader 127
El Oufia, Algerian tribe 119
Emerson, Rupert (1899–1979), American IR Professor 79
Empire 9, 20, 30–33, 35–8, 42–3, 47–60, 65–72, 75–6, 79, 81–7, 91–100, 108, 116–9, 125–6, 143, 146, 149, 154, 158–9, 166–7, 169, 172, 186, 206, 232, 236–8, 242–3, 245, 254, 256, 276–7, 283, 286–7, 310–317, 337, 342–46, 352, 385–7, 389
  African 58, 146, 166
  Asante 56
  British 31, 37, 57, 71–2, 81, 87, 346
  Buddhist 94–5, 98
  European 82
  expansion of 66
  French 126, 238, 245
  future of 83
  Ghazni 277
  Han 242
  Hindu 94
  history of 60, 84
  Ming 243
  Mongol 242
  multi–ethnic 43
  Ottoman 43, 125, 346, 352
  Portuguese 36
  Roman 9, 20, 91, 232, 276, 385
  sentiment 71
  size of 37, 60
  Soviet 154, 310, 312
  Spanish Habsburg 91
  Srivijaya 94, 96
  territorial 36
  United 71
  Wassoulou 55, 66
  Zulu 56–7
Empire–makers 30–31, 38, 47, 52, 60, 65–7, 75–6, 81, 86, 108, 117

creation of 65, 76
rivalries 65
war and 66
Empire–making 30, 38, 59, 69, 83, 91
Empire lost and 81, 83
Marxist view 83
modus operandi 69
Entick, Rev. John (1703–1773), British imperialist 37
*The Present State of the British Empire* 37
Erasmus, Desiderius (1466–1536), Dutch humanist and Catholic theologian 21
Eridu (c. 3,500 BC), Sumerian city 342
Estado da India 35
Ethiopia 35, 58–9, 196–8, 293, 294, 309, 342
Provisional Military Administrative Council (PMAC), 197
Europe 2, 6–8, 15, 21–4, 28, 34–6, 38, 40–41, 43–4, 47–51, 66, 70–72, 77, 81, 83, 86–7, 92, 105, 112, 117, 149–50, 153, 156–7, 166, 180–86, 216, 223–4, 249, 267, 270, 276, 278, 290, 296, 310–11, 345, 375–6, 383
American military and civilian involvement 184
conduct of war in 7
expansion of 51, 86
pacification of 28
powers of 23, 48, 156, 180
Renaissance 6
sovereign powers of 23
supremacy 37
European Union 318

Fabin–Leveque, Captain (mid-19th c.), French colonialist 237
Faizullah, Maulana Taliban leader 327
Fall, Bernard B. (1926–1967), French war correspondent 255
*Street Without Joy* 255
Fanon, Frantz (1925–1961), FLN's theorist 51, 54, 100, 140
Farah, Muhammed, *see* Aideed
Faraj, Mohammed Abdel al Salam, Islamic radical 323
Feisal, Amir (1883–1933), King of Iraq 353, 355
Ferrand, Gabriel (1864–1935), French orientologist 95
Fidayeen 6
Finland 156
Fissile Material Cut–off Treaty 179
FLN (1954–), Algeria, National Liberation Front 135–46
Foch, Marshall Ferdinand (1851–1929), French military theorist 12
Fontaine, Andre (1921–), French historian 181
*Foreign Affairs* 316, 333
Foreign Legion 134
*Foreign Policy* 316
Fort Jesus 36
Foucault, Michel (1926–1984), French philosopher and sociologist xiv–v
France 9–10, 14, 20, 23, 28, 31, 36, 41–2, 48–9, 60, 73, 83, 116–26, 130–8, 141–9, 151, 158–61, 177, 185, 195, 228, 236–54, 275, 296, 311, 338–9, 385, 387
anti–colonialist 133
disaster of Macta 127
French Communist Party 121, 130
National Assembly 136
revolutionary 9–10, 14, 36, 41
Royal 36
Franco–German war 12–3
Frederick, Charles William (1735–1806), Duke of Brunswick, 8
French Revolution 9–10, 41, 80
Fuller, General J.F.C. (1878–1910), British military historian 66
*The Conduct of War* 5, 66

G–7 179
Gailani, Sayyed Ahmed Mujahidin, commander 304
Gairy, Eric (1920–1997), Grenadian Premier 211

Galileo, Galilei (1564–1642), Italian astronomer xx
Gatling (mid-19th c.), early rapid fire gun 67
Geertz, Clifford James (1926–2006), American anthropologist 73
Gelb, Leslie (1937–), US academic 347
Gellner, Ernest 75, 76
Gemayel, Bashir (1947–1982), Lebanese President 195
Gemayel, Amine (1942–), Lebanese President 195
Geneva 142, 169, 182, 254, 256, 310
Genghis Khan (1162–1227), Mongol conqueror and Emperor 47, 149, 346
Genouilly, Admiral Rigault de (1807–1873), French colonialist 238, 244
Geoffrey of Monmouth (c. 1100–1155), British clergyman, populariser of the King Arthur tales 43, 66
Germany 13, 22, 31, 48, 58, 77, 119, 135, 137, 141–2, 151, 158, 204, 209, 228, 230, 268, 275, 322, 338, 355, 387
  Nazi 119, 135, 355
Ghana 55, 56, 166
Ghazi (1930s), Iraqi King 355
Ghita, Ayatollah Mohammed Kashifa al, Iraqi nationalist 354
Ghose, Aurobindo (1872–1950), Indian freedom fighter 79
Gibbon, Edward (1737–1794), English historian 276
Gidir, Habar 198
Gilgamesh, Sumerian epic hero 342, 350
Gilpin, Robert American IR scholar 229
Girard, Comte, French War Minister, 1830s 119
*Gita*, The 95–6
Gladstone (1809–1898), British Premier 58, 71, 286
Globalisation 39, 76
Glubb, John Bagot (1897–1986), British soldier 161
Goethe (1749–1832), German polymath 13
Gokalp, Ziya (1876–1924), Turkish sociologist and political activist 43
Gorbachev, Mikhail Sergeyevich (1931–), last Sovier President 308
Gowon, Yakubu (1934–), Nigerian Head of State 68
Great October Socialist Revolution 85
Greece 3, 156–7, 183–4, 381
  Greek communist party (KKE), 183, 184
  National Liberation Front (EAM), 183
  National Republican Greek League (EDES), 183
Grenada 206, 208, 210–11, 219
  People's Revolutionary Army 211
Guatemala 204
Guattari, Felix (1930–1992), French philosopher 278
  *A Thousand Plateaus* 278
Guerilla tactics 135, 242, 259
Guha, Ranajit (1922–), Indian historian 53
Guinea 55, 158
Gujarat 34, 95
Gulf of Basra 160
Gurion, Ben (1886–1973), first Israeli Premier, 162
Guzman, Jacobo Arbenz (1913–1971), Guatemalan military officer 204

Hadj, Messali (1898–1974), Algerian nationalist 132–3, 135, 137
Hague Code of Conduct 179
Haile Mariam, Mengistu (1937–), Ethiopian leader 293
Haiti 206–8
Hakim, Ayatollah Mohammed Baqir al (1939–2003), Iraq 181, 359
Ham Nghi (1872–1943), Vietnamese Emperor 243, 246, 248
Hammurabi, (mid-18th c. BC), Babylonian King 342, 350

Haq, Zia-ul (1924–1988), Pakistan President 300
Haqqani, Jalaluddin (1950–), Afghan nationalist 308
Haqqani, Sirajuddin (1970–), Taliban leader 328
Harthi, Abushiri ibn Salim al 19th c. Tanzanian nationalist, 49
Hashim, Khalid Ibn, grandson of Abdel Kader, 131
Hatta, Mohamed (1902–1980), Indonesian leader 105, 111–2
Heathenism 48
Heeren XVII, Board of Directors of the VOC 92
Hegel, Georg Wilhelm Friedrich (1774–1836), German philosopher 11, 73, 74
Hekmatyar, Gulbuddin (1947–), Afghan Mujahidin leader 281, 302, 304, 326, 328
Henry IV of France (1553–1610), 20–22
  Grand Design 20, 22
Heraclitus, (c. 535–475 B.C.), Greek philosopher 3, 154
Herbert, Sydney 20th c. historian of modern Europe 43
Hereros, Bantu ethnic group, mostly Namibian 71
Heroism 6, 10, 91
Wells, H.G. (1866–1946), English author 152
Hich Can Vuong, (late 19th c.), Vietnamese national movement 244–6
Hieu, (19th c.), Vietnamese nationalist 246
Hinduism 94–6
Hitler 81, 160, 167, 323, 355
Hiyari, General Ali, Jordanian Chief of Staff, 1950s 191
Hizb–e–Islami 281, 302, 304, 326, 328
Hoang Hoa Tham, (1858–1913), Vietnamese nationalist 248
Hobbes, Thomas (1588–1679), English political philosopher xx–xxii, 6, 13, 23
Hobsbawm, Eric (1917–), British historian 40, 78, 122
  *The Age of Extremes* 78
Hobson, John Atkinson (1858–1940), English economist, 84
Holland 8, 31, 37, 92, 100, 112
Hormuz 32
Howe, Jonathan (1935–), US admiral 202
Hulagu, (1217–1265), Mongol ruler 346
Humanity 12, 153
Human rights 27, 146, 177, 222, 270, 318, 338, 365, 387
Hume, David (1711–1776), Scottish philisopher and economist 42
Huntington, Samuel (1927–2008), American political scientist 388
Hussein, King (1935–1999), Jordan 161, 191
Husein ibn Ali, (1854–1931), Sherif of Mecca, 353
Hussein, Saddam (1937–2006), Iraqi President 337, 359
Hutton, Chief Staff Officer Brigadier William 161

Ibn Hashim, Khaled *see* Hashim
Ibn–Nafi, Uqbah, Ummayad General 123
Ibn–Tashfin, Yusuf (1061–1106), founder of Almoravid dynasty 125
Ibrahim, Qaid (mid-19th c.), Algerian nationalist 128
Ibrahim, Sidi 128
I–Ching (634–712), Chinese pilgrim 94
ICRC 200, 329
Ideology 52, 104, 151, 155, 172–3, 175, 184, 198, 260, 302, 312, 318, 322–3, 350, 375–6, 386–7
  socialist 175
Ikha, Hizb al (1930s), Iraqi nationalist party 354–5

Imam or Imamat, Islamic, leader or leadership 5
Immigration 42
Imperialism 38, 45, 47, 49, 52, 57, 60, 67, 82–5, 102, 110, 164, 293
collapse of 85
denunciation of 84
European 82
outburst of 67
Imperium Britannicum 36
India 4, 31–6, 45–6, 48, 53, 59, 66, 70, 77–8, 80–2, 85, 92, 94, 99, 103, 107–8, 116, 151, 159, 167, 172, 179, 187–9, 221–2, 229, 275–6, 278, 280–90, 301, 304, 345, 366
British expansion in 70
British rule in 46
Congress party 54
independence in 1947 159
Indian National Army (INA) 54
Muslims of 77
princely states of 116
religious violence in 221
Indian National Congress 80
Indian Ocean 32–6, 48, 87, 92–3, 166–7, 189
Portuguese excursion 33
Indochina 82, 185, 237, 245, 250, 252, 254–5
Indonesia 31, 54, 78–9, 82, 91–114, 124, 137, 236, 340
Buddhist and Hindu empires 94
central leadership 101, 110
colonial school system 93
colonisation of 91
Communist Party of the Indies (PKI) 101–02, 110
currency 112
Dutch occupation 91, 97–8, 100
Dutch–sponsored federal United States of 110
Indonesian Communist Party 110
Linggadjati Agreement 107
Marshall Plan 107, 157
national upsurge 109
Partai Nasional Indonesia (PNI) 103
Pemuda 109
Pendidikan Nasional Indonesia 98
Peta 105
Republic of 105, 114
Unitarian Constitution 114
United States of 107, 110, 114
war and empire 91
Industrialisation 39, 75, 84, 228, 230, 249
Institutionalisation 41
Internationalism 102
International relations (IR) 14–5, 21, 26, 155, 157, 174, 181, 183, 215, 218, 222, 224, 227, 228, 230–33, 257, 270, 312, 315–6, 366–70, 384–5
Asia and Africa 31, 39, 45, 52, 59–60, 67, 69, 71–2, 75, 86, 157, 166, 172, 180, 216, 227
India and Europe 34
India and Pakistan 187, 222
India–Pakistan 187
US and Latin America 203
US and Pakistan 299
Invasion 46, 47, 52, 82, 117, 126, 161, 193, 211, 216, 219, 221, 243, 275, 286–7, 292, 305, 309, 315, 336–9, 346, 356–7, 359, 362
French 117, 126
Iran 78, 124, 157, 179, 219–20, 275, 297, 301, 304–5, 309, 339, 351, 354–5, 359, 365, 373–4
Safavis in 124
Iraq 160–63, 165, 178, 180, 219–20, 304, 315, 317, 324–5, 336–74, 388–9
educational system 350
effects of defeat 269, 365
infrastructure 339
invasion and after 336
US incursion in 315
eight–year war with Iran 339
Iraqi revolution 193

Ireland 220
Isandlwana, Battle of (1879), 57–8, 66
defeat of British forces 66
Ishtar, Sumerian goddess 342, 350–51
ISI, Inter Services Intelligence, Pakistan 300, 302–4, 319, 327
Islam 5–6, 46, 76, 95–6, 101, 124–5, 131–2, 135, 277, 280, 291, 297, 301, 303–4, 323–4, 327, 344, 360, 383
purification of 124
Islamisation 125
Ismail Pasha, Khedive (1830–1895), ruler of Egypt 49, 282, 303–4
Israel 161, 164, 181, 194, 196, 219, 222, 376
Italy 23, 31, 59, 73, 151, 195, 204, 317, 364, 378
liberation of 73

Jaafari, Ibrahim al (1947–), Iraqi Premier 359
Jafar, Caliph Abu 344
Jaffar Naderi 139, 282
Jahns, Max 19th c. German military theorist 13
Jainism 4
Jakarta 93, 105, 109
Jamaat–e–Islami 302, 304
Jamaat–ul–Ulema Islam (JUI), 327
Jammu and Kashmir 275, 301
*Jane's Fighting Ships* 294
Janisssary/Yenicheri, Ottoman troops, 125
Japan 15, 31, 54, 82, 87, 105, 154, 158, 179, 185, 224, 227–8, 248, 251, 364, 366, 387
Java 91, 93–5, 97–8, 100, 103–4, 107–10
Jerusalem, recovery of 20
Jihad, Jehad, Islamic, struggle 5, 6, 280, 290, 298, 303–4, 323, 325–6, 360, 364
Jiminez, Dominican President, 1903 208
Jinnah, Muhammad Ali (1876–1948), founder of Pakistan 77
Jobert, Michel (1921–2002), French Foreign Minister 181
Jogjakarta 95, 97, 111–3
Johnson, Lyndon B. (1908–1973), US President 209–10, 257, 264, 267–8
Johnston, Philip 200
Jonassaint, Emile (1913–1995), Haitian President 207
Jordan 160–61, 164, 189, 191, 194, 358
Jugurtha, (160–104 BC), ruler of North Africa 123
Justice 3–4, 22–3, 26, 123–4, 321, 375, 377, 383
means of 22
standard of 4

Kabul 281–90, 295, 298–9, 303, 307, 319–20, 326–7, 332–3, 365
Kader, Abdel, *see* Abdel Kader
Kahn, Herman (1922–1983), American futurist 228
Kampuchea 221
Kandahar 281, 284–5, 288–90, 295, 318–20, 327–29, 332
Kantian peace argument 149
Kant, Immanuel (1724–1804), German philosopher 24–8
*Perpetual Peace* 19, 23, 25–6, 28
propositions 26
*The Science of Right* 25
Karna, hero in Indian mythology 96
Kassim, General Abdul Karim (1914–1963), Iraqi Premier 162, 350
Kateb Yacine, (1929–1989), Algerian writer, 123
Katzman, Kenneth American IR analyst 331
*Afghanistan: Post–War Governance, Security, and U.S. Policy* 331
Kaunda, Kenneth (1924–), First President of Zambia 47
Kautilya, also Vishnugupta, Chanakya (c. 350–283 B.C.), Adviser to Chandragupta Maurya xii–iii, xvi, 2, 4–6, 36

*Kedjawen* 96
Keegan, John (1934– ), British military historian 66
*A History of Warfare* 66
*Keeping the Peace* 166
Keletigui 54
Kennan 173, 269, 382
Kennan, George (1904–2005), American diplomat 173
Kennedy, John F. (1917–1963), US President 138, 146, 176, 181, 186, 230, 255–7, 268, 292, 387
Kennedy, Paul (1945–), British historian 229, 292, 387
*The Rise and Fall of British Naval Mastery* 229–30, 235
*The Rise and Fall of the Great Powers* 229
Kennedy, John F., (1917–1963), US President 138, 146, 176, 181, 186, 255–7, 268
Kenya 57, 166, 200
Kertarajasa Jayavardhana, (ruled 1293–1309), founder of Majapahit Kingdom, 95
Khaled, Emir, see Ibn Hashim 131
Khalili, Karim Afghan Mujahidin Commander, 1980s 282
Khalis, Maulvi Yunus (1919–2006), Afghan Mujahidin leader 328
Khan, Abdur Rahman (1840–1901), Afghan ruler, 229
Khan, Amanullah Afghan ruler 47, 88, 95, 149, 187–8, 242, 282–3, 285–90, 303–4, 346
Khan, Ayub (1907–1974), President of Pakistan, 288–9
Khan, General Yahya (1917–1980), President of Pakistan 187–8
Khan , Dost Mohammed (1793–1863), Afghan ruler, 283–6, 289
Khan, Ismail (1946–), Afghan nationalist, 49, 282, 303–4
Khan, Yakub (late 19th c.), Afghan ruler 287–8
Kublai Khan, (1215–1294), Mongol Emperor 88, 242
Khrushchev, Nikita (1894–1971), Soviet leader 164, 181–2, 186, 294
King Arthur, (early 6th c.), legendary Briton, 9, 111
Kinjikitile, Ngawale, late 19th c. Tanzanian nationalist 58
Kissinger, Henry (1923–), US Secretary of State 182, 188–9, 216, 269, 316, 338
Kitchener, Field Marshall Horatio Herbert (1850–1916), British army officer 48–9, 68–9
KKE, (1918–), Greek Communist Party 183–4
Knorr, Klaus (1911–1990), American political scientist 216
Konadu, Nana 56
Koran 118, 124
Korea 77, 179, 185, 190–91, 222, 364, 366, 373–4, 389
Krauthammer, Charles (1950–), American political commentator 384
Krim, Belkacem (1922–1970), Algerian nationalist 136, 138
Ksatriyas, Kshatriyas, Military and ruling class of India 4
Kuhn, Thomas S. (1992–1996), American philosopher of science 232
Kunjali III, late 16th c. Calicut admiral 33
Kuwait 339, 359, 366
Kwa Zulu Natal 56–7
Laden, Osama Bin (1957–), Saudi Arab terrorist 277, 319–25, 362
Lanessan, de Governor-General of Vietnam, 239
Latin America 157, 203, 208, 210, 221, 224, 309
Lebanon 160, 164, 181, 190–6, 219, 359
army 193, 194

Christian militia (LF), 194
National Pact of 1943 192
Le Bon, (6th c.), King of Vietnam 242
Lefebvre, mid-19th c., French Bishop 237
Lenin, V.I. (1870–1924), Soviet revolutionary statesman 84
*Imperialism: The Highest Stage of Capitalism* 84
Leninism 176, 226
Leopold, King 50
*Les Etats hinduise d'Indochine et d'Indonesie* 94
Le Truc, (19th c.), Vietnamese nationalist 246
Lewis, Bernard (1916–), British American orientalist and historian 5
Liberalism 8
Libya 58, 125, 373
Li Phat Tu, 7th c. Vetnamese nationalist, 242
Lisbon 34, 35
Lloyd, Selwyn, (1904–78), British Foreign Secretary, 160–61
*Los Angeles Times* 339
LTTE 378
Lugard, Captain Frederick John Dealtry (1858–1945), British soldier and explorer 85
Lytton, Lord (1831–1891), Viceroy of India 287–8, 297

MacArthur, General Douglas (1880–1964), American Army officer 155
Machiavelli, Niccolo (1469–1527), Italian political philosopher xvi, xix, 2, 6–7, 36
*The Prince* 6
Mackinder, Halford (1861–1947), English geographer 86
*The Geographical Pivot of History* 86
Macnaghten, Sir William (1793–1841), British army officer 284
Mahdi army, (2003–), Iraqi paramilitary force 4, 95–6, 101
Mahaz-e-Milli 304
Mahdi, Islamic, the Great Redeemer 68–9, 199–200, 358–9
Mahdi army, (2003–), Iraqi paramilitary force 200
Mahieddine, Sheikh (19th c.), son of Abdel Kader 130
Mahmud, Sheikh Kurdish leader (1920s) 354
Mahsud, Baitullah (1974–2009), Pakistan Taliban leader 325
Majapahit Kingdom, (1293–1520), Indonesia 95
Majid, Zabiullah Taliban spokesman, 2000– 327
Maji Maji war 57–8
Malacca, straits of 32–3, 35, 94–5, 99, 189
Malaya 82, 166
Malay peninsula 95, 99
Malaysia 54, 221
Mali 55, 125, 158
Malik, Abdul, Uzbek warlord, 1990s 282
Maliki, Noori al (1950–), Iraqi Premier 359, 364
Mallaby, A.W.S British commander, World War II, 106
Manchus, (17th c.), Chinese rulers 386
MAN–PADS, Man Portable Air Defense Systems 180
Mansur, Caliph al *see* Abu Jafar 1, 344, 350
Manu, India, law giver 4
Law book of 4
Manuel, King 35
Marchand, Jean Baptiste (1863–1934), French military officer and explorer 48
Marhaenism, Sukarno's political philosophy 103
Marini, Antoine (15th c.), chancellor to the King of Bohemia 20
Marrakesh 125
Marxism 75, 176, 226
Marxist–Leninist Party 176

Karl 73
.cara, Abdel Kader's capital 58, 119, 126–8
Massawa 58
Massinissa, (2nd c. BC), Berber King 123
Massu, General Jacques (1908–2002), French Army 139, 142, 144
Masud, Ahmed Shah (1953–2001), Afghan nationalist 303–4, 307–8, 317, 326
Matabele, or Ndebele Branch of Zulus 68
Mataram Sultanate, (16th to 18th c.), Java, 95
Maude, Major-General Sir Stanley (1864–1917), British Commander 346
Maududi, Maulana (1903–1979), Jamaat–e–Islami founder 297, 323
Maxim gun, (invented 1884), First self-powered machine gun 67
Maurya, Chandragupta (340–290 BC), founder of the Māurya Empire xiii
Maynes, Charles William (1939–2007), American foreign policy expert 316
Mayor, Lord 166
Maza, Bu 129
Mazar–i–Sharif 282
Mazari, Abdul Ali, Afghan leader, 1990s 305
Mboya, Tom (1930–1969), Kenyan political leader 47
McNamara, Robert (1916–2009), US Secretary of Defense 257
Mecca 126, 324, 353
Medina 126, 324
Megasthenes (c. 350–290 BC), Greek Ambassador to Maurya Court xiii–iv
Megawati Sukarnoputri, (1947–), Indonesian President 380
*Mein Kampf* 160, 323
Melians 4
Mendes–France, Pierre (1907–1982), French Premier 144
Menelik II (1844–1913), Ethiopian Emperor 58
Merlin, Martial Henri Governor-General of Vietnam (1923–25) 240
Messali Hadj, Ahmed (1898–1974), Algerian nationalist, 132–3, 135, 137
Mexico 207
Michael, Archangel 48
Middle East 161–3, 184, 191, 221, 363, 374
Middle East defence organisation (MEDO), 161
*Military Balance* 232
Mill, John Stuart (1806–1873), British philosopher and economist 11
Minh Mang, (1791–1841), Vietnamese Emperor 243, 248–9, 251, 253–4, 256, 258–60
Minh, Ho Chi (1890–1969), Vietnamese leader, 243, 248–9, 251, 253–4, 256, 258–60
Missile Technology Control Regime 179
Modernisation 42, 76–7, 291, 297
Modernity 8, 15, 19–30, 39, 44, 53, 60–61, 65–91, 94, 97, 111, 116, 118, 121, 132, 134, 145, 159, 164, 184–5, 203, 205, 207, 210, 215–236, 287, 312, 332–3, 346–7, 372–389
  arguments of 132, 347
  interpretations of 145
Mogadishu 199–203
Mogadishu Syndrome 203
Mohammedi, Mohammed Nabi (1920–2002), Mujahidin commander 304, 328
Mokrani, Sheikh Mohammed el (late 19th c.), Algerian nationalist 129
Mollet, Guy (1905–1975), French Premier 142, 144, 162
Monopoly 34, 82, 84, 175, 197, 311
  imperialist 175
Montagnac, Colonel de, French colonialist, 19th c., 120, 128
Montoneros, Argentine guerilla group, 1960s–1970s 378

Mook, Van, (1894–1965), Governor–General, Indonesia 108
Morales, Carlos, Dominican President, 1903 208
Morality 2, 4–6, 8, 10, 73, 383
  international 2
  kind of 2
  virtue and 6
Morgenthau, Hans (1904–1980), German American IR theorist 155, 227–9, 232–3
  *Politics among Nations* 227
Morocco 125, 142, 146, 158, 339
Moscow 102, 110, 130, 163, 165, 197, 221, 230, 250, 260, 293, 298, 305–6, 312
Mountbatten, Louis (1900–1979), British admiral 105
Mozambique 176
MTCR, (1987–), Missile Technology Control Regime 179
Muawiyah, Caliph (602–680), first Umayyad Caliph 123
Mujaddedi, Maulana Sibgatullah Afghan Mujahidin leader 304
Mullen, Admiral Michael (1946–), American Navy officer 332
Muqtadir, Caliph (early 10th c.), Abbasid ruler 344
Muscat 32, 36
Muslim Umma 123
Musso 110
Mussolini 59
Musso, Indonesian communist leader 110
Myos Hormos, Ptomelaic Red Sea port, circa 3rd c. BC 34
Myth 43, 117
Mythology 40, 43
  Saxon 43

Nabulsi, Suleiman Jordanian Premier, 1950s 191
Naderi, Jaffar Afghan Commander, 1990s 282
Najaf 305, 351, 354, 358–9
Najibullah, Mohamed (1947–1996), Afghan President 281
Nasser, Gamal Abdel (1918–1970), President of Egypt 49, 137, 160–65, 181, 183, 191
  *Egypt's Liberation, The Philosophy of the Revolution* 160
Nasserism 161, 191
Natal 56, 57
National consciousness 42, 51, 86, 102, 104, 140, 241
National identity 42, 346, 349
Nationalism 30, 38–81, 82, 86, 93–7, 100, 102, 122–6, 130, 132, 134, 140, 160, 173, 175, 187, 216, 240–41, 244, 249, 251, 271, 279, 283, 291, 323, 326, 344–52, 356, 361
  Afghan 280
  African 57
  Algerian 122, 132
  Arab 124, 167, 192, 351
  Asian 82
  assertion of 79
  British 42
  components of 72
  construction of 349
  creation in Asia and Africa 45
  creation in Europe and Turkey 40
  creation of 40, 45, 97, 123, 126, 249, 348
  ethnicity 39, 41, 72, 74, 93, 103, 122, 155, 282
  French 41
  Gellner's theory 75
  growth of 38, 41
  Indian 53, 77, 78, 80
  Indonesian 93, 96–7, 124
  Iraqi 346, 350–51, 356, 361
  Italian 73
  kinds of 39
  mainstream 100, 130
  making of 39, 41, 44
  narrow 86
  nation–building 40–42, 46, 52, 349, 351

Soviet retaliation against 300
struggle for the creation of 187
Palestine Liberation Organisation (PLO) 194, 195
Pamuk, Orhan (1922–), Nobel laureate 44
Pannikar, K.M. (1895–1963), Indian scholar and diplomat 33
Parker, Geoffrey (1943–), English military historian 66
*The Cambridge History of Warfare* 66
Parmelee, Jennifer 201
Parochialism 79
Parthians, (c.105 BC), ruled Iran, Iraq 343
Pasquier, Pierre (1876–1934), Governor-General of Vietnam 239–40
*Patterns of War* 66, 222
Pattimura, (1783–1817), Indonesian nationalist, 98
Peace 2–9, 11, 19–28, 35, 65, 82, 85, 92, 108, 144, 149, 152–3, 162, 166, 174, 176, 183, 186, 191, 195, 199–200, 203–4, 207, 218, 222, 230, 245, 251, 257, 268, 270, 272, 317–9, 322, 329, 333, 338, 374–5, 380, 384, 388
advantages of 22–4
calm and tranquillity of 20
democratic 27
enforcement 199
establishment 82
ideas of 25
Kantian perpetual 2
liberal 25
maintenance of 20
perpetual 2, 11, 19, 22–8
plans 9, 19, 21–2
European 19–20
modernity 21
pre–Westphalian 19
reasons for 25
universal 20
world 19, 191, 222
Peace–keeping force 195
Peace of Westphalia (1648), 19, 21, 36
Pearson, Charles (1830–1894), Oxford historian 47
Pearson, Karl von (1857–1936), English professor of eugenics, social darwinist 14
Pelissier, Colonel French colonialist, 19th c.
Pendidikan Nasional Indonesia, Indonesian nationalist party 120, 129
Penn, William (1644–1718), English Quaker 22
*Essay Towards the Present and Future Peace of Europe* 22
*Perestroika* 309–10, 312
Pericles, (c. 495–429 B.C.), Athenian statesman and general 3–4
Peril, Yellow 48
*Periplus of the Erithraean Sea* 34
*Perpetual Peace: A Philosophical Sketch* 25
Persia 35, 95
Persian Gulf 34
Petraeus, General David (1952–), US Central Command 357
Petrov, V.I. 293
Peureulak (early 9th. c.), Indonesian Islamic Kingdom 98
Pflimlin, Pierre (1907–2000), French Premier 142
Phan Boi Chau, (1867–1940), Vietnamese nationalist 247, 249
Phan Dinh Phung, (1847–1896), Vietnamese nationalist, 246
Philippines 81, 95, 185, 221, 271
Philippines, the US forces in 185
Phung, Phan Dinh 246
Picq, Ardant du (1819–1870), French military theorist 12
Pizzeghetone, Siege of (1793), 8
Plato (c. 428–347 B.C.), Greek philosopher and mathematician 3
Podgorny, Nikolai (1903–1983), Soviet leader 164
Podhoretz, Norman (1930–), American neoconservative 375

Poland 20, 151, 157, 275, 311, 340, 364
Popular Movement for the Liberation of Angola (MPLA), 293
Porto Novo, Benin 68
Portugal 31–2, 34–5, 60, 82, 172
  extra-terrestrial assistance 32
Power aggressive 94
  American 217, 233, 317
  balance of 14, 36, 81, 163, 223, 228, 381, 388
  civil and military 36
  coercive 24
  colonial 45, 47, 53, 72–3, 75, 78, 80, 82–3, 101, 105, 124, 126, 140, 172
  concept of 223–6
  extension or protection of 154
  French 237
  great 14, 30, 38, 81, 138, 153, 155–8, 164–5, 172–3, 175, 177, 182–4, 186–7, 203, 216, 218–9, 223–5, 269, 316–7, 356
  Great 15, 116, 153, 158–9, 172, 185–6, 190, 215, 217–8, 227, 253, 291, 316, 366, 387
  hierarchy of 153, 229
  imperial 54, 58–9, 116, 159, 315
  international 11, 224, 231
  kingly 15
  latency of 2
  measuring 226–32, 383
  military 5, 15, 36, 196, 203, 205, 208, 215–6, 226, 228–32, 237, 294, 309, 315, 386
  Muslim 21
  nation 14, 227–8
  national 227, 230–31
  naval 33, 94
  physical, mental, moral and political 13
  possession of 1, 2, 227, 233
  priestly 15
  relative 14, 157, 384
  revolutionary 15
  sea 36
  state 110, 279
  super 173, 177, 181, 220–22, 241, 300, 315, 369
  temporal 20
  western 14
  world 157, 166, 228, 292, 384–5
Power and war 14
  relation 14
Power gap 67
Puerto Rico 211

Qadirite, Islamic sect 126
Qutb, Mohammed 323
Qutb, Sayyid (1906–1966), radical Islamist theoretician 323

Rabbani, Maulana Burhanuddin (1940–), leader, Jamaat–e–Islami Afghanistan 282, 304
Rahmat Ali, Chaudhary, see Ali
*Ramayana*, Indian epic 96
Raphel, Robin US diplomat 317
Rapoport, Anatol (1911–2007), French strategic thinker, author of game theory 12
Rashid Ali, (1892–1965), Iraqi Premier 355
Rawlings, Jerry 56
Reagan, Ronald (1911–2004), US President 176, 196, 220–21, 380
Realism 227, 229, 232–3
Red Sea 33–4, 58, 167, 343
Renan, Ernest (1823–1892), French philosopher and writer 74
Rhodesia 68
Rice, Condoleezza (1954–), US Secretary of State, 374
Rivalries 65, 81, 84, 198
Rivalry 21, 183, 217–8, 225, 293, 383
Riza, Mohammed Iraqi nationalist, 1920 revolt, 353
Robin, Rene, Governor-General of Vietnam (1934–36) 239
Rome 31, 37, 117, 122–4, 276, 315, 365, 385–6
Romney, Mitt (1947–), US politician 375

Roosevelt , Franklin D. (1882–1945), US President 174, 204, 381
Rostow, Eugene (1913–2002), American official 181
Rostow, W.W. (1916–2003), American economist 80, 228, 292
Stages of Economic Growth 80, 292
Rousseau, Jean Jacques (1712–1778), citizen of Geneva, philosopher 8, 23–4
Rovigo, General, French colonialist, 19th c. 118
Royal Geographical Society 86
Rumsfeld, Donald (1932–), US Secretary of Defense 337
Rusk, Dean (1909–1994), US Secretary of State 169
Russell, Bertrand (1872–1970), British philosopher and mathematician 15, 25
Russia 31, 74, 163–4, 173, 228, 230, 256, 283, 287, 289, 309, 345, 382, 387

Saadi, Yacef (1928–), Algerian nationalist 139
Sadat, Anwar (1918–1981), Egyptian President 165
Sadr, Muqtada Al (1973–), Iraqi nationalist 358–9
Safavids, (1501–1722), Persian Empire 346
Said, Edward 51
Said, Nuri (1888–1958), Iraqi Premier 193
Sailendra Empire (8th to 11th c.), Java 94
Saint Arnaud, (1798–1854), French colonialist 120
Saint Pierre, Abbe Charles–Irene Castel de (1658–1743), French writer and radical, 23, 24
Salisbury, Lord (1830–1903), British statesman 85
Samori Toure, (1830–1900), founder of Wassoulou Empire, West Africa, 54, 57, 66, 158
Sam, Vilbrun Guillaume, Haiti President, 1915 206
Sandracotta/Sandracottos, Greek name for Chandragupta Maurya xiii
Sardinia 73
Sarekat Islam, (founded 1911), Indonesian party 101
Sargon I, (c. 2,400 BC), conqueror of Sumer 342
Sarraut, Albert 240
Sarrauton, Henry de (late 19th c.), French author 118
Sassanians, (224–651), Persian Empire 343
Saudi Arabia 191, 283, 301, 318, 322, 323–4, 339, 358
Saud, King 191
Schelling, Thomas C. (1921–), American economist
*The Strategy of Conflict* 218
Schelling, Thomas C. 218
Scott, Ridley (1937–), English film director 203
SEATO 271
Seleucids, (312–63 BC), Hellenistic Empire 343
Seleucus Nicator, (c. 358–281 B.C.), Founder of the Seleucid Empire xiii, 343
Senegal 46, 58, 125
Senghor, Leopold (1906–2001), President of Senegal 46
Separatism 86
religious 86
Shah, Ahmad, see Abdali
Shah, Mugayat 99
Shah Waliyullah, (1703–1762), Islamic reformer, 124
Shah, Zahir (1914–2007), Afghan King 291, 298, 302, 317, 328
Shining Path, Senderoso Luminoso, (1980–), Peruvian revolutionary movement, 378
Shaka 56, 57
Shakespeare, William (1564–1616),

English poet and playwright 9
*Henry V* 9
Shangani river, Battle of (1893), Zimbabwe 68
Shawcross, William (1946–), British journalist 318
Sheikh, Sidi 120, 130
Sher Ali, (1825–1879), Amir of Afghanistan 287–8
Shevardnadze, Eduard (1928–), Soviet Foreign Minister 301, 309, 310
Shirazi, Ayatollah al (1892–1984), Iraq 352
Shuja, Shah (1785–1842), Afghan ruler 284–5
Shultz, George (1920–), US Secretary of State 211
Sidqi, General Baqr (1890–1937), Iraqi nationalist 354
Singapore 82, 99, 166–7, 237, 366
Singasari Kingdom, (911–1007), Eastern Java, 95
Singer, J. David (1925–), American IR scholar 222
*The Correlates of War* 222
Singh, Ranjit (1780–1839), North Indian ruler 283–4
SIPRI, Stockholm International Peace Research Institute 219–21, 232
*SIPRI Yearbook* 219–21
Sjahrir, Sutan (1906–1966), Indonesian leader 111
Slave 31, 68–70
labour 70
trade 69
Slave trading 31
Smith, Adam (1723–1790), Scottish pioneer of political economy 8, 74, 82
Smith, Anthony (1933–), Academic, known for studies on nationalism 8, 82
Social Darwinism 10, 12, 60, 66, 68, 71–2, 383
Socialism 104, 155, 174, 176, 197–8, 226, 260, 293
proclamation of 176
scientific 174, 176, 197–8, 226, 293
Soetomo, (1888–1938), Indonesian nationalist 101
Sogato 242
Sogato, Marshall 242
Somadeva, political commentator of the Gupta period 4
Somalia 196–202, 293
Somali National Movement (SNM), 198
United Somali Congress (USC), 198–9
UN operation in 200
US interests in 201
Sonnenfeldt, Helmut (1926–), US official 182
Soustelle, General Jacques (1912–1990), Governor-General of Algeria 136
South Africa 56–7, 116, 180, 220, 293
South–East Asia Collective Defence Treaty 185
South Korea 185, 364, 366, 389
South Sea 36
Sovereignty 41, 46, 52, 127, 204, 289, 311
national 46
Soviet Union 45, 84–5, 102–3, 110, 138, 143, 146, 151, 154–65, 172–86, 188–91, 196–8, 205–6, 209, 211, 216, 219–20, 222–7, 229, 231, 249–51, 256, 260, 262–3, 268–70, 275, 280–312, 315, 322–3, 325–6, 328, 333, 356, 362, 365, 367, 382
Congress of the Communist Party 164, 368
Marxist–Leninist Party 176
US and 156, 163–4, 172, 177, 180–81, 185, 223
Vanguard Party 176, 197, 298
Spain 23, 31, 47, 60, 82, 125, 167, 209, 338, 340
Spanish Habsburg Empire, (1506–1700), zenith of Spain's global power and influence 91

Sparta (dominant c. 650–362 B.C.), Greek city state 3, 24, 36
Spear, Percival (1901–1982), English historian, 78
Spinoza, Baruch (1632–1677), Dutch philosopher xx–xxi
Sputnik 181, 294
Sri Lanka 221
Srivijaya Empire, (7th to 13th c.), Sumatra 94
Stalin, Joseph (1878–1953), Soviet leader 75, 102, 155, 184
*Marxism and the National Question* 75
Stanley, Edward (1799–1869), English statesman 84
Star of North Africa (ENA) 130, 132–3
St. Augustine (354–430), Algerian philosopher, Christian theologian 9
St. George Red Cross, England's national flag from 16th c. 41
St. Lucia 211
Stockholm Institute of International Peace Research (SIPRI), 219–21, 232
St. Thomas Aquinas, (1225–1274), Italian Roman Catholic priest of Dominican order, 211
St. Vincent 211
Strabo (63 BC–24 AD), Greek geographer xiii–iv
Sudan 58, 68, 159
Suez Canal 160
Suez Canal Company 160
Suffren, Pierre Andre de (1729–1788), French admiral 48
Suharto, Mohamed (1921–), Indonesian President 96–7, 101–6, 112, 114
Sukarno, Ahmed (1910–1973), first President of Indonesia, 96–7, 101–6, 112, 114
Suleiman, Hikmat, Iraqi Premier, 1930s 191, 346
Sultan Ali Mugayat, ruler of Aceh Darussalam (1511–1530) 99
Sulzberger, C.L. (1912–1993), American columnist 155
Sumatra 94, 97–9, 107–9, 111
Sweden 31, 156
Switzerland 135, 145, 156, 178, 275, 279
Syria 82, 129, 161–3, 164, 191–2, 339, 351, 358

Tafna, Treaty of (1837), Algeria, 127, 128
Taliban 277, 281–3, 317–37, 365, 383, 388
Afghan 325–9, 333
Tamer Lane, (1336–1405), Mongol conqueror 346
Tamuz–Dumuzi, Mespotamian spring God 350
Tanzania 58
Taraki, Noor Mohammed (1913–1979), Afghan President 281
Tarnoff, Peter (1937–), American IR expert 316, 336
Tashfin, Yusuf ibn (1061–1106), founder of Almoravid dynasty, 125
Taylor, A.J.P. (1906–1990), radical English historian 15
Teijn, Van 99
Tenth Inter–American Conference 204
Terra Australis 36
Terrorism 324, 365, 373–4, 376–81
Tet, (1968), Vietnam 243, 261, 264–71, 357
TF–74, US naval task force of 1971 189
Thailand 185, 221, 366
*The Battle of Algiers* 139
*The Project for the New American Century* 337
*The Ugly American* 256, 258
Thirty Years' War, (1618–1648), xix, xxii, 6–8, 14, 21, 150, 152
Thorez, Maurice (1900–1964), French communist 121
Thucydides, (c. 460–395 B.C.), Greek historian xv, 3–4
Tiglath Peleser III (8th c. BC), Assyrian King 343
Tilly, Charles (1928–2008), American sociologist 77
*Time*, The 66

Tito, Josip Broz (1892–1980), Yugoslav leader 184
Tjokroaminoto, Haji Omar Said (1883–1934), Indonesian nationalist, 101
TNI 113
Tocqueville, Alexis de (1805–1959), French historian, 119
Tontons Macoute, Haitian private army 208
Toure, Ahmed Sekou (1922–1984), President of Guinea 46, 55, 158
Tourane, now Da Nang, Vietnamese port, 237–8
Toynbee, Arnold J. (1889–1975), British historian 153, 276, 385
  *A Study of History* 153
Tran dynasty, (1295–1407), Vietnam, 242–3
Treaty of Peace, Friendship and Cooperation, Indo–Soviet, 1971 188
Trieu Da, founder of Vietnam, 208 BC 241
Truman, Harry S. (1884–1972), US President 110, 154, 173, 184–5, 381–2
Trung Nhi, Trung Trac, Vietnamese nationalist sisters (1st c.) 242
Tuanku Imam Bonjol, (1772–1864), Indonesian nationalist 98
Tunisia 132, 139, 142, 146, 158, 324
Tupamaros, (1960s), Uruguayan guerillas 378
Turkey 40, 43–4, 78, 157, 161, 184, 290, 338, 346–7, 356, 361, 381
Turkmenistan 282
Tzu, Sun (c. 544–496 BC), Chinese military strategist 8

UK 141, 169, 322, 338–40, 356, 362
Umara, Amir Al 346
Umayyad, (661–750), Caliphate 123
Umkhonto We Sizwe 57
Umma, Islam, community of believers, 123–4
UN 113–4, 137, 160, 179, 192, 195, 199–203, 207, 221, 231, 319, 333, 338–40, 367–8, 373–4, 387
  Charter 200
  UN Mission in Haiti (UNMIH), 207
UNDP 202
UNESCO General History of Africa 52
UN General Assembly (UNGA), 137–8, 179, 373–4
UNICEF 340
Union Oil Company of California (UNOCAL), 317
United Arab Republic (UAR), 162, 163, 164, 192
United Kingdom (UK), 23, 28, 31, 37, 42–3, 49, 54, 57, 60, 69, 71, 74, 80, 82–3, 85, 141, 143, 149, 151, 158–61, 166–7, 169, 172, 177, 204, 287, 289, 318, 322, 325, 338–40, 346, 352, 356, 362, 387
  Defence White Paper, 1962 167
  Egyptian adventure 159
  *The Next Five Years* 167
United Nations 108, 182, 208, 310, 338–9, 380, 382–3
United Nations Security Council (UNSC), 108, 200–202, 207, 338
  Article 39 108
  Good Offices Committee 108
United Nations Stabilisation Mission in Haiti (MINUSTAH), 208
United States 13, 31, 60, 87, 105, 107, 110, 112, 114, 119, 151, 155, 157–8, 163, 176, 181, 185, 191, 193, 203–5, 208, 210, 216–7, 219, 221, 224, 228–30, 264, 266, 268, 270–71, 292, 294, 309, 339–40, 362, 375, 380–85, 387–8
  9/11 317, 319, 322, 324–5, 327, 331, 337, 375, 379–80, 384, 387
  aid programmes 211
  Army of Cuban Pacification 205
  CIA 260, 300, 319
  Congress 183, 191, 318–9, 321, 337–8, 383
  Construction of freedom 381–3

effects of defeat 365–69
in Afghanistan 315–35
in Iraq 356–65
in Vietnam 255–74
Marines 193, 200, 369
Man–Portable Air Defence Systems (MAN–PADS), 180
Measure of power 383–88
military intervention 216
Monroe doctrine 203–4, 211
National Security Council paper 68 of April, 1950 173
policy to Pakistan 188
politico–military structure 267
Soviet Union and 156, 163–4, 172, 177, 180–81, 185, 223
Tarnoff doctrine 316, 336
Truman Doctrine 184
US War Department annual report of 1912 13
United Task Force (UNITAF), 201
Universal hospitality 28
UNOSOM (UN Operation in Somalia), 200–203

UNSC ( UN Security Council), 113, 160, 200, 319, 339–40
Resolution 794 200
Resolution 814 201
*UN Statistical Yearbook* 231
Uprising 49, 57, 111, 130, 133, 182, 239, 242, 246, 250, 285
communist 111
Kabul 285
Kabyle 130
Ur, Uruk, Sumerian cities, 342
Urban the Second, Pope, 1035–1039, 9
Uruguay 207, 378
U.S. 185, 196, 210, 217, 270, 331, 366

Van Meerdervoort, Pompe 99
Vasquez, John (1945–), American IR expert 232
Vedrine 385
Venezuela 204, 207, 340
Venice 20, 34
Versailles Conference 131
Vienna 47, 181
Vietminh, (1941–), Vietnamese national lilberation movement 251–2, 254–5
Vietnam 31, 54, 79, 95, 137, 158, 182, 191, 216–7, 219, 229, 236–72, 294, 305–6, 309, 315–6, 333, 362–3, 365
Chinese attack on 222
endless struggle 240
Hich Can Vuong movement 246
impact of Tet 264
power, war and empire 236
resources 244
struggle against China, France and then the US 236
US in 255
Vietnamese Communist Party 250
war against france 250
Vijayadoorg 37
Violence 4, 50–53, 100, 103, 123, 133, 136, 150, 154, 192, 196, 206, 208, 218, 221, 266, 324, 330, 364, 375–9, 389
direct 150
global 51
uncontrolled 51
Violette, Maurice Governor-General of Algeria 131
Vitkavich, Captain 283
Vo Nguyen Giap, (1912–1991), Vietnamese leader 251, 253
VOC, (founded 1602), Vereinigde Oost–Indische Compagnie, the Dutch East India Company, 92

Wahid, Abdul Mujahidin commander 303
Walewski, Count French Foreign Minister, 1850s 237
Waliyullah, Shah, see Shah
Walt, Stephen M. (1955–), American IR professor 386
Waltz, Kenneth (1924–), American IR professor 229

War 1–18, 20–45, 48, 52–100, 104–130, 134, 137–8, 140–72, 173–5, 181–90, 194, 196–99, 203, 206–7, 210, 215–36, 241–80, 286–93, 296, 300–39, 342–3, 346, 351, 356–7, 359–76, 379–89
  1914–18 82, 84, 149, 150–53, 249, 290
  1914–18 European 84, 149, 290
  1939–45 83, 143, 151
  1956 166, 217, 222
  1956 Suez 138, 146, 159
    Chinese classic 8
  actual 7
  Afghan 280, 306, 310
  African 58
  air 259–66
  Arab–Israel 222
  art of 3, 8, 153
  Boer 66
  casualties 7–9, 12, 69, 93, 118, 128, 141, 149–50, 156, 168, 195, 202, 253, 261, 266, 269, 296, 305, 307–8, 320, 330, 332, 341, 357, 364, 380
  cause of 23, 228
  causes for or of 14, 19, 22–5, 28, 152, 155–6
  chances of 15, 28
    actual 9
  Civil 42
  Cold 30–31, 45, 68, 87, 110, 146, 149, 157, 162–65, 172, 175, 181, 183–4, 186, 207, 215–35, 256, 268–9, 287, 301, 312, 316, 368–89
  colonial 69
  conduct of 5, 7, 9, 66
  crimes 106
  desperate and ruinous 127
  destructiveness of 1
  Eighty years of 91
  European 84, 149, 290
  future 25
  glorification of 13
  glory and honour of 9
  guerilla 53, 100, 107, 127, 128, 166, 198, 243, 253
  history and function of 11
  Holy 10
  influence of 154
  Iran–Iraq 220, 359
  Japanese 104
  justification for 3, 7, 10, 12
  kinds of 67
  Korean War (1950–53) 155, 174, 190, 216, 381, 383
  liberation 158
  making of 1, 227
  motivations for 22
  nomadic 278, 288, 290
  offensive and defensive 4
  Pattimura 98
  posture of 7, 23
  renaissance idea of 11
  revolutionary 130
  South Yemen 166
  state and 11, 43
  successful 2–3
  success in 8
  tactic of 33
  total 10, 137, 150, 152
  trade and 93
  Vietnam 222, 267, 271
    waging of 10
    Warre 7
  Zulu 66
War and peace 5, 25, 218
War and power 1, 3–4, 10, 30, 65, 153, 155, 215, 316
  equation of 4, 155
  links 1, 10, 316
    historical 10
    normative 10
Wardak, General Ghulam Haider Khan (1880s), ruled northern Afghanistan 288
Warfare 2, 4, 8, 58, 66, 69, 113, 143, 150, 168, 184, 253, 255–6, 266, 276, 296, 298, 306, 362–3
  guerilla 58, 113, 168, 184, 255

histories of 66, 69
prolonged 8
trench 150
urban 113, 266
Warnier, Dr. French consul in Mascara, mid 19th c. 128
*Washington Post* 201, 338, 362
Wassenaar Arrangement, (1996–), 180
Wassenaar Arrangement on Export Controls for Conventional Arms and Dual–use Goods and Technologies 180
Wassoulou Empire, (1878–1898), West Africa 55, 66
Weber, Eugen (1925–2007), American historian and sociologist 43
Weber, Max (1864–1920), German sociologist 73
Weinberger 219
Wells, H.G. (1866–1946), English author, 152
Westmoreland, Gen. William (1914–2005), US Army 259, 264, 267
Westphalia, Treaty of (1648), ended the Thirty Years' War 19, 21, 36, 124
Wheeler, Gen. Earle (1908–1975), US Army officer 267
*White Man's Burden* 10
William, Prince of Orange (1533–1584), founder of the Netherlands 91
Wilson, Harold (1916–1995), British Premier 169
Wilson, Woodrow (1856–1924), US President 131
Wolf, Eric (1923–1999), Austrian anthropologist 41
Wolfowitz, Paul (1943–), American official 336–7
Woolf, Leonard (1880–1969), English political theorist and author 83
*World Armaments and Disarmament Yearbook* 219
World Bank 211, 367, 387
*World Handbook of Political and Social Indicators* 231
World War I 149
World War II 54, 59, 81, 152–3, 158, 185, 196, 228, 256, 259, 264, 270, 311, 385, 387
Wright, Quincy (1890–1970), American political scientist 14, 152, 155
WSAG, Washington Special Action Group 189
WSLF, Western Somali Liberation Front 197

Yacine, Kateb Algerian nationalist author 123, 129
*Nedjma* 123
Yavadvipa, name for Java, early Indian 94
Yemen 77, 159, 166–7, 176, 217, 309, 322
Ying Ling, Lt. Paul US Army officer 362
Yohannes, Emperor 58, 59
Ypres 150
Yugoslavia 151, 156, 183–4, 311

Zachariadis, Nikos (1903–1973), Greek communist 184
Zakaria, Fareed (1964–), American IR expert 333
Zakharov, M. (1898–1972), Soviet army chief 164
Zaki, Amin Iraqi Chief of Staff, 1930s 355
Zambia 47
Zamorin 33
Zangger, Committee (1970–), 178–9
Zanzibar 49
Zarqawi, Abu Musab al (1966–2006), leader of Al Qaeda in Iraq 362
Zatcha, Algerian tribe 120
Zawahiri, Ayman (1951–), Al Qaeda leader 322
Zelaya, Nicaraguan President, 1909, 205
Ze Min, Jiang (1926–), Chinese President 368–9
Ziggurat, Babylonian raised structure 350, 351
Zimbabwe 117
Zouagla, Algerian tribe 120
Zululand 57